REGIONAL MAPS

Road number

Point of interest

Important featured town

Drive start point

Map reference

Important featured point of interest

Regional name

Adjoining chapter

- A locator map accompanies each regional map and shows the location of that region in the country.
- Adjacent regions are shown, each with a page reference.

WALKING TOURS

Walk route

Point of interest (not on route)

Featured site (in bold) on walk route

Start point

Direction of walk route

Red numbered bullets link site on map to descriptions in the text

Building outline

- An information box gives the starting and ending points, time and length of walk, and places not to be missed along the route.
- Where two walks are marked on the map, the second route is shown in orange.

DRIVING TOURS

Red numbered bullets link site on map to descriptions in the text

Road number

Important featured town

Region name

Point of interest

Important point of interest

Drive route

- An information box provides details including starting and finishing points, time and length of drive, places not to be missed along the route, and tips on terrain.

NATIONAL GEOGRAPHIC

TRAVELER

Ireland

About the author

Christopher Somerville is one of Britain's best-known travel writers, with some 25 books to his name—including the *National Geographic Traveler: Great Britain*. He writes regularly for the travel sections of *The Times*, the *Sunday Times*, and the *Daily Telegraph*, and also broadcasts on radio and TV. His love affair with Ireland was kindled on his first trip to the island, an 800-mile (1,280 km) walk through the rugged and romantic west. Since then, he has written four books and countless words of travel journalism about the country, and returns whenever he can to hook up with old friends, walk the mountains and coasts, play traditional music, and continue his search for that place "just around the corner, now," where the crack is mighty and the pub never closes.

History & culture

The penny whistle drives many an Irish jig.

Ireland today

A LEATHERFACED COUNTRYMAN IN A CLOTH CAP AND AN OLD PATCHED jacket, pitchforking his hay in a tiny stonewalled field against a timeless backdrop of mountains and sea: That's Ireland today. His green-haired daughter striding out of a Dublin cappuccino bar, networking to the United States on her mobile phone: That's today's Ireland, too, on the move and on the change.

ROMANCE WITH A HARD EDGE

Romantics have no trouble at all in finding what they're looking for in Ireland. Few countries project such a seductive image as this rainwashed little island off the northwest coast of Europe, and few fulfill their visitors' dreams so faithfully—the green fields, the soft rain, the quick-tongued and open-handed people, the Guinness-drinking and laughter against that eternal backwash of irresistible Irish music.

But there is a hard edge, too, not far underneath the fun and fancy. During the past 10 years no western European country has undergone such a profound economic and social change as Ireland. Everywhere people talk of the Celtic Tiger, the boom economy in the Republic during the 1990s that has seen business and optimism swell. "Ireland of the Welcomes," the laid-back land where hospitality is the watchword and no one's in a hurry, still flourishes, of course, as much in visitors' minds as anywhere. You can feel more relaxed, more welcome here than in almost any other country in the world. Ireland is famous for just this atmosphere, with good reason. But the signs of change are all around, too— money jingling in Dubliners' pockets, farmland sliced by superhighways built with European development grants, extravagant modern houses sprouting on remote hillsides, and a confidence in the attitudes of youngsters who no longer need to emigrate to find a decent job and some freedom to live their lives as they see fit.

The image of Ireland as a gently backward, rural, and mystical land, and of the Irish as a rustically humorous community of God-fearing, thrifty peasants (seeded with a few erratically brilliant novelists and poets) was deliberately fostered in the 1930s and '40s for nationalistic reasons by Eamon de Valera, prime minister of the newly and proudly independent Eire. It wasn't without a basis in truth. And it served the Irish tourist industry well, fixing southern Ireland in the world's mind as the ideal soft landing for an escape from reality. What it disguised, though, was an all-too-real rural poverty, economic and social, which drove young, vigorous men and women to emigrate in droves up to the mid-1990s. Now, at the turn of the 21st century, many are returning to Ireland, or have never had to leave in the first place.

This new, shiny-faced, and thrusting young Republic, transformed into one of Europe's most dynamic economies, has been built on a foundation of development money from the European Union and from the International Fund for Ireland. Agricultural and pharmaceutical chemicals and information technology have been particularly big players, with multinational companies settling in Irish towns on a featherbed of tax breaks, subsidies, and start-up grants. They like the Irish willingness to work hard for moderate wages, and the brightness of the motivated school leavers.

TROUBLESOME TIGER

The Celtic Tiger has turned out to be a troublesome and uncertain beast to ride, all the same. Too many of these new high-tech industries have been found to flit out from under when times get tough or when the global market gives a twitch, with little sense of loyalty to their host country or workforce. Older homegrown industries such as textiles, car assembly, and agriculture, more labor-intensive and inward looking, haven't done so well. Some visitors find an un-Irish offhandedness and arrogance in the new

Old-fashioned traditional ways of agriculture are still practiced in many isolated pockets of rural Ireland.

breed of entrepreneurial young highflyers; others complain of Dublin, traditionally the very stamp and form of a city on a human scale with plenty of relish for human idiosyncrasies, losing its intimacy, its sense of proportion, and sense of humor in the rush for wealth.

Then there's the crude, often laughable effect of too bright and insensitive a spotlight being shone on Ireland's deceptively simple but in fact extremely subtle cultural heritage. Riverdance, for example, that internationally

successful stage show that drew the world's attention to Irish dancing: Many think it cheapened this very formal, highly technical connoisseur's art by coating it in an alien, glitzy sexuality. And can you really find the true "crack," that absolutely and uniquely Irish version of a high old time, in Beastie O'Shagg's Irish Theme Pub in Salzburg or Bangkok?

You could call this snobbery or cultural elitism, but there's probably some justification for these concerns—just as there was for the

unease that discerning visitors felt with Ireland's "leprechaun-and-shamrock" tourist image of the 1950s and '60s. The fact is that the Republic has been through enormous changes in a very short space of time—changes that have shaken and stirred both place and people. And if the Celtic Tiger has given the Republic a rough ride over the past decade, how much more intense has been the shaking and stirring north of the border during the same period of time.

The Celtic Tiger rests a while: Dublin's cafés have come bang up to date with the recent boom in prosperity.

NEW HOPE FOR THE NORTH

The island of Ireland contains 32 counties. The six northernmost counties of Antrim, Derry, Tyrone, Fermanagh, Armagh, and Down make up the province of Northern Ireland, which remained politically a part of the United Kingdom when the other 26

Clean, modern lines of Belfast's Waterfront Hall reflect the emergence of Northern Ireland's chief city from post-industrial shabbiness ...

counties of Ireland split away to form the Irish Free State in 1921 after the Irish War of Independence (see pp. 32–33). You may hear Northern Ireland called Ulster—the six counties formed part of the ancient Irish province of that name. Ancient Ulster contained three additional counties (Donegal, Cavan, and Monaghan), but these joined the infant Free State (later the Irish Republic) in 1921 and have remained politically apart from Northern Ireland ever since.

Almost everyone in Northern Ireland in the mid-1990s would have given their eyeteeth to enjoy an image as benign, if misleading, as the Republic's leprechaun winsomeness, instead of the dour and deadly reputation—equally false—that they had been cursed with through the activities of a few bitter bigots. Thirty years of being unwillingly strapped to the careering headless horse of sectarian and politically motivated terrorism made all moderate folk—and they constitute the majority of people in the North—heartily sick of being classified with extremists. They knew only too well the damage it was doing to their province's economy, with visitors and overseas investors reluctant to consider a place tarred with the deep-staining brush of violence and

intolerance. The North's traditional heavy industry, following a pan-European trend, was in decline, the economy stagnant. Emigration of bright, ambitious youngsters, always seen as a purely southern Irish scourge, was getting a grip of Northern Ireland, too.

What the Good Friday Agreement of April 10, 1998 (see pp. 294–295), with all its flaws and uncertainties, has brought about is a new perspective on Northern Ireland. The outside world, looking in, is beginning to see growing shoots of hope for peace and a settled society, rather than yet more uprooted aspirations. European Union and United Kingdom taxpayers' money, along with the U.S.-supported International Fund for Ireland, have put some much needed foundations under the province's rocky economy. There has been a dip in unemployment and emigration as high-tech businesses have begun to settle in, much as they did in the Republic in the late 1980s.

Even more to the point, there is a significant and continuing melting of the frozen sectarian divide. Ever since the English monarchy began to "plant" Northern Ireland with Protestants in the early 17th century, tensions between Catholics and Protestants

... while in the Republic's western counties, things go on much as they always have—at a steady, easy pace.

have risen and fallen (see p. 26). Since the start of the most recent spate of Troubles, relations have frequently descended to the poisonous. Even now, with the peace process in place, sectarian confrontations and bitterness can still flare up in the more contentious areas of Belfast. But the social conditions that exacerbated these problems have largely improved. The old inequalities in incomes and social benefits that favored Protestants at the expense of Catholics are narrowing, even if there are still pockets of injustice. Good news doesn't hit the headlines like bad news does, of course. But outside the handful of extremist enclaves you'll find Protestant and Catholic, unionist and republican, indistinguishable.

Stability is a catching habit. It has helped outsiders—holidaymakers and business investors alike—to hear what the Northern Irish have been saying all along: theirs is a beautiful place with extremely hospitable people, only too keen to welcome all comers.

RURAL CHARM & CITY BUZZ

Few enough visitors yet know about Northern Ireland's gorgeous secret countryside, or the warmth of the welcome in the music pubs and bed-and-breakfast houses of the province. Their expectations are vague, their image of the North distorted by the Troubles (see p. 35). But south of the border it's a different story. Three million visitors a year flock to the Republic, one tourist for every inhabitant. Tourism is big business here.

Visitors planning a trip to southern Ireland have a seductive image in mind—the beauty of the mountains and sea coasts of the west and southwest, the sophistication and humor of Dublin, outdoor fun on golf courses, horse tracks, and fishing lakes, and the laid-back pleasures of the talk, the music, and the general lifestyle everywhere. Famous beauty spots and tourist honey pots lie thick on the ground, and those who come to Ireland to find the fantasy Island of the Leprechauns don't go home disappointed. Buying shamrocks and shillelaghs in the crowded gift shops of Killarney, crawling bumper to bumper around the Ring of Kerry's over-popular scenic route, fighting for a table in a Kinsale fish restaurant, or watching stage Irishwomen at their spinning wheels in Bunratty Folk Park, you could be forgiven for thinking that all Ireland was out to sell itself lock, stock, and barrel to the tourist trade.

The real living country, you'll find, lies along the lane just off the main road, in the street behind the harbor, ten minutes' walk up the mountain track, out along the bog road. Explorers and wanderers get the best out of Ireland—so do talkers and listeners, hikers and drivers, laughers and quaffers, and those who like the odd angle and the elliptical way.

That easygoing image, of course, is only half the story. It's true that there are still thousands of small traditional farms in rural Ireland, especially out in the Irish-speaking Gaeltacht areas of the west, working their picturesquely tiny, intensely green stonewalled fields, with EU subsidies to prop the businesses up. Country towns still tend to be charming and sleepy in equal proportion, retaining their old-fashioned grocers and butchers' shops and tiny dark pubs. But cities such as Galway and Cork, where many of the Celtic Tiger youngsters have injected a healthy dash of loud life, buzz with modern energy these days.

KEEPING AN EYE ON THINGS

Irish politics, both local and national, have always been riven by scandal. Bribes, cronyism, secret accounts, and nod-and-a-wink deals behind closed doors were so much the order of the day by the early 1990s that they were becoming an embarrassment to the Irish themselves, as well as an international talking point. An Ethics in Public Office Act was passed in 1998 to try to get a grip on this shady side of things, with mixed success to date.

Clouds drift across Croagh Patrick, Ireland's holy mountain, as a County Mayo farmer shifts his flock along a bog road.

During the same period a very noticeable growth in concern for the environment, both built and natural, has led to lively debate about planning, development, and design, notoriously unchecked in Ireland until recently. Traveling through rural areas you'll hardly fail to spot the much reviled "Irish

hacienda" style of architecture—a sprawling ranch-style bungalow fronted by an enormous prairie of slate patio behind raw brick arches, usually posed on an otherwise pristine hillside. Around city streets the main culprit has been the over-enthusiastic use of garish plastic and eyeball-tingling paint. In areas of outstanding natural beauty and historical interest, European development money has paid for several interpretive centers of more or less obtrusive design. Few would have raised a

murmur 20 years ago; now, thanks to the emergence of a better educated and more sophisticated electorate, the powers-that-be are obliged to take notice of objectors.

Perhaps the best example is the growing protest over the destruction of the vast boglands by Bord na Mona, the Peat Board (see pp. 258–259). Seen until recently as barren wastelands fit only to be exploited for cheap fuel, today they are regarded by many as a wonderful, strangely beautiful refuge for wildlife.

WOMEN TO THE FORE

Change is sweeping through Irish life, and nowhere is this more clearly shown than in the rise in status that women achieved during the last decade of the 20th century. When Mary Robinson, a liberal-minded barrister with strong feminist allegiances, was elected President of the Republic of Ireland in 1990, she became an inspiration to many women, who were still taking pretty much a back seat in Irish political and business life, and they

Mary McAleese has stretched out across religious and cultural divisions in her role as President of Ireland.

quickly became much more assertive and self-confident. She proved an indefatigable traveler in her own country and through the wider world, keen to gain a hearing for unpopular or ticklish subjects such as unmarried mothers, drug abuse, gay rights, and religious intoler-ance. By her warm and genuine personality

she raised the profile of the presidency and of Ireland, and especially of Irish women. In 1997 she was appointed United Nations High Commissioner for Human Rights, and another woman—Mary McAleese, a Roman Catholic law lecturer from Northern Ireland—took her place. Times had changed indeed.

A CHURCH IN CRISIS

The business of who lines up on which side of the religious divide has come to mean less and less in the modern Ireland. In Eamon de Valera's backwoods Ireland of the 1930s, the Roman Catholic Church was king of the castle, dispensing welfare and education, laying down strict rules of behavior that the largely poor and rural populace disregarded at their peril. Anyone who crossed the priest in some country parish would become an untouchable. Respect for the Church and adherence to Christianity—Church of Ireland or Roman Catholic—was almost universal.

Aran Islands girls at prayer. The Roman Catholic faith is struggling to maintain its influence at the center of community life.

But social change, greater affluence, international travel, and a wider education have put an end to all that. These days, after a series of well-publicized sexual and financial scandals, the Roman Catholic Church is in a very reduced state. A parish priest no longer has the automatic respect of his flock: He has to earn it.

THE "OLD FAITH"

What some call superstition and others name the "Old Faith"—belief in the power of holy wells and woods, offerings to natural gods, ceremonies at standing stones and circles—continues unabated, a powerful hidden tide still surging below the surface of modern life. Often it works side by side with Christianity, or is bound up with music and dance. You won't have to look too hard to find it. ■

Fauna, flora, & climate

IRELAND'S CLIMATE IS FAMOUSLY MILD AND WET, WITH RAIN FALLING somewhere almost every day of the year. In the west, on a series of what locals euphemistically term "soft" summer days, it can seem as if most of it is falling on you. The prevailing damp westerly air stream off the Atlantic is what makes Ireland so beautifully green.

Bloody cranesbill flushes the naked grey limestone of the Burren, in County Clare, a springtime paradise of wildflowers.

Ireland is like a great geological wheel, with a hub of carboniferous limestone filling the interior and a rim of ancient volcanic rock. You'll find schists and gneisses up in parts of the far north and out in western Connemara, basalt in spectacular formations along the Antrim coast, and the oldest stuff, granite, along the north shore of Galway Bay, in west Donegal and southwest of Dublin.

The famed bogs that have formed in the central, poorly drained region are still cut and milled for turf—as the Irish call their horticultural and fuel peat—but exploitation is in its final phase now (see pp. 258–259).

Ten thousand years ago the meltwaters of ice age glaciers heaped parts of the landscape with eskers (long ridges) and drumlins (round hillocks) of rubble, now greened over to form attractively bumpy little hills and islets. Monaghan, Cavan, and Clew Bay in County Mayo are great examples.

All of these areas support a variety of wildlife (famously lacking in snakes), though Ireland's four-legged creatures—wild goats, hares, deer—tend to be too wary to be spotted easily. However, during the late autumn mating season you will be able to smell the goats long before you see them.

The most spectacular groupings of the bird population, the seabird colonies of the west coast cliffs and islands, are matched by tremendous gatherings of overwintering wildfowl on east coast estuaries such as Strangford Lough, east of Belfast, and the North Slobs mudflats and marshes near Wexford. It's the mountains and moorlands of Ireland—the Sperrins in County Tyrone, Macgillycuddy's Reeks in Kerry, the Wicklow Mountains south of Dublin, and the wild hills of Donegal way out northwest—that will give you the best opportunity to spot birds of prey, including hen harriers, peregrines, little bullet-like merlins, and the wheeling buzzards. The boglands offer anyone with binoculars the chance to spot buntings and warblers, while along the hayfields around Killala Bay where Sligo meets Mayo, and in remote Inishowen in northern Donegal, you might just hear the grating *crex-crex* of the rare and very elusive corncrake.

As for wildflowers, you'll find beautiful pink bogbean, insect-eating sundews, and wonderfully colored rushes and grasses in the bogs, primroses in the narrow country lanes in springtime, and blood-red fuchsia in the hedges of the southwestern counties in summer. Ireland's showpiece for wildflowers, however, is the Burren in County Clare (see pp. 170–171), a unique environment of limestone pavement where acid-loving and lime-loving plants, arctic and Mediterranean flowers all exist abundantly together. ∎

Blocks of turf, dug for fuel from the boglands of Achill Island, County Mayo, are laid neatly in long rows to dry.

History of Ireland

IRELAND'S HISTORY HAS BEEN A TURBULENT AFFAIR. THE ISLAND'S GOLDEN
Age of spiritual influence and artistic achievement reached its zenith more than a thousand years ago, bolstered by a rich mythic tradition and a flowering of passionate evan-
gelical Christianity. Echoes of that magnificence sustained the Irish over the ensuing
centuries of cultural dilution and dissipation brought about by British settlement, and
through the long, bitter struggle for emancipation and independence. The stories of
Ireland and Britain, uneasy neighbors and bedfellows, have been intimately bound up
together for the past ten centuries.

Ancient myth, that potent source of national
identity and pride, has Ireland's original
inhabitants, the Firbolgs, overcome by a
race of mystical and magical conquerors
known as Tuatha de Danaan, the People of
Danu, Mother of the Gods. This version of
the island's story gets off to a flying start
with tales of wooings, betrayals, battles, feasts,
and mighty deeds of derring-do by heroes
and heroines such as Fionn MacCumhaill
(Finn McCool), Diarmuid and Gráinne (see
p. 266), Deirdre of the Sorrows, and
Cúchulainn (see pp. 338–339).

More prosaically, it was a hardy bunch
of fishermen and food-gatherers who first
crossed to the Antrim coast from Scotland
about 10,000 years ago, at the end of the last
ice age. Little is known about this thin population who made their settlements by lakeside
and seashore.

By the time the first Celts from central
Europe began to arrive around 500 B.C., Irish
culture had progressed through successive
Stone, Bronze, and Iron Ages that left the
landscape scattered with splendid chambered
tombs, stone circles, and field systems. Irish
became the universal language in a country
divided among rival noble families who elected their own kings from among themselves.
Families lived in wooden homesteads surrounded by earth banks, well strengthened
with stone walls. Land was held in common;
cattle became the main measure of wealth,
with cattle-raiding endemic. Warfare between
family "kingdoms" was a way of life.

Balance and a sense of justice were encouraged by the liberal set of rules known as
Brehon Law—the experts who codified the
law were known as brehons—by which society
more or less abided.

COMING OF CHRISTIANITY

Into this fertile, vigorous society came
Christianity, brought to Ireland by the itinerant
preacher Patrick in A.D. 432. By now Ireland had
divided into the four major kingdoms, or
provinces, of Ulster (north), Connacht (west),
Leinster (east), and Munster (south), each ruled
by its own king. St. Patrick and the early
Christian missionaries wisely decided to work
with, not against, the established druidic religion of the Irish Celts. They built many of their
churches and monasteries on sites already considered holy, and showed respect for the leaders
of Irish society. Their reward was to see Ireland
embrace Christianity fervently.

GOLDEN AGE

Along with Christianity came literacy and
a flowering of the arts. Monasteries became
centers of culture, from which Irish monks
went out to spread the word all over Europe
and far beyond. Poetry, song, stone-carving,
the arts of jewelry and gold-working all
flourished. The seventh and eighth centuries
were Ireland's Golden Age, culminating in
the production of such glorious works of
art as the Ardagh Chalice and the Tara
Brooch, both from the eighth century (now
in the National Museum of Archaeology
and History, see pp. 58–61), and the incompa-
rable Book of Kells around 800 (now in
Trinity College, Dublin, see pp. 54–55).
The Vikings were unwelcome visitors from
around that time onward; Brian Boru, High
King of Ireland, finally defeated them and
broke their power at the Battle of Clontarf

**The King of Connacht commissioned the
Cross of Cong in 1123, a treasure now on
display in the National Museum in Dublin.**

in 1014. Another century was to pass before even more effective invaders began to cast their eyes across the Irish Sea.

SETTLERS FROM ENGLAND
The Normans had occupied mainland Britain in 1066, but it took another hundred years for them to invade Ireland. They came to support

English soldier-statesman Oliver Cromwell earned himself an everlasting reputation for brutality for his savage repression of Irish insurgents in the 1650s.

Dermot MacMurrough, King of Leinster, who had been banished by Rory O'Connor, High King of Ireland (not without cause—he had stolen the High King's wife). At first the Normans made a great show of force, building castles on land they seized. But after various military setbacks, with the passing of centuries and some intermarriage, they settled down—mostly in a strip of land around Dublin known as the Pale, defended with palings, or palisades—to a more or less neighborly accommodation with the Irish.

REPRESSION & REBELLION
It was King Henry VIII of England and then his daughter Queen Elizabeth I, both fearing a Roman Catholic invasion of the mainland from Irish soil, who set the fire under the

cauldron of Ireland in the 16th century with a series of punitive taxes, confiscations, and legal exclusions of influential Irish Catholic families. In 1541 King Henry VIII had himself proclaimed King of Ireland, and unleashed a wave of repression that in its turn bred resentment and rebellion. The Catholic countries of Europe, keen to blunt the supremacy of England on the high seas and to bring the newly Protestantized country back into the Roman Catholic fold, saw Catholic Ireland as a potential springboard for the invasion and subjection of the British mainland. A mixed Spanish and Italian landing on the Dingle Peninsula in 1580 was defeated with savagery by Elizabeth's Crown forces, and more repressions followed. Repression bred rebellions, each put down with the mailed fist. The last uprising of this period, an insurrection headed by Hugh O'Neill, Earl of Tyrone and backed by 4,500 Spanish soldiers, was crushed in 1601.

By 1610 the leaders of the great families of Ulster had fled overseas, and in what was known as the Plantation of Ulster, Protestant farmers from Scotland and England were encouraged with grants of money and land to settle all over the north of Ireland, in order to keep land and influence out of Catholic hands.

If things were bad for Irish Catholics, they got a great deal worse in the mid-17th century when ripples from the English Civil War ignited more trouble in Ireland. After ten years of confused fighting, Oliver Cromwell arrived with his battle-hardened Ironsides and instituted a repression that put even the Elizabethan brutalities in the shade. Towns such as Drogheda and Wexford were sacked; rebels were executed en masse. Catholic landowners all over the country were stripped of their property and rights and driven west across the River Shannon "to Hell or Connacht," to the poorest land in the west, while "planters" took their place in the fat lands of the east and the midlands.

FROM PENAL TIMES TO SWAGGERING DAN
The infamous penal times continued through the late 18th century. After the Cromwellian repressions, there was a surge of Catholic hope when King James II, the Roman Catholic monarch deposed from the English

throne, tried to gain support for his cause in Ireland. Though James was defeated at the Battle of the Boyne on July 12, 1690, his conqueror King William III seemed to hold out promise of better and more equal opportunities for Irish Catholics. But William soon went back on his word, and within a few years the miserable penal laws had been introduced.

The penal laws enshrined Catholic disenfranchisement; no Catholic was allowed to vote, to educate his children as Catholics, or to hold property. The intention of the penal laws was clear—to perform a kind of ethnic cleansing on the Catholic majority by squeezing them out of political, social, and economic life. The ban that really hurt, though, was that on celebrating Mass. Roman Catholicism became a clandestine faith, practiced in out-of-the-way places, its priests in fear of death, its adherents increasingly politicized through poverty and desperation. Risings came and went, each harshly suppressed. Rebel groups formed in secret, plotting insurrection. The United Irishmen mounted the final rebellion of the 18th century in 1798, bolstered by 1,100 Frenchmen who landed at Killala Bay on the Sligo/Mayo border. It started successfully with a crushing defeat of the English at Castlebar; but ended as all the other uprisings had, in defeat for the rebels and death for their leaders.

Intolerance of Catholics as a general practice had been softening toward the end of the 18th century. The penal laws were not being applied as rigorously as they had been at the outset. In 1782 a qualified parliamentary independence was granted, but the 1798 Rising put an end to all that. The new century opened with the 1801 Act of Union that abolished the Irish parliament and imposed direct rule from London. Discrimination against Catholics was tightened, not to be relaxed again until the forceful Kerry lawyer Daniel O'Connell won his famous long-drawn-out struggle to force Westminster to attend to the grievances of the Irish poor. "Swaggering Dan," or "The Liberator" as his followers styled him, finally gained a seat in Parliament as a Catholic MP (member of Parliament) in 1828.

THE GREAT FAMINE

The history of 19th-century Ireland—and 20th-century Ireland, too—was shaped by the overarching tragedy of the Great Famine of 1845 to 1849. The potato fungus *Phytophthora infestans* struck a country with a population of nine million, the majority of them poor, illiterate peasants living in enormous families on tiny patches of rented land in remote regions, entirely dependent on the potato for food. When the fungus turned their potatoes to

Swaggering Dan O'Connell led the poverty-stricken Roman Catholics of rural Ireland to political emancipation in 1828.

black slime in the ground, four seasons out of five, they had no defense against the disaster.

The British government's response has frequently been condemned as cruelly indifferent, even deliberately so. Initially, in fact, measures were taken to relieve the famine. Food depots were established, maize was put on the market, hospitals were opened, and relief works started. But the authorities were soon overwhelmed by the scale of the catastrophe, the sheer numbers of people involved, the lack of infrastructure—hospitals, relief centers, port facilities, even roads—within rural Ireland, and the rapidity with which disease and death spread. A hard-hearted change of policy after the first year of the famine saw the government at Westminster throw much of the responsibility for dealing with the disaster onto the shoulders of the local Poor Law

Overcrowded workhouses and hospitals turned away starving peasants in the thousands during the disastrous Great Potato Famine of 1845-49.

Unions, charitable organizations, and the individual landlords.

It is tempting to see all the landlords as absentee exploiters, feathering their own nests and harshly evicting those tenants who failed to pay their rent. Some certainly fitted that bill. Others, such as the Marquess of Sligo, however, suspended rents and sold their own possessions to aid their tenants. But it was the peasants of Ireland who paid the highest price for the government's past policy and present pragmatism. Workhouses and temporary hospitals were filled to overflowing. Sick and starving people were turned away. Typhus, cholera, relapsing fever, and diarrhea spread like wildfire through the crowded cabins and hovels of the rural poor, and through the unsanitary streets of the towns. Families died where they lay together, unattended by doctor or priest. It is impossible to collect accurate figures, but a million men, women, and children probably died during the five years of the Great Famine—either from disease, or literally starving to death.

EMIGRATION & ANGER

Emigration, which had been a means of escape from poverty for the rural Irish for a century or more, swelled to a flood during and after the famine. Anyone who could scrape up the price of a ticket boarded one of the emigration

Brotherhood, established in the U.S. in the 1850s, and sees its expression today in support among many expatriate Irish communities for extremist causes in Northern Ireland.

LAND REFORM & HOME RULE

As for the movement for political change in post-famine Ireland, it continued down its

Charles Stewart Parnell, heir to the political imperatives of Swaggering Dan O'Connell, championed the causes of land reform and Home Rule in the 1880s.

ships—leaky, dirty old buckets as many of them were—in hopes of a better life elsewhere, in mainland Britain, the U.S., Canada, Australia. The Irish diaspora spread all over the world during the following century, draining the young and active lifeblood of Ireland, especially in the poor rural west. Today the population of the Irish Republic is about three million—one-third of its pre-famine level.

As the emigrants picked up the threads of strange new lives, powerful feelings of attachment to their homeland were mingled in many cases with bitterness and anger toward Britain, the country they held responsible for their plight. This mixture of sentiment and politics grew stronger as time went on. It was to fuel the activities of 19th-century anti-British organizations such as the Fenian

well-worn track of clandestine groupings organizing boycotts, sporadic attacks on landlords and their agents, and a string of brief and unsuccessful risings. But the grievances of poor Catholic Ireland were coming more and more to the fore in mainstream politics. Michael Davitt's nonviolent Land League movement eventually forced a Land Act, passed in 1881, which ensured fair rents and security of tenure for tenants. And the ever more vociferous Home Rule movement found a powerful mouthpiece in one of the Land Act's keenest supporters, Protestant landowner and MP Charles Stewart Parnell, heir to Daniel O'Connell's crown as champion of the Catholic poor.

Parnell was brought down by a sexual scandal in 1890, but the impetus he gave to the

Home Rule movement meant that the government could no longer consign the issue to the back burner. As the new century dawned, militant pressure for independence from Britain grew irresistible. Yet in Northern Ireland the Protestant people, descendants of the 17th-century planters with a clear interest in preserving the status quo, were lining up

Padraic Pearse, a gentle, dreamy poet— and Home Rule hardliner—paid with his life for his role in the Easter Rising of 1916.

behind charismatic Dublin MP Sir Edward Carson to repudiate the notion of political severance from the United Kingdom. This stance of separation by the Ulstermen was made far worse in the eyes of many Northern Catholics by Carson's decision to agree to the establishment of an Ulster that excluded three of the nine counties of the historic province. Catholic voters were in a majority in Monaghan, Cavan, and Donegal, and Protestant dominance of those three counties looked uncertain. So they were "let go" to the putative independent free state of southern Ireland. Their Protestant inhabitants were not happy to be included in what appeared to them a hostile and backward country. Home Rule-minded Catholics in Antrim, Derry (called Londonderry by Protestants), Tyrone, Fermanagh, Armagh,

and Down, the Six Counties of the proposed Ulster, resented being severed from the political freedom that their southern brethren seemed about to enjoy. Seeds of cross-border bitterness and resentment were sown.

A compromise Home Rule Act, excluding the Ulster counties of Antrim, Londonderry, Tyrone, Fermanagh, Armagh, and Down, was passed in 1914. But this effective partition of Ireland was then immediately suspended upon the outbreak of World War I. This was the final straw as far as radical Home Rule advocates were concerned. They drew together under the umbrella of the Irish Republican Brotherhood (first formed in the 1850s in the aftermath of the Great Famine) and began preparations for an armed rebellion.

THE EASTER RISING

The Easter Rising of 1916 was planned by a small group of people dedicated to gaining independence from Britain. They were organized and led by socialist trade unionist James Connolly, and Christian schoolteacher Padraic Pearse. They argued, philosophized, organized, and drilled their small bands of volunteers, looking for the right moment to make their move. "England's difficulty is Ireland's opportunity," ran the republican mantra; and it was to Germany that the activists dispatched Sir Roger Casement, looking for support, on the eve of the uprising they planned for Easter 1916. Casement's realistic assessment was that they could expect no help and should call off the Rising. But they went ahead anyway, hoping for simultaneous action from 10,000 sympathizers all over Ireland.

Owing to confusion, poor coordination, and lack of communication among widely scattered groups, only 2,000 rebels joined the Rising, with almost all the action taking place in Dublin. The initial action that Easter Monday morning took the authorities by surprise, and about 1,000 armed insurgents installed themselves in various key administrative buildings across the city. Standing on the steps under the portico of the General Post

The GPO building on Dublin's O'Connell Street, besieged and bombarded by British troops in the fierce fighting of Easter 1916, became a powerful symbol of freedom.

Delegates from Ireland went to London in 1921 for discussion of peace terms to end the War of Independence.

Office on O'Connell Street, Padraic Pearse read out the rebels' proclamation: "We hereby proclaim the Irish Republic as a Sovereign Independent State, and we pledge our lives and the lives of our comrades in arms to the cause of its freedom, of its welfare and of its exaltation among the nations."

Fine words and fine aspirations, which were soon crushed. The rebels did not have the resources—although they certainly had the bravery—to withstand the British Army for long, once it had recovered from its shock and rolled its troops and hardware into action. A week of bombardment, and many deaths on both sides, saw the GPO shattered by shellfire and the activists forced to surrender. If the British Government had played it cool from then on, benefiting from a wartime public mood in Ireland that initially saw the rebels as misguided hotheads—if not downright traitors—rather than heroes, a lot of subsequent bloodshed would have been avoided. Instead they enshrined the insurgents as martyrs by shooting 15 of the leaders, drawing out the executions over the following weeks in a manner that outraged decent opinion.

TWO WARS

Republican sentiment coalesced around Sinn Fein (Ourselves Alone), a small political sect that quickly grew to wield real power. Immediately after the end of World War I in

establishing an independent Irish Free State that excluded those six contentious counties of Northern Ireland.

Now came a split between followers of Michael Collins, reluctantly prepared to accept the partition of Ireland—and even the prospect of basing some British troops there in time of war—and the less accommodating

Eamon de Valera, leader of the IRA during the Civil War of 1922–23, became known around the world when he entered his long period as Taoiseach and then President of Ireland.

1919, with half its MPs in jail, it forced Ireland to the top of the British Government's agenda again by declaring independence, forming its own parliament under Eamon de Valera, and making a demand that Westminster could not agree to—a withdrawal of all British troops from Ireland. There followed two years of war between the official military forces of Britain and the irregular battalions of the nationalists' Irish Republican Army, of bombs and ambushes, interrogations, and ransackings, during which the British paramilitary force known as the Black and Tans gained notoriety for their brutality, and the republican leader Michael Collins developed from a dashing, romantic Robin Hood-style guerrilla fighter into a charismatic political figure. In 1921 the Anglo-Irish Treaty put an end to the fighting,

republicans behind de Valera, who held out for a united Ireland and denial of all military concessions to Britain. The Civil War that broke out between the two factions in July 1922 claimed the lives of thousands more Irish men and women, including Collins himself, generated internecine bitterness that lasts to this day, and ended in May 1923 with defeat for the hard-line republicans.

FROM FREE STATE TO REPUBLIC—DECADES IN A RURAL BACKWATER

Eamon de Valera went to jail, and the brand new Irish nation began to lick its wounds. In 1924 de Valera was released and in 1926 quit Sinn Fein and started his own Fianna Fail (Warriors of Destiny) party. Six years later

Bitter anger erupts on the streets of central Londonderry: A young boy hurls a missile during civil disturbances.

Fianna Fail came to power, and de Valera started a mammoth term as Taoiseach (prime minister) that would last until well after World War II. The Free State renamed itself "Eire," a good indication of the folksy-nationalist direction it was heading in: a direction inspired by de Valera's vision of "a land whose countryside would be bright with cozy homesteads, whose fields and villages would be joyous with the sounds of industry, with the rompings of sturdy children, the contests of athletic youths and the laughter of comely maidens, whose firesides would be forums for the wisdom of serene old age …" Fianna Fail abolished the oath of allegiance to the Crown, and claimed sovereignty over the north (a bone of contention not resolved until the Good Friday Agreement of 1998—see pp. 294–295). Meanwhile the Roman Catholic Church tightened its grasp on all aspects of life south of the border. In the north, Protestantism stayed in the ascendancy while the economy took a nosedive along with the rest of the industrial world.

Eire declared itself neutral for the duration of World War II, though thousands of men and women from both sides of the border volunteered to fight in the Allied cause. Belfast was badly bombed—in one terrible night in

April 1941 more than 700 civilians were killed. In 1949 Eire—now calling itself the Republic of Ireland—left the British Commonwealth, and all through the '50s it stagnated, stuck in an agricultural and social backwater, with increasing censorship of books, films, and plays by a Church and State unwilling to come to terms with the modern world. Emigration soared as younger Irish people left to find better-paid work and greater artistic, sexual, and moral freedom than small-time farming or backwoods town life in Ireland could provide.

From the perspective of Protestants north of the border, life in the Republic seemed backward and unappealing, although the slow and steady rundown of Ulster textile and shipbuilding industries was beginning to make itself felt. Northern Catholics were still enduring a position of economic and social inferiority cemented in place by the inbuilt majorities of Protestant local politicians.

PROGRESS IN THE REPUBLIC

In the 1960s the Republic became a more energetic and outward-looking place under the leadership of Taoiseach Sean Leamass—Eamon de Valera, by now the grand and rather out-of-touch old man of republicanism, had

Nowadays the mood in Londonderry is better expressed in the hands-across-the-divide message of the Peace Statue on the city walls.

been "moved upstairs" to occupy the presidency. In the '70s the country joined the European Union and began to benefit from a flow of economic development money and a healthy agricultural economy. The 1980s saw a faltering in progress and a rise in emigration, but the following decade became a gallop to economic glory on the back of the Celtic Tiger and a remarkable boom in tourism and international popularity.

NORTHERN IRELAND THROUGH THE TROUBLES

As for Northern Ireland in the 1970s, '80s, and '90s, rarely can a country have undergone such a thoroughly publicized rollercoaster ride through such depths of misery and despair. Discrimination against Roman Catholics in the workplace, in housing, and in health, education, and social services had been enshrined in those Protestant political majorities since 1921—and for centuries before that, too. The Civil Rights movements of the late 1960s aimed to force change through popular protest, in as peaceful a way as possible. But with so much mutual mistrust and bitterness, contempt and bigotry on hand, the marches became the flashpoint for full-blown civil

strife. From the moment in August 1969 that British troops were deployed on the streets of Londonderry and Belfast, the Troubles were on every television set and radio. They were to stay center stage, making Northern Ireland a byword for sectarian hatred and terrorism for almost 30 years (see pp. 292–295), until the historic paramilitary ceasefires and the signing of the Good Friday Agreement in 1998.

Reflecting on the state of affairs at the start of the 21st century, no one would claim that all the problems of the north have been solved, but great changes for the better have taken place. People from all traditions and shades of political and religious opinion are learning to live with each other in a new spirit of realism. Peace is catching, and looks more secure with each passing year.

Above all, the people of Northern Ireland want to let the outside world know that they are not all like some of the opinionated sectarians who have grabbed headlines during the past 30 years or so of the province's difficulties. In fact, the absence of tourist overkill has left Northern Ireland and its people with a fresh, welcoming approach that every visitor can appreciate. ∎

Arts & culture

NOVELISTS, PLAYWRIGHTS, POETS, SHORT-STORY WRITERS; ROCK BANDS, fiddle players, opera stars, traditional singers; TV soap stars and comedians, film directors and actors; dancers, painters, street performers … Ireland has them all, in numbers and of a quality that would be the envy of a country ten times the size. Just think of James Joyce, Samuel Beckett, W. B. Yeats, Seamus Heaney, Edna O'Brien, U2, the Chieftains, John McCormack, Mary Black, Ballykissangel, Father Ted, The Commitments, *Ryan's Daughter,* Maureen O'Hara, *Riverdance,* Jack Yeats …

The oral tradition of Irish folk tales dates back 2,000 years or more, and it is embedded deep in the national sense of identity. It's not by random selection that the influential traditional music group De Danaan named themselves after a mythical race of magic-makers, or that the cultural activities center in Mullaghbane in County Armagh is named Ti Chulainn, the House of Chulainn, the legendary blacksmith of nearby Slieve Gullion mountain. Such names, and the tales that are associated with them, still carry considerable power.

THE MIGHTY DEEDS OF FIONN MACCUMHAILL

The best known of Irish heroes must be Fionn MacCumhaill—Finn McCool—not in fact a giant, although his mighty deeds make him seem one. Stories were beginning to be made up about him in the fourth and fifth centuries. Fionn's most famous act was to establish the band of knightlike heroes known as the Fianna, the Warriors. Entry requirements were tough. Anyone who wanted to join the Fianna had to be able to defend himself against nine spears hurled simultaneously, while buried up to his waist in the ground and armed only with a hazel stick. Candidates also had to prove themselves capable of escaping a band of the Fianna while running through the woods, without cracking any twig or having any of their hair dislodged from its braid. While running full tilt they must also leap over a head-high stick, duck under a knee-high one, and pick a thorn out of the sole of their foot. And, of course, each aspirant member had to show himself matchlessly brave and honest, while also producing per-fectly polished poetry to order. There were not many Fianna.

Perhaps the best tale of all concerns Fionn MacCumhaill's love in old age for the beauti-ful Gráinne, daughter of Cormac the High King of Tara (see pp. 266–267), and his pur-suit of her after she had eloped with hand-some young Fianna member Diarmuid. This is a great-chase saga, and you'll find rocks and hollows known as "Diarmuid and Gráinne's Bed" all over Ireland. Fionn got his woman in the end, but only after wreaking his revenge on the dying Diarmuid (see p. 216) on Benbulben Mountain.

FROM TELLING TO WRITING

Tales like these were the bedrock on which Ireland's long-standing tradition of fireside storytelling was based. Literacy, education, and modern ways of entertainment have all but eclipsed such domestic tale-spinning, although it is reviving in a new generation of "ceilidh houses" in which people gather to swap songs and stories. But when this lyrical talent with words hits the page, it deepens into a very characteristic Irish magic. Ireland has produced four winners of the Nobel Prize for Literature—William Butler Yeats (1923), George Bernard Shaw (1925), Samuel Beckett (1969), and Seamus Heaney (1995)—a truly astonishing accolade for such a small country. The writer whom most regard as the greatest of the lot, James Joyce (1882–1941), never did win a Nobel Prize: His output was far too controversial. But it was Joyce with his dense, convoluted, and brilliant 1922 masterwork *Ulysses*—unbelievably daring with its sexual frankness and open challenge to the "Celtic

Great big smiles and plenty of energy from young Irish dancers, whose beautifully embroidered dresses carry intricate designs based on ancient Celtic symbols.

Twilight" quaintness of most Irish writing of the time—who set the stage, and made the template, for the modern novel.

James Joyce may head Ireland's roll call of 20th-century literary genius, but it bulges with other talent too. Among short-story writers of note are Liam O'Flaherty (1897–1984), Sean O'Faolain (1900–91), Corkman Frank

Oscar Wilde: Searing, flamboyant wit

O'Connor (1903–66), with his superb stories of the 1919–21 War of Independence such as "Guests of the Nation," and the Kerry pub owner and gentle humorist John B. Keane (born 1928). Older-guard novelists who have caught the nuances of Irish life include Brian Moore (born 1921), Edna O'Brien (born 1932), the wonderfully subtle John McGahern (born 1934), and the masterfully funny and erudite Brian O'Nolan (1911–1966), who wrote under the names Flann O'Brien and Myles na gCopaleen.

STRUGGLE FOR LITERARY FREEDOM

These groundbreakers did not have it easy in the repressive cultural atmosphere of the Ireland in which they were trying to get their work published. Edna O'Brien had her 1960 novel *The Country Girls* banned for encourag-

ing immorality, while John McGahern's second novel, *The Dark,* treating as it did homosexual child abuse, was likewise banned in 1966. James Joyce himself wrote *Ulysses* abroad in self-imposed artistic exile, and had it published abroad, too—publication in its home country of what many regard as the most influential novel ever written would have

Samuel Beckett: Enigmatic brilliance

been unthinkable. When he died in 1941 his countrymen were still unable to buy his masterpiece in Ireland; they would have to wait until the 1960s.

Later writers to benefit from the freedom of expression won by these trailblazers include such as Roddy Doyle (born 1958) with *The Commitments, The Snapper,* and *The Van,* his sharp and funny working-class Dublin trilogy; Eoin McNamee (born 1960) with the dark Belfast Troubles novel *Resurrection Man;* Maeve Binchy (born 1940) and her string of "intelligent doorstopper" blockbusters; and Frank McCourt (born 1930), who was awarded the Pulitzer Prize in 1997 for *Angela's Ashes,* his searing account of a sad childhood.

Mention must also be made of a trio of writers who wrote not novels or short stories but remarkable autobiographies—Tomas

O'Crohan with *The Islandman* (1929), Maurice O'Sullivan with *Twenty Years A-Growing* (1933), and Peig Sayers with *Peig* (1936). These three native Irish-speakers from County Kerry's remote Blasket Islands represented an astonishing flowering of talent within a tiny, culturally isolated, and largely illiterate community.

Seamus Heaney: Nobel laureate poet

POETRY—FROM YEATS TO HEANEY

As for poetry—the line from William Butler Yeats (1865–1939) through Patrick Kavanagh (1904–1967) to Seamus Heaney (born 1939) glints with genius. Much of Yeats's poetry is undergoing a recession in popularity at present, part of a natural cycle; many see him as important as much for his catalytic effect on the Gaelic Revival of the late 19th century, and his articulation of an Irish sense of independent nationhood, as for his actual verses. In fact, the poet's painter brother Jack is seen nowadays as far more of an innovator, with his vivid expressionist art so profoundly influenced by the landscapes of Sligo where the Yeats boys spent much of their childhood.

Patrick Kavanagh's poetry, expressive of the backbreaking work and rural poverty—financial and spiritual—of his native County

Monaghan, cut away the myth of the dignified, happy peasant Ireland so dear to Eamon de Valera's heart and opened the way for the accessible, uncomplicated, yet profound insights of Seamus Heaney's work.

Heaney, a Northerner from Bellaghy in County Derry, found ways of exploring the tensions and anxieties of the Troubles with-

Roddy Doyle: raw Dublin humor

out climbing onto an overtly political soapbox; but it is his cameos of rural life and his journeys through the nature of faith and humanity that distinguish him as Ireland's foremost living poet.

THE STAGE ...

Among Irish playwrights to have influenced the world stage (often from positions of cultural exile) are household names such as Oscar Wilde (1854–1900), George Bernard Shaw (1856–1950), Sean O'Casey (1880–1964), with his great trilogy *Shadow of a Gunman, Juno and the Paycock,* and *The Plough and the Stars,* and the man who became James Joyce's secretary in 1932 before finding one or two things to say on his own account—Samuel Beckett (1906–1989), author of the world's least-understood famous play, *Waiting for Godot.*

"The way yeh love me is frih'nin ..." Brother Deco howls it out in *The Commitments* (1991).

... AND THE SCREEN

The classic early Irish film documentary, Robert O'Flaherty's *Man of Aran*, came out in 1934. But it wasn't until the establishment of the Irish Film Board in 1981 that Ireland really came into its own as a filmmaking country. Neil Jordan has triumphed with a tale of an IRA man tormented over his execution of a hostage *(The Crying Game, 1992)*, an account of the life and death of a War of Independence leader *(Michael Collins, 1996,* starring Liam Neeson), and an adaptation of Patrick McCabe's fable of small-town oppression *(The Butcher Boy, 1998)*.

Meanwhile, Jim Sheridan's star rose to international acclaim with his version of Christy Brown's *My Left Foot* (1989), starring Daniel Day Lewis and featuring the coasts of Killiney and Bray just south of Dublin; John B. Keane's sardonic rural parable *The Field* (1990), filmed in the spectacular scenery of the mountains around Killary Harbour on the Mayo/Galway border; and the story of the unjust imprisonment of the Guildford Four for an IRA bombing they did not commit, *In The Name Of The Father* (1993), also starring Daniel Day Lewis and partly set in the grim surroundings of Dublin's Kilmainham Gaol (see pp. 76–81).

Three sprightly, very funny films have been made of Roddy Doyle's Barrytown trilogy, *The Commitments* by Alan Parker in 1991, and *The Snapper* (1993) and *The Van* (1996), both by Stephen Frears. Meanwhile Hollywood has not forgotten the photogenic nature of Ireland's landscape—Mel Gibson filmed some wild "Scottish" scenes for his 1995 Anglo-bashing *Braveheart* around Trim in County Meath, while the beaches of County Wexford took a pounding during the making of Steven Spielberg's 1997 D-Day epic *Saving Private Ryan*.

IRISH AS SHE IS SPOKE & PLAYED

The Irish language, after a post-famine decline to the point where barely one in ten could speak it, has undergone a revival thanks to being allotted a place in the school curriculum. These days, while only 3 percent of people in the Irish Republic use Gaelic as their first language, more than 10 percent are fluent, and most educated people have at least a smattering. The language's strongholds—west Donegal, northwest Mayo, Connemara and

Blood, guts, and determination: Hurlers battle for glory in one of Ireland's most popular sports.

the Aran Islands, west Kerry, and a few other hotspots—are termed Gaeltacht areas, and receive subsidies to prop up their Gaelic-speaking communities. That's where you are most likely to hear Gaelic, although you'll read it all over the Republic in the form of place-names on bilingual road signs. Radio na Gaeltachta and Teilifís (TV) na Ghaeilge, both based in Connemara, cater specifically to Gaelic-speakers.

Pronunciation

á (bodhrán) = "aw" ("bow-rawn")
ane (cloghane) = short "an" sound ("cloch-an")
bh (cobh) = "v" ("cove")
ch (Achill) = "ch" as in Scottish loch
dh (bodhrán) is silent
eagh or **eigh** (Glenveagh, Glenbeigh) = "ay" ("Glenvay, Glenbay")
gh is silent at the end of a word, and softer than the "ch" sound in "loch" in the middle of a word—almost "h," but slightly harder.
h is slightly harder than "h," slightly softer than loch.

The revival of the language is one symbol of pride in Irish nationhood. Another is the huge popularity of traditional Irish games such as hurling and Gaelic football, administered by the powerful, and chiefly Catholic, Gaelic Athletic Association. You'll see children playing with hurley (wooden stick) and *sliotar* (leather ball) in most town parks on weekends. However, this traditionalism hasn't prevented soccer from becoming a ruling passion throughout Ireland, with the Republic's team reaching the World Cup quarterfinals of 1990, 1994, and 2002.

Another very popular pastime around south Armagh and in rural County Cork—to name it formally a "sport" might be stretching a point—is road bowling, in which players have to project an iron ball along the road for an agreed distance (up to a couple of miles in some cases) using as few throws as possible. Shortcuts over hedges and through the angles of bends in the road are all part of the skill. If, on your travels, you find an informal road block set up, the chances are that one of these keenly contested matches is going on. Take the opportunity and hop out of your car to see a very Irish bit of sport.

ON THE HORSES

Big bets can be laid at a road bowling match; but not as big as when thousands of people are gathered together for horse racing, Ireland's grand sporting passion. The Curragh in County Kildare is the place to go if you want to worship at the high temple of Irish racing (see pp. 96–97), but throughout the country you have your pick of nearly 30 courses and dozens of meetings, from the unique thrill of Laytown Races on the beach near Drogheda and the genial holiday atmosphere of Galway Races to the "dukes-and-dustmen" democracy of the Irish Derby at the Curragh in June.

There's a great sense of democracy at these occasions, as the drink and bonhomie flow. One word of warning—keep your wits about you, or you may find you have been sold a spavined nag by the friendly man in the greasy plus fours. If you really do want to buy a horse, try the Clifden Show in August for a Connemara pony (see p. 185).

TRADITIONAL MUSIC—ALIVE AND KICKING

Of all branches of art, it's the country's traditional music that most ostensibly carries the flag for Irish culture today—that infectious, irresistible forward rush of tunes that were originally created simply to help dancers keep in time, but proved to have a joyful life of their own as performance and "all-join-in" pieces.

The Dubliners and the Clancy Brothers promulgated Irish songs and ballads in the

The fair, the fat, and the freaky: Everyone's welcome in a session of traditional music, provided they know how to carry the tune.

1960s, the Chieftains burst onto the scene with brilliant musical dexterity in the early seventies and still play to worldwide acclaim, and younger bands such as De Danaan, Planxty, the Bothy Band, Dervish, Lunasa, Danu, and Patrick Street then found they could make a living by playing their native music all over the world. Masters of their craft such as *uillean* pipers Liam O'Floin and Davey Spillane, singers Dolores Keane, Mary Black, Cara Dillon, and Cathal McConnell, and fiddlers Tommy Peoples, Kevin Burke, and the young, dynamic Martin Hayes command a reverence among aficionados of the music that most rock stars could only envy.

Boy from Belfast: Van "The Man" Morrison hammers out another bluesy masterpiece live on stage.

The astonishing international rise of interest in Irish traditional music in recent years has a lot to do with the sheer size and geographical spread of the Irish diaspora, and is particularly noticeable in the United States. And Irish theme pubs that feature live traditional music can be found worldwide, sometimes in the most unlikely of places. Modern media have been enormously influential, too. Like it or not, the slick styling of shows such as *Riverdance* and *Lord of the Dance* have made a huge impact all over the world, drawing attention not only to the costumes and dancing but to the wild music that drives the whole thing along. And when listeners and watchers find themselves hooked, and decide to come over to Ireland to see where it all started, they find to their delight that the music has never been more healthily alive and kicking in its homeland.

PLEASURES OF THE SESSION

Well-honed music by professional troupes is laid on at Bunratty Castle and other such commercial venues that cater to the tourist trade. You may also find some of the big names in concert in the main towns and cities. But you'll find the best and most enjoyable traditional music—rough edges, occasional blemishes, and all—in the sessions that take place in pubs all over the country (see p. 43).

Anyone in town or village can tell you where and when you'll find a session. They tend to start around 9:30 in the evening and go on till 11:30 (or much later); they may be entirely spontaneous, but will probably be based round one or two musicians that the pub landlord has asked to turn up. The instruments will tend to be some combination of

fiddle, flute, squeezebox, *bodhrán* (round goatskin drum), tin whistle, traditional *uilleann* (literally "elbow") pipes, guitar, bouzouki, and banjo. Anyone is welcome to join in, provided they have the courtesy to ask first, and as long as they are skilled enough not to spoil the tune. Session music is rarely humdrum; frequently it touches great heights. Occasionally it goes into another dimension altogether, giving birth to a roaring beast of a medley that gathers its own unstoppable momentum, or a heart-meltingly emotional song or air that produces a pin-drop silence in a crowded bar. At such moments you wouldn't want to be anywhere else in the world.

Ireland seems an inexhaustible breeding ground for rock and pop performers—superstar Van Morrison from Belfast, boy bands

Hup-two-three-four! Opinions are divided over the *Riverdance* show: Is it a liberating breath of fresh air, or a crass travesty of traditional Irish culture?

Boyzone and Westlife, powerful women singers such as Mary Black and Sinead O'Connor, pop acts from the Corrs to the Cranberries, rock bands from Rory Gallagher's R&B outfits to world-straddling U2, and maverick wildman rock poets like Shane MacGowan of the Pogues and Phil Lynott of Thin Lizzy.

Great things can happen, too, when innovators mix traditional music with rock (The Pogues, The Waterboys), jazz (Moving Hearts, Davy Spillane) or more classical influences (Michael O'Súilleabháin). ■

Food & drink

NOT SO LONG AGO IRISH FOOD WAS FAMOUS FOR JUST ONE THING—ITS plainness. But affluence and tourism changed things, and palates became a lot less easy to please. In the 1990s there was a phenomenal growth in the number of restaurants serving international cuisine—and in the number of fast-food outlets, too. Homespun Irish dishes were regarded as peasant food and fell into disfavor. But that trend has been reversed with the onset of a new sophistication and a more demanding class of visitor.

A marriage made in heaven—a pint of creamy-headed Guinness, and a plate of fresh oysters with a zest of lemon.

Today's young kitchen supremos are wise enough to use the very best fresh ingredients that a mostly unpolluted island like Ireland has to offer, including wild Atlantic salmon, mountain lamb, shellfish, and organically grown vegetables and herbs. They take pleasure in adding a touch of modern magic to such traditional Irish fare as *champ* (mashed potatoes and scallions), *drisheen* (black pudding), *colcannon* (potatoes, cabbage, onions, and cream), *brack* (fruity tea bread), or the famous Irish stew that can have pretty much anything in it along with the four vital ingredients: neck of mutton, potatoes, onions, and a pinch of serendipity.

Visitors with their preconceptions still intact are always surprised to learn that the Irish national drink is not Guinness but tea. God alone knows how much tea is drunk in Ireland every day, but it's plenty. In the cities these days you can also get a very respectable cup of coffee, from cappuccino to espresso with all the variations in between. As far as alcoholic drink is concerned, there is a smallish but good selection of Irish whiskeys (County Antrim's Bushmills and Jameson's of Cork head the smoother brands, generally sweeter than their Scottish counterparts), and a growing number of "real ales" or unpasteurized, unfiltered beers brewed by small, independent breweries and served from a hand pump.

But it's the famous strong black stout with its creamy head, poured with ritual slowness from a tap rather than a bottle, that rules the pub roost. Beamish and Murphy's (favored in Cork) are sweeter, Guinness heavier and more bitter. What the Irish tell foreigners about Guinness is absolutely true—if you have tried it in your own country and disliked it, give it another go when you come over to Ireland. Guinness drunk in an Irish pub is one of the world's most nectarous delights.

You can certainly come across the famed poteen or home-distilled spirit if you know where to look and how to ask—generally the farther west and the more remote you are. Poteen-distilling is illegal, but the tradition is strong. So is the liquor, which can vary from smooth to extremely rough. If badly distilled it could turn nasty or even fatal, but the good stuff is characterful with a very special effect—including impromptu musicmaking. ∎

Smart young waiters whiz among the Dublin diners at one of Temple Bar's trendiest restaurants, the Eden Restaurant in Meeting House Square (see p. 356).

A festivals sampling

Specific dates can vary from year to year.
Contact www.festivals.travel.ie.

January
Lord Mayor's New Year's Day Parade—
Marching bands from around the world convene on Dublin. Tel 01 679 9144.

February
Imbolc, February 1—kicks off Londonderry's
Celtic seasonal festivals. Tel 028 7126 4132.

March
St. Patrick's Day, March 17—the world's
favorite party. Tel 01 676 3205.

April
City of Belfast Spring Fair—magnificent
floral displays. Tel 02890 270467.

**Public figures are satirized during a parade
on Ireland's famous St. Patrick's Day.**

May
Fleadh Nua, Ennis, late May—the cream of
Irish traditional music and dance in the county town of Clare. Tel 065 684 0406.

June
Irish Derby, late June—lords and layabouts
rub shoulders at the Curragh for Irish racing's
Big Day Out. Tel 045 441205.

Bloomsday, June 16—a literary Dublin pub
crawl in commemoration of Leopold Bloom,
hero of *Ulysses.* Tel 01 878 8547.

July
Orangemen's Day, July 12—with flute and
drum, Protestants celebrate the victory of
"King Billy," William III at the Battle of the
Boyne in 1690. July 12. Tel 02890 246609.

July/August
Galway Races (tel 091 753870) and
Galway Arts Festival (tel 091 509700)—
fun and games at the horse track, spilling over
into music, theater, films, and literary events
all round Galway city.
Connemara Pony Show, third Thursday
in August—festival fun at Clifden, County
Galway, based round buying, selling, and
exhibiting semi-wild ponies. Tel 095 21863.

September
**Matchmaking at Lisdoonvarna,
County Clare,** all month—enjoyable
lonely-hearts hokum for visitors, and a
chance for the west of Ireland's bachelors and
spinsters to get together. Tel 065 7074005.

October
Kinsale Gourmet Festival, mid-
October—great seafood celebration in a beautiful coastal location in County Cork
Tel 021 4772234 or 021 4273251.

November
Wexford Opera Festival, late
October/early November—some of the great
names of opera perform in front of a highly
enthusiastic audience. Tel 053 22144.
Cork Arts Festival, all month—arts,
dance, drama, music, film. Tel 021 4326445.

December
Downpatrick Christmas Festival, early
December—crafts, song, and good cheer. Tel
02844 610854.
Dingle Wren, December 26—boisterous
fun in Dingle; extravagant costumes and wild
music. Tel 066 9151188. ■

Whatever you'd most enjoy as your first taste of Ireland—a thought-provoking introduction to the country's history, fabulous collections of national treasures, or just a roaring good time—you'll find it here in Dublin.

Dublin

Georgian door knocker, Dublin

Molly Malone, or the Tart with the Cart, as Dubliners call this statue of their city's heroine

Dublin

THE BEST THING ABOUT DUBLIN IS THAT THERE IS NO ONE BEST THING. Each of a hundred aspects of Ireland's agreeable national capital helps to build a picture of a city that has seen a lot of history—hard times and prosperity, dignified consolidation and brash expansion—while somehow retaining a manageable pace and scale.

Those who remember Dublin "in the rare old times" will tell you that it has lost the cozy intimacy and humanity that inspired James Joyce. Certainly Ireland's wild 1990s ride to economic boom time on the back of the Celtic Tiger has transformed the center of the once sleepy city on the River Liffey into a place rattling with new money and smart new businesses, and stiff with the chic kind of eateries, wine bars, and dance clubs that young go-getters love to frequent.

Equally, there is still poverty in parts of the city where the new money doesn't reach and the visitors don't go. But those who come to Dublin as first-time visitors will be delighted to discover a city bustling with new confidence and energy, yet still conserving its time-warp pockets of peace in traditional back-street pubs and out-of-the-way gardens; a city so lively at nighttime that it hardly knows what to do with itself.

One of the key factors in Dublin's favor is that everything is built low around the city center, with the great Georgian and Victorian civic buildings such as the General Post Office, the Custom House, and the buildings of Trinity College dominating the scene, rather than anonymous modern office buildings. This definitely helps to put visitors in the mood for the mythic Dublin that so many expect to find—the Joycean old city where time runs slow and there's always time for another pint and a bit more chat.

Another advantage the city enjoys is its relationship with the River Liffey. They used to tell you that the superiority of Guinness over other porters and stouts was due to the use of Liffey water in its brewing. You might even believe it if you have never seen the muddy waterway—rather more turbid than limpid. However, the Liffey is close to Dubliners' hearts, and it makes a fine spectacle as it flows

Area of map detail

Belfast

Dublin

CENTRAL IRELAND
p. 235

0   6 kilometers
0   4 miles

⊲6

Balscaddan   Balbriggan
R122
R127
Rockabill

Naul
M1
Skerries   St. Patrick's
Island

Garristown
R127
R128   Shenick's
Island

R130   Loughshinny   ⊲5

Oldtown   Ballyboghil
R108   Lusk
R122   R128   Rush   Irish Sea

Broad Meadow Water
Portraine

Killsallaghan   Donabate   Lambay
Island

Ward
Swords   Malahide   Malahide
Castle   ⊲4

St. Margaret's   Dublin
Airport   Cloghran

CENTRAL IRELAND
p. 235   D U B L I N   N1   Kinsaley   Portmarnock

N2   M50   N32   Ireland's
Eye

Corduff   Santry   M1   Coolock   Sutton   Howth
Harbour

N3   Killester   Howth
Mulhuddart   Blanchardstown   Glasnevin   ST. ANNE'S
PARK   R105

Royal Canal   National Botanic   Casino   North Bull
Gardens   Marino   Island

EAST IRELAND
p. 89   Liffey   Lucan   PHOENIX
PARK   Clontarf   Isle of Man   ⊲3

N4   See map pp. 52-53   Holyhead, Liverpool

Grand Canal   DUBLIN   Dublin Bay

M50
Clondalkin   Rathgar   R131

R120   R118   Booterstown   Holyhead

Newcastle   N7   Rathfarnham   N11
R113   N81   N31   Dun Laoghaire   James Joyce
Rathcoole   Tallaght   Ballyboden   Tower

Saggart   Ballinteer   R113   Sandycove   Archibald's
Castle

Dodder   R113   153m   Dalkey
Killiney Hill ▲   Dalkey Island   ⊲2
N81   Stepaside   Killiney

R115   Golden Ball   N11   Killiney
Bay

Brittas   THE WICKLOW WAY   R119
582m   R117
648m   Glendoo   Shankill
Seahan ▲   Mountain   Glencullen   M11
618m   R116   to Bray
Corrig
Mountain   EAST IRELAND
p. 89   ⊲1
752m
Kippure ▲

△   △   △   △
A   B   C   D

Wisdom, blarney, and nonsense are staple conversational fare over the pints in Dublin's wonderful talking pubs.

through the heart of the city, between handsome old quays and beneath a series of fine bridges on its eastward journey to the sea in Dublin Bay. These Dublin bridges, favorite meeting places for Dubliners, are more like lively thoroughfares than mere river crossings.

Central Dublin is small enough to visit almost everything on foot, and most of its celebrated attractions—Trinity College, St. Stephen's Green, St. Patrick's Cathedral, shops and cafés on Grafton Street, the trendily renovated quarter of Temple Bar—lie south of the Liffey. North of the river things gets less polite, but just as much fun, with the sassy market vendors of Moore Street and Mary's Lane.

East of the city center the Liffey quays take you into an area that boasts a number of fine eating and drinking places with wonderful

views of the river. To the west you come to the great national monument of Kilmainham Gaol—a must-visit place—and Europe's largest urban green space, the magnificent open miles of Phoenix Park. This is a marvelous place to relax when the pace of city life is getting too much for you.

Although the city of Dublin is far and away the main attraction of the county to which it lends its name, the Irish capital is not the be-all and end-all of County Dublin. The DART, Dublin's swift suburban railway, will take you out of the city center, farther south or north to Dublin's outer pleasures. To the north you can enjoy walking in St. Anne's Park at Killester or

round the promontory of Howth Head—the Howth Head walk in particular is a beauty, with very fine views over miles of mountains and green countryside as well as far prospects out to sea. Rhododendron season at Howth Castle is a famous day out for Dubliners.

Driving on northward you'll find the handsome town of Malahide, well-known for good restaurants. Malahide Castle, home of the Talbot family for nearly eight centuries, is a romantic dream of battlements and turrets, on a core of late Norman work. Northward again is Skerries, a pretty fishing town where you can enjoy more brilliant sea views.

South of the city the DART runs through

some handsome Georgian and Victorian seaside towns—Dun Laoghaire, Dublin's main ferry terminal, is a pleasant place to idle and watch the world go by, while Dalkey with its narrow streets still retains something of an old-fashioned village air.

Other delights of south County Dublin are visiting the James Joyce Tower at Sandycove where the writer once stayed—it features at the opening of his masterpiece *Ulysses*—and spotting the millionaire residents of exclusive and expensive Killiney from the top of Killiney Hill. At the end of the DART you can pick up the flavor of a traditional Irish day by the sea at the old resort of Bray. ■

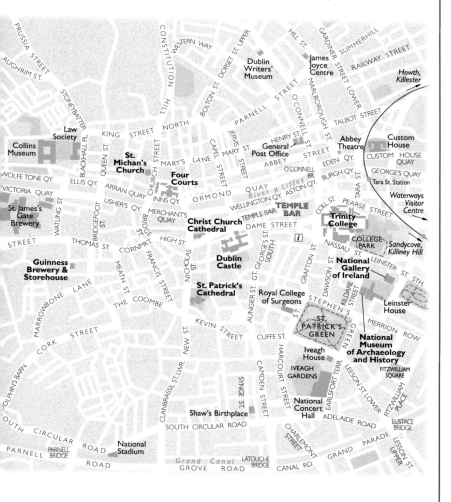

Trinity College

MOST PEOPLE SETTING OUT TO EXPLORE DUBLIN HAVE Trinity College at or near the top of their "must-see" list. It claims not only the finest set of university buildings in Ireland, but a roll call of alumni that embraces fierce polemicist Jonathan Swift and Ireland's first female President Mary Robinson, satirical humorists Oscar Wilde and Brian O'Nolan (Flann O'Brien), rebel leader Wolfe Tone and statesman Edmund Burke, *Dracula* author Bram Stoker and playwright Samuel Beckett. It also houses the Book of Kells, judged by many to be the most beautiful book in the world.

Trinity faces College Street, its entrance a low doorway far more modest than the grandeur of the buildings behind would lead you to expect. After the buzz of modern-day Dublin, everything seems very peaceful once you enter the cobbled quadrangles and university build-ings spanning four centuries.

Queen Elizabeth I founded Trinity in 1592. Her aim was "to civilize Ireland with both learning and the Protestant religion, for the reformation of the barbarism of this rude people." Certainly Protestants long ruled the roost

here; the Roman Catholic Church, although its adherents were in practice studying at Trinity from the early 19th century, did not give its official approval until the 1960s. (Until 1966 Catholics had to obtain the permission of their diocese to study at Trinity.) The admission of women undergraduates as long ago as 1903, however, shows that the university was far from hidebound over gender discrimination.

On your left as you enter the first quadrangle is the **university chapel,** a peaceful paneled church with beautiful painted windows under a stucco ceiling of subtle grays and greens. The chapel was built to an oval design in the momentous year of 1798, when the United Irishmen launched their doomed rebellion. On the far side of the quad you pass a 100-foot-high (30 m) Victorian campanile before heading right into the **Old Library,** a fine early 18th-century building. Inside on the first floor is a permanent exhibition entitled **Picturing the Word.** This explains the technicalities of how religious manuscripts were written and illustrated, preparing you for the kernel of the exhibition, the **Book of Kells** (see pp. 56–57).

On the upper floor of the Old Library is the truly impressive **Long Room,** a vast shadowy tunnel some 200 feet long (60 m) under a barrel-vaulted roof whose pillars turn out on close inspection to be huge stacks of books—about a quarter of a million in all. Aside from the books, two items here claim attention. One is an ancient harp of dark willow wood; it has been dated from 1400, although legend makes it 400 years older and places it in the hands of Brian Boru, the High King of Ireland who was killed as he led his men to victory over the Danes at the Battle of Clontarf in 1014.

Right: A quarter of a million books line the vaulted chamber of the Old Library's Long Room.

Book of Kells
www.tcd.ie/Library/kells.htm
- ✉ Trinity College, College St., Dublin 2
- ☎ 01 608 2320/608 2308
- 💲 $$

Dublin Experience
- ✉ Trinity College, Dublin 2
- ☎ 01 608 1688
- 🕐 Closed Oct.—mid-May
- 💲 $

The other historic treasure here is an evocatively tattered and roughly printed poster, a rare original copy of the Proclamation of the Republic of Ireland, pasted up around Dublin by the rebels during the Easter Rising of 1916 (see pp. 30–32) in a burst of splendidly sonorous phrases: "The Provisional Government of the Irish Republic, to the People of Ireland … We declare the right of the people of Ireland to the ownership of Ireland, and to the unfettered control of Irish destiny, to be sovereign and indefeasible … We hereby proclaim the Irish Republic as a Sovereign Independent State, and we pledge our lives and the lives of our comrades in arms to the cause of its freedom, of its welfare, and of its exaltation among the nations."

Two other attractions of Trinity are worth a look—the **Dublin Experience** in the Arts and Social Science Building, an audiovisual trot through Dublin's history, and the weird and wonderful flora and fauna carved in the Victorian stonework of the **Museum Building** on New Square. ■

Book of Kells

This glorious 680-page book of the four Gospels was crafted by monks at Kells Monastery (see p. 264) in County Meath around 800, at the height of Ireland's golden age of monastic talent and influence. It is the world's first example of an illuminated manuscript—a handwritten text beautified with handcolored illustrations. In 1953 it was rebound in four volumes, of which two are always on display—one open at a sumptuously illuminated page, the other at a page of text. The pages chosen for display are changed every

Close study of the illuminated letters in the Book of Kells reveals allegorical tableaus, along with scenes from everyday life in eighth-century Ireland.

few months to prevent the illuminated script fading from over-exposure to light. But in fact the eggwhite fixative employed by the monks 1,300 years ago has proved remarkably effective in keeping details sharp.

The book lies under glass in its own special display area at the heart of the Picturing the Word exhibition in the Old Library at Trinity College (see pp. 54–55). Whichever page is displayed when you visit, you can't fail to be dumbstruck by the beauty, humor, and force of imagination that come shining through the patina of the centuries. The Kells' illustrators must have been strongly influenced by the artistic brilliance of the monks of Iona (a monastery established off the west coast of Scotland in about 563), because the freedom of line and intricacy of detail so characteristic of Iona work of that era are all present here.

Each of the illuminated capital letters looks at first sight like an inextricable riot of circles, rectangles, and curlicued bits of foliage in gold, red, and blue. But as you stare you begin to see more—beasts with open mouths, misshapen devils, little domestic cameos, men passionately embracing, huge-eyed angels, heavenly flowers and fruit, all cunningly sneaked into uprights or packed into round spaces. The single page becomes an admonitory or encouraging sermon on the pitfalls and pleasures of life in the real world. What infinite pains the monks of Kells took in making their wonderful masterpiece—and what evident delight, too.

For colors they used what they had on hand, or could get by barter, purchase, or gift—gold leaf, chalk for white, copper verdigris for green. Red came from lead, black from charcoal, blue from either ground-up lapis lazuli, or woad, a European plant. How much eyesight the Book of Kells consumed, and how many monkish migraines the crafting of its minuscule details provoked, one can only guess.

Don't forget to admire the other superbly beautiful ancient Gospel books on display: the eighth-century pocketsized Book of Mulling made for some missionary monk, the Gospel made by Dimma the scribe around the same time, the Book of Armagh made in 807 for Torbach, Bishop of Armagh—and the oldest decorated Gospel book in existence, the Book of Durrow, created around 675.

On summer holiday weekends it's a very good idea to plan your visit as early in the day as possible to avoid a tedious half-hour's waiting in line. ∎

Opposite: The monks who created the Book of Kells used dozens of natural sources of color to complement their exquisite artistry.

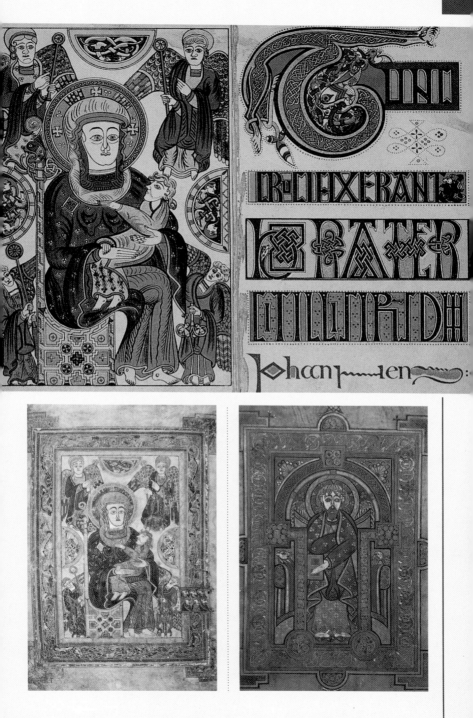

National Museum

www.museum.ie

53

Kildare St., Merrion Row, Dublin 2

01 677 7444

Closed Mon.

Bus: 7, 7A, 8 (Burgh Quay), 10, 11, 13 (O'Connell St.); Rail: Pearse Station, DART

National Museum of Archaelogy and History

INSIDE DUBLIN'S SPLENDID NATIONAL MUSEUM IS gathered the majority of the nation's most significant archaeological finds, brought here from the peat bogs, fields, and hillsides where they have been dug up or stumbled across over the years by turf cutters, ploughboys, and amateur archaeologists. The best of Ireland's treasure-trove of religious art is here, too. The museum itself was built in 1890, its grand entrance hall floored with a giant mosaic of the zodiac.

THE EXHIBITIONS

There are seven permanent exhibitions. The Treasury (the museum's chief attraction), Prehistoric Ireland, Ór—Ireland's Gold, and The Road to Independence are sited on the ground floor in the Great Hall, while the first-floor gallery and its side halls contain Viking Ireland and Ancient Egypt, along with The Church.

Prehistoric Ireland

On entering the Great Hall you will find the Prehistoric Ireland exhibition directly in front of you. Exhibits that catch the imagination are the **Lurgan log-boat,** 52 feet long (19 m), fashioned from a tree trunk nearly 5,000 years ago; the tiny **Knowth mace head** crafted of flint with whorls shaped like an astonished human expression, which came from Knowth burial chamber at Brú na Bóinne (see p. 268); and the **wood and leather shields** with which Stone and Bronze Age Irishmen protected themselves.

Ór—Ireland's Gold

Beyond Prehistoric Ireland in the center of the hall is Ór—Ireland's Gold, a wonderful exhibition of gold ornaments made in Bronze Age Ireland between circa 2000 B.C. and 700 B.C. One of many peaks of

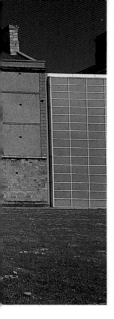

skill and artistry comes in the form of the **Gleninsheen Gorget—** a heavy, many stranded gold collar with circular shoulder pads found near the Gleninsheen wedge tomb in the Burren, County Clare.

The Treasury

The right-hand side of the hall contains the fabulous Treasury exhibition. Perhaps the three most famous exhibits here are the Tara Brooch, the Broighter Hoard, and the Ardagh Chalice.

The shape of the bejeweled eighth-century **Tara Brooch,** with its circular gold clasp and long pin, is familiar as the inspiration for countless pieces of modern Celtic jewelry. The brooch was found by chance in 1850 on the seashore at Bettystown near Drogheda, just south of the mouth of the River Boyne. The museum has it displayed above a mirror so that you can see the exquisite gold filigree work on both sides.

Another wonderful collection

Above: The early 18th-century Royal Barracks once housed 3,000 men; renamed Collins Barracks, it is now an annex of the National Museum.

Right: Another glory of Ireland's golden age, the eighth-century Ardagh Chalice was dug up in 1868 in a potato patch in a "fairy fort" in County Limerick.

Opposite: The Tara Brooch, a treasure of eighth-century Irish art, was found by chance in 1850, when a seashore wanderer picked it up on the beach.

Chalice cheat

In the 1860s a west Limerick man named Quinn was in the habit of planting his potatoes in the soil inside Reerasta ring fort at Ardagh. One day in 1868, while digging, he unearthed an astonishing hoard of treasure—the Ardagh Chalice itself, four brooches, a wooden cross, and a bronze cup that he smashed by mistake with his spade. The uneducated Quinn had only a hazy idea of the true value of his find, and sold the lot to a sharper-eyed neighboring doctor for £50—an enormous sum to an Irish peasant back then, but a raw deal all the same. Eight years later the hoard was on display in Dublin, its worth having risen many hundred-fold. Quinn was dead by then, his widow furiously campaigning for compensation. In 1878 a payment of £100 was made—not to the Widow Quinn, but to the Bishop of Limerick, on whose land the potatoes had been planted. It was left to the Bishop and his conscience to deal fairly with Mrs. Quinn. To his credit, he handed over half his windfall to her. ∎

of treasures is the **Broighter Hoard,** discovered in the 1890s near Limavady in County Londonderry. This is pre-Christian goldwork at its finest—leaf-thin hollow necklace balls, disks with hammered indentations, crescent-shaped lunulae to wear round the neck, and a model boat of sheet gold so thin it looks as if a touch would break it.

The **Ardagh Chalice—**a wide-bowled, two-handled cup of softly glowing silver-copper alloy banded with finely chased gold and set with crystal, enamel, and amber—was made in the eighth century, Ireland's golden age. The story of its discovery near Ardagh in west Limerick (see p. 59) is one that tells plenty about 19th-century society and its values.

Other glories of the Treasury exhibition are the **Derrynaflan Hoard,** which contains a silver chalice, paten and other treasures of the eighth and ninth centuries found as recently as 1980 by casual seekers wielding a metal detector at Derrynaflan in County Tipperary.

Among the the Treasury's extensive collection of reliquaries and shrines is the bronze **Shrine of St. Patrick's Bell,** ornamented with crucifixes, gold, and gemstones. It was made around 1100 to hold the sturdy iron bell (ca 406) also on display.

Other wonderful reliquaries include several gem-encrusted shrines to hold the crosiers of 11th-century bishops, the eighth-century **Moylough belt-shrine** of bronze plated with silver

Above: Dignified Leinster House; Below: The shrine that housed St. Patrick's bell for centuries

that was found near Tobercurry in County Sligo, and an assortment of book-shrines that includes one made to hold a psalm-book said to have belonged to St. Columba. Strangest of all to modern sensibilities are the shrines for such objects of veneration as St. Lachtin's arm, St. Bridgid's shoe, and St. Patrick's tooth.

The Road to Independence
This is the fourth exhibition on the ground floor, occupying the left-hand side of the Great Hall opposite the Treasury. It tells the story of Ireland's struggles to break political ties with Britain in the early 20th century, from the Easter Rising of 1916 through the guerrilla warfare that followed, the 1919–21 War of Independence, and the disastrous Civil War of 1922–23 between the army of the newly born Irish Free State, backed by the British government, and the forces of the IRA. Of all the deaths in the Civil War, none was more poignant than that of Michael Collins, charismatic young commander-in-chief of the Free State Army. On display is the uniform that Collins was wearing when he was shot by an IRA sniper near Bandon in County Cork on August, 22, 1922.

Viking Ireland
Upstairs you'll find Viking Ireland in the gallery on the right side, directly above the Treasury. Giving the lie to the Vikings' enduring image as bone-headed philistines intent only on plunder and slaughter, this fine exhibition reveals them as sensitively skilled artists in metal—particularly the decorative pins and brooches swirling with interlacing patterns.

Medieval Ireland 1150–1150
Alongside Viking Ireland is this fascinating exhibit that explores the era when power shifted from the

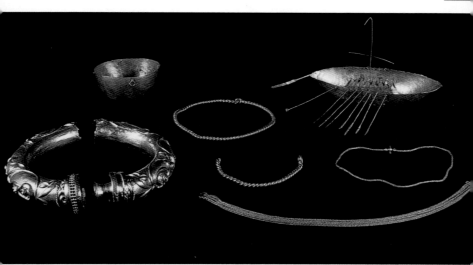

Irish to English kings, when the land was settled by English lords. A unique collection of artifacts, many never before on show, illustrates the lifestyles, trades, and activities of the people of Ireland—kings, lords, and warriors in the **Power Gallery,** farmers, artisans, and townspeople in the **Work Gallery,** and bishops, priests, and their parishioners in the **Prayer Gallery.**

Ancient Egypt

At the front of the upper gallery, next to the curve of the Rotunda, is the last of the permanent exhibitions, Ancient Egypt, containing everything you'd expect on this theme from painted mummy cases to dog-headed gods.

NATIONAL MUSEUM OF DECORATIVE ARTS AND HISTORY

Collins Barracks, just north of Wolfe Tone Quay on the River Liffey 1.5 miles (2.4 km) east of the parent museum, is home to a decorative arts collection.

The building itself is impressive in its unadorned simplicity, a flat-faced gray stone barracks block with a pedimented central section, built in 1704 (when it was known as Royal Barracks) to house 3,000 men and 1,000 horses. These days it holds a fine collection of Irish ceramics, silverwork from elaborate 17th-century goblets to swirly modern jewelry, costumes through the ages, weapons, and a great range of furniture from solid ancient carved chairs to up-to-the-minute contraptions.

LEINSTER HOUSE

Massive Leinster House, housing the Irish Parliament, Dáil Éireann, stands next to the National Museum. To look at the workings of Irish democracy, buy a ticket for the visitors' gallery from the entrance when the Dáil is not in session.

The house was built between 1745 and 1748 as the Dublin seat of the Earl of Kildare. Twenty years later, when the earl became Duke of Leinster, its name was changed. It became the seat of the Irish Parliament in 1922, shortly after the War of Independence, when the Free State Government established itself there. ■

The first-century B.C. Broighter Hoard shows early Irish gold working of astonishing skill and delicacy.

Leinster House
www.irlgov/oireachtas
🄰 53
✉ Kildare St., Dublin 2
☎ 01 618 3000

National Museum of Decorative Arts and History
🄰 53
✉ Collins Barracks, Benburb St., Dublin 7
☎ 01 677 7444
🕐 Closed Mon.
 Bus: 25, 25A, 66, 67 (Middle Abbey St.); Rail: Heuston Station; Museumlink bus from National Museum of Archaeology and History

Shoppers and browsers flock down Grafton Street, Dublin's dispensary of retail therapy.

Walk: Through central Dublin

This stroll through the heart of Dublin leads from the bustling riverfront to the leafy green oasis of St. Stephen's Green and on through the trendy quarter of Temple Bar. From there it runs along the characterful quays of the Liffey to reach the city's grandest and most handsome Georgian building, the Custom House.

Starting on **O'Connell Bridge,** walk south to cross the River Liffey and keep ahead to pass the entrance that leads to **Trinity College ❶** and the Book of Kells (see pp. 56–57). Bear east along Nassau Street, then turn right down Kildare Street to pass the **National Museum of Archaeology and History ❷** (see pp. 58–61). At the bottom of Kildare Street, bear right through the gardens of **St. Stephen's Green ❸,** then turn right up Dublin's prestigious shopping thoroughfare of **Grafton Street,** stopping at the sidewalk tables of **Bewley's Oriental Café ❹** *(78 Grafton St., tel 01 677 6761)* for a cup of coffee.

At the top of Grafton Street, bear left along Suffolk Street past the old church that houses the **Dublin tourism center,** and left again along Dame Street to reach **Dublin Castle** and the **Chester Beatty Library and Gallery of Oriental Art ❺** (see pp. 66–69). From here steer northeast through the

kaleidoscopic colors, sounds, and streetscapes of **Temple Bar** (see p. 64) until you hit the River Liffey. Bear left along the south quays of the river to the end of Merchant's Quay, where you cross the Liffey on **Father Matthew Bridge** to find the Georgian dome and facade of the **Four Courts** facing you to the right. The building still houses Dublin's High Court and Supreme Court.

Turn right along the river past the Four Courts to make your way back to the south end of O'Connell Street. A little way up on the left you'll find the great colonnaded portico of the **General Post Office** or **GPO ❻** *(O'Connell St., tel 01 705 7000),* a fine Palladian building of 1814–18, now a national monument and symbol of the Easter Rising of 1916. It was from the GPO's steps that the Proclamation of the Republic was read.

Return down O'Connell Street, and near the bottom turn left along Abbey Street Lower to find the **Abbey Theatre** ❼ *(Lower Abbey Street, tel 01 878 7222, box office closed Sun., theater open for performances only)*, Ireland's national theater, founded in 1898 by poet W. B. Yeats and his patron Lady Gregory.

Now turn down to the river. Before veering

Shoppers take a break in Bewley's elegant Oriental Café on Grafton Street.

right back to O'Connell Bridge, walk a block downriver to see the **Custom House** ❽ *(Custom House Quay, tel 01 888 2538, closed Mon. & Tues. Nov.–mid-March)*, built between 1781 and 1791, Dublin's grandest building with its arcaded wings and central dome. ■

🗺 See area map p. 51 C3
▶ O'Connell Bridge
↔ 4 miles (6 km)
🕐 From 2 hours to a whole day, depending on which attractions you decide to explore
▶ O'Connell Bridge

NOT TO BE MISSED

- Trinity College & the Book of Kells
- Ór—Ireland's Gold exhibition in the National Museum
- Chester Beatty Library & Gallery of Oriental Art
- General Post Office
- Custom House

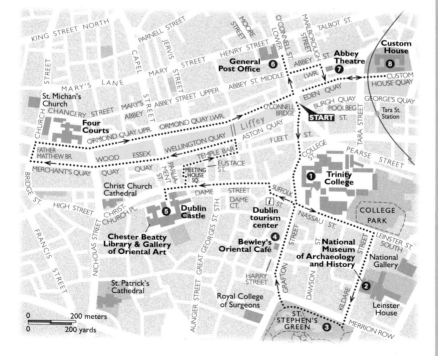

Temple Bar

Temple Bar

53

Bus: All city-center
buses; Rail: Tara St.
Station, DART

IF YOU HAD MENTIONED TO A GROUP OF DUBLINERS 20 years ago that you were going to hang out in Temple Bar, a lot of funny looks would have come your way. These days all you'll get is advice as to where to shop and which street has this great little restaurant, and there's this Georgian dance group on at the Arthouse …

The happy-go-lucky atmosphere of Temple Bar extends to its exterior decor.

Not so long ago Temple Bar (named after a local landowner, Sir William Temple, whose property included a sand bank, or bar, on the south side of the river) was due to be flattened to make way for a bus depot. The area just west of Trinity College had become so run down and seedy that no one wanted to live or work there, much less visit for pleasure. Then Group 91, a group of young architects, came up with some radical plans for the district. They designed a compact mix of galleries, theaters, and an arts center around a market square. Rooflines became fun, sprouting twisted rods like punk hair; balconies curved and snaked; buildings lost their drab brick and whitewash in favor of hot orange or Mediterranean blue.

Temple Bar suddenly became the trendiest place in Dublin. New boutique and lifestyle shops proliferated. Artists, photographers, and filmmakers began to frequent the area and exhibit. And at night a tide of over-refreshed youngsters spilled between dance clubs and pubs.

This is the place to come during the day for a good cup of coffee or a meal in an ethnic restaurant, if either snappy or flea market shopping suits the mood, or if you just feel like people-watching for a while. At night you'll still get the mad crowds, though, with plenty of noise and rowdy behavior.

The heart of Temple Bar is **Meeting House Square,** scene on Saturday mornings of an open-air market, a great place to stock up on fabulous olives, cheeses, sushi, homemade bread, and sausages. Around the square are a school of acting and a children's activity center, The Ark, along with a gallery and center for photography, Temple Bar Music Centre, the Arthouse arts center, and the Irish Film Centre and Archive. ∎

St. Stephen's Green

AT THE FAR END OF GRAFTON STREET FROM TRINITY
College lies St. Stephen's Green, 22 acres (9 ha) of gardens at the heart
of southside Dublin. Generations of Dubliners have come here to
sunbathe, stroll, and flirt among the flowerbeds and under the trees.

You'll find monuments here to
heroes of Ireland's long struggle
for Home Rule—notably the 1798
leader Wolfe Tone, and Constance
Gore-Booth, Countess Markiewicz
(see pp. 214–215), who fought
tigerishly against British rule and
was imprisoned for her activities
during the 1916 Easter Rising and
subsequent conflict.

Georgian buildings surround the
Green, including the pedimented
Royal College of Surgeons on
the west side, where, in 1922, the con-
stitution of the new Irish Free State
was drafted under the chairmanship
of Michael Collins. The big hotel on
the north side, with its sculptures of
princesses lording it over bond
maids, is the **Shelbourne,** a
mid-Victorian extravaganza.

More of Dublin's handsome
Georgian architecture graces

Upper Merrion Street and
Merrion Square just northeast
of St. Stephen's Green, and
Harcourt Street to the south.
Take plenty of film on your stroll—
it's impossible to resist the famous
double doorways, side-by-side
entrances to neighboring houses,
flanked by columns, with elaborate
semicircular fanlights above. ■

Timeless elegance
is the keynote of
Georgian Dublin,
in the fountains
and lawns of St.
Stephen's Green
(top) and the
doorways of
surrounding
streets (above).

Dublin Castle

FOR SEVEN CENTURIES THE PRIME SYMBOL OF ENGLISH dominance over Ireland, Dublin Castle has long had its medieval grimness dressed up in mellow Georgian brick. There are elaborate 18th-century State Rooms, an undercroft, and various towers to explore. The castle's Clock Tower is home to one of the world's great collections of Middle Eastern and Oriental manuscripts and art.

Dublin Castle
www.dublincastle.ie
🅰 53
✉ Dame St., Dublin 2
☎ 01 677 7129
🚌 Bus: 50, 54A, 56, 77 from Eden Quay; Rail: Tara St., DART
💲 $$

The castle was built in the early 13th century as the seat of power for the English rulers of Ireland, a function it served for the following 700 years right up until the establishment of an independent Irish Free State in 1922.

There were at least two sieges of Dublin Castle—one in 1534 by "Silken Thomas" Fitzgerald, whose forces were driven off when the garrison made a gallant sortie, and the other a hopelessly brave attack by the republican rebels during the Easter Rising of 1916, who succeeded for only a few hours in penning up the British Army soldiers.

Not much remains of the original castle, which was redesigned internally in good Georgian style with a range of buildings added at the elegant height of the 18th century. Down in the **Undercroft** you can inspect the ancient footings of the Norman castle's Powder Tower, bedded on walls that the Vikings raised round a fortress of their own three centuries before, along with ancient segments of city wall and moat—a real sense here of a hidden past under your hand.

The main focus of a tour around the castle, though, is a circuit of the opulent 18th-century **State Rooms,** still sometimes used to entertain foreign dignitaries. The tour has to be taken with a guide, who follows a fixed route. It includes **St. Patrick's Hall,** almost 100 feet long and festooned with banners of the long-disbanded Knights of St. Patrick under a fine painted and paneled ceiling, the gorgeous powder-blue **Wedgwood Room,** the great **Drawing Room** entered between gilt Corinthian columns and barred with light from tall windows, and a **Throne Room** stiff with gold and lit by golden chandeliers.

CHESTER BEATTY LIBRARY & GALLERY OF ORIENTAL ART

The real treasure of Dublin Castle, however, resides in the gardens at the back of the castle beyond the State Apartments (enter by the Ship Street gate), home to the incomparable Chester Beatty Library and Gallery of Oriental Art. Dublin is lucky to have this fabulous collection, put together over the best part of 60 years by the agents of Canadian mining tycoon Sir Alfred Chester Beatty (1875–1968). Beatty moved to Dublin in 1953 and gave his collection to the Irish nation in 1956.

Beatty was primarily interested in Oriental art and in religious manuscripts—he owned more than 300 copies of the Koran—and eventually amassed some 22,000 manuscripts as well as thousands of paintings, printed books, maps, and carved objects.

Right: The bride prepares to jump on a pyre—one of the illustrations in the Chester Beatty collection.

Chester Beatty Library & Gallery of Oriental Art
www.cbl.ie
✉ Dublin Castle, Dublin 2
☎ 01 407 0750
🕐 Closed Mon. Oct.–April
🚌 Bus: 50, 54A, 56, 77 from Eden Quay; Rail: Tara St., DART

The **Clock Tower** displays, occupying two floors of the tower, are arranged in seven exhibitions that pick and choose among the highlights of this huge mass of material. They are so absorbing that you will certainly want more than half a day to appreciate them. You'll find a good magnifying glass enhances your enjoyment, too, since there is so much delicate detail in the Oriental work.

Gallery Floor 1

On entering Gallery Floor 1 you'll find an exhibition outlining the life and work of Sir Alfred Chester Beatty. Beyond this the gallery is simply but effectively laid out. Most of the material on this floor comprises manuscripts and printed books, bindings, calligraphy and typography, miniature paintings, prints, and drawings.

On the left side of the gallery are exhibits from the **Western and European traditions.** From the Egypt of 1160 B.C. a papyrus screed has somehow survived; love poems, said to be the most important example of ancient Egyptian poetry in existence, are written on it in Hieratic text. There's also a wonderfully illuminated 15th-century Book of Hours. In the center is the Islamic material—Arabic, Persian, and Turkish. Here is a unique treatise written by a medieval Iraqi expert on engineering, the use of artillery, astronomy, and geometry. On the right you'll find treasures from India and East and Southeast Asia. They include Tibetan ceremonial swords and a magic dagger with a carved deity on the pommel; also many Indian paintings and examples of jeweled work.

This section also contains **decorative arts from China and Japan.** Because of the miniature size of much of the work, you'll benefit from taking plenty of time over these collections. From China are cups carved from rhinoceros horn, lacquered boxes, finches painted on silk, and a number of tiny snuff bottles in jade, lacquer, porcelain, and mother-of-pearl.

The Japanese items form the cream of the Chester Beatty Gallery's non-manuscript displays. Notable are dozens of **netsuke—** toggles made to weigh down the ends of a kimono cord—little men, animals, trees, and birds carved from ivory, wood, or jade.

But it is the Japanese paintings that fascinate, intrigue, and inspire. Here are dozens of hand-painted scrolls of paper or silk, dating from the early 17th to the late 19th centuries, telling stories or recounting courtly and military history. Some are up to 80 feet long (29 m), each scene shown in utmost detail—a young girl daydreaming on a rock, a poets' meeting at which everyone is trying to look wiser than the next man, the courtesan Konami gripping her handkerchief between her pearly little teeth in a carefully staged flood of emotion.

Then you come across a whole

"Three Men Standing beside a Pool"

selection of prints—the tranquil "Plum Garden at Karneido," the actor Sawamura Sojuro caught pulling a face in 1794. Such works of art form a bridge between cultures and ages across which it is a breathtaking privilege to step.

Gallery Floor 2

Upstairs in Gallery Floor 2 the great spiritual traditions of the world are explored. The layout is the same as on the floor below. To the left are items illustrating the **Western and Christian tradition**—pre-Christian texts, Judaic scrolls, and early Old and New Testament manuscripts. Here Christian treasures include a double papyrus page of St. Luke's Gospel, copied early in the third century; also a segment of the Book of Revelations of around

the same date, the oldest fragment of the final New Testament chapter yet discovered. Even more astonishing is the version of St. Paul's Epistles written around 200—only three or four generations separated scribe and author. Out of the Middle Ages come wonderfully illuminated bibles, and a copy of St. Augustine's *City Of God* dated from around 1100.

In the centrally sited **Islamic section** are illustrated manuscripts of the Koran, miniature paintings of the life of the Prophet, and Islamic history and traditions within the Arab, Persian, Mughal Indian, and Turkish worlds. The Arabic calligraphy of the richly gilded Koran texts is of stunning beauty as an art form, as are the ancient jeweled Koran stands and

the tiny gold cases inlaid with enamel that were made to hold miniature copies.

The right of the gallery houses the **Eastern religions—** Buddhist, Hindu, Jain, Sikh, Daoist, and Shinto. In Southeast Asia Sir Alfred Chester Beatty collected Thai paintings of the life of Buddha, including one of the saint as a golden elephant in flight, and gilded lacquer statues from Burma.

Tibet yielded elaborate prayer wheels, and a Thanka painting on cotton cloth of the four-armed Avalokitesvara.

A good tip to ensure maximum enjoyment of this unique and remarkable collection—don't try to see it all in one day. Set aside two half days, and give your senses time to recover in between. ∎

"Snow at Night"—a detail from one of the Chester Beatty Library's wonderfully evocative Oriental paintings

Literary Dublin

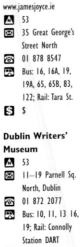

Seated as a statue on a canalside bench, poet Patrick Kavanagh receives a little less than his due respect from a young Dubliner.

James Joyce Centre

www.jamesjoyce.ie

- 🚇 53
- ✉ 35 Great George's Street North
- ☎ 01 878 8547
- 🚌 Bus: 16, 16A, 19, 19A, 65, 65B, 83, 122; Rail: Tara St.
- 💲 $

Dublin Writers' Museum

- 🚇 53
- ✉ 11–19 Parnell Sq. North, Dublin
- ☎ 01 872 2077
- 🚌 Bus: 10, 11, 13 16, 19; Rail: Connolly Station DART
- 💲 $$$

IF THERE'S ONE ART ABOVE ALL OTHERS FOR WHICH Dublin is celebrated, it is the city's astonishingly rich literary heritage. The old saying that there's the making of a great novel on the back seat of every Dublin cab has some truth to it. Dubliners seem to be born with a feel for rhythms and cadences of language. Conversations in the bars and on the street corners of the city are rich in imagery and imagination to the eavesdropping outsider. In such fertile ground, many seeds of genius have flourished.

THE WRITERS

James Joyce (1882–1941) towers over literary Dublin. His shadow has hardly diminished in the 80 years since his 1922 masterpiece and love-letter-in-exile to the city, *Ulysses,* was first published.

These days, Joyce fanatics from all over the world descend in fancy dress on Dublin each "Bloomsday"—June 16, the date on which all the action in *Ulysses* takes place—and embark on a **James Joyce Trail** that faithfully follows the perambulations of the novel's hero Leopold Bloom around the city's streets and pubs. You can join in (details from Dublin Tourism),

but make sure your digestion is in good shape as along with the pints of Guinness and the *Ulysses* readings, one ritual is immutable—the reenactment of Leopold Bloom's lunch of a gorgonzola cheese and mustard sandwich and a glass of burgundy in **Davy Byrne's pub** on Duke Street. Alternatively, enjoy the trail at any time of year and at your own pace by following the bronze plaques set into the sidewalks of central Dublin.

Dublin carries the mark of a host of literary giants besides Joyce. Dean Jonathan Swift (1667–1745), author of *Gulliver's Travels, Tale of a Tub,* and much other furiously indignant polemic and political satire, lies buried next to his platonic lover Esther Johnson, or "Stella" (1681–1728), in the nave of St. Patrick's Cathedral.

The **Abbey Theatre** on Abbey Street Lower saw historic opening nights of plays by Nobel Prize-winners W. B. Yeats (1865–1939) and Samuel Beckett (1906–1989). Near Baggot Street Bridge a **sculpture** of Monaghan-born poet Patrick Kavanagh (1904–1967) contemplates the turbid water of the Grand Canal, as Kavanagh himself loved to do while recuperating from lung cancer operations in the 1950s.

THE PUBS

So much of Dublin's literary life, high and low, has been conducted in the city's pubs. Patrick Kavanagh frequented **McDaid's** (see p. 73), whose Moorish frontage looks out on Harry Street, a pedestrian-only lane off Grafton Street. Acid-witted columnist and novelist Brian O'Nolan (1911–1966), writing like an avenging angel with a great sense of humor under the pseudonyms Flann O'Brien and Myles na gCopaleen, also drank in McDaid's, as did rambunctious playwright Brendan Behan (1923–1964).

Nearby on Lower Baggot Street is **Toner's** (see p. 73). North of the River Liffey are the working-class estates whose life and speech have been brilliantly captured by Roddy Doyle (born 1958) in his "Barrytown Trilogy"—*The Commitments, The Snapper,* and *The Van.*

THE MUSEUMS

A couple of literary museums are well worth visiting. The **James Joyce Centre** has an excellent reference library, first editions, memorabilia, and tapes of the great man reading from *Ulysses* and other works; James Joyce walking tours leave from here.

The modest birthplace of Nobel Prize-winning playwright George Bernard Shaw, at **33 Synge Street,** is evocative of (outwardly) stiflingly respectable Victorian life with a kind father who drank like a fish and a very strong-willed mother. You'll find the strands of many of these literary Dublin lives pulled together in the displays, portraits, and memorabilia in the **Dublin Writers' Museum,** just north of the top end of O'Connell Street.

Or you could opt for one of Dublin's organized Literary Pub Crawls (*details from Dublin Tourism, $$$*) and make a round of half a dozen pubs where actors bring Dublin writers to life. ■

Photographs, first editions, and other memorabilia commemorate Dublin's greatest novelist in the James Joyce Cultural Centre on Great George's Street.

St. Patrick's Cathedral

St. Patrick's Cathedral

www.stpatrickscathedral.ie

🅼 53

✉ Patrick's Cl., Dublin 8

☎ 01 453 9472

🚌 Bus: 49, 50, 54A, 77 (Eden Quay); Rail: Pearse Station DART

💲 $$

ST. PATRICK'S IS A BEAUTIFUL, UNCOMPLICATED BUILDING, much of it dating back to the 12th century, with a west tower and spire that soar to 225 feet (69 m). It was built on the site of a well where St. Patrick was said to have baptized converts, and there was probably a church on the site from the fifth century onward.

Inside you'll find the side-by-side graves of Dean Jonathan Swift and his companion "Stella." They lie under brass plaques set into the floor of the nave just beyond the entrance. On the south wall opposite hangs the self-penned Latin epitaph of Swift, "laid ... where fierce indignation can no longer rend the heart. Go traveller, and imitate, if you can, this earnest and dedicated Champion of Liberty." In the north transept is a little Swift exhibition.

There are some splendid tombs—notably the enormous 17th-century **Boyle Monument** with its three tiers of Westons, Fentons, and Boyles, and some fine 16th-century brasses in the aisle south of the choir—as well as a rather feeble likeness of Ireland's most revered musician, the blind harpist Turlough O'Carolan (1670–1738). Brass rubbings in the church can be made by arrangement (*tel 01-453-9472, $$$*).

Don't miss the old wooden door displayed with its central panels missing. In 1492 this was the door of the cathedral's chapter house, behind which the Earl of Ormond barricaded himself against his enemy the Earl of Kildare. Ormond refused to come out, even though promised safe passage, so Kildare hacked a hole in the door with his spear and stuck his unprotected arm through in a brave gesture of trust. Ormond grasped the hand thus offered, the feud was ended, and the expression "chancing one's arm," meaning taking a risk, entered the language. ∎

Great pubs
of Dublin

DUBLIN AND PUBS ... NOW WHY WOULD THEY COME TO mind together? Ireland is justly famous for its pubs—not as drinkers' dens, but as centers of social life, conversation, information, music, and fun. Here's a handful of suggestions to get you started.

At 8 Poolbeg Street, between Trinity College and the River Liffey, you'll find **Mulligan's;** the Guinness is superb. East of Grafton Street are **Davy Byrne's** at 21 Duke Street (see p. 70), **McDaid's** (see p. 71) at 3 Harry Street, and the traditional **Kehoe's** at 9 Anne Street South.

West of St. Stephen's Green lie three contrasting pubs. On Lower Baggot Street you'll find **Doheny & Nesbitt's,** a popular spot-the-politician pub at No. 5; and the plain-fronted **Toner's** at No. 139, the only pub, reputedly, that W. B. Yeats ever brought himself to enter, considering himself too refined for such places; and at 15 Merrion Row a traditional music pub, **O'Donoghue's.**

In Temple Bar you'll get tourist tunes in the **Oliver St. John Gogarty** at 58–9 Fleet Street. The modern **Porter House** at 16 Parliament Street brews its own delicious beer, while the **Stag's Head** in Dame Court off Dame Street has a cozy atmosphere.

At 3 Great George Street South **The Long Hall** is another pub full of character. Along eastward, two great traditional music pubs face each other across Bridge Street Lower, **O'Shea's Merchant** and the **Brazen Head.**

North of the river is a splendid trio of pubs with music: the **Cobblestone Bar** on King Street North and **Hughes** at 19 Chancery Street for traditional sessions, and **Slattery's** at 129 Capel Street for rock and ballads. ∎

If it's a nice day, you can take your drink out on the sidewalk—but then you might miss spotting some famous face inside Doheny & Nesbitt's popular pub.

Guinness Brewery & Storehouse

Guinness Storehouse
www.guinnessstorehouse.com

🅐 53

✉ St. James's Gate, Dublin 8

☎ 01 408 4800; 01 453 8364 (recorded information)

🚌 Bus: 51B, 78A (Aston Quay), 123 (O'Connell St.); Rail: Heuston Station

💲 $$$$

What's black and white and comes from copper?—the riddle that's solved millions of times a day all over the world. That's the Black Stuff!

HALF OF ALL THE BEER DRUNK IN IRELAND IS BREWED IN the sprawling Guinness Brewery at St. James's Gate on the Liffey's north bank. Altogether some 2,500,000 pints of the black stout with its creamy white head are drunk daily in 120 countries in all parts of the world—not bad for the little family brewery that Arthur Guinness established on the site in 1759. They are still black-roasting the malt here, and the popularity of Guinness continues to grow.

The brewery itself is not open to the public, but the company's spanking new **Guinness Storehouse** attraction nearby will tell you all you want to know, and then—fulfilling Guinness's proud boast—serve you the best pint and the best view in Dublin.

The Guinness company has always excelled at marketing itself through clever advertisements. They engaged some of the best commercial artists, and what they produced for the company were masterpieces of the genre—the

ostrich with the Guinness glass stuck halfway down its neck; the pelican with its bill crammed with bottles of stout; the toucan balancing a pint of Guinness on its orange bill ("See what Toucan do!"). All of these and more, many in full street hoarding size and color, are displayed in the Storehouse.

Inside one of Guinness's former fermentation and store plants, a handsome 1904 building in cast iron and brick, the company has developed a six-story exhibition based around a giant atrium—shaped like a pint glass. You'll find out exactly what goes into making the black nectar—ingredients, techniques, plant, and manpower—in a replica brewery with a giant "kieve" or mash tun, a big gleaming copper fermentation vat, and displays on the malting process and hop growing. Old photographs of the brewery during the 19th century are fascinating, with heavily moustachioed employees hauling casks into tottering mountains. Until after World War II the Guinness casks were mostly handmade especially for the brewery, and there is an exhibit of the cooper's art.

There's a retail store, of course, with a huge range of Guinness merchandise, and a restaurant. And then there's the pint itself—after the tour you'll be offered a taste of the Black Stuff in the viewpoint Gravity bar on the top floor. ■

Phoenix Park

Europe's largest urban green space

PHOENIX PARK IS THE GREEN LUNG OF DUBLIN—A VAST oasis of trees and grassland, which grateful Dubliners use for walking, bicycling, and playing games in the fresh air.

Surprisingly few visitors to Dublin get out to Phoenix Park, although it lies only just over a mile (1.6 km) upriver of the city center and conveniently close to the national monument of Kilmainham Gaol. The park never feels crowded—after all, this is the largest walled city park in Europe, with 1,750 acres (700 ha) of open space enclosed by 7 miles (11 km) of wall.

Displays in the **visitor center** near the northern edge trace the history of the park through various monastic and aristocratic owners to its 18th-century landscaping and opening to the public.

The President of Ireland lives in the park in a mansion called **Áras an Uachtaráin;** the residence of the U.S. ambassador is here, too, and there's a zoo and a hospital.

By far the best thing to do in Phoenix Park is to bring a picnic and wander through woods and over grassland, watching for fallow deer and stopping to enjoy the spectacle of Gaelic sports such as hurling and Gaelic football that are played on weekends. ■

Phoenix Park

🅰 52

✉ Main entrance on Parkgate St., opposite Heuston Station

🚌 Bus: 25, 26, 51, 66, 67, 69, 69X from city center; Rail: Heuston Station

Phoenix Park Visitor Centre

☎ 01 677 0095

🕐 Closed weekdays Nov.–mid-March

🚌 Bus: 37 from Abbey St. to Ashtown Gate

 $

Kilmainham Gaol

FOR ANY NEWCOMER WHO WANTS TO GET BENEATH THE skin and understand what has shaped the modern country, for anyone with the smallest interest in Irish history and the centuries of strain and strife between Ireland and England, this tour of Ireland's most famous jail is a must. The guides are young, enthusiastic, and passionately interested in their subject. You will come to appreciate why Kilmainham Gaol is a national monument, a keystone in the building of an independent Ireland, once you have walked its cold, echoing corridors, stood silently in one of the tiny, chilly cells, and stared around the blank-walled execution yards.

Certain dates resonate around Kilmainham—1798, 1803, 1848, 1867, 1881, 1883. These were the years of abortive uprisings and rebellions in an Ireland ruled from mainland Britain: Wolfe Tone's United Irishmen and their French allies in 1798, Robert Emmett's short-lived rising of 1803, the quickly-crushed Young Ireland rebellion in the famine year of 1848, the Fenian rising of 1867 backed by American money.

Leaders and activists of all these revolutionary groups, along with suspects and innocent parties, were held in this prison; so were Charles Stewart Parnell and Michael Davitt, leading lights of the reform-hungry Land League during the "Land War" of 1879 to 1882.

But 1916 is the most poignant date in Kilmainham, because it was during May of that year that 15 of the leaders of the Easter Rising were shot for treason in the prison yard. The General Post Office on O'Connell Street, scene of the first proclamation of the Irish Republic and the subsequent week-long siege of the Easter rebels, is one icon of the Irish struggle for independence. Kilmainham is an even more potent symbol, because its story goes back more than two centuries and represents the continuing struggle.

Building of the prison started in 1786, on open fields to the west of the city center, and it was designed to look as grimly forbidding as possible. That's the impression you still get as you approach the looming gray bulk of the complex and come to the thick entrance door with its spyhatch, set in a massive stone surround. Above the door are carved the Five Devils of Kilmainham, five hissing snakes chained by the neck to represent evil under strict control.

Kilmainham Gaol

⚑ 52

✉ Inchcore Rd., Kilmainham, Dublin 8

☎ 01 453 5984

🚌 Bus: 68, 69, or 79 from Aston Quay; Rail: Heuston Station

💲 $$

Left: Many nefarious necks entered the noose in Kilmainham Gaol's execution block.

A GUIDED TOUR

Kilmainham Gaol was not built purely to house political prisoners, but as an all-purpose prison for general malefactors. The guided tour begins in the **prison museum** with an introduction to street-level Dublin of Georgian and Victorian times, a place of crowded, unsanitary slums, mass unemployment, rampant disease, ignorance, alcoholism, child abuse, and early death. Most of the inmates of Kilmainham Gaol were debtors and petty thieves, with a sprinkling of sheep stealers, prostitutes, rapists, and murderers. This was where the flotsam of Dublin life ended up, often for many months or years. Neglect was the norm, beatings commonplace. Executions took place week in, week out, in the prison or before large public crowds out at Blackrock on the southern arm of Dublin Bay.

With such scenes in mind, you move off from the museum along the gloomy corridors of the east wing, to emerge into the frigid light of the prison's enormous **Central Hall,** a horseshoe-shaped structure built in 1862. With its 100 cells stacked in four tiers and looking inward to a cats' cradle of iron walkways and stairs, it is the echoing embodiment of control. The wardens would muffle the walkways with carpet so that the prisoners never knew when they were being observed.

The guide shows you a cell decorated with a mural, the "Madonna of the Lilies." It was painted in 1923 by Grace Plunkett while she was

Grim, gray, and threatening, the claustrophobic facade of Kilmainham Gaol sent an abandon hope signal to every manacled prisoner who entered its door.

Thanks to the defining drama that the Easter Rising prisoners played out within its walls, Kilmainham Gaol has become a symbol of Irish independence and national pride.

held here as a republican prisoner during the Irish Civil War. Seven years earlier, as Grace Gifford, she had married Joseph Plunkett in the chapel of Kilmainham Gaol at 1:30 a.m. on May 4, 1916, with 20 British soldiers as witnesses. Two hours later her bridegroom was dead, shot for treason as one of the leaders of the Easter Rising. Thinking of this, you can't help but be moved as you inspect the chapel. A carpenter who was serving a seven-year sentence made the altar: His crime was stealing a cartwheel.

Bleak dark corridors lead to flights of steps, their granite treads hollowed by convict feet. The guide tells of the Williams family, sentenced to one month's imprisonment in 1850 for fare-dodging on the railway; they all had to serve the

sentence, including the youngest, a boy of six.

The **cells** where the Easter Rising rebels were held are in the older part of the prison, on a particularly chill and dark passage. You can have yourself shut into one of these stark, claustrophobic boxes where the insurgents were penned up while the authorities decided their fate. The cells had their final use during and just after the Civil War of 1922–23, when the Sinn Fein leader Eamon de Valera—later in life to become both Taoiseach (Prime Minister) and President of Ireland—was incarcerated here. The guide points out the cell from which de Valera was released on July 16, 1924, Kilmainham's last prisoner. Afterward the old prison was abandoned and left to rot until

long week between May 3 and 12, 1916. Connolly could not stand, his ankle having been shattered, so he was shot sitting tied in a chair.

When details of these long-drawn-out executions began to emerge, the public mood in Ireland swung behind the rebels. The British had succeeded only in creating martyrs out of men whose actions the majority of ordinary Irish men and women had been inclined to view with bafflement or contempt. Standing in the cold shadow of the execution yard walls,

A mural in one of the bare rooms in the gaol shows the scene of a prison visit there in former times.

its restoration in the 1960s.

Outside you walk through a grim, gray enclosure walled with stone—the **"Invincibles' Yard,"** named after members of a secret organization who were hanged in the yard in 1883.

And so to the most resonant, most chilling place on the whole tour—the high-walled **prison yard,** once used as a place for con-victs to break stones in hard labor, where 15 of the Easter Rising lead-ers were executed by firing squad for treason. The signatories of the original Proclamation of the Republic—Padraig Pearse, James Connolly, Joseph Plunkett, Sean MacDermott, Thomas MacDonagh, Eamonn Ceannt, and Thomas Clarke—were shot, along with eight others, in ones and twos over the

Famine refugees

Kilmainham Gaol in mid-Victorian times was as grim a place as could be imagined. Even so, to many desperate and starving men and women during the Great Famine (see pp. 27–28) it seemed a refuge. They would break windows or steal fruit in order to be sent to Kilmainham and qualify for a straw bed in a cold cell and a spoonful of the prison's anemic gruel. ∎

**Central Hall
(19th-century cell block)**

Exercise yard

you can almost hear the
echoes of history.

Near the Invincibles' Yard
stands the hull of the yacht
Asgard. She figured in an incident
in 1914 when her owner, Erskine
Childers, author of the classic sea
yarn *The Riddle of the Sands* and a
committed Home Rule activist,
landed guns and ammunition at
Howth Harbour (see pp. 82–83) for
the rebels. Childers himself, one of
the most passionate supporters of
the IRA, was executed for possess-
ing a revolver—shot not by the
British, but on the orders of his
sworn enemies the newly installed
Irish Free State Government in
November 1922, during the Irish
Civil War. ■

Main entrance

Outer wall

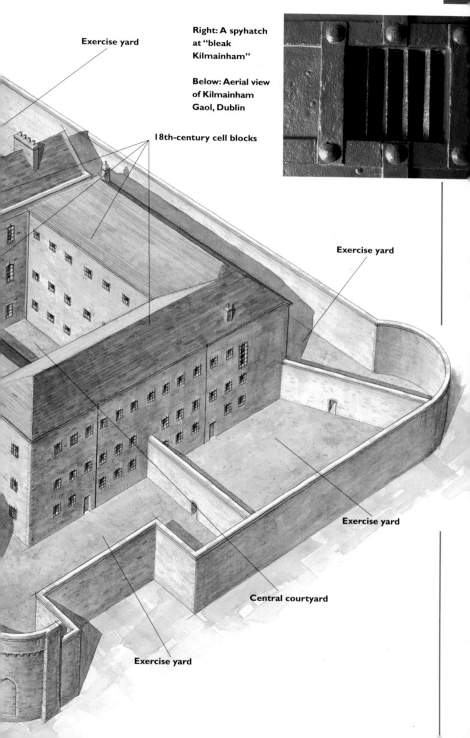

Exercise yard

Right: A spyhatch at "bleak Kilmainham"

Below: Aerial view of Kilmainham Gaol, Dublin

18th-century cell blocks

Exercise yard

Exercise yard

Central courtyard

Exercise yard

Sea and coast views under huge skies enhance the bracing walk around **Howth Head.**

Walk: Hill of Howth

Feel like taking a break from the city and getting a lungful of fresh sea air? This half-day stroll around a beautiful coastline is a favorite with Dubliners, being easily reached by suburban DART train in less than half an hour from the city center.

Disembark from the **DART** *(visitor information: tel 01 836 6222)* at **Howth Station.** Turn left out of the station along **Howth Harbour** ❶, scene of Erskine Childers's gun-running exploits (see p. 80). In a third of a mile (0.5 km) turn right up Abbey Street. **Ye Olde Abbey Tavern** ❷ on the right serves

good lunches. Take the steps beside the pub to reach the ruined shell of **Howth Abbey** ❸, famous throughout medieval Europe for the brilliance of its monks. The view from here over Howth Harbour is excellent.

Spies from Paris University once landed at Howth, intending to entice away the abbey's students. But the abbot, forewarned, had cunningly posted monks disguised as dock laborers on the harbor. The spies returned to France empty-handed, saying that it was useless to bring offers of education to a place where even the dockers conversed in Latin!

Return to Abbey Street and continue uphill, then turn right along St. Lawrence's Road. In about 100 yards (90 m), continue along Grace O'Malley Road, then turn left up Grace O'Malley Drive. Where the road bends to the left (by a phone booth), keep walking straight up the path, and then follow the road to the top. Turn right at the top. A ramp next to house No. 53 leads to a grassy slope; climb it to go through trees and on up a steep bank

---

- See area map p. 51 D3
- Howth DART railway station, a 25-minute run from Connolly Station, central Dublin
- 7 miles (11 km)
- 3–4 hours
- Howth Harbour

NOT TO BE MISSED

- Howth Harbour
- Ye Olde Abbey Tavern
- View from Howth Abbey ruins
- Shielmartin summit
- View of Baily Lighthouse

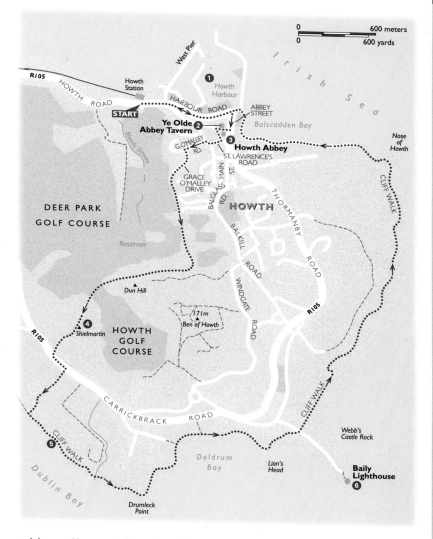

and then a golf course. At the top bear right along the top edge of the course and follow the path under craggy Dun Hill. Cross the golf course and climb the slope ahead (aim for red-and-white striped poles) to the top of **Shielmartin** ❹.

The best view of the walk, taking in Dublin Bay, the city, and the Wicklow Mountains, is from this summit. Follow the path seaward off the hill, descending to turn left on Carrick-brack Road. In about 300 yards (250 m) cross

the road and go through a gate, ignoring the ominous "Dangerous Cliffs" sign as the cliffs are perfectly safe, and continue along a foot-path down to the shore. Turn left here and fol-low the **cliff walk** ❺. Narrow in places, it runs for about 5 miles (8 km) around the bul-bous nose of the Howth Peninsula.

You pass the 1814 **Baily Lighthouse** ❻ and continue on the coast path among seabirds and wonderful sea views until it deposits you safely back at Howth Harbour. ■

Attractions out of town

BY FAR THE BEST WAY FOR VISITORS TO GET A FEEL FOR what lies beyond O'Connell Street and St. Stephen's Green is the DART—Dublin Area Rapid Transit. These little green trains are not just cattle trucks for commuters; they bring the pleasures of outer Dublin within easy reach of the city center. The DART is punctual, quick, and handy, with city-center stations north of the River Liffey at Connolly, and south at Tara Street and Pearse Street.

Riding the DART northward of the city center you come to **St. Anne's Park** *(Killester or Harmonstown Station)*. A footpath dips down on the west side of the park through a wooded valley, past a number of eccentric architectural follies, before reaching the coast and some fine views across the flat wedge of North Bull Island to the rounded peninsular hump of Howth Head.

North Bull Island, often known as Dollymount Strand, has an east-facing coast of fine sandy beaches where you can swim in a bracingly fresh sea. More to the point, the island is a great favorite with birdwatchers. Its location is a good spot for migrating birds to

descend and rest mid-journey, and many species of northern ducks, geese, and waders come to spend the winter here. Bring your binoculars for a stroll along the beach, and if you want to find out more about the wildlife visit the interpretive center.

The terminus of the DART lies farther along the coast at **Howth**— the start point for a superb 7-mile (11 km) walk (see pp. 82–83).

Southward from the city center, the DART reaches **Booterstown Station** on the shores of St. George's Channel. Here at low tide you can hop over the sea wall and enjoy a superb bird-watching beach stroll on a great scimitar of sand. Farther along is **Dun Laoghaire**

Above left: **Bathers launch themselves— clothes and all— into the sea at Sandycove.**

DART information
☎ 01 836 6222

James Joyce Tower
▲ 51 D2
✉ Sandy Cove Point, Dublin
☎ 01 280 9265
🕐 Open April—Oct., by appt. rest of year
💲 $$

(pronounced "Dun Leary"), a lively port town well known for its ferry services to Holyhead (Wales) and Liverpool (England), with handsome Georgian terraces and fine granite harbor walls.

Next comes **Sandycove,** where the granite-built Martello tower now known as the **James Joyce Tower** is an object of pilgrimage for fans of *Ulysses.* It was in this fortification, built in 1804 against the threat of a Napoleonic invasion of Ireland, that Joyce stayed with Oliver St. John Gogarty for a week in August 1904. Joyce set the opening scene of *Ulysses* here, with Buck Mulligan (Gogarty) at his early morning toilet on top of the tower. Views from up there are wonderful, and there's enough Joyceiana collected in the little museum to make

this an enjoyable side trip.

Beyond Sandycove the DART reaches the nicely preserved old seaside town of **Dalkey,** with its stubby fortified house called Archibold's Castle. Flann O'Brien made merry with Dalkey's genteel atmosphere in his bitingly funny book *The Dalkey Archive.* Dalkey lies around the foot of **Killiney Hill** *(Killiney Station),* worth climbing for its stunning views around the giant curve of Dublin Bay to far-off Howth Head.

In the well-heeled village of **Killiney** itself there's always the sport of celebrity spotting; plenty of rock stars, writers, and TV persons have migrated out here. And farther along the coast you can enjoy some great clifftop and beach walks around the resort of **Bray.** ■

Above: Pop idols, film stars, famous writers, and other Dublin millionaires have settled around the beautiful bay under Killiney Hill.

More places to visit in & around Dublin

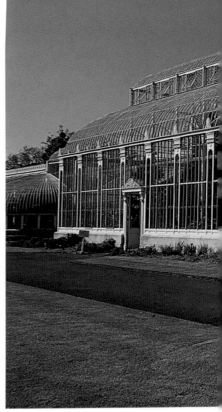

CASINO AT MARINO

This 18th-century folly must rank as Dublin's oddest building. It is famed as the masterpiece of leading Scottish classical architect William Chambers (1726–1796), who designed it for the Earl of Charlemont. The casino was built between 1758 and 1776 as a miniature palace of pleasure, its three stories of harmonious rooms with their stucco ceilings and inlaid floors lit cleverly by concealed sources of light, all hidden away inside what seems from the outside to be a single-roomed Greek temple. The corner columns are hollow, concealing rainwater pipes; funerary urns on the roof disguise chimneys; curved windowpanes act as one-way mirrors, concealing those inside from passersby. All is trickery, conceit, and trompe l'oeil, a rich man's fantasy—and it bankrupted the Earl.

🅰 51 C3 ✉ Off Malahide Rd., Marino, Dublin 3 ☎ 01 833 1618 🕐 Open daily May–Oct.; and Sun. & Thurs. Feb.–April and Nov. 🚌 Bus: 20B, 27, 27B, 42, 42A, 123; Rail: Clontarf, DART 💲 $

CHRIST CHURCH CATHEDRAL

Christ Church was stone-built in the late 12th century, replacing a wooden church founded on this site in 1038 by the splendidly named Norse king Sigtryggr Silkenbeard. In the enormous crypt that runs the full length of the church you'll find carvings and statues, and the grisly tableau of the "cat and the rat"—their mummified corpses were found in an organ pipe, where they had become trapped during their last chase.

🅰 53 ✉ Christ Church Pl., Dublin 8 ☎ 01 677 8099 🚌 Bus: 49X, 50, 50X, 51B, 54A, 77X, 78A, 123, and 206; Rail: Tara St., DART 💲 Donation requested ($$)

IRISH MUSEUM OF MODERN ART

Here you can see stimulating, sometimes baffling exhibitions from a big collection of

The Georgian folly of Merino's casino, where a house is hidden inside a mock Greek temple

Regal air: A Dublin girl dressed up for the magnificent Victorian glasshouses of the National Botanic Gardens

Irish and worldwide modern art. They are housed in part of the finest 17th-century building in Ireland—designed in the 1680s as a colonnaded, courtyarded retirement home for old soldiers and only decommissioned from that role in 1927.
www.modernart.ie  52 ✉ Royal Hospital, Kilmainham, Dublin 8 ☎ 01 612 9900 🕐 Closed Mon. 🚌 Bus: 51B, 78A, 206; Rail: Tara St.

IVEAGH GARDENS

This quiet green enclave in the heart of southside Dublin, a five-minute walk from St. Stephen's Green, is never overcrowded. There are sunken lawns and graveled paths beneath mature trees, secluded little arbors, and a beautiful fountain whose basin is held aloft by winged angels.

🔺 53 ✉ Clonmel St., off Harcourt St., Dublin 2 ☎ 01 475 7816 🚌 Bus: 14, 14A, 15, 15A, 15B, 15C, 48A 🕐 Closed at dusk (6 p.m. in summer)

MALAHIDE CASTLE

Out to the north of Dublin, in the seaside town of Malahide, this old castle sits on 250 acres (100 ha) of parkland. The Talbot family lived here from 1185 until 1973, and the whole place—with its fully restored interior—is steeped in strong, rather cranky atmosphere. In the Great Hall a huge painting by Jan Wyck depicts the Battle of the Boyne on July 14, 1690; 14 Talbot cousins were killed. Be sure to stroll the grounds and their prized gardens.

🔺 51 C4 ✉ Malahide, Co. Dublin ☎ 01 846 2184 🚌 Bus: 32A, 32X, 42; Rail: Northern Commuter rail from Pearse, Tara St., or

Connolly Station to Malahide, DART to Malahide  $$

NATIONAL BOTANIC GARDENS

These gardens have limestone pavements, an arboretum, decorative beds, and more than 20,000 plant species. 🅰 51 C3 ✉ Botanic Ave., Glasnevin, Dublin 9 ☎ 01 857 0909 🕐 Closed at 6 p.m. (winter at 4:30 p.m.) 🚍 Bus: 13 or 19 from O'Connell St., 83 from College

NATIONAL GALLERY OF IRELAND

Highlights here include some of J. M. W. Turner's watercolors, a vigorous, dark "Taking of Christ" by Caravaggio, a Rubens "Annunciation," Irish landscapes and portraits that form a kind of history of Anglo-Irish Ireland, and a number of Dutch masters and French and English Impressionists. A room is devoted to the blurred, hallucinatory work of Jack Yeats (see pp. 210–211).

City-goers take to the water aboard the good ship *Viking Splash*.

🅰 53 ✉ Merrion Sq. West, Dublin 2 ☎ 01 661 5133 🚍 Bus: 10 to Merrion Row and Pembroke St., 5, 7A, 45, 46, 63 to Merrion Sq. North and Clare St., 13 to Merrion Sq. South, 46, 48A, 86 to Merrion Sq. West; Rail: Pearse St., DART (5-minute walk)

ROYAL CANAL & GRAND CANAL

These two canals were built in the 18th century (Grand Canal started in 1765, Royal Canal in 1789) in a fantastically ambitious move to connect Dublin by water with the northwest and west of Ireland via the Shannon system, and with the southeast by way of the River Barrow. They ring the center of the city, the Royal to the north, the Grand to the south, and these days are used for fishing, boating, and strolling. 🅰 51 B3 **Waterways Visitor Center** ✉ Grand Canal Quay, Dublin 2 ☎ 01 6777510 🕐 Closed Mon.–Tues. Oct.–May 🚍 Bus: 2

ST. MICHAN'S CHURCH

St. Michan's, on the north side of the Liffey, contains two remarkable features— a gloriously carved organ case and, in the vaults, a macabre collection of "mummified" bodies, including those of crusaders that date from the 12th century. They have been preserved by the water-absorbing qualities of the magnesian limestone foundations. 🅰 53 ✉ Church St., Dublin 7 ☎ 01 872 4154 🕐 Closed Sun. 🚍 Bus: 83 💲 $ (tour)

CHILLING CHURCHES

Dublin has several churches with more or less macabre item on display. The mummified corpses in **Mt. Michan's Church** (see above) are well known, but there are others to seek out. Two of the most interesting are the bones of that patron saint of lovers, St. Valentine, and the cast of Dean Jonathan Swift's skull.

St. Valentine's remains are contained in a handsome black-and-gold chest under an altar in **Whitefriar Street Church** (*57 Aungier St., tel 01 475 8821, buses 16, 16A, 19, 19A, 22, 22A*). They were given to Father John Spratt by Pope Gregory XVI as a reward for Spratt's excellent preaching when the Dublin Priest visited Rome in 1835.

In **St. Patrick's Cathedral** (see p. 72), the Jonathan Swift display in the north transept features a plaster cast of the writer's skull. The original skull was removed from Swift's grave in the 1830s and started a bizarre 100-year circuit of the drawing rooms of fashionable Dublin as a conversation piece. It was reburied in the 1920s. ■

From the horse-racing plains of Kildare to the Wicklow Mountains, from the sandy bird-watching coast of Wexford to the green Tipperary farmlands, the easy-paced, sunny southeast of Ireland is made for soft times and relaxation.

East Ireland

**Eastern love affair:
The Irish and horses**

East Ireland

THE COUNTIES OF KILDARE, WICKLOW, CARLOW, KILKENNY, WEXFORD, Waterford, and Tipperary comprise the East of Ireland region. It takes in everything south of Dublin; the mountains, grassy plains, sandy coasts, and rich green farmland that make up the southeast part of the island. This is an area that is instantly likeable, its pleasures easily accessible. All you'll need hereabouts is plenty of time to take the narrow back roads, explore the little country towns, and bask in the good weather of what is Ireland's driest, sunniest region.

Leaving Dublin you enter Kildare, the most celebrated county for horse racing and breeding in the whole of Ireland. If you are a horse fanatic, the county town of Kildare will entrance you with its National Stud and Horse Museum and its world-famous racing and training ground of the Curragh. But even if you do not care for horses, these characterful places will fascinate.

Kildare's neighboring county on the east is Wicklow. The Wicklow Mountains are a rugged range, heather-clad and wild, crossed by a fine network of footpaths based on the well-marked Wicklow Way long-distance trail, with the beautiful old monastic settlement of Glendalough hidden in their heart. Most visitors to Wicklow content themselves with Glendalough and never get out of the hills and down to the uncrowded coast, pebbly nearer Dublin, sandy the farther south you go.

Two rivers in lovely surroundings cross the rolling farmland of little County Carlow—the Barrow in the west and the Slaney in the east. The westerly neighbor of Carlow is County Kilkenny, which has the finest medieval town in Ireland as its capital. South is County Wexford, with its fine sandy coast and superb winter bird-watching on the marshes; also the old-style county town of Wexford, full of music from traditional to opera, and Enniscorthy with its stirring evocations of the bloody Rising of 1798.

So to the two most westerly counties of the east—County Waterford with its rugged cliffs and its well-preserved old county town where they make the finest crystal glassware in Ireland; and inland Tipperary, whose ecclesiastical sites culminate in the wonderful assembly of churches, monastic houses, and round towers on the Rock of Cashel. ■

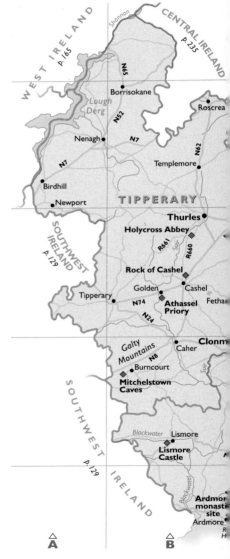

Area of map detail

Belfast

Dublin

CENTRAL IRELAND
p. 235

Maynooth

Carbury

Castletown House

Lexlip

Celbridge

Grand Canal

R403 Clane

Liffey

DUBLIN
p. 49

**Irish National Stud,
Horse Museum, St. Fiachra's
Garden, & Japanese Garden**

Bog of Allen

**Russborough
House**

Enniskerry

Bray

Naas

Blessington

Powerscourt

Kilmacanoge

**Powerscourt
Waterfall**

501m

**Grey-
stones**

M7

Newbridge

Kildare

Kilcullen

*Pollaphuca
Res.*

Sally Gap

*Great
Sugar Loaf*

Monasterevin

**The
Curragh**

R413

R750

WICKLOW
MTS. N.P.

R759

Roundwood

R761

**Newtown Mt.
Kennedy**

**Dan Donnelly
obelisk**

R756

Hollywood

N81

R755

R115

Ashford

Rathnew

N78

N9

Wicklow Gap

Vartry

KILDARE

Glendalough

Devil's Glen

Athy

R418

Slaney

Laragh

Avonmore

R752

Wicklow

*Wicklow
Head*

Baltinglass

Wicklow Mountains

▲925m
Lugnaquilla

Rathdrum

R750

**Castledermot
high crosses**

R418

WICKLOW

**Meeting of
the Waters**

*Brittas
Bay*

CENTRAL IRELAND
p. 235

Hackestown

R747

Avoca

Mizen Point

Carlow

**Browne's
Hill dolmen**

**Millmount
Mills**

Castlecomer

Graiguecullen

Tullow

Arklow

Ballyragget

CARLOW

Leighlinbridge

*Kilmichael
Point*

Freshford

**Black
Castle**

N8

Ballyfogle

**Ballymoon
Castle**

Urlingford

**Dunmore
Cave**

N10

Bagenalstown

Bunclody

N11

Gorey

Kilkenny

Kells

Borris

Blackstairs Mts.

793m
*Mount
Leinster*

Slaney

Bann

Courtown

KILKENNY

N75

Callan

Kings

N10

Thomastown

Borris House

R741

*Cahore
Point*

Knocktopher

R697

Graiguenamanagh

**National 1798
Visitor Centre**

R742

St. George's Channel

N9

**Jerpoint
Abbey**

St. Mullin's

Enniscorthy

**Ahenny
high crosses**

Nore

Vinegar Hill

Urrin

WEXFORD

St.

**Ormond
Castle**

N30

New Ross

N11

Carrick-on-
Suir

Mullinavat

N25

**Irish National
Heritage Park**

**Wexford
Wildfowl
Reserve**

WATERFORD

Barrow

Waterford

Ballyhack

R734

Wexford

N25

Rosslare

**Waterford
Crystal Factory**

Wellingtonbridge

Fishguard, Pembroke

**Rosslare
Harbour**

Kilmacthomas

N25

Mahon

R737

Waterford

Fethard

Kilmore
Quay

*Carnsore
Point*

Roscoff, Cherbourg

◁**2**

Tramore

**Dunmore
East**

Slade
Hook Head

SALTEE
ISLANDS

Dungarvan

Celtic

Sea

0   20 kilometers

0   10 miles

△
C

△
D

△
E

△
F

Market Day in
the shadow of
St. Brigid's
Cathedral; Kildare
has plenty of time
for browsers and
chatters.

County Kildare

COUNTY KILDARE HOLDS A SPLENDID VARIETY OF treasures: a fine cathedral in a friendly town, the Irish National Stud with its flawless Japanese garden and Horse Museum, and the Curragh—hundreds of acres of grassland to run wild. You'll see horses, horses everywhere, because the Curragh is the home of Irish horse racing and a world-renowned bloodstock breeding center.

Kildare town

🗺 91 D5

Visitor information

✉ The Square, Kildare, Co. Kildare

☎ 045 521240

🕐 Closed Oct.–May

At the Irish National Stud paddocks

Christianity—courtesy of St. Patrick—had been in Ireland for less than 60 years when in 490 St. Brigid founded a mixed-sex monastery on the wide plains of the **Curragh** (see pp. 96–97), some 30 miles (50 km) from the east coast.

KILDARE TOWN

In the friendly little town of Kildare, you can get an idea of what the Curragh must have looked like from the scale model of the walled settlement that stands in the present-day **St. Brigid's Cathedral**—thatched round wattle-and-daub huts for the monks and nuns, dining and kitchen buildings, a big wooden church in the middle.

A handsome gray stone cathedral stands on the monastery site today. It dates from the 13th century, although it was heavily restored in 1875. Some amusing modern gargoyles adorn the corbel table—they include two bespectacled men, one wearing a cow across his shoulders, the other clutching a pair of moneybags. Along with the monastery model in the south transept is the fragmented but beautiful tomb of Bishop Walter Wellesley (died 1539), with stone carvings that include a very poignant figure of Christ stripped for scourging, sitting with hands bound, his head bowed in sorrow and exhaustion. Under the eaves of the tomb, sharp-eyed explorers will spot a *sheela-na-gig* dancing with her legs lasciviously astraddle— and maybe a similarly unabashed sister, too. The guard/guide will show you a so-called "pardon stone" with a penitential prayer carved on it. The carving also features a rare depiction of two angels holding jars to catch streams of the crucified Christ's blood. The cathedral font is a tremendous piece of work, a crude and plain upright stone rectangle with a recessed top that might have been created any time over the history of Christianity—and possibly long before that.

Beside the cathedral rears Kildare's impressive **round tower** (*tel 045 521 229*), 108 feet tall (33 m), an orange-gray finger of stone now shaggy with innumerable clumps of grass. Some date it to the 10th century, some to the 12th. The fine recessed Romanesque doorway—unusually ornate for a round tower—was let into the tower 15 feet (5 m) above ground level to secure it against Danish attack. Inside you ascend wooden ladders (103 steep steps, so not for the unfit) to reach the tower's original cap, a shallow ribbed cone inside inauthentic 19th-century battlements. The view is tremendous, 30 miles (48 km) across the plain of the Curragh and north over the vast Bog of Allen to distant hills.

If you find the cathedral and the round tower closed during the lunch hour (*1–2 p.m.*), a great place to sit it out is **Nolan's pub** near the churchyard gates. Ancient wooden shelves behind the bar sag under their freight of vintage Guinness bottles and rolls of long-deleted brands of toilet paper, as if some past landlord had stocked up in the 1960s against nuclear war— a peculiarly Irish view of how to survive the apocalypse.

IRISH NATIONAL STUD

In 1900 Colonel William Hall Walker selected the village of Tully, a mile (1.6 km) south of Kildare, as the ideal place to start a stud farm—mainly because of the high levels of calcium carbonate (good for bone strength) in the waters of the River Tully and in the Curragh grass. Walker was phenomenally successful; so much so that when he gave the stud to the British Crown in 1915, he was created Lord Wavertree for his generosity with such a valuable asset.

A guided tour around the Irish National Stud (state property since 1943) makes for a fascinating hour, even for non-horse-lovers. Among the attractions are the **Foaling Unit** with its intensive care stable, and the **Stallion Yard** with ten roomy boxes for the stallions whose fertility is the real business of the National Stud (covering fees can top $320,000 for a single impregnation). Mating takes place in the **Covering Shed**. The **Oak and Tully Walks** pass the railed paddocks where the beautiful creatures graze contentedly—mares and

Good water, good grass, good breeding— the triumvirate of essentials for success at the Irish National Stud.

Irish National Stud, Irish Horse Museum, St. Fiachra's Garden, & Japanese Garden
www.irish-national-stud.ie
🅰 91 D5
✉ Tully, 1 mile (1.6 km) S of Kildare, Co. Kildare
☎ 045 522963/521617
🕐 Closed mid-Nov.–mid-Feb.
💲 $$$

foals in small groups, the naturally aggressive stallions with a private paddock each.

Along the way you learn plenty: that the Irish National Stud offers its breeding service to small-scale breeders at special cut-rate prices; that 90 percent of foals are born at night; that stallions work hard during the January to June breeding season, covering four mares a day (and being photographed while in action, to prove paternity), six days a week. You'll become acquainted with Colonel Hall Walker's notions about astrology—he designed the stallions' stalls with special skylight roofs so that the moon and stars could infiltrate their beneficial influences, and he ordered all foals with inauspicious birth horoscopes to be sold, regardless of how successful their bloodline might be.

Between 1906 and 1910 Walker engaged one of Japan's top gardeners, Tassa Eida, to lay out a **Japanese Garden** to reflect a

"Journey through Life." From the Stallion Yard you enter the garden by way of the Gate of Oblivion, and make your way along the narrow Path of Life through gorgeous flower banks and trees both dwarf and full size. There are childhood's Tunnel of Ignorance, the Bridge of Engagement (broken in the middle!) and Bridge of Marriage, the mazelike Hill of Ambition, and the scarlet Bridge of Life to negotiate before you walk the smooth lawns of the Garden of Peace and Contentment in old age.

A recent addition to the attractions at the Irish National Stud is **St. Fiachra's Garden,** opened in 1999 by President Mary McAleese. In its way, this is as artificial as the Japanese Garden, with mock-ups of hermit huts and a "drowned forest" of imported bog oak. It lacks the subtlety of its senior cousin, but it still makes a pleasant stroll under silver birch and conifers.

There is also the **Irish Horse Museum** to enjoy—the prize

Trees, water, and stone buildings combine in relaxing style in the leafy hideaway of St. Fiachra's Garden.

Castletown House

The finest country house in Country Kildare is undoubtedly Castletown House (*at Celbridge off the R403, tel 01 628 5252, map p. 91 E6*), built between 1722 and 1732 for William Connolly, speaker of the Irish House of Commons, as a no-holds-barred piece of Palladian splendor. The enormously long colonnaded facade is a breathtaking sight. Much of the interior—the hand-blown Venetian chandeliers in the pale blue Long Gallery, the elaborate stucco on the staircase walls—reflect the exuberant 18th-century taste of Lady Louisa Lennox. Aged 15, she married Connolly's great-nephew, who inherited the estate, in 1758. More intimate are the black-and-white prints that Lady Louisa herself selected and pasted on the wall of the Print Room. The follies in the park—the piled domes and curly exterior staircase of the conical Wonderful Barn, and the 140-foot (40 m) obelisk on tiers of arches that commemorates William Connolly—were the contribution of Connolly's wife, Katherine. ∎

Severely formal, symmetrical, and dignified, County Kildare's Castletown House shows off Palladian architecture at its peak.

attraction here is the large but fragile preserved skeleton of Arkle, Ireland's great steeplechaser of the 1960s, a rather bizarre but impressive item. Other exhibits include ancient pieces of horse equipment, a portrait of Colonel Hall Walker with stiffly upswept moustache alongside one of his horse horoscope books for 1914, an enjoyable gallop through the history of the horse, and an entertaining account of the "pounding matches" of the 18th and 19th centuries. These challenges between country gentlemen—proxy dueling, in fact—involved each man in turn choosing a difficult or dangerous obstacle to jump, the other contestant being obliged to follow on behind. Needless to say, much money was wagered and many necks broken in pursuit of such macho honor and glory. ∎

The Irish, horses, & the Curragh

What is it with the Irish and horses? Set up a horse race anywhere in the world and there'll be an Irish interest, and presence, more knowledgeable and intense than that of any other nation. Sales of Irish Thoroughbred horses in Ireland alone approach 160 million dollars annually, and hundreds of millions of pounds change hands each year in covering fees at Irish studs. Attendance at classic horse races swells year by year, while down at the other end of the scale you'll find ragged men with rusty old trotting rigs competing on country roads while onlookers bet as if money and common sense were going out of style.

The origins of good relations between the Irish and horses go back into pre-Christian times, with evidence that horses had been domesticated—perhaps for the table as much as for transport—as far back as 2000 B.C.

Steeplechasing had its origins in north County Cork in 1752, when Lord Doneraile staged a 4.5-mile (7 km) race between the two church steeples of Buttevant and St. Leger. By the mid-19th century there were nearly 30 flourishing race tracks in this small and poor country. Today, Irish men and women from all walks of life are as bound up as ever with the fortunes of horses, and Ireland still has the same number of race tracks.

Little of the elitism generally associated with racing obtains in Ireland—top hats rub along with cloth caps, morning coats with greasy anoraks at meetings as prestigious as the Irish Derby or the 1,000 and 2,000 Guineas. These three premier races all take place at Ireland's best known race track, the Curragh (the very name means what it says in Gaelic—*cuirrech*, a racecourse), just outside Kildare. The track is iconic among race-goers, and the broader expanse of the Curragh proper—6,000 acres (2,400 ha) of unfenced, gently rolling grassland around Kildare town—is the very heartland of Irish racing. ∎

Above: Thundering down the final stretch—another exciting day at the races!

Dan Donnelly, the Curragh bruiser

In a hollow on the south side of the R413 road, 3 miles (5 km) west of Kilcullen, stands a railed obelisk. It commemorates a bare-knuckle fight that took place on December 13, 1815, between Curragh-trained Dan Donnelly and "the famous English pugilist" George Cooper. Donnelly won, after a tremendous battle. In 1818 he was dubbed "Sir Dan" by the Prince Regent in a Surrey pub after another victory. Less than two years later Donnelly died, penniless. His body was exhumed and sold to a surgeon, who preserved the fighter's phenomenally long right arm. ∎

Left: All bets are on as the tote boards are lifted high at McBrierty's.

Below: Jockey's gear at John Oxy's stables, Kildare

A hiker contemplates the day's route as she looks toward the high peaks of the Wicklow Mountains.

Wicklow Mountains

IF YOU HAVE BEEN EXPLORING DUBLIN, YOU WILL ALMOST certainly have seen the Wicklow Mountains already, rising enticingly in tall blue humps right on the southern doorstep of the capital. Inevitably, the mountains see a lot of visitors; they are the Dubliners' country playground, after all, being less than half an hour's drive to the south of the city.

But most day-trippers are making for a very small handful of destinations, the "must-see" sites: either the beautifully located monastic site of Glendalough, the picturesque village of Avoca with its photogenic handloom weavers, or the two great Anglo-Irish houses of Russborough and Powerscourt (see pp. 106–107) with their stunning gardens.

Once clear of them, however,

you will find great tracts of upland and hillside, valley and coast where you'll have only the birds—and maybe the occasional hiker or two—for company.

GETTING THERE
There are several ways to drive into the Wicklow Mountains from Dublin, all of them increasingly beautiful the farther into the hills

you go, all becoming steeper, slower, and more twisty. This is definitely not country for speed demons. The main coast road to Wexford, the N11, skirts the Wicklow Mountains on the east. Side roads from the N11 include the R755 from Kilmacanoge under Great Sugar Loaf, and the R765 from Newtown Mount Kennedy—these both reach Roundwood on the shore of Vartry Reservoir.

Another beautiful way into the hills is via the R763 from Ashford near Wicklow town, which goes west to Laragh and Glendalough. Three miles (5 km) west of Ashford you can take a narrow side road on the right that leads to the entrance to the **Devil's Glen,** a spectacularly rugged cleft threaded by a footpath from which you can

see the Vartry River tumble 100 feet (30 m) into the agitated pool called the Devil's Punchbowl.

Alternatively, you could take the R115 from central Dublin through Rathfarnham and up over the wild **Sally Gap pass;** here the road divides, with the R759 swinging off to the left and down to Roundwood, while the R115 wriggles on down to Laragh and Glendalough. Or you could start out southwest from Dublin on the A81 Baltinglass road and follow it down to Hollywood, where the R756 cuts off eastward to Laragh over the **Wicklow Gap** in superb hill country scenery of bare, heathery moorland rising to mountain ridges and peaks.

A lovely alternative to this last route is to leave the A81 at

Blessington, 5 miles (8 km) north of Hollywood, and make your way on a minor road over narrow bridges and around the north shore of the Pollaphuca Reservoir to join the R758, then the R756.

GLENDALOUGH

Whichever route you choose, all roads in the Wicklow Mountains seem to lead inevitably to Glendalough. This remarkable monastic site, tucked down in its lake valley among steep mountainsides, well repays half a day's exploration. St. Kevin, its patron saint and lodestar, was an awkward young monk of the early sixth century, so embarrassed at his unwanted fame as a miracle worker that he gave up monastic life to live in a hollow tree in the utter seclusion of Glendalough, the Valley of the Two Lakes.

In 570 Kevin became abbot of the slowly growing monastic community in the valley, which had consolidated into a sizeable frater-

nity by the time he died about 617. The lonely valley was not immune from outside attack, however; the community was plundered by Danes in 922, and again by Norman adventurers in 1176, but as a counterbalance there was a great period of rebuilding under Abbot Lorcan O'Tuathail (St. Laurence O'Toole,

St. Mary's Church

**Right:
Reconstruction of
the Lower Lake
portion of the
Glendalough
monastic site in
the 12th century**

**Left: The tiny
oratory of St.
Kevin's Kitchen is
backed by the
rocket-shaped
tenth-century
Round Tower.**

Glendalough

91 E5

Visitor information
at entrance to
Glendalough, Bray,
Co. Wicklow

0404 45325

$

1128–1180). In 1398 a party
of English soldiers razed the
monastery, but the church continued in use. By then pilgrimages
to Glendalough, attracted by St.
Kevin's piety, had become a fixture,
and these continue to this day.

It is not just the beautiful
enclosed setting that makes

Glendalough so special; equally
remarkable are the number and
density of the monastery's dozen or
more 10th-, 11th- and 12th-century
buildings. A well-marked footpath
leads through a sturdy granite
double arch—the only surviving
monastic gateway in Ireland, with
a big sanctuary cross just inside—
and runs round the riverside site.
Here you will find **St. Kevin's
Kitchen**, a cramped little oratory
that might perhaps date as far back
as the time of St. Kevin, with a
round 11th-century belfry. Nearby,

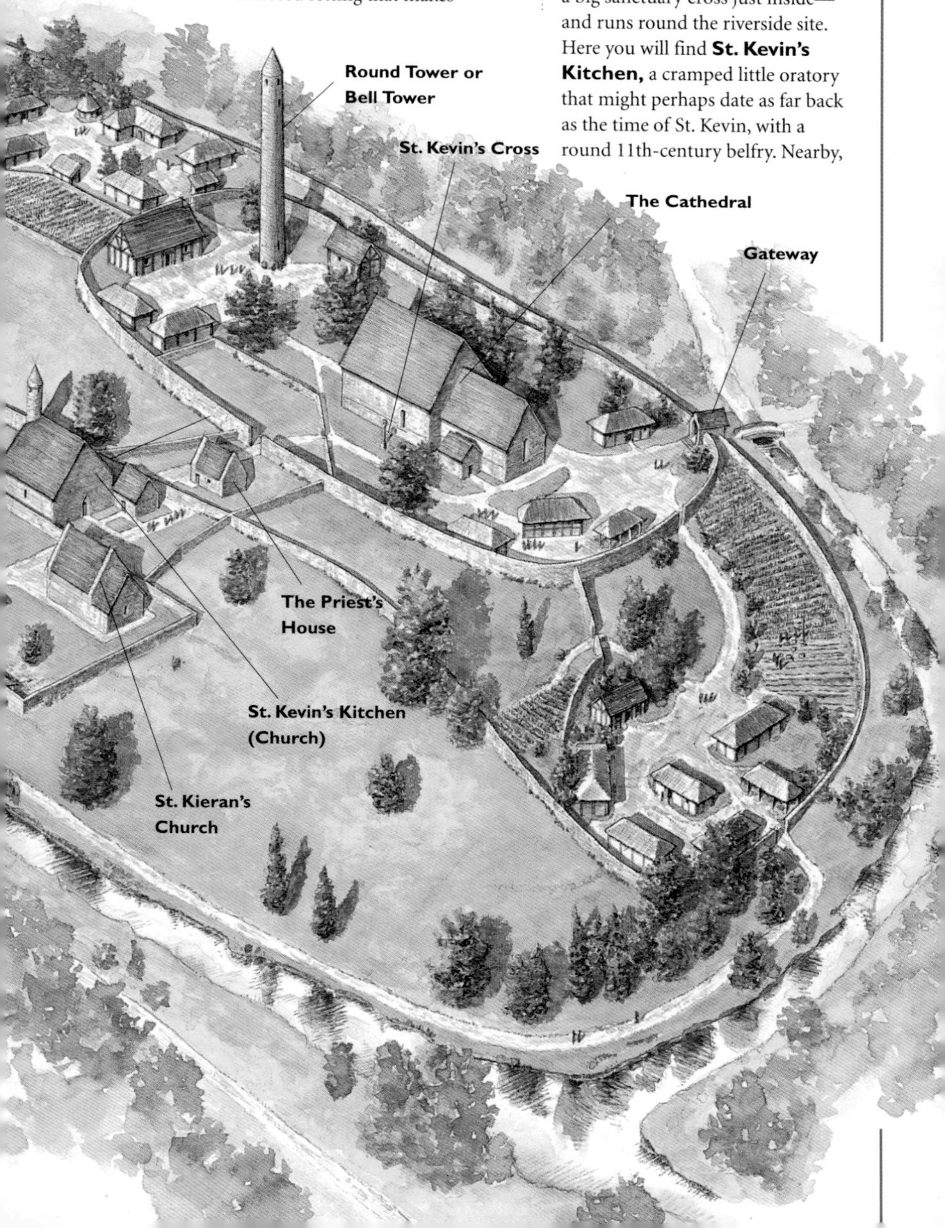

Round Tower or
Bell Tower

St. Kevin's Cross

The Cathedral

Gateway

The Priest's
House

St. Kevin's Kitchen
(Church)

St. Kieran's
Church

among the remains of other buildings and a forest of graveslabs, are the shell of a ninth- or tenth-century cathedral, a 12th-century priest's house whose east wall contains a fine dogtooth arch, and a splendid tapering rocket of a tenth-century round tower, built 110 feet high (33 m) to give the Glendalough monks a good look-out, its stairless door some 12 feet (3.5 m) above the ground to keep besiegers at bay.

LEAVING GLENDALOUGH

From Glendalough's neighboring village of Laragh, you take the R755 to Rathdrum, the snaky road threading the lovely tree-lined Vale of Clara; then on south on the R752, stopping 4 miles (6 km) south of Rathdrum to enjoy the spectacle of the confluence of the Avonbeg and Avonmore Rivers, an often crowded beauty spot known as the **Meeting of the Waters.**

Avoca lies a mile (1.6 km) or so downstream, a village of white-washed houses under slate roofs with wooded hills rising at its back. The old mill here has been working since 1723, and inside you can see weavers clacking and shuttling away at their rattly handlooms as they produce woolen cloth; the mill shop sells a good variety. The R752 and R747 lead on southeast down the Vale of Avoca to Arklow, a quiet little town on the Wicklow coast.

The coast of county Wicklow stretches north for 40 miles (64 km) from Kilmichael Point, a few miles below Arklow, to the jaded but enjoyable seaside resort of **Bray**

Sea-watchers love the breezy open spaces of the Promenade at the resort of Bray, on the north Wicklow coast.

**Avoca
Handweavers**
www.avoca.ie
🅰 91 E4
✉ Millmount Mills, Avoca Village, Co. Wicklow
☎ 0402 35105

just south of Dublin. Generally overlooked by visitors in favor of the mountains, this is a coast for connoisseurs of moody, lonely shores and seascapes.

The old R750 road along the coast from Arklow to Wicklow town, followed by the R761 a mile or so inland all the way up to Bray, have long been superseded by the fast N11, but they offer a largely traffic-free saunter up the coast for those in no particular hurry. **Mizen Head** and **Wicklow Head** are two fine promontories, and the harbor town of **Wicklow** makes a good place to stop for a cup of tea. As for the beaches—they are mostly sandy as far as Wicklow, with **Brittas Bay** the pick of them, and mostly pebbly from there on up. Any side road to the right from the R761 will land you after a more or less potholed mile on the low cliffs of the northern Wicklow coast, the perfect place to gaze at the sea and daydream with not another soul to bother you. St. Kevin himself could not have asked for more. ■

Walking in the Wicklow Mountains

The Wicklow Mountains are wonderful country for hill walking. The usual precautions about keeping an eye on the weather and taking proper hiking gear and a good map need to be observed. They may look small in comparison with other mountain ranges—Lugnaquilla, the highest, only reaches 3,038 feet (927 m)—but the Wicklow Mountains and their notoriously changeable weather should be treated with proper respect. The Wicklow Way is well marked, and any number of paths cross and climb the mountains.

Hill Walkers Wicklow by David Herman (Shanksmare Publications, 2000, ISBN 0-953143-1-7) is widely available locally; it details 30 full-day walks in the area (wear good walking boots). Irish Ordnance Survey 1:50,000 sheets 56 and 62 cover the mountains. The Wicklow Mountains National Park information point between Glendalough's Upper and Lower Lakes (closed Oct.–May) has details of walks, or you can get books and maps from the visitor information offices at Glendalough (*tel 0404 45325*, see p. 100), Wicklow town (*tel 0404 69117*), or Arklow (*tel 0402 32484*). ■

A boardwalk winds through the boggy Spink, overlooking the cliffs of Glendalough.

St. Kevin's Kitchen could date back to the time of St. Kevin, in the early sixth century A.D.

Walk: Glendalough & the Glenealo Valley

An easy, level walk among the remains of monastic and mining activity in Glendalough, with an upward climb into the upper Glenealo Valley. The first part of the walk is very popular. To avoid crowds, set off early morning, or wait until late afternoon.

Before you start, make sure that you look around the excellent display on St. Kevin and the Glendalough monastery in the **visitor center ❶** *(tel 0404 45325)*. From the visitor center parking lot, cross the river by a footbridge and turn right along the track. In about 300 yards (300 m) recross the river to view **St. Kevin's Kitchen ❷**, the **round tower ❸**, and the other features of the main monastic site (see pp. 100–102).

Return across the river, where "Green Road to Upper Lake" signs guide you along a surfaced track on the south side of the **Lower Lake ❹**. Follow this for 1 mile (1.6 km), admiring the mountainside and white houses reflected in the lake, until you reach the

Saintly slayer

St. Kevin, good with wildlife, was hopeless with women. When an over-zealous female follower came too close, the pious saint stung her cheeks with nettles to warn her off. Another story (probably a Victorian invention) tells how St. Kevin, meditating in the coffinlike cave (now called St. Kevin's Bed) above the Upper Lake, fell asleep and dreamed that one of his female acolytes, Kathleen, was standing between him and the Gates of Heaven. Waking to find Kathleen bending over him, and taking her to be a temptress sent by the Devil, he plunged her in the lake and drowned her. ∎

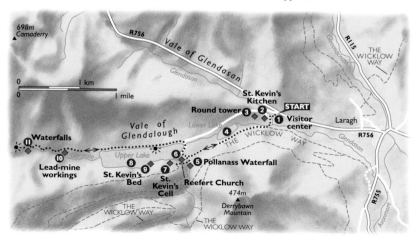

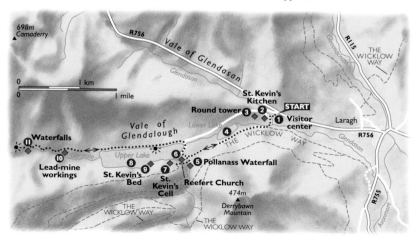

- See area map p. 91 E5
- Glendalough visitor center (see pp. 100–102)
- 6 miles (10 km)
- Allow 3 hours
- Glendalough visitor center

NOT TO BE MISSED
- Visitor center display
- St. Kevin's Kitchen
- Round tower
- Kevin's Bed View
- View down Glenealo Valley from waterfall above the old mine workings

ground between the Lower and Upper Lakes.

Just past the **Pollanass Waterfall ❺,** where the track swings right to cross between the lakes, continue to the **Reefert Church ❻** ruins among weathered crosses and gravestones. Just beyond here, well signposted, is the semi-circle of stones on a little promontory that marks the site of **St. Kevin's Cell ❼.**

Return to cross between the lakes and bear left on a path between tall pine and larch trees along the north shore of the **Upper Lake ❽**. A sign, "Kevin's Bed View," leads to a viewpoint that looks across the lake to the tiny square black mouth of a partly man-made cave known as **St. Kevin's Bed ❾**.

Continue beyond the lake end, through the ruined buildings and spoil heaps of 19th-century **lead-mine workings ❿.**

You can retrace your steps from here back to the visitor center, but if you have waterproof footwear and sufficient energy, continue forward to reach the zigzag track up beside the **waterfalls ⓫** of the Glenealo River. The path leads to a memorable view back over the Upper Lake. ■

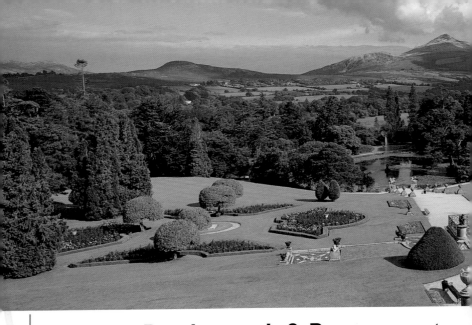

Russborough & Powerscourt

THESE TWO TREMENDOUS PALLADIAN HOUSES FLANK THE northern Wicklow Mountains—Powerscourt near Bray to the east, and Russborough near Blessington on the west. Built in the mid-18th century, they trumpet the wealth and power of the Anglo-Irish gentry of British origins who owned great tracts of Ireland. Some were absentee landowners who rarely set foot in Ireland. Others lived on their Irish estates and would move mountains—literally, in some cases—to get the landscape effects they wanted.

Russborough House

- 91 E5
- Blessington, Co. Wicklow
- 045 865239
- Open daily May—Sept.; also open Sun. & public holidays last two weeks of April & Oct.
- $$

The interiors of the grandest Anglo-Irish houses, too, reflected what money, sophisticated taste, and influence could achieve. Powerscourt House, never as grand as Russborough, was burned out in a fire in 1974, while Russborough's grounds were always intended to be wild and green rather than meticulously organized; so it is the house at Russborough and the gardens and grounds at Powerscourt that are the main attractions today.

RUSSBOROUGH HOUSE

Russborough was built in the 1740s for Joseph Leeson, Earl of Milltown and heir to a brewery fortune. He spent his money on creating one of the most impressive-looking houses in Ireland. Its immense **facade,** 900 feet long (275 m), is topped with heraldic lions and features a twin sweep of curving colonnades.

Inside, all eyes turn to the richly unrestrained plasterwork. Italian brothers Philip and Paul Francini, the leading exponents of plaster ornamentation at the time, were commissioned to do the work and filled the house with intricate floral sprays, swags, fruit, faces, and foliage Another artist, less delicate but more fantastical, created the hounds enmeshed in sprays and flowers who career up the main staircase.

The house contains an astonishing **art collection**—Vermeer and Rubens, Goya, Velazquez, Thomas Gainsborough, Hans Hals. Sir Alfred Beit, cofounder of the De Beers diamond mining empire, initially put it together. The Beit collection has suffered two high profile robberies: in 1974, 16 paintings stolen to raise funds for the IRA were quickly recovered; in 1986 several pictures were removed and have not yet been retrieved.

POWERSCOURT

The glory of Powerscourt is its setting, best seen from the uppermost of the five terraces that drop away to the **Triton Lake** and its 100-foot (30 m) fountain in the valley below. From here you look out over the lake, cradled in tall trees, to the peak of the 1,643-foot (501 m) **Great Sugar Loaf Mountain,** 2.5 miles (4 km) away across a patchwork of farmland. The "wildness" of this prospect only enhances the artistry of the 50 acres (20 ha) of gardens.

The steeply sloping terraces were designed in the 1840s by Daniel Robertson, a martyr to gout who stimulated his genius with copious drafts of sherry while being trundled from one vantage point to the next in a wheelbarrow. Walking down the terraces between formal gardens, you pass a superb mosaic pavement featuring the planets, created with colored pebbles and enclosed by elaborate cast-iron screens. Beautiful Austrian cast-iron work appears beyond the upper terrace, too, in the 18th-century Bamberg Gate. The peaceful, terraced **Japanese Gardens,** screened from the Triton Lake by bamboos and shapely conifers, contain delicate temples and bridges.

After all this artifice, a visit to the **Powerscourt Waterfall,** a signposted 3.5-mile (6 km) walk or 3-mile (5 km) drive from the gardens, is refreshing. At 425 feet (130 m), this is the highest waterfall in Ireland. "The longest" might be more accurate, as the River Dargle tumbles from one ferny rock face to the next. This is a great place to picnic, especially on a sunny afternoon a day or so after heavy rain when the fall is at its most spectacular. ■

Powerscourt

🅜 91 E5

✉ Powerscourt Estate, Enniskerry, Co. Wicklow

☎ 01 204 6000

💲 $$$

County Carlow

Carlow town

91 D4

Visitor information

Tullow St., Carlow, Co. Carlow

059 913 1554

TINY COUNTY CARLOW IS LANDLOCKED AND SURROUNDED on all sides by more glamorous counties—horse-mad Kildare, Kilkenny with the finest medieval town in Ireland, Wicklow and its mountains, and Wexford's sandy coast and superb bird-watching. Carlow tends to be overlooked. Yet there's plenty in this easy-going agricultural county to please you, if you are content to wander at a slow pace and listen to some fairly elastic local tales.

Balancing act: The great 100-ton capstone of Browne's dolmen in County Carlow stands propped precariously on its supporting stones as it has done for nearly five millennia.

The town of **Carlow,** up near the county's northwest border, was for centuries a frontier town between the Norman English of the Pale (the defended area of British influence around Dublin; see p. 26) and the troublesome Irish "beyond the Pale."

Early in the 13th century, Carlow was provided with a sturdy stone castle, which from certain viewpoints still looks impregnable. However, closer inspection reveals a solitary castellated wall suspended between two towers, all that was left after a local doctor blew it up in 1814. He was trying to reduce the thickness of the walls, with the intention of turning the place into a refuge for psychiatric patients.

Carlow also boasts a handsome **courthouse** of 1828 to 1830.

Small wonder if the Ionic columns of the portico look as if they should be gracing some Greek temple—they are modeled on the Parthenon.

On May 25, 1798, about 640 "Croppy," or Catholic, rebels supporting the United Irishmen's rebellion were massacred on Tullow Street. Their mass grave (the Croppy Grave), marked by a Celtic cross, lies across the River Barrow at **Graiguecullen.**

Father John Murphy, a priest who led a contingent of the rebels, was hanged in the market square at **Tullow,** 9 miles (14 km) east of Carlow; a memorial commemorates him there.

Two miles (3 km) east of Carlow, **Browne's Hill dolmen** is signed from the Hacketstown road. This is a wonderful site, the 4,500-year-old burial place of some leader important enough to have his tomb sealed with a capstone that weighs many tons. The weathered capstone lies propped on three of its original curbstones.

The threat of unrest and even insurrection in this frontier region led to the building of several castles in County Carlow. You can find the ruins of the 12th-century **Black Castle** at Leighlinbridge in the lovely valley of the River Barrow, and near Bagenalstown the ruggedly massive ruins of **Ballymoon Castle.** Later, when things became quieter in County Carlow, symmetrical plantation villages were built, each with its

dominating "Big House." At **Borris**, this was **Borris House,** dating from the late 18th century. Its owner in mid-Victorian days, Arthur MacMurrough Davanagh (1831-89), was a determind and courageous man. Born with only stumps of arms and legs, he nevertheless succeeded in becoming not only an excellent shot and horseman, but also a career politician—quite a feat for someone with such handicaps in mid-19th-century Ireland.

County Carlow tapers southward from Borris toward the rolling heights of the **Blackstairs Mountains.** These bleakly beautiful hills, straddling the border country between the counties of Carlow and Wexford, rise to the 2,600-foot (793 m) peak of Mount Leinster. A great way to enjoy the Blackstairs is to stroll along the well-marked **South Leinster Way,** a long-distance footpath that skirts Mount Leinster on its way northeast to link up with the Wicklow Way.

The River Barrow forms all but a snippet of the western boundary of County Carlow. There is great coarse fishing (fishing for any freshwater fish other than salmon or trout) on the Barrow, and good towpath walking along the **Barrow Way.**

River, minor roads, and paths all lead more or less southward to the village of **St. Mullin's,** 3 miles (5 km) north of the Wexford/Kilkenny border, where remnants of a monastery founded in the late seventh century lie around the present-day church. ■

Around the village of St. Mullins on the Carlow-Kilkenny border, the landscape smooths out into rolling, tree-dotted farmland.

Kilkenny Castle

✉ The Parade,
    Kilkenny,
    Co. Kilkenny

☎ 056 772 1450

🕐 Closed Mon.
    Oct.–March

💲 $$

Kilkenny town & around

COUNTY KILKENNY LIES TO THE WEST OF COUNTY
Carlow, with its county town, Kilkenny—by far the most complete
medieval city in Ireland—at its heart. This is a small-scale town, a
place with character stamped on its old buildings and narrow lanes.

Set on the west bank of the River
Nore, Kilkenny town lies between
its two chief landmarks, the castle
and the cathedral. Most visitors
to Kilkenny make straight for
Kilkenny Castle, dominant on
its bend of the river. This three-
sided fortress (Oliver Cromwell's
men knocked down the fourth in
the 1650s) is built of local gray
limestone, with castellated battle-
ments and drum towers at the
corners. Richard de Clare, the
Norman baron better known as

Strongbow, first built a wooden fort
on this site in 1172 to guard the
river crossing; his son-in-law
William le Mareschal built the
stone castle. When the Butler fami-
ly, Earls of Ormond, bought the
castle and the lordship of Kilkenny
in 1392, the city was already an
important place, a fortified strong-
hold where parliaments were held.
The parliament of 1366 to 1367
passed the famous Statutes of
Kilkenny, aimed at keeping the
Anglo-Norman heritage free from

taint by the Irish. Their prohibitions on marrying Irish partners, speaking Irish, or playing Irish games or music were honored more in the breach than the observance.

For nearly 600 years the Butlers continued to live in Kilkenny Castle, suffering all the vicissitudes of fortune that flowed from being stubbornly loyal to the royal house of Stuart. The Butlers lost wealth and influence by backing the deposed king, James Stuart, in his defeat at the Battle of the Boyne in 1690, and when the 2nd Duke of Ormond supported a Stuart-inspired plan in 1714 to invade England with Spanish troops, he was actually attainted for treason and lost his earldom. It took the rest of the 18th century for royal memories to fade sufficiently to allow the Butlers to resume their ancient title.

A tour around the castle takes in the Victorian library and drawing room, the bedrooms with their hand-painted wallpaper and beautiful Georgian furniture, and the showpiece **Long Gallery.** Here Butler portraits frown darkly down below a delicately carved 19th-century hammerbeam roof (braced with arches), painted with trails of foliage in pre-Raphaelite style and furnished with a central skylight to admit the daylight. Outside there are terraces, gardens, and walks by the river and through woodland.

Across the road from the castle entrance are the handsome 18th-century stables that now house the **Kilkenny Design Centre** *(tel 056 22118),* a showcase for good modern design in textiles, jewelry, furniture, and ceramics.

From the castle you cross the top of Rose Inn Street to enter **High Street,** the first part of a crooked old road that changes its name to Parliament Street and then Irishtown as it runs north through

the heart of the city. On the right you'll see the **Tholsel** or toll stall with its octagonal pepperpot clock tower and round-arched arcade projecting into the roadway. It was built in 1761 as an office where market users, traders, and others could pay dues and tolls, and it is still in use as the offices of Kilkenny's city council. The Tholsel is only one of Kilkenny's many handsome medieval buildings, rare survivals in Ireland due to the country's history of poverty and destructive strife.

Follow the narrow "slips" or alleyways, some of them so steep they require steps, to seek out these remnants of historic Kilkenny, from humble cottages to churches and merchants' houses. The one with the best story attached is the 13th-

In Kilkenny, High Street's medieval thoroughfare leads through an archway under the old Tholsel toll house.

Kilkenny town
🅰 91 C3
Visitor information
✉ Shee Alms House, Rose Inn St., Kilkenny, Co. Kilkenny
☎ 056 775 1500

century **Kyteler's Inn** *(tel 056 772 1064)* on St. Kieran's Street, which runs in from the right to join High Street at its juncture with Parliament Street. It was in this house that Alice Kyteler, the famed Witch of Kilkenny, was born. Alice was charged with being a

Kilkenny's famous stonework monuments are not confined to St. Canice's Cathedral; the Black Abbey contains several, along with some really notable medieval stained glass.

Rothe House Museum

✉ Parliament St., Kilkenny, Co. Kilkenny

☎ 056 772 2893

$ $

witch in 1324 after she had been overheard offering peacocks' eyes and nine red cocks to her familiar, a sprite named Robin Artysson whom she would meet at the crossroads. She was also reported to have gone through the streets of the city at night with her broom, sweeping the dirt toward her son's house while chanting: "To the house of William, my son, Lie all the wealth of Kilkenny town." Dame Alice was convicted, but pardoned. However, this did not stop her persisting in her witchy ways. Sentenced to death after reoffending, she escaped and left her unfortunate maidservant Petronella to be burned at the stake as a substitute. The Tholsel was later built on the place of execution on High Street.

Farther along Parliament Street

are two notable medieval buildings. On the west side is **Rothe House Museum,** another arcaded building with a tall central gable, linked by tiny courtyards to two other houses. The whole complex—open as a museum of Kilkenny history these days—was built in the 1590s as a rich merchant's dwelling.

On the east stands **Grace's Castle,** built as a fortified tower in 1210, a prison since Tudor times and a courthouse from the late 18th century to the present day. United Irishmen, supporters of the failed Rising of 1798, were executed here.

Like every prosperous medieval city, Kilkenny had several monastic houses in its heyday. Along Abbey Street (running west from Parliament Street) you'll find the very well restored church of the 13th-century **Black Abbey,** with some beautiful medieval glass. Toward its northern end Parliament Street becomes Irishtown. In Norman times the native Irish were confined to this ghetto outside the city walls, an area already sacred to them because of its holy well dedicated to St. Kenny or Canice, the founder of Kilkenny's first monastery in the sixth century.

On a rise of ground at the top of Irishtown you'll see the squat bulk of **St. Canice's Cathedral** *(tel 056 776 4971),* built in the 1250s on the site of St. Canice's monastery. It's a massive building, its central tower pulled down low into the roofs like a square head tucked into hunched shoulders.

Beside the cathedral rises a slender 101-foot-high (31 m) **round tower** *($),* built by the monks some time between 700 and 1000. You can climb its wooden ladders (weather permitting) to enjoy a stunning panorama over Kilkenny and around.

When Oliver Cromwell's troops captured the city in 1650, they used

the cathedral as a stable, broke the font while letting their horses drink out of it, shot guns into the roof, and smashed stained-glass windows and other furnishings. Despite this, however, most of the church's glories survived, including its wonderful collection of carved memorial slabs and effigies in the shiny local limestone known as Kilkenny Marble.

The tombs of the ruling Butler family in the south transept are wonderful examples of the carver's art, particularly the smiling effigies of Piers Butler, Earl of Ormond and Ossory (died 1539), in his domed helmet and elaborate breastplate, and his wife, Margaret Fitzgerald, with billowing sleeves and horned headdress.

Dozens of humbler memorials can be enjoyed, too, many of their images rubbed smooth and shiny by centuries of hands and feet. They include the graveslab of Jose de Keteller (died 1280), probably the father of Dame Alice the Witch; slabs showing the tools of trade of a cobbler, a weaver, and a carpenter; and the slab to Edmund Purcell (died 1600), the captain of the Earl of Ormond's gallowglasses or mercenary army, whose carving includes the tiny image of a bird perched on the rim of a cauldron—the cock that crowed twice as St. Peter denied Christ for the third time.

When you have had enough of sightseeing, you could pop into a pub for a pint of Kilkenny ale. This fine beer, brewed in the town, owes its reputation to its creamy texture. Be patient—it

The thick stone walls of Rothe House on Parliament Street guard treasures of antique furniture and fine paintings.

Dunmore Cave

🅰 91 C4

✉ Ballyfoyle,
Co. Kilkenny

☎ 056 775 1500 &
056 776 7726

🕐 Closed Mon.–Fri.
Nov.–mid-March

💲 $

Jerpoint Abbey

🅰 91 D3

✉ Thomastown,
Co. Kilkenny

☎ 056 772 4623

🕐 Closed Dec.–Feb.

💲 $

The ruins of 12th-
century Jerpoint
Abbey are rich in
medieval stone
carvings that
portray angels
and saints with
more than a
touch of humor.

takes almost as long as Guinness
to settle in the glass.

DUNMORE CAVE

A steep descent on foot takes you
into this well-lit and exciting cavern
located 7 miles (11 km) north of
Kilkenny town, reached via the N77
and N78. It contains several rock
formations—including the Market
Cross, at 23 feet (7 m) reckoned to
be the tallest stalagmite in Europe.

Dunmore Cave has a dark history. In 1973 spelunkers found the
skeletons of 46 women and children
who had taken refuge in the caves
during a Viking raid in 928 in
which their menfolk—more than a
thousand of them—were slaughtered. There were no signs of
violence on the bones, suggesting
that the victims either starved to
death or were suffocated with smoke
from fires lit by the attackers.

JERPOINT ABBEY

Ten miles (16 km) south of
Kilkenny town via the N10 then the

N9 eastward are the finest
Cistercian abbey ruins in Ireland.
Donal MacGiollaphadruig, King of
Ossory, founded the **Jerpoint
Abbey** in 1158 and its first abbot
was Felix O'Dulany, founder of St.
Canice's Cathedral in Kilkenny.

O'Dulany's tomb lies in the
barrel-vaulted choir of the abbey,
the carving showing his bishop's
crosier being swallowed by a snake.
More finely carved tombs of the
15th and 16th centuries can be seen
in the transepts; one carries effigies
of fiercely staring and heavily
bearded Apostles, with their bare
toes poking out appealingly under
the hems of their robes.

Carving is also rich on the inner
and outer faces of the double pillars
in the cloister arches. Here you will
find beasts and soldiers, a grinning
knave in a hooded tunic, a woman
in a long gown with deep pleats,
and St. Christopher with a long
staff, his face as meditative as an
Easter Island statue, raising one
hand in blessing. ∎

Wexford town & around

The quays of
Wexford

STRETCHED OUT BEHIND ITS LONG QUAYS BESIDE THE
Slaney Estuary, Wexford town has no glamour, but its lack of hurry
and worry and the friendliness of its people draw visitors back time
and again. Not that the town is uncrowded—narrow, undulating, and
winding Main Street, parallel with the river, is usually thronged with
customers of the old-fashioned stores. The sweet whiff of turf smoke
from domestic fires hangs around the streets, and pubs such as Tim's
Tavern, Kelly's, and Simon's Place make cozy, cheerful watering holes.

Wexford town

🅰 91 E2

Visitor information

✉ Crescent Quay,
Wexford, Co. Wexford

☎ 053 23111

**Memorial to the
1798 Rising**

Vikings founded Wexford town
down in the southeast corner of
County Wexford in the ninth century, and their street plan survives
in the narrow covered alleyways
such as Keysers Lane that run down
from Main Street to the quays.

Wexford's history has been
spectacularly bloody. When Oliver
Cromwell captured the town in
1649, his men destroyed the 12th-
century Selskar Abbey (its fine red
stone ruins still stand off Abbey
Street), and slaughtered 1,500
citizens—three-quarters of
Wexford's population—and in the
1798 Rising (see p. 27) there were
many brutalities on both sides. A

heroic statue of a peasant pikeman
in the Bullring commemorates the
United Irishmen rebels. You can
learn more about all this in the
Wexford Experience exhibition in the Norman-era Westgate
Tower, or you can take your time
over the small 1798 display in the
beautiful and peaceful late 17th-
century **Church of St. Iberius**
on High Street, parallel to and one
block higher than Main Street.

WEXFORD WILDFOWL RESERVE

Tidal wetlands are known in
Ireland as "slobs," and those along
the estuary of the River Slaney

The way they lived: Replica dwellings from many eras of Irish history help bring the past alive at Wexford's Irish National Heritage Park.

Wexford Wildfowl Reserve

⚑ 91 E2
✉ Visitor center, North Slob, Co. Wexford
☎ 053 23129

Irish National Heritage Park

www.inhp.com
⚑ 91 E2
✉ Ferrycarrig, Co. Wexford
☎ 053 20733
💲 $$

northeast of Wexford town are internationally famous as breeding and wintering grounds for ducks, geese, and waders.

The North Slob, some 4,500 acres (1,800 ha) of marsh reclaimed for agriculture during the Great Famine years of 1847 to 1849, is the site of the Wexford Wildfowl Reserve, where you can spot numbers of mallards, shelducks, black swans, goosanders, greenshanks, and redshanks, as well as reed warblers and reed buntings in the extensive reed beds. The best bird-watching is in winter, when some 10,000 Greenland white-fronted geese (about 35 percent of the world population) overwinter here, along with 2,000 light-bellied brent geese and large flocks of lapwings and pochards.

Leave the visitor center at dusk and perch yourself on the sea wall with a pair of binoculars; you'll never forget the extraordinary sight and sound as several thousand white-fronted geese rise into the air all at once with a mighty roar of wings and gabble of voices and fly low overhead to their nighttime sea roosts.

IRISH NATIONAL HERITAGE PARK

This 30-acre (12 ha) open-air park, created on the marshes of the Slaney Estuary just west of the Wexford Wildfowl Reserve, gives an easily digestible run-through of Irish history up to medieval times by way of reproduced sites—a Stone Age encampment and stone circle, a *rath* (ring fort) and a *crannóg* (lake island stronghold) from the native Celtic culture, a Viking shipyard (complete with longboat moored on the river), a Norman castle, and more. Trails connect the sites and a guided tour is available.

ENNISCORTHY

Fifteen miles (24 km) north from Wexford along the N11, the lively small town of Enniscorthy holds the **National 1798 Visitor Centre,** an excellent and detailed exhibition that is based around the events and circumstances of the United Irishmen's 1798 uprising. This attempt to win independence for Ireland by force of arms was carried along on a wave of revolutionary fervor that was sweeping Europe, and fuelled by widespread resentment of the oppressive penal laws (see p. 26–27).

The Rising started in mid-May of 1798, when rebels and government forces set about slaughtering each other. Thousands were maimed, raped, and killed in Wexford, Carlow, and Kildare, as they were all over the country, before the insurrectionists in the southeast of Ireland were finally crushed on June 21 at the Battle of Vinegar Hill on the east bank of the River Slaney outside Enniscorthy. Five hundred people were killed there, many of them the wives and children of the fleeing rebels. The punitive measures that followed served only to stoke up more bitterness and resentment.

Wexford Opera Festival

Opera lovers in their tens of thousands come to Wexford town in the autumn for the three-week Wexford Opera Festival *(Theatre Royal, 27 High St., tel 053 22400 or 053 22144, www.wexford opera.com)*. It generally runs from mid-October until the first week in November and offers three full-length operas staged in the Theatre Royal, as well as fringe events and other kinds of music ranging from blues and jazz to traditional concerts and informal sessions.

At Wexford you're more likely to hear some seldom-performed opera than the famous old favorites. The festival prides itself on rescuing and reviving these neglected pieces, so it's something of a connoisseur's treat. But there's no snobbery about Wexford Opera Festival. The town's shop-keepers dress up their front windows, performers and festival-goers drink elbow-to-elbow in the bars, and there's music in and out of the pubs. ■

Glorious light and sound at a **Wexford Opera Festival** church concert featuring choir and orchestra

All this is told graphically with animated and static displays, light and laser effects, contemporary accounts, and cartoons. You can drive up to the battle site on **Vinegar Hill** (signposted from the town), where there is a round tower, a memorial plaque, and a fine prospect over Enniscorthy.

SOUTH OF WEXFORD

The N25 leads south from Wexford to **Rosslare** *(visitor information: tel 053 33232)*, a busy harbor town with ferry connections to Fishguard and Pembroke in Wales. Beyond here minor roads reach a coast that is partly muddy, partly sandy. **Kilmore Quay** has thatched cottages in a small harbor setting, looking out to the **Saltee Islands.** From March to June the islands are home to a quarter of a million puffins, kittiwakes, gannets, razor-bills, and other nesting and breeding seabirds. Boat trips from Kilmore Quay take bird-watchers out to see, hear, and smell it all. ■

National 1798 Visitor Centre
www.1798centre.com
🅰 91 E3
✉ Millpark Rd., Enniscorthy, Co. Wexford
☎ 054 37596
💲 $$

Courtown Bay and its sandy beach make a popular family resort.

Drive: The old coast road from Dublin to Wexford

You can dash from Dublin to Wexford in an hour and a half by the fast N11, or you can saunter the old coast road through quiet towns and villages, flirting with a coast-line of low cliffs, lonely pebble strands, and splendid sandy beaches. This is real back-country travel—motoring just for the pleasure of it.

Setting off from central Dublin, head east along the south bank of the River Liffey to Ringsend, where you pick up the R131 for Dun Laoghaire. This is the old coast road, easing south for 12 miles (19 km) through the seaside towns of south Dublin.

Pass through Sandymount to join the R118 at Merrion, continuing through Booterstown past the vast, low-tide sand and mud flats in Dublin Bay. Then join the N31 to head through Blackrock to the bustle of **Dun**

Laoghaire ❶, with its Georgian terraces and busy ferryport. Continue on the R119 through Sandycove, in whose Martello tower (see p. 85) James Joyce set the opening part of *Ulysses;* past Dalkey and under the seaward flank of Killiney Hill, to reach Ballybrack and Bray.

Now on the R761 in open country, the landscape on your right lifts exhilaratingly into the eastern outliers of the Wicklow Mountains. There's the first exciting sight of sharp-peaked **Great Sugar Loaf ❷**, with

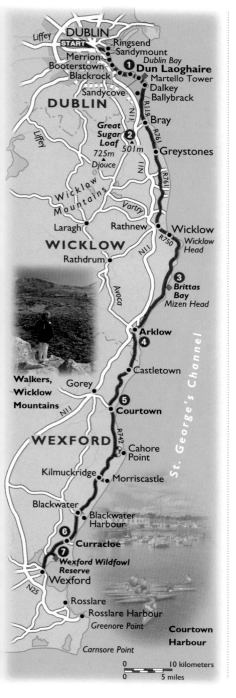

- See area map p. 51 C3
- Central Dublin
- 85 miles (136 km)
- Half a day
- Wexford town

NOT TO BE MISSED
- First sight of Great Sugar Loaf & the Wicklow Mountains
- Brittas Bay's sandy strand
- Arklow town
- Fishing harbor at Courtown
- Wexford Wildfowl Reserve

the rounded flanks of 2,380-foot (725 m) Djouce glimpsed away beyond. Past Greystones, a former fishing village whose charming harbor and old cottages are now surrounded by modern housing projects, the road enters flattish, well-wooded country. Just four side roads lead to the sea between here and Wicklow town; each will land you on a bleak strand of red, gray, and yellow pebbles.

At Rathnew you join the R750 for the run through Wicklow town and on along the lovely sandy curve of **Brittas Bay** ③, where duckboard trails through the dunes around Mizen Head may tempt you to stop for a breath of salt sea air.

Arklow ④ (*Arklow visitor information: tel 0402 32484*) is a pleasant, slow-paced little town, just right for a cup of coffee and a hazelnut slice from the Stone Oven bakery on Lower Main Street. From here, head on south from the harbor on a minor road, aiming for Castletown and the fishing harbor of tiny **Courtown** ⑤. Here you pick up the R742 and follow it for 25 miles (40 km) to Wexford.

Curracloe ⑥, 5 miles (8 km) short of Wexford, is the classically pretty fishing village of thatched cottages, although now spoiled by a hotel monstrously out of sympathy with its surroundings. If you're after seashore peace and quiet, however, you'd do better to take the side lanes to coastal hamlets such as Cahore Point, Morriscastle, or Blackwater Harbour.

Before plunging into Wexford town, follow signs from the R742 to the **Wexford Wildfowl Reserve** ⑦ (see pp. 115–116). At any time of day, but especially at dusk, there will be wildfowl in spectacular numbers. ■

Waterford town & around

LOOKING AT WATERFORD TOWN FROM THE QUAYS THAT line both banks of the River Suir, many visitors feel a sense of disappointment. They don't expect a place with such a varied history to look so workaday. But that is part of the charm of the chief city of southeast Ireland; the gritty bustle of shipping along its river, and the old streets and buildings of its historic heart hidden away just behind the southern quays.

The Vikings, no mean judges of a decent anchorage, settled **Waterford town** in the mid-ninth century, calling it Vadrafjord, the Weather Haven. Their three centuries of occupation, and their leather boots, dinner bowls, jewelry, and daggers, are displayed in the splendid **Waterford Museum of Treasures** next to the Tourist Office. Not confined to the Vikings, the museum also gives a comprehensive account of Waterford's dramatic history. The Vikings built walls around the town in 1000 A.D., and many fragments still stand. The best stretch leads from the Watch Tower, where Castle Street meets Parnell Street at the apex of the old city's triangular layout.

The cylindrical **Reginald's Tower** (tel 051 873501), founded by Ranguald the Viking in 1003, stands a little way from here, at the waterfront end of the Mall. In the adjacent Reginald's Bar is an arched section of the old city wall. Boats entered the city here along a waterway now replaced by the Mall. The bulk of the tower is Norman, built shortly after these new invaders had captured the city in 1170. They revamped the city walls and added a string of watchtowers, many of which still stand.

In medieval times Waterford became the most prosperous city in Ireland, and Georgian money built the fine houses along the Mall and O'Connell Street, as well as the

Roman Catholic Holy Trinity Cathedral, lit by Waterford crystal chandeliers, on Barronstrand Street. East, on Bailey's New Street, another addition was the **Protestant Christ Church Cathedral,** with its rich stucco ceiling; the morbid effigy of James Rice, seven times Lord Mayor of Waterford in the 15th century, is shown as a sunken corpse being burrowed by toads and worms.

Today, the city has a buzz to it, perhaps because of the student population, the commercial activity of the port, and the light industry around the outskirts.

ARDMORE MONASTIC SITE

Down in southwest County Waterford, the resort of Ardmore boasts a superb monastic site. On the hillside above the town, with wonderful coastal views, you'll find a 12th-century round tower standing 97 feet tall (29 m) next to ruined **St. Declan's Cathedral,** dating from the 10th to 14th centuries.

The chief attraction is the stone tableaus, probably ninth century, on the outside of the cathedral's west wall. Framed in a double row of arcades, they include a winged Archangel Michael weighing souls in his scales, Adam and Eve being banished from Eden, and St. Declan converting the heathen Irish. The eighth-century oratory of the saint—he came from Wales some time between 350 and 420—stands nearby.

Just along the path toward the cliffs of Ram Head, beside the ruins of Dysert Church, you'll find **St. Declan's holy well** guarded by rough-hewn crosses. Down at this southern end of Ardmore beach is **St. Declan's Stone,** on which his bell and vestments floated to Ireland from Wales in his wake. It is said that rheumatics who manage to squeeze under the stone on the Feast of St. Declan, July 24, will gain a miraculous cure—even if they hurt their back in the process. ∎

Ardmore

🅰 90 B1

Visitor information

✉ Seafront parking lot, Ardmore, Co. Waterford

☎ 024 94444

Pre-Norman stone arches filled with sculptures decorate the west end of St. Declan's Cathedral, Ardmore, in the shadow of the 12th-century Round Tower.

Waterford crystal

Waterford crystal is the Rolls Royce of crystal. It sets the standard to which all other glassmakers aspire. The factory is the town's main employer and about 1,600 Waterford people work here, many of them in big echoing sheds, to a constant background of machine roar and the tinny blare of pop music. Even if the prospect of a tour around such a factory seems unappealing, you shouldn't miss this opportunity to see genuine craftsmen and women at work.

Crystal itself is greatly superior to ordinary glass, its lead content (Waterford is around 30 percent) giving a special sheen, weight, and workability. The tour around the factory (*Kilbarry, Cork Rd., Waterford, tel 051 332500, www.waterfordvisi torcentre.com, gallery closed Jan. Sat. & Sun., no tours Sat. & Sun. Nov.–March., $$*) shows you the process by which litharge (lead monoxide), silica sand, and potash are blended in furnaces. One of the most enjoyable parts of the tour is watching the blowers puffing and twirling their tubes to form brilliant orange balloons of molten crystal. These are gently patted and smoothed into the desired shape— a globe, a slim-waisted vase, a goblet, a bowl— in molds, while the color of the crystal fades from violent orange to lemon-peel yellow and then smoky gray. It's a process that hasn't changed much since English brothers George and William Penrose first set up the glassmaking business in Waterford in 1783.

The crystal goes into the cooling oven;

It takes a lot of puff and much experience to produce a piece of Waterford crystal.

trophy pieces such as highly decorated flower vases and engraved plaques can take up to 26 hours to cool. When it's ready the crystal is taken to the cutters at their diamond-tipped wheels—wedge cutters or flat cutters. Patiently the plain shape is steered against the revolving blade, cutting arcs and straight lines deep into the thick crystal in characteristic Waterford patterns that catch every nuance of light. One mistake here is one too many; a slip of the wheel and the piece is destroyed. Master cutters are employed on special trophy pieces at piece-work rates.

Now the crystal comes to the engravers who use an array of tiny wheels to cut delicate patterns or details of leaves, faces, and hair, or whole scenes such as a foxhunt or a garden full of individually engraved flowers. One hardly likes to break in on their silent concentration, but visitors are welcomed and encouraged to ask questions. If you are too shy, you can save your queries for the workshop area at the end of the tour, where blowers, cutters, and engravers display and discuss their skill. Provided your group is not too big, you may be able to have a go yourself.

To finish up with, of course, there is the showroom with its beautifully lit pieces, just waiting to part you from your money. Note though that, unlike most factory shops, Waterford does not sell damaged products as "seconds." In order to preserve the firm's reputation, any crystal with a flaw, however slight, is smashed on-site and recycled. ∎

Making the finished pieces (above) requires the skill of master cutters and engravers (below).

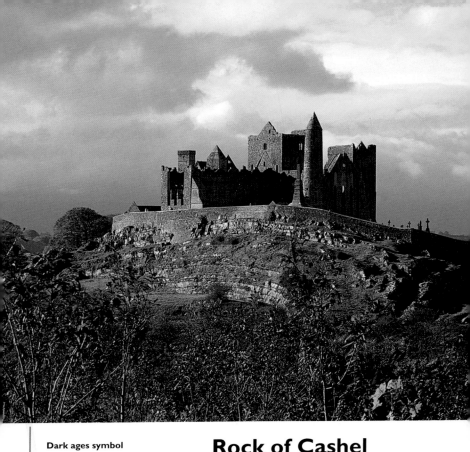

Rock of Cashel

YOUR FIRST SIGHT OF THE ROCK OF CASHEL RISING OUT OF the Golden Vale of Tipperary, its domed top tightly packed with towers, spires, and pointed gables, will be unforgettable. During the first millennium the Rock was indeed a kind of secular and spiritual capital, the seat of the Kings of Munster and a rival to the power of Tara where the High Kings of Ireland held sway. Great and grim history clings to the Rock, and there's a resonance about the place that is enhanced at night when floodlights throw it all into brilliant relief.

Rock of Cashel

- 90 B3
- Cashel, Co. Tipperary
- 062 61437
- $

The limestone outcrop on which the walled citadel stands is 200 feet high (60 m). Legend has it that the devil, who had just taken a bite out of the Slieve Bloom Mountains (they still call the place Devil's Bit), saw St. Patrick about to build a church in the Golden Vale. In disgust, he spat his mouthful out and

it landed at Cashel. But this rock was already fortified in the fourth century, when it was known as "Cashel of the Kings." In the fifth century it became the coronation place for the Kings of Munster, and St. Patrick came here to baptize King Aengus in 450. During the ceremony he inadvertently jabbed

pleasantly with the dour gray of the great cathedral looming behind, is considered the earliest and finest surviving Romanesque church in Ireland. Outside is a corbel frieze of the heads of men and beasts, and more of these look down from the pillar capitals of the arcade inside. The round Norman chancel arch is studded with heads, too, and there are highly colored fragments of the original frescoes in the chancel. At the west end stands a sarcophagus, probably that of King Cormac.

Even more impressive is the carving in the tympanum over the north doorway. It shows a wild scene of a grinning monster, its clawed feet trampling two unidentifiable animals, while a centaur in a Norman helmet (complete with nose-guard) twists his upper body back to fire an arrow at it.

The cold, echoing shell of the 13th-century **St. Patrick's Cathedral** stands roofless and loud with jackdaw cries. Cobbled on to its west end is the fortified palace of the archbishops of Cashel.

The cathedral was burned in 1495 by the Earl of Kildare, who excused himself to King Henry VII by confessing with much honesty, "I thought the archbishop was in it." Cashel's prelates were as powerful and unpopular as any monarch. Archbishop Myler Magrath (1523–1622), whose tomb is in the choir, held one archbishopric, four bishoprics, and 77 other livings, making him extremely wealthy.

Tragedy came in 1647 when up to 3,000 people were sheltering from attack by Cromwell's army under "Murrough of the Burnings," Lord Inchiquin. The attackers piled sods of turf against the outside of the cathedral and set them ablaze, killing everyone inside.

Beside the cathedral rises a round tower of the 11th or 12th century, 92 feet high (28 m). ■

Below the Rock, statuesque dancers leap at the moon outside the Brú Ború center for traditional Irish culture.

his crosier through the king's foot, but stoical Aengus, thinking the saint was testing him, did not flinch.

By the 11th century Cashel was held by Brian Boru, High King of Ireland, but in 1101 King Murtagh O'Brien gave it to the Church, after which the great buildings that now crowd the summit were erected.

You enter the complex through the **Hall of the Vicars Choral,** built in 1420 for the choristers of Cashel's cathedral. It houses an exhibition and the weathered 12th-century high cross of St. Patrick. Outside you pass a reproduction of the cross en route to **Cormac's Chapel** (1127–1134), built by King Cormac MacCarthy. This sturdy little building under a steeply pitched roof, its pinkish stone contrasting

County Tipperary

TIPPERARY IS OFTEN GLOSSED OVER BY TRAVELERS RACING through impatiently to get to the dramatic coasts and peninsulas of the southwest. But there are plenty of hidden delights hereabouts, just off the beaten track, for those who take the time to slow down.

Athassel Priory

🅰 90 B3

✉ Golden, Co. Tipperary

Caher

🅰 90 B2

Visitor information

✉ Castle parking lot, Caher, Co. Tipperary

☎ 052 41453

Caher Castle

✉ Caher, Co. Tipperary

☎ 052 41011

💲 $

Swiss Cottage

✉ Kilcommon, Caher, Co. Tipperary

☎ 052 41144 or 052 41011

🕐 Closed Mon. mid-Oct.–April

💲 $

ATHASSEL PRIORY

The substantial ruins of what was once the largest priory in Ireland occupy a very peaceful location beside the River Suir. Rising above trees on the riverbank are the tall gray walls of the abbey church, pierced with lancet windows, and its shattered 15th-century tower. Other remains include the priory gatehouse, the cloister ruins, and the stump of the chapter house.

William Burke founded the priory for Augustinian canons in 1192, only a few years after the Normans had arrived in Ireland. His tomb lies inside. Irish marauders burned the priory in 1319 and again in 1329, and 1447.

CAHER

The **castle** at Caher is one of Ireland's most impressive—and most complete, having surrendered to Oliver Cromwell's forces in 1650 before they could set about battering it to pieces. It stands on a rock in the River Suir, a natural defensive site, first built on by Conor O'Brien in 1142. The fortified tower he erected is incorporated into the inner ward of the present castle, a two-stage rebuilding—first in the 13th century when the Anglo-Norman keep was built, and secondly by the Butler family, Earls of Ormond, once they had acquired the site in 1375. In the middle ward stands the keep, complete with its portcullis, and a chilling prison cell.

A stroll along the river, 1.5 miles (2.5 km) south of the town center, will bring you to the **Swiss Cottage,** designed in 1810 by celebrated English Regency architect John Nash for Richard Butler,

12th Baron Caher. Nash used the *cottage ornée* style, then extremely fashionable, to suggest that this crooked little hunting and fishing retreat, with its rustic timbering, artfully asymmetrical windows, and roses round the door, had somehow been engendered by the spirit of the surrounding countryside.

CARRICK-ON-SUIR

One building distinguishes this quiet market town—the splendid ensemble of **Ormond Castle** and its satellite mansion, the finest Tudor domestic building in Ireland. The castle was built in 1309 and contains a brace of 15th-century fortified towers as proof of turbulent times in medieval Ireland. But when Black Tom Butler, 10th Earl of Ormond, built a new mansion onto his ancestral castle in 1568, he felt confident enough to dispense with any fortifications. The castle is lit by an almost continuous run of mullioned windows under the gables and is glorified inside by a tremendous carved fireplace and some wonderful ornate plasterwork in the Long Gallery.

MITCHELSTOWN CAVES

This 2-mile-long (3 km) cave system, the longest in Ireland, is the one to visit if you abhor "touristification" of such natural attractions. Mitchelstown Caves are not overburdened with tourist developments or gimmicks—you simply walk through the three enormous caverns and admire the extraordinary mineral formations of stalactites, stalagmites, and calcite flows.

Although the caves lie in the sandstone Galtee Hills, they themselves are part of an intrusive band of limestone. Rain and stream water burrowing along cracks and fault lines in the rock have hollowed out the caves, and its chemical interaction with the limestone has formed their pinnacles and flows over countless million years. ■

Greyhound racing is popular in Irish country towns.

Ormond Castle
🅰 91 C2
✉ Castle Park, Carrick-on-Suir, Co. Tipperary
☎ 051 640787
🕐 Closed Oct.—mid-June
💲 $

Mitchelstown Caves
🅰 90 B2
✉ Burncourt, Cahir, Co. Tipperary
☎ 052 67246
💲 $$

More places to visit in East Ireland

AHENNY HIGH CROSSES
In Ahenny churchyard you'll find two high crosses dating from the eighth and ninth centuries. Each 13 feet high (4 m), their arms of equal length, they are covered with intricate decoration.
 91 C3 ⊠ Signed off the R697, 3 miles (5 km) N of Carrick-on-Suir, Co. Tipperary

CASTLEDERMOT HIGH CROSSES
These two tenth-century high crosses, standing near a lovely Romanesque arched doorway and a 67-foot (20 m) round tower with a crenellated top, are carved with biblical scenes.
91 D4 ⊠ Off the N9, 10 miles (16 km) SE of Athy via the R418, Co. Kildare

Big Raymond's big tower: The oldest lighthouse in Ireland stands on Hook Head.

HOLYCROSS ABBEY
This is a Cistercian abbey, founded in 1168 by Donal Mor O'Brien, King of Munster, as a shrine for a splinter of the True Cross and enlarged in the 1430s. The north range of the cloister has been carefully restored, as has the abbey church—it is now the parish church. The south transept contains two chapels, one with vaulting elaborate enough to suggest it was here that the sacred relic was venerated. The choir holds a beautiful late 14th-century

sedilia or priest's seat, elaborately carved— it's known, strangely, as the Tomb of the Good Woman's Son.
90 B3 ⊠ On the R660, 4 miles (6 km) S of Thurles, Co. Tipperary ☎ 0504 43241 or 43118

HOOK HEAD
The circular 30-mile (48 km) Ring of Hook Drive, well signposted with brown-and-white signs, is reached via the Passage East to Ballyhack car ferry 7 miles (11.4 km) east of Waterford. You'll find yourself driving down a lovely peninsula of green farmland and dark cliffs. Attractions of the Hook Peninsula include the gaunt gray shells of two 13th-century monasteries, Dunbrody Abbey and Tintern Abbey. You'll enjoy the vast sandbanks of Bannow Bay, the big star-shaped Tudor fort at Duncannon, and the craggy ruins of Slade Castle standing over its pretty little harbor. All roads eventually lead south to the **lighthouse** on Hook Head's dusky red sandstone cliffs. The modern light sits atop a 100-ft (33 m) tower, built by Raymond le Gros—"Big Raymond"—in 1172. This is far and away the oldest lighthouse in Ireland. The coast and sea views from the top *(tel 051 397055 and 051 397054, March–Oct., daily, $$)* are sensational.
91 D2 ⊠ SE of Waterford via the R737, the R734, and minor roads, Co. Waterford
Hook Head visitor information ☎ 051 397502 ⏱ Seasonal **Waterford visitor information** ☎ 051 875823 ⏱ All year

LISMORE CASTLE
Lismore, a huge, impressive castle on a hill above the River Blackwater, is mostly 19th-century but based on a 12th-century strong-hold. Elizabethan adventurer and pioneer American colonist Sir Walter Raleigh owned it from 1589 to 1602, and physicist and chemist Robert Boyle was born here in 1627. The castle is private, but the 800-year-old Yew Walk, the Pleasure Grounds with their flowering rhodo-dendrons *(May–June)*, and the other gardens are open.
90 B2 ⊠ On the N72, 15 miles (24 km) W of Dungarvan, Co. Waterford ☎ 058 54424 ⏱ Castle not open; grounds closed Oct.–Easter 💲 $$ ∎

Wander through the small-scale pastoral landscapes of Counties Cork and Limerick, through the historic water-girdled city of Cork, and down to where the coast divides into the five peninsulas of west Cork and Kerry.

Southwest Ireland

Southwest magic: Kings in the wood

Southwest Ireland

THREE COUNTIES MAKE UP SOUTHWEST IRELAND: CORK, KERRY, AND Limerick. Hereabouts the landscape begins to break up and the edges of the land become ragged, splitting apart into five great peninsulas that push out into the Atlantic. These fracture further into headlands and islands, giving the map of this region the appearance of blobs of liquid streaking out from some central spillage.

Dramatic skies, dramatic scenery at the Gap of Dunloe near Killarney, Co. Kerry

Cork is a fine city. Some call it Ireland's "second city," but Cork thinks that title should be Dublin's. Certainly Cork has plenty of Dublin's zip and zing, and not too much of the capital's recently acquired impatience and glitziness. Eastern County Cork is well wooded with wide farmlands, cut into on the south by the great lagoon of Cork Harbour with its historic town of Cobh.

The farther west you go, the more appealing County Cork becomes, with a gorgeous south coast indented with bays and dotted at regular intervals with seaside villages, until the three southernmost peninsulas—Mizen, Sheep's Head, and Bear (Beara)—break away and spear out to sea between their inlets of

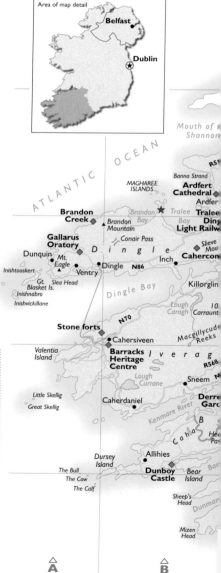

Area of map detail

Belfast

Dublin

△
A

△
B

Roaringwater, Dunmanus, and Bantry Bays.

The southwest has one other big city, Limerick, a place with a vivid history that somehow can't quite match the warmth and intimacy of Cork. But the rest of County Limerick makes up for what its capital lacks with a whole scatter of charming picture-book villages and fine houses, and a swath of under-discovered backcountry out west.

As for County Kerry, it shares the Bear (Beara) Peninsula with County Cork and boasts two more of its own—Iveragh, whose mountainous spine is formed by Macgillycuddy's Reeks and whose beautiful coast is circled by the spectacular Ring of Kerry road, and rugged, otherworldly Dingle, with the remote Blasket Islands at its outermost tip. Kerrymen are the butt of the rest of Ireland's jokes for their supposed backwoods gullibility. Don't let that fool you—the Kerrymen themselves make the same jokes about Corkmen …. ∎

Cork city

ALTHOUGH THE MOST IMPORTANT CITY IN THE SOUTH-west of Ireland, Cork wears a relaxed air. The best way by far to get the most out of this civilized place, and its "softly sharp" people with their distinctive roller-coaster intonation, is to take your time and stroll about, letting the city under your skin by slow degrees.

The physical shape of Cork is easy to grasp. The city center occupies a long island in the River Lee that is connected by numerous bridges to 19th-century suburbs on the steep-ish hills to north and south.

The low-lying land in the Lee Valley was always a good spot to settle. St. Finbarr established a monastery at Corcaigh, the "marshy place," in 650, and once the Vikings had ceased plundering the monks they, too, settled and established a town during the ninth and tenth centuries. With its fine river frontage and its great natural harbor just to the southeast, Cork prospered in Norman and medieval times on trade, and it developed an independent political spirit based on this mercantile confidence. Wisely the city admitted Oliver Cromwell's forces in 1649; not so wisely it backed the deposed King James II during his unsuccessful comeback bid against King William

The River Lee, spanned by handsome bridges and lined with fine old houses, lends dignity and character to the city of Cork.

Cork city

⬛ 131 E2

Visitor information

✉ Áras Fáilte, Grand
Parade, Cork,
Co. Cork

☎ 021 4255100

THE CITY SIGHTS

Some of what you see in the city center today is a rebuilding of what was burned in 1920, but many of the fine Georgian houses remain. The chief thoroughfare and shopping street is **St. Patrick's Street,** which curves from the North Channel of the River Lee south and then westward through the center before resuming its southward course as Grand Parade to reach the South Channel.

As a base marker for a walk around Cork, off Grand Parade you'll find the **English Market,** a handsome Georgian covered hall on the site of a 400-year-old market where Cork's citizens still go to meet, greet, and eat. Sounds and sights are on the vivid side around stalls such as the Real Olive Company, the Meat Centre, and On the Pig's Back (a French deli stand), as well as the numerous vegetable stands, joke stores, and clothing booths, while smells are a rich jumble of bread, fish, apples, spices, leather, and earthy potatoes. After plunging

III in 1690, and had its town walls and many of its buildings flattened when the Protestant army broke in.

The 18th century brought prosperity to Cork—not least thanks to the industry of French Huguenot refugees who settled here at a time when newly dug canals were bringing improved trade. In the 19th century the city became a refuge for Home Rule activists, while in the 1919–1922 War of Independence it was one of the hottest of hotbeds of IRA plotting and action—a period brilliantly caught in *Guests of the Nation,* a selection of short stories by Cork's great writer Frank O'Connor. In 1920 the Black and Tans, a brutal paramilitary British regiment, murdered the mayor in front of his family and later burned and ransacked much of Cork.

Right: The English Market in the city center, where you can get anything from a stuffed olive to traditional tripe and drisheen

St. Finnbarre's Cathedral shows off High Victorian Gothic decor at its most extravagantly overblown.

in among all this, it's enjoyable to climb to the first-floor balcony and look down on the bustle below as you enjoy a meal at the outside tables of the Farmgate Restaurant.

Going south from English Market along Grand Parade, take a right turn down Tuckey Street and a left into South Main Street to pass two Cork institutions on your way to the South Channel of the River Lee—on your left is **An Spailpin Fánai,** one of the best pubs in the city for sessions of traditional music (generally a 9:30 p.m. kick-off), and opposite it the bulk of **Beamish and Crawford's Brewery** *(tours: tel 021 491 1100),* generally known simply as Beamish's. This velvet-black beer is drunk all over Ireland by those who prefer a sweeter stout than

Guinness. Cork's other stout, Murphy's, is said to be smoother than Guinness.

Cross South Gate Bridge and turn right along the river to find the gray rocket tower of **St. Finnbarre's Cathedral** *(tel 021 496 3387),* its exterior walls carrying statues of saints, angels, and demons. The medieval cathedral was shattered during the siege of 1690, and this church, dating from 1878, is an exuberant example of high Gothic exterior and something more artsy-craftsy within. It has walls of blood-red Cork marble, a beautiful rose window on the theme of Creation, a finely colored mosaic floor in the choir, and glorious gold, blue, and red angels in the roof of the sanctuary. Don't forget to lift the seats of the choir stalls to

enjoy the carvings of grasshopper, butterfly, stag beetle, and dragonfly under the misericord ledges—on which choristers can recline while seeming to remain upright.

Back at English Market, a north-ward walk would start with a right turn along St. Patrick's Street, from which Carey Lane and French Church Street lead north into the old **Huguenot Quarter.** Now a chic part of the city, it's a peaceful area of high stone walls, small 18th-century houses, and brick-paved pedestrian alleys. The heart is **Rory Gallagher Square,** honoring the Stratocaster-wielding bluesman (who spent his young days in Cork) and featuring a sculpture of a twist-ed guitar with Gallagher's words and music streaming out of it.

North of the Huguenot Quarter, Paul Street runs east to pass the **Crawford Municipal Art Gallery.** Don't be surprised to find more people eating in the gallery's café than looking at the pictures—the fabulous food is provided by the Ballymaloe School of Cookery at Midleton to the east of Cork. Once you have had your fill, the paintings are definitely worthy a look as well—among them an icy 1955 por-trait of writer Elizabeth Bowen by Patrick Hennessy, a sentimental Victorian "Letter from America" by James Brenan, a thoughtful Barrie Cooke study of modern Irish poet John Montague, and a blazing yellow-and-blue "The Rice Field" (1989) by William Crozier.

Just north of the Crawford Municipal Gallery, Christy Ring Bridge crosses the North Channel of the River Lee to reach the north-ern suburb of **Shandon.** From its perch high on the hillside, the tall tower of St. Anne's Church calls you up twisty, steep old lanes. The tower contains the famous Bells of Shandon that can be rung by any-one paying the small fee. You can make up your own composition or "read" a tune off a crib card.

At the foot of the tower stands **Shandon's Butter Exchange,** built in 1770 to cope with the grading of hundreds of thousands of casks of prime Cork butter. It now houses a craft center, where you can watch makers of fiddles and fishing flies, crystal goblets and ceramic mugs—and buy their products, naturally.

A half-hour walk west of Shandon leads to Sunday's Well and the former **Cork City Gaol.** It houses a chilling exhibition about the harsh conditions in the jail, and the even harsher social conditions in 19th-century Cork that drove prisoners such as Mary Sullivan to steal the twopence-worth of calico that earned her a seven-year sen-tence, or that sentenced Edward O'Brien to gaol and a twice-weekly lashing for stealing brass—his 52nd offense, and he was only nine. ∎

Crawford Municipal Gallery

www.crawfordartgallery.com

🖼 139

✉ Emmet Pl., Cork, Co. Cork

🕐 Closed Sun.

☎ 021 427 3377

Shandon's Butter Exchange craft center

🖼 139

✉ Shandon, Co. Cork

☎ 021 430 2303

Cork City Gaol

✉ Convent Ave., Sunday's Well, Cork, Co. Cork

☎ 021 430 5022

💲 $$

Talk & tipple at the Hi-B

South of English Market down Grand Parade, a left turn into Oliver Plunkett Street would take you east all the way to the tip of the "island." No need to go farther than the General Post Office, though, if you are in search of a drink, for above the chemist's shop opposite you'll find the wonderful Hi-B bar up a flight of steps. The Hi-B is everything you look for in an Irish town pub—cheerful, friendly, comfortable, firelit, a bit old-fashioned, a place where connoisseurs can pass a pleasant hour trying to decide which is better—the talk or the ale. Both are among the very best in town. ∎

A somber monument in Casement Square remembers the 1,198 people who drowned when the Cunard liner RMS *Lusitania* was torpedoed off the Old Head of Kinsale on May 7, 1915.

Cobh & the Queenstown Story

West of the city of Cork, Great Island all but fills the northernmost portion of Cork Harbour. This is one of the world's finest natural sheltered havens, and the port known as Queenstown that developed during the 19th century along the seaward-facing side of Great Island became Ireland's premier port for commerce and communications with the British colonies and ex-colonies.

Queenstown—or Cobh (Cove) as it was called before the visit of Queen Victoria in 1849—meant many things to many people. To sailors at the Admiralty station established here during the Napoleonic Wars, it was a strategic communications post in the North Atlantic. To the troops embarking for the Crimean War in the 1850s or the Boer War 40 years later, it was their last sight of home territory and the launch point to death or glory. For most of those who boarded *Titanic* here in 1912, it was their last contact with Earth. For prisoners such as the rebel United Irishmen condemned to transportation (banishment to a penal colony in Australia) for their part in the 1798 Rising, it meant the start of six months chained in the lightless, airless hold of a leaky convict ship. Above all, it was the point of

holding "American wakes" on the waterside before parting from relatives and lovers as they board the emigrant ships. These ranged from well-appointed vessels to the rotten old coffin ships, apt to founder in bad weather, that those fleeing the Great Famine of 1845–49 were only too glad to scramble on board.

We learn of the bad water and food, vomiting and cursing, the dances and *ceilidhs* in the steerage-class holds; the daunting strangeness of the arrival on a foreign shore weeks or months later, weak and filthy from the voyage, with only the name of an already-emigrated relative or the vague suggestion of a promise of work to sustain them.

Between 1815 and 1970 some 3,000,000 emigrants—roughly the population of Ireland today—left Cobh in search of a better life. It is the ceaseless movement of this vast anonymous army, which enriched so many other countries while it drained the lifeblood of Ireland, that is the real Queenstown story. ■

Irish emigrants on their way to the New World: A poignant sculpture at the Queenstown Story exhibition, Cobh

embarkation for many millions of poor Irish emigrants seeking a new life in Canada, the United States, England, or Australia, away from the poverty or oppression that had dogged them in their native land.

In the beautifully refurbished former railway station at the old port—now once more named Cobh—the Queenstown Story exhibition *(Cobh Heritage Centre, Cobh, Co. Cork, tel 021 4813591, www.Cobhheritage.com, $$)* tells the tale of those who left Ireland over the course of two centuries through this thronging gateway. Here are ship models of every shape and size, tableaux, photographs, letters, and the poignant personal effects of emigrants—locks of loved ones' hair, rosaries, pocket watches. It is the stories of the men, women, and children, leaving Ireland because there was no other option, that strike home the hardest.

We see these mostly reluctant travelers, bold or frightened, optimistic or downcast,

Walk: Around Cork city

Although Cork is Ireland's "second city," and by far the largest conurbation in the south-west of the country, it's an extremely manageable city to walk around. The center of Cork amounts to a spearblade-shaped island between the North and South Channels of the River Lee. Everything that makes for an enjoyable city walk is contained within this island and on the river banks just north and south of it.

Start your walk amid the bustle and color of the **English Market ❶** (see p. 133) at the heart of Cork's island center. You could pick up provisions for the walk at some of the delicatessen stands in the market, but with a pub, café, or food shop on every corner it's scarcely worth carrying your food with you. Better to grab a coffee and then set off from the Prince's Street entrance, turning right along Prince's Street to reach South Mall at the bottom.

Turn right to the foot of Grand Parade, where you turn left over the South Channel of the River Lee. Bear right along the south bank of the river with the water on your right hand for 500 yards (457 m) to reach the tall gray bulk of **St. Finnbarre's Cathedral ❷** (see p. 134) on the left side of Bishop Street.

After looking around the cathedral, retrace your steps along Bishop Street and beside the

- **See area map p. 131 E2**
- **English Market**
- **2 miles (3 km)**
- **Half a day**
- **St. Anne's Church**

NOT TO BE MISSED

- English Market
- St. Finnbarre's Cathedral
- Huguenot Quarter
- Crawford Municipal Art Gallery
- Quays along the River Lee
- Bells of Shandon

South Channel, turning left over South Gate Bridge and on up South Main Street. On your left you'll pass the **Beamish and Craw-ford's Brewery ❸** (see p. 134), while on your right opposite the brewery is the great music pub of **An Spailpin Fánai ❹** (see p. 134).

Halfway up South Main Street, turn right along Tuckey Street, then left up Grand Parade past another entrance to the English Market. At the top of Grand Parade take a right turn and make your way through the crowds along the shopping thoroughfare of St. Patrick's Street, crossing the road in 200 yards (182 m) to turn left along French Church Street into the quieter pedestrian lanes of the **Huguenot Quarter ❺** (see p. 135).

You can wander here at will, soaking up the atmosphere of the brick-paved lanes around **Rory Gallagher Square ❻** (see p. 135). The walk continues northward along French Church Street or Carey's Lane to reach Paul Street, where you turn right.

At the end of the street, bear right for a few yards, then turn left along Emmet Place. Soon you see on your left the **Crawford**

A lively music pub in the city of Cork: Bring your *bodrhán* here, and welcome!

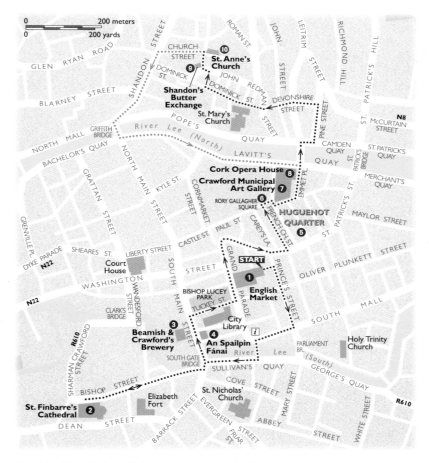

Municipal Art Gallery ⑦ (see p. 135). This is the place to stop if you are feeling hungry or thirsty, as the Gallery Café serves exceptionally good food.

Just beyond the gallery you pass **Cork Opera House ⑧.** Then cross the North Channel of the River Lee—there are great river views from the bridge along Lavitt's Quay and Camden Quay.

Reach the far bank of the river and continue up Pine Street. Turn left along Devonshire Street and continue west along the hillside on Dominick Street. Take a right to climb Exchange Street and you will find yourself outside the handsome Georgian **Shandon's Butter Exchange ⑨** (see p. 135). Take time to enjoy the wide range

of crafts being expertly practiced in the Shandon Craft Centre, which is housed in the Butter Exchange, before climbing on for another few yards to reach the tall tower of **St. Anne's Church ⑩,** parish church of the hilly Cork suburb of Shandon. Announce your arrival by striking a tune out of the famous Bells of Shandon (see p. 135).

From Shandon you could get back to the English Market the way you came. Or, walk west along Church Street opposite St. Anne's, turning left down Shandon Street to regain the North Channel of the River Lee at Griffith Bridge. Cross the bridge, then bear left along the quays to reach the Opera House and Emmet Place, from where you retrace your steps to the English Market. ■

Blarney Castle

EVERYONE KNOWS THAT THOSE WHO KISS THE BLARNEY Stone at Blarney Castle are magically endowed with the gift of the gab. In fact the castle and its grounds are imbued with legends—so much so that a stroll about will introduce you to the Rock Close and its "druidical foundations," the Fairy Glade with its "sacrificial altar," and the Wishing Steps that will grant you your heart's desire if you can negotiate them backwards with your eyes closed.

Blarney Castle itself is a battlemented keep standing on a rock outcrop overlooking the River Martin 6 miles (10 km) northwest of Cork city. Dermot Laidhir (Strongman) McCarthy built it in 1446 on the site of an earlier 13th-century fortified tower. Other towers rise as outposts, giving the whole ensemble a formidable look.

"Blarney" as a synonym for charming claptrap originated with an evasive McCarthy, Lord of Blarney, who was quizzed by the Earl of Leicester, Queen Elizabeth I's emissary. Either the Queen had demanded the handing-over of the castle, or there was some dispute about land ownership, but whatever the disagreement the loquacious McCarthy just kept talking and never came to the point. When Leicester reported the stalemate to Queen Elizabeth, she burst out: "But this is just more Blarney!"

The Queen's forces never did take Blarney Castle; it fell to Oliver Cromwell's commander Lord Broghill in 1646, but the garrison escaped during the siege by underground passage. There were reputed to be three of these, one running to the nearby lake, one to Cork, and one—not very feasibly—to County Kerry 50 miles (80 km) to the west.

As for the **Blarney Stone,** you have to climb right to the top of the old keep to find that, past the Great Hall with its enormous fireplace, the Earl's bedroom lit by big windows, and the Young Ladies' Room. Once out on the oval-shaped open top of the castle, you'll spot the location of the Blarney Stone easily enough—it's where the line ends amid much giggling and gasping. Kissing the Blarney Stone is one of Ireland's prime visitor activities, as the bus tour operators know well. Come early in the morning to avoid lines that can stretch right down the castle stairs.

The stone, cloaked in legends, is set into the outer face of a gap in the battlements. You'll have to lie on your back and wriggle your upper body outward and downward to kiss the stone. It's quite

Above: Bloody history and feisty legend cling to the 15th-century stronghold of Blarney Castle, on the River Martin near Cork city.

Blarney Castle
www.blarneycastle.ie
🅰 131 E2
✉ Blarney, Co. Cork
☎ 021 438 5252
💲 $$

Left: It's not all about the stone, you know— Blarney Castle also has beautiful grounds.

safe, as you perform the feat while gripping two safety bars, supported by a sturdy guard and shielded by a metal grille from the 83-foot (29 m) drop to the ground.

Two words to the wise—take all your coins out of your pockets, or they'll shower through the grille, and don't wear a miniskirt if you value your modesty. ■

Below: Easy now! Yet another eloquence-seeker kisses the Blarney Stone.

Legends of the stone

Legends surround the Blarney Stone. One says that it was brought to Ireland by the prophet Jeremiah, and claims it as the stone pillow on which Jacob slept in the desert when he had his dream of angels on a ladder—although that is also said of the Lialh Fail or Stone of Destiny at Tara (see pp. 266–267). Other tales tell of the stone being given to Cormac McCarthy, King of Munster, either by an old witch whom he had saved from drowning, or by Robert the Bruce of Scotland as a thank-you present for sending 4,000 men to help Bruce defeat the English at the Battle of Bannockburn in 1314.

A (marginally) more credible account is that the stone was brought to Ireland by some crusader who had acquired it in the Holy Land as a curiosity, probably already the focus for legends—hence, perhaps, the Jacob's dream connection. ■

Kinsale & the west Cork coast

EXPLORE THIS AREA WHEN YOU HAVE ADJUSTED TO THE slow tempo of the southwest. It's no good hurrying over the 100-mile (160 km), in-and-out coast of west Cork, because the twisty roads won't let you speed along, and the seaside villages and windy headlands will do their darndest to detain you. Better to take two days over it than one—better still to take three, or a week ....

Kinsale
🏔 131 E2
Visitor information
✉ Pier Rd., Kinsale, Co. Cork
☎ 021 477 2234

Kinsale Regional Museum
✉ Market Sq., Kinsale, Co. Cork
☎ 021 477 7930
🕐 Closed Nov.–March

The town of **Kinsale,** spread around a tight waterfront of green hills at a bend in the River Bandon's estuary 15 miles (25 km) south of Cork city, is the perfect jumping-off point for the beautiful, unspoiled coastline of west Cork. For one thing, you are guaranteed a great meal—Kinsale is reckoned the gourmet capital of the southwest, if not of all Ireland, thanks to the excellence of its fish restaurants.

Kinsale is made for wandering, with its waterfront and snaking Main Street full of color-washed buildings. Lanes and narrow streets climb the hills behind the harbor, and the houses are spread attractively above the water. The only

eyesore is a development of close-packed green-and-pink apartments on the east bank of the estuary, brutally out of keeping with everything else in view.

Two notable buildings in Kinsale are **St. Multose's Church** (tel 021 477 2220) and the **Desmond Castle** (tel 021 477 4855). St. Multose's Church stands in from the harbor, where Higher O'Connell Street meets Cork Street—a squat church dating from the 12th century, whose sturdy Irish Romanesque tower has a curious top, smaller than the lower stories, awkwardly fitted on.

The Desmond Castle, halfway up hilly Cork Street, is a fine late

medieval fortified tower with craggy crenellations and stone mullioned windows. At various times it has served as a customs house and a jail for French prisoners-of-war—and as a powder magazine during the Siege of Kinsale. This episode took place toward the end of 1601 when 4,000 Spanish troops under Don Juan del Aguida landed at Kinsale to support a rebellion by Hugh O'Neill, Earl of Tyrone. The rebels held the town for three months, but when the Spanish failed to back the Irish during the decisive battle the rebellion quickly crumbled. It was the last throw of the dice for the Gaelic chiefs of Ireland: In 1607 O'Neill and his fellow-rebel the Earl of Tyrconnell fled to the Continent, the famous "Flight of the Earls"— and the English Crown took full control of Ireland.

Much Kinsale history is expounded in endearingly ramshackle style at the **Kinsale Regional Museum** in the old Court House on Market Square. Here are ice picks and fish boxing hammers, boatbuilder's tools and

Easter Rising rifles, ships' guns and Kinsale lace, all packed into the museum's few rooms. Most affecting are the mementoes of the British passenger liner *Lusitania,* torpedoed by German submarine *U-20* on May 7, 1915, off the Old Head of Kinsale promontory. Of 1,951 passengers, 1,198 died, many of them women and children. A striped mail bag, a German commemorative medal, a cane deckchair, and a facsimile of the log of *U-20*, translated into English, all bring the tragedy up close.

For light relief there are the vast kneeboot and the unnecessarily massive knife and fork of Patrick Cotter O'Brien (1760–1806), the celebrated "Kinsale Giant." At 8 feet 7 inches (2.5 m), O'Brien was certainly phenomenally tall. He was also a sad figure, unable to walk properly or even rise from his chair without pain, obliged to exhibit himself as a freak to earn a living.

Any exploration of the west Cork coast from Kinsale ought to start with the short trip along the east side of the estuary to **Charles Fort**, an eerie and

Enjoy the magnificent panorama from Charles Fort over the town of Kinsale, which spreads across the hills in a bend of the Bandon Estuary.

Charles Fort

🅰 131 E2

✉ Summer Cove, Kinsale, Co. Cork

☎ 021 477 2263

🕐 Closed weekdays Nov.–mid-March

💲 $

striking star-shaped fort built in the 1670s to be impregnable from the sea. Designed on the principles of the French military engineer Vauban, the fort fell in three days when actually put to the test by King William III's army in 1690—they attacked it from the land.

The extensive interior of Charles Fort is filled with ruined barracks, magazines, officers' quarters, an armory, a cooperage—all massively constructed, but all now roofless and blank-eyed. Strolling around these lifeless monuments to defense is a surreal, gripping experience. The view from the headland over Kinsale, the boats on the river, and the estuary mouth is sensational.

From Kinsale a scenic drive, signposted Coast Road, wriggles and snakes for something like 80 miles (128 km) westward to Skibbereen, making use of byways and lanes in which you are almost bound to lose yourself. Don't worry: There's always someone to ask when the signposts give out. In any case this is one of the most beautiful corners of Ireland, a gentle coastal landscape that simply begs you to put the car in low gear and wander aimlessly, simply enjoying the scenery.

Don't bother going down to the Old Head of Kinsale—a golf club has taken over the historic headland and access is no longer possible. Instead, high-banked lanes colorful with poppies, ragwort, fuchsia, and bindweed will take you on to **Timoleague,** one of a number of attractive color-washed villages

sited around the estuaries whose shining mudflats are haunted by seabirds and crossed by narrow causeways. Timoleague's 14th-century **Franciscan friary** is astonishingly complete—Cromwell despoiled it in 1642, but the shell stands almost perfect in lichen-green stone. Lancet windows, tomb niches, a tall arched nave, and fragments of cloister echo to the somnolent cooing of nesting pigeons.

It is worth sidetracking through pretty Courtmacsherry and on around the maze of lanes that crisscross the **Seven Heads Peninsula.** O'Neill's pub in sleepy Butlerstown is a good pit-stop, and the moondaisies, roses, and silver sand beaches around Dunworley are a delight. You can swim here, or wait until you have passed through the small but lively town of **Clonakilty** to cross the causeways to Inchydoney Island with its broad strands.

Three miles (5 km) west of Clonakilty, the **Four Alls pub** and Sam's Cross are signposted off the N71. The dark and cozy Four Alls is where the Commander-in-Chief of the Free State Army, Michael Collins, stopped on August 22,

1922, for his last drink on Earth before an IRA bullet felled him in an ambush. The pub walls are covered in photographs, drawings, and newspaper clippings relating to the hero.

The **Birthplace of Michael Collins** stands at Woodfield nearby (ask at the pub for directions), and is the object of many a pilgrimage. A bronze bust of Collins generally has a posy of fresh flowers on its plinth.

Across another estuary stands **Ross Carbery** with the spire of its cathedral beckoning. This has a splendid heavy Victorian chancel roof, and contains some excellent 19th- and 20th-century stained glass, notably the pre-Raphaelite young knight in the south transept who commemorates a dead soldier of World War I.

The **Drombeg Stone Circle** (ca 150 B.C.) is well signposted along the Glandore road. Seventeen slim, man-sized stones stand in a tight circle, and nearby you'll find an ancient cooking pit with a primitive boiling oven.

Before reaching Skibbereen, seek out the erratically signposted **Ceim Hill Museum** (see below) and its remarkable curator. ■

Ceim Hill Museum

The cottage that houses Ceim Hill Museum (*Union Hall, Skibbereen, Co. Cork, tel 028 36280, $*), crooked and cracked and sunk in a leafy dell, looks as if it has sprouted out of the earth.

Inside, everything is set out higgledy-piggledy on tables, shelves, floor, and walls. Miss Therese O'Mahony, owner and curator, collected everything herself from the land around her cottage: fragments of boar tusk incised with pictures by Stone Age man, ancient stone tools, segments of bone

sharpened and rubbed in the long ago. The guided tour of the museum is de rigueur.

A War of Independence room has displays of old photos and cuttings about Michael Collins (Miss O'Mahony's father was an Irish Volunteer), a bathtub full of shipwreck remains, gorgeous handmade lace, old caps and kettles, and lanterns galore.

Miss O'Mahony is a herbalist, a healer, and a West Cork countrywoman to her fingertips, and her museum is an absolute gem. ■

Birthplace of Michael Collins
 131 D2
✉ Woodfield,
Clonakilty, Co. Cork

Islands of southwest Cork

Roaringwater Bay, poetically and aptly named, forms the underbelly of the Mizen Head Peninsula. There are said to be 127 islands scattered in the bay, and the two largest—Sherkin Island and Clear Island—are accessible by ferry.

Islands of southwest Cork
131 C1–C2, 130 B2
Visitor information
Áras Fáilte, Grand Parade, Cork, Co. Cork
021 425 5100

Sherkin Island *(10-minute ferry ride from Baltimore or Schull, tel 028 20125)* is some 3 miles long (5 km), a great island for swimming from safe, sandy beaches. The 70 inhabitants run a couple of pubs: the Jolly Roger, and Murphy's beside the ruins of an O'Driscoll castle. There's also the ruin of a 1460 Franciscan friary to explore, along with the enjoyable little island museum in the volunteer-run Marine Station, which monitors the marine environment around the island.

Irish speaking **Clear Island,** or Cape Clear, as some call it (*ferry from Baltimore, tel 028 28278*), lies 6 miles (10 km) out from land at the mouth of Roaringwater Bay. It is roughly the same size as Sherkin, but more mountainous and bulky. The island, which has a bird observatory with a worldwide reputation, is a landfall for millions of migrating birds and sees spectacular flypasts in summer of gannets, kittiwakes, shearwaters, guillemots, cormorants, and storm petrels.

North Harbour, where the boat docks, has a couple of pubs, and there's a third one on the potholed road over to the sheltered South Harbour. Here on the south side of the island—Ireland's southernmost point—are splendid cliffs from which to gaze out at the rugged hump of the Fastnet Rock 4 miles (6 km) out into the Atlantic.

In Bantry Bay, northward beyond the Mizen Head and Sheep's Head Peninsulas, lie four islands. **Whiddy Island** *(ferry from Bantry, tel 027 50310 or 027 51066)* is little visited, mostly because it holds the ugly remains of an oil storage depot abandoned when the tanker Betelgeuse blew up in January 1979 with a roar that was heard 15 miles (24 km) off, killing 51 people.

Garinish Island, also known as **Garnish** or **Ilnacullin** *(ferry from Glengarriff, tel 027 63116 or 027 63333),* is a different kettle of fish— a scrap of an island of 37 acres (15 ha) that was a bare rock until transformed by the English landscape gardener Harold Peto for the owner Arran Bryce. Between 1910 and 1913 he planted on imported topsoil a garden of plants and shrubs from all over the world. Among the lush growth is a formal Italian garden.

Farther down the bay lies **Bere** or **Bear Island** *(ferry from Castletownbere, tel 027 75009),* a former British naval base that has a sailing school and some fine hilly walking and scrambling based on a 13-mile (21 km) stretch of the circumpeninsular Bear (Beara) Way.

Out at the tip of the Bear (Beara) Peninsula you can sway in a cable car over a furious tidal race to lonely **Dursey Island,** a rugged finger of island where some 50 people live without shop, pub, or other mainland amenities.

Follow a 7-mile (11 km) loop of the **Bear Way** around this beautifully peaceful slip of land, pausing at the seaward end to look out over the three sea islets of the Bull, the Cow, and the Calf—a wild and glorious prospect. ∎

Opposite: A touch of Romanesque elegance in the Italian garden on Garinish Island in Bantry Bay. It's hard to believe this lush haven for plants was a barren rock before Harold Peto got to work on it in 1910.

Three peninsulas: Mizen, Sheep's Head, & Bear

COUNTY CORK BOASTS THREE OF THE FIVE GREAT peninsulas of southwest Ireland—south to north: Mizen, Sheep's Head, and Bear (Beara). Each has a quite distinctive character, and individual magic. Try to take a day, at least, on each peninsula; they tend to hide their secrets from those who rush through.

Mizen Peninsula
🅰 130 B1
Skibbereen visitor information
✉ Town Hall, Co. Cork
☎ 028 21766

Mizen Head visitor information
✉ Mizen Head, Co. Cork
☎ 028 35115
🕐 Closed weekdays Nov.–March

Sheep's Head Peninsula
🅰 130 B1

Bantry visitor information
✉ Old Courthouse, Co. Cork
☎ 027 50229
🕐 Seasonal

Traveling the **Mizen Peninsula** clockwise from pretty Ballydehob, you enter a sparse world of gorse-covered bog, rock outcrops, and high hills. Roses, purple flowering heather, and brilliant orange montbretia grow in the roadside hedges.

Schull and Goleen are sleepy villages on coastal bays, while charming Crookhaven sits on an isolated mini-peninsula. Barleycove, just beyond, is a huge, fabulous beach system backed by enormous grassy dunes and spreads of machair (shell-sand turf). Out at the end, **Mizen Head** is the southernmost point of mainland Ireland, with impressive vertical cliffs. You can walk beyond the visitor center and

cross a bridge over a rocky sea chasm to see a display of charts, photographs, and signal flags in the old fog station. There's a fine view, too, and maybe a sight of dolphins, whales, and any number of seabirds.

The village of Durrus is where you turn left for the **Sheep's Head Peninsula**, another clockwise circuit. There are no attractions in the tourist sense; this only adds to the magic of this slim and low-rolling promontory with its scatter of tiny villages and well-ordered farmland that turns wild as you approach the lighthouse at the tip. The scenic drive back to Bantry along the north side is called the Goats Path, with good reason.

The **Bear Peninsula** is another matter altogether, a great ragged leg of land, 30 miles long (50 km), shared between Cork and Kerry—though Cork has the lion's share. The purple slabs of the Caha Mountains march along the spine of the peninsula, rising to 2,251 feet (685 m), and the Slieve Miskish Mountains are in the west—lower, but no less impressive—rising above inhospitable bog and stony fields. The shoreline is heavily indented. Southward it looks to Bantry Bay and its islands (see p. 146), on the north is the Kenmare River, with more, smaller islands and the tremendous backdrop of Kerry's mountainous Iveragh Peninsula (see pp. 152–155).

Tour the Bear in an open-ended figure-of-eight route, starting at the pretty but rather over-run Victorian health resort of Glengarriff. In a beautiful location, backed by wooded mountains, the town is full of hydrangeas and palm trees, with 19th-century villas peeping out. Going west along the southern coast road, you soon reach the right turn for the Healy Pass. Try to pick a really clear day for the ascent of the narrow, zigzag mountain road to the pass at just under 1,100 feet (334 m), because the view from the big white Crucifixion shrine at the top is stupendous.

At the northern foot of the pass you'll find beautiful **Derreen Garden,** with walks to the shore through flowering shrubs and giant feathery tree ferns from Australia. Continue west in stunning coast scenery, to wriggle by a narrow, winding road over the end of Slieve Miskish to **Allihies** on the black cliffs of west-facing Ballydonegan Bay. Allihies was a copper-mining center in the 19th century, and above the village you can explore the remains of mine buildings.

Out at the end of Bear is the swaying cable car ride to **Dursey Island** (see p.146). Back along the south coast, have a look at the extraordinary ruin of **Dunboy Castle** west of Castletownbere—the IRA torched this giant chateau-like mansion in 1921, leaving a Gothic horror set of vaults, huge blank windows, and grand rooms open to the sky. ■

Whorls and windings of the sea around the shores of the Beara Peninsula, one of five that stick out like fingers from the coast of southwest Ireland

Bear Peninsula
🅐 130 B2
Glengarriff visitor information
✉ Eccles Hotel parking lot
☎ 027 63084
🕐 Seasonal

Derreen Garden
✉ Lauragh
☎ 064 83103
🕐 Closed Oct.–March
💲 $$

Killarney National Park

SOME OF IRELAND'S MOST BEAUTIFUL LAKE AND mountain scenery falls within the boundary of Killarney National Park. The heart of the park is the 10,000 acres (4,000 ha) of the Muckross Estate around Lough Leane, given to the Irish nation in 1932 by the philanthropic American landowners Mr. and Mrs. William Bowers Bourn and their son Senator Arthur Vincent of California. Careful purchases by the Irish State and some more donations of land in subsequent decades have safeguarded a total of 25,000 acres (10,200 ha) of wonderful country from development.

Killarney National Park

131 C3

Victorian and Edwardian holiday-makers eulogized the Killarney landscape as "the Mecca of every pilgrim in search of the sublime and beautiful in Nature—the mountain paradise of the west." Yet all were agreed that Killarney town itself was far too touristy for its own good. Located at the northeast corner of the park, it is still an all-out tourist town where the sales of leprechauns, shamrocks, and shillelaghs keep the gift shops ticking over nicely. The problem with Killarney is that, while the town is just the place to rent a horsedrawn

thick on the ground here, too, if you feel like a horsedrawn tour.

As a contrast to the civilized surroundings of Muckross, head northward along the lakeshore to reach the restored 15th-century fortified *bawn,* or walled tower, of **Ross Castle** *(tel 064 35851).* Hire a rowboat here and pull out across the lake to **Inisfallen,** a lovely little island whose thick woods conceal a church and the ruins of monastic settlements.

From Ross Castle head south again along the N71 to reach the start of the succession of lakes (Middle and Upper). Boatmen are ready, able, and only too willing to row you about.

The star attraction of Middle Lake (also known as Muckross Lake) is the **Meeting of the Waters,** set in a flowery and shrubby dell. Next you climb past the beautiful little Upper Lake to reach Ladies' View, a famous viewpoint looking back north over the spectacularly narrow Gap of Dunloe and the Killarney Lakes.

Torc Waterfall, another classic Killarney sight, is signed off the N71 beside Middle Lake. Getting to the fall, a fine 60-foot (18 m) cascade down a staircase of rock overhung with sycamore and mountain ash, involves a short climb up a stepped path. If you feel like a moderate stretch of the legs from this point, you can leave the crowds behind in a twinkling if you carry on up the path beyond the waterfall. Turn around when you've had enough. This is the old road over the mountains to Kenmare (12 miles/19 km away) by way of Esknamucky Glen and Windy Gap, now part of the long-distance **Kerry Way.** It will lead you up through mossy woods of dwarf oaks and ancient holly trees to an exciting fording of a mountain torrent by way of stepping stones. ∎

Jaunting car and jarvey: You'll need a great love of gossip, or a good pair of earplugs.

jaunting car with a silver-tongued *jarvey*, or driver, to trot you out to the lakes, there are no views of the lakes themselves. The best thing to do is to refuel and head straight for the **Muckross Estate** on the shores of Lough Leane.

This car-free estate is extremely popular and perhaps best avoided on public holidays in summer. At other times of the year, Muckross is a great place to stroll by the lake or through the beautifully kept rhododendron and azalea gardens. Muckross House is a Victorian mock-Elizabethan mansion with an appealingly cranky museum of folklore and rural life, and to the north of the house you'll find the largely 15th-century cloisters and ruined church of Muckross Abbey. Jarveys and their jaunting cars are

Muckross Estate
www.muckross-house.ie
✉ Muckross, near Killarney, Co. Kerry
☎ 064 31440
🕐 Farms closed Nov.–Feb. & weekdays March, April, & Oct.; house & gardens open year-round
💲 House & farms: $$$

Drive: Ring of Kerry

This looping route around the coast of the Iveragh Peninsula, known as the Ring of Kerry, is Ireland's best-known scenic drive. Here are the mountains, craggy coasts, and charming small towns and villages depicted in chocolate-box photographs of the west of Ireland, but close-up and for real. In spite of the possibility of becoming stuck behind a caravan or crawling line of cars—and you stand a better chance of avoiding that the earlier you make your start, especially in the summer holiday season—the Ring of Kerry is one treat you must not miss. A few diversions along even narrower roads are suggested here, to give you the chance of a bit of exploration and a respite from any traffic jams on the main road.

Start your full day's drive by leaving **Killarney** for Killorglin along the N72, with great views to your left on the outskirts of town down the wide, mountain-framed expanse of **Lough Leane.** In 12 miles (19 km) you reach **Killorglin ❶,** a characterful small town where each year in August a

wild goat is enthroned as master of an extremely enjoyable three-day revel called Puck Fair.

Leave the main N70 Ring of Kerry route here and enter the town across its bridge, driving up the hill and taking the second street on the right (signed Caragh Lake), which soon

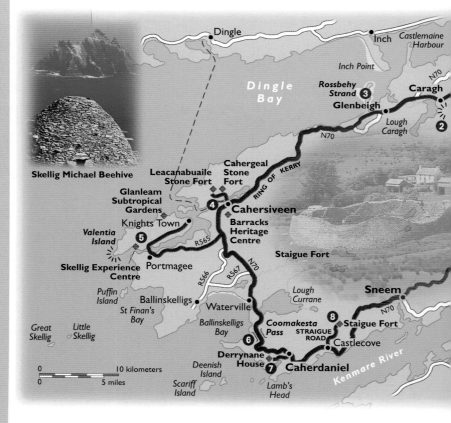

becomes a bumpy road across forested bog-lands. At O'Shea's shop in **Caragh** village fork left (signed "Hotel Ard Na Sidhe"), and in 1 mile (1.6 km) bear left up a forest track (wooden sign: "Loch Cárthaí; Caragh Lake") for half a mile (0.75 km) to a **viewpoint ②**. The view here sweeps over Lough Caragh to the mountains—a great place for a picnic.

Return to Caragh and turn left to reach the N70, bearing left through Glenbeigh village. A right turn just before you reach the end of the village leads to **Rossbehy (Rossbeigh) Strand ③**, with a wonderful view of a giant spit of shaggy dunes stretching 3 miles (5 km) north across Dingle Bay toward the mountainous spine of the Dingle Peninsula. The narrow road continues in a loop back to the N70.

Continue on the N70 down the northern coast of the Iveragh Peninsula through glorious hilly scenery. Just before crossing the

Cahersiveen's old police barracks looks like a Bavarian castle—reputedly because plans, intended for a building in India, got lost in the mail and ended up here instead.

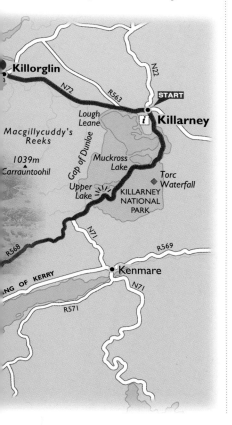

▲ See area map pp. 130–131
► Killarney
⟳ 150 miles (240 km)
◔ 1 day
► Killarney

NOT TO BE MISSED
- Cahergeal & Leacanabuaile stone forts
- Valentia Island
- Views over the Skelligs and Kenmare River
- Derrynane House

bridge into the village of **Cahersiveen ④**, glance to your left to see the ruins of the birthplace of Daniel O'Connell (1775–1847), champion of Ireland's poor and the first Irish Catholic to be elected to the Westminster parliament in London.

Turn right in the village to pass the **Barracks Heritage Centre** (*tel 066 947 2777*), where there are exhibitions and displays of local interest, then cross a bridge and go left, following brown "Stone Houses" signs,

Out on a limb: Puffin Island stands in the Atlantic off the tip of the Iveragh Peninsula, a rugged neighbor of the rocky Skelligs.

to find **Cahergeal** and **Leacanabuaile** stone forts. Leacanabuaile—certainly inhabited during the Bronze Age, and maybe dating back more than 4,000 years—is especially impressive. Perched on a rock outcrop, it is a great stone-built enclosure 80 feet across (25 m), with a square building in the center and the remains of three beehive huts, all inside a circular 6-foot (2 m) wall.

Three miles (5 km) beyond Cahersiveen, a side road (R565) leaves the N70 and makes for Portmagee, where you cross the causeway onto **Valentia Island** ❺. This is a most delightful island of tiny patchwork fields, with fine high cliffs on the west and north, and the small but beautiful **Glanleam subtropical gardens** *(tel 066 947 6176, $)*. From the western tip of the island the view looks down to the remote, needle-towered rocks of **Great Skellig** and **Little Skellig**. These towering rocks in the Atlantic are seabird sanctuaries, but until the 12th century hardy monks inhabited Great Skellig. Inquiry about boats in Portmagee or Ballinskelligs may yield a fisherman willing to run you out to Great Skellig, where you climb 1,000-year-old steps to the sixth-century beehive huts and tiny oratory chapels of the

monks, 700 feet (215 m) above the waves. If you can't get hold of a boatman to land you, or sea conditions are too rough, you can always visit the **Skellig Experience Centre** *(tel 066 947 6306, closed Dec.–March, $)* near the Valentia causeway. Or you can join one of the regular nonlanding cruises around the islands from Knights Town, the downbeat "capital" village of Valentia Island.

Return from Valentia Island to the N70, where you turn right to continue your Ring of Kerry circuit. The seaside resort of Waterville stands on the beautiful sandy Ballinskelligs Bay, from where the road climbs (more very fine views of the Skelligs from here) to the classic **viewpoint from Coomakesta Pass** ❻—back to the Skelligs, then forward to Scariff and Deenish Islands, with the prospect improving all the time as you come in sight of the mighty, islet-fringed Kenmare River, far more like a great bay than an estuary as it opens in front of you.

At **Caherdaniel** take a right turn, signposted Derrynane House, stopping if you're hungry and thirsty at the Blind Piper or Freddie's Bar, both excellent pubs.

Derrynane House ❼ *(tel 066 947 5113, closed Mon. in April & Oct., Mon.–Fri. Nov.–March, $)* was the home of Daniel O'Connell from 1825 onward and is now a museum to Swaggering Dan, or "The

Liberator," as his fans preferred to call him. O'Connell was a great Irishman, passionate and persevering, and inside the slate-hung house you get a good idea of the Kerry lawyer who inspired such devotion and raised such expectations among the poorest of the poor.

In the dining room a table is set with silverware presented to O'Connell by grateful supporters; upstairs in a display case is a silver cup voted to him in December 1813 by the "Catholics of Ireland." Also here are portraits, contemporary cartoons, the dueling pistols with which he killed an opponent, D'Esterre, in 1815, and, most poignantly, the bowl he was baptized in and the bed he died in.

Outside, the wooded grounds of Derrynane House are threaded by walking trails that will lead you to a ring fort and to a Mass Rock. It was here, during the 18th century when practicing the Roman Catholic religion was outlawed, that local faithful would gather clandestinely to hear Mass.

Return to the N70 and in 4 miles (6 km) bear left in Castlecove to find the magnificent **Staigue Fort ❽.** Set in a beautiful lonely valley, this wonderfully well-preserved ring fort of 1500 B.C. is well over 100 feet (30 m) in diameter, with great thick walls in which steps lead to some fine sea and mountain views.

Back at the N70, turn left and continue as far as **Sneem** village, where you fork left on the R568 for a wild and lonely 30-mile (50 km) mountain run, later passing the lakes of Killarney National Park (see pp. 150–151) and back to Killarney. ■

Transporting turf by donkey and creel: The old ways persist in County Kerry.

Dingle Peninsula

Dingle Peninsula
www.dingle-peninsula.ie
 130 A3, B3

**Dingle visitor
information**
✉ The Quay, Dingle,
   Co. Kerry
☎ 066 915 1188

**Tralee visitor
information**
✉ Ashe Memorial Hall,
   Denny St., Dingle,
   Co. Kerry
☎ 066 712 1288

THE DINGLE PENINSULA IS THE CONNOISSEUR'S CHOICE
among the five peninsulas of southwest Ireland. Here are beautiful
sandspits, beaches, and mountains, and Ireland's greatest concentration of early Christian sites—not to mention the laid-back charm of
Dingle town, and the extraordinary literary hothouse of the remote
and rugged Blasket Islands. The 105-mile (168 km) Kerry Way long-
distance footpath circumnavigates the peninsula.

The gateway to the Dingle
Peninsula is **Tralee,** a sizeable
country town with a bloody history,
having been sacked and destroyed
in 1583, and again in the 1640s
and '50s during the Cromwellian
repressions. These dark deeds are
recalled in the excellent **Kerry
County Museum** on Denny
Street, a fine street of handsome
Georgian buildings that leads to

Tralee's trademark rose gardens.
The annual **Rose of Tralee
Festival** *(tel 066 712 1322),* held
in August to the delight of the
media and the tourist board, pits
lovely girls from all over the world
against each other (they are supposed to be of Irish extraction) in
what is essentially an old-fashioned
beauty contest with some PC trimmings thrown in. Tralee is a town

Above right: Good pubs, great atmosphere, and brilliant music: Dingle town is on the rise.

Kerry County Museum

✉ Ashe Memorial Hall, Denny St., Dingle, Co. Kerry

☎ 066 712 7777

💲 $$$

Blennerville Windmill

✉ West edge of Tralee

☎ 066 712 1064

🕐 Closed Nov.–Dec.

💲 $$

of narrow streets, usually crowded, with good traditional music sessions in several pubs—try Paddy Mac's or Bailey's.

The Dingle Peninsula had its own eccentrically delightful railway until 1953, which connected Tralee with Dingle town. A short section of track has been reopened *(Tralee to Blennerville Steam Train, tel 066 712 1064),* and you can rattle behind a steam locomotive as far as the grand restored **Blennerville Windmill,** 60 feet tall (20 m). It's a landmark for miles around with its big white cross of sails that whirl round when the wind is right.

From Tralee, the N86 follows the northern flank of the Slieve Mish Mountains. The western end of this high ridge is dominated by the ancient stone-walled promontory fort of **Caherconree,** perhaps built around 500 B.C. You can scramble up to the fort from a minor road, signed to the left off the R559 at the eastern edge of Camp village. According to legend Caherconree was the stronghold of King Cu Roi MacDaire, a warrior

who made the fatal misjudgment of stealing and "marrying" beautiful Blathnaid, girlfriend of the Ulster hero Cúchullain. Shut up in Caherconree, Blathnaid waited until an auspicious moment arrived for her lover to attack the fort, then summoned him by pouring milk into the springs of the Finglas River. Cúchullain saw the sign, stormed the fort, slew the king, and was reunited with his beloved.

From the south coast of the peninsula, the superb 4-mile (6 km) sand and dune spit of **Inch** curves out into Dingle Bay—a wonderful sight at low tide with the whorls and channels of sand and water backed by the spectacular Macgillycuddy's Reeks across the bay. West of here is Dingle.

Dingle has earned itself a reputation as a hippyish sort of place, and there certainly are plenty of bangle, bead, and magic crystal shops. However, this is still a working fishing town, and a shopping and socializing center for the wide Gaeltacht area toward the end of the peninsula. It's also a tourist town, often crowded in summer—

The beautiful stone walls and corbeled roof of the Gallarus Oratory, out near the tip of the Dingle Peninsula

Blasket Islands interpretive center

- 130 A3
- Dunquin, Co. Kerry
- 066 915 6444 or 066 915 6371
- Closed Nov.–May
- $

especially around August, with the Dingle Races, Dingle Show, and Dingle Regatta hard on each other's heels. Each St. Stephen's Day, December 26, the town is given over to the Dingle Wren, when "Wren Boys" dress up and play tricks on each other, with plenty of alcohol thrown in.

Boat rides run around the sheltered, almost enclosed harbor, enlivened if you are lucky by a sighting of Dingle's fabled resident dolphin, Fungie—on contract to the Irish Tourist Board, cynics say. Try the Small Bridge pub for traditional music and don't forget to sample a Dingle Pie, a squashily delicious mutton pie served with a jug of mutton broth to pour over it.

Farther west again on the R599, into Irish-speaking territory, you'll come to **Ventry** on its glorious curve of sand, and then to the rich archaeological treasury of the hillsides under **Mount Eagle.** Here, a few steps off the road to either side, are standing stones and cross-inscribed slabs, beehive huts, and souterrains (underground storehouses) built by early Christian

hermits on these slopes.

As you near Slea Head at the peninsula's end, the four **Blasket Islands** swim into view—Inisvickillaun, Inisnabro, the big green hump of Great Blasket, and Inistooskert, with its sleeping-man shape. There were no modern amenities for the hundred or so islanders who lived on Great Blasket, and life was simple; yet within one decade they produced three of Ireland's most respected writers (see p. 159). The island was evacuated in 1953 because the disparity between island poverty and mainland prosperity was too stark, and the island's young women had all left to seek jobs, men, and fun ashore.

In Dunquin village on the mainland, you can learn something of what Blasket life was like at the modern **interpretive center.** However, a far better idea of the island can be got by crossing the sometimes lively Blasket Sound on one of the regular boats from Dunquin and wandering through the ruined village and over the island for yourself.

From Dunquin the R559 takes you northeast to the well-signposted **Gallarus Oratory,** a beautifully built, boat-shaped chapel some 1,500 years old. Nearby is **Kilmalkedar Church.** If you can rise to the challenge of squeezing through the narrow east window, they say, you'll never suffer from a bad back. Unless you hurt your back squeezing through the window, that is …

Soon you come to a signpost pointing right for **Brandon Creek,** a long 5 miles (8 km) to the north. This is a wonderfully peaceful and lonely spot, under the slope of the 3,127-foot (953 m) **Mount Brandon,** second highest mountain in Ireland after Carrantuohill (3,414 feet/1,039 m) in Killarney National Park. A ruined oratory at the sum-

mit (reachable from nearby Ballyhack via a stiff 3.5-mile/5 km climb up the waymarked Saint's Road—but only in clear weather) is said to be the one St. Brendan prayed in before his epic sixth-century transatlantic voyage in a leather *curragh*. It was from Brandon Creek that the adventurer Tim Severin set sail for Newfoundland in 1976 in his replica boat (see p. 169),

following the wake of Brendan.

There are wonderful views from the steep road over the Conor Pass and a warm welcome to be had in O'Connor's pub in Cloghane on the north side of the peninsula before you set course eastward for Tralee. First, though, take a quick stretch of the legs around the tip of the beautiful and windswept **Magharee sandspit** (see pp. 160–161). ∎

Dog meets dolphin, an everyday Dingle Bay delight

THE BLASKET WRITERS
By any reckoning, the literary flowering that took place on Great Blasket between the two World Wars of the 20th century was an extraordinary event. When Brian O'Kelly brought pen to paper, and the novelty of writing to the island, it resulted in three classics; Tomás O'Crohan's *The Islandman* (1929), Maurice O'Sullivan's *Twenty Years A-Growing* (1933), and Peig Sayer's *Peig* (1936). All are widely available in paperback. ∎

Tralee & Dingle Light Railway

The Tralee & Dingle Light Railway (T&DLR), opened in 1891, was one of the world's great eccentric railways, fulfilling every stereotype of an Irish—and more specifically a Kerry—backcountry branch line. The T&DLR was seldom on time, never worked to capacity or made a profit, and operated with increasingly antiquated locomotives and carriages. It was a friendly, informal line, whose engineers were known to emerge from Fitzgerald's Bar at Castlegregory Junction wiping porter froth from their moustaches as they prepared to drive their

trains; a railway whose firemen were valued just as much for the accuracy with which they could throw lumps of coal from the footplate at sheep grazing on the tracks as for their skill in firing the locomotives. The 20-odd-mile (30 km) line itself incorporated very steep gradients and sharp curves, which added to the delays, as did the grass that often smothered the rails. Somehow the Tralee & Dingle Light Railway prolonged its existence until 1953, when its closure was widely mourned by steam enthusiasts and connoisseurs of curiosities. ∎

Early Christian hermits lived and prayed in the wildflower fields of the Dingle Peninsula.

Walk: The Magharees

This is an easy stroll, all on the level, in the flat but remarkable landscape of the Magharees sandspit that divides Tralee Bay from Brandon Bay on the north side of the Dingle Peninsula.

Start in the tiny village of **Fahamore** and follow the road north to **Scraggane Bay** ❶ at the tip of the scimitar-shaped spit. Local men paid by the Congested Districts Board, a body set up to aid poverty-stricken and over-populated rural Ireland, built **Scraggane pier** in 1887. At that time the United States was taking as many barrels of salted mackerel as Ireland could supply. In the bay you'll see moored the black fishing canoes, tough and responsive in lively seas, that are so characteristic of the west of Ireland; they are built here at Fahamore. Elsewhere this kind of craft is known as a *curragh*, but hereabouts it is called a *namhog* (pronounced na-VOGUE).

Clustered offshore you will see the **Magharee Islands**, also called the **Seven Hogs**. On the largest, **Illauntannig**, a wall encloses two tiny oratories and three *clochans*, or stone huts, the remnants of an early Christian monastery. You may be able to persuade a local boatman to take you out there at a price. Farther out is

🗺 See area map pp. 130–131 B4
▶ Fahamore
🔁 6 miles/10 km (11 miles/18 km with extension to Lough Gill)
🕐 2 hours (4 hours)
▶ Fahamore

NOT TO BE MISSED
- Scraggane Bay with its *namhogs* & pier
- View of the Magharee Islands
- St. Senach's Church, Kilshannig
- Brandon Bay

Inishtooskert, off which the German vessel *Aud* idled for a day and a night during Easter Week of 1916. She was waiting for an all's-well signal from accomplices on Inishtooskert, when they were to bring ashore weapons to support the planned Easter Rising, but the signal never came. At last *Aud* departed, and a

day later the crew scuttled her off Cobh Haven in County Cork (see pp. 136–137) when they were accosted by the Royal Navy.

Follow the shore to your left around the curve of Scraggane Bay for 1 mile (1.6 km). Halfway around the bay, turn briefly inland where the road makes a right-angle to see a fine, tall **standing stone** ❷, a pagan monument carved with a rough cross by some early hermit to appropriate its power.

Continue along the shore, then turn inland through the hamlet of **Kilshannig** to reach the ruin of **St. Senach's Church** ❸. Look inside the 16th-century building to see an incised slab marked with a Chi-Rho crucifix symbol, dating from the seventh century.

From Kilshannig head east for the shore and turn right for 1.5 miles (2.5 km) along the beach until you come opposite **Lough**

Inishtooskert

Illaunimmil

Listooskert

Illaunboe

Reennafardarrig

Gurrig Island

Illauntannig

Mucklaghbeg

Illaunturlogh

M a g h a r e e   I s l a n d s
(S e v e n   H o g s)

Doonagaun Island

Rough Point

Illaunnanoon

Minnaun

Scraggane pier

❸ **St. Senach's Church**

Kilshannig

Scraggane Bay

Kilshannig Point

Fahamore

❶

START

❷ **Standing stone**

The Dingle Way

❹

Lough Naparka

B r a n d o n
B a y

❺

The Dingle Way

T r a l e e
B a y

❻

Lough Gill

0   1 kilometer
0   1 mile

The great curved sandspit of the Magharees, seen from the summit of Beenoskee Mountain

Naparka ❹. Cross the spit here (looking out for sea holly and pyramidal orchids in the splendid dunes), and return to Fahamore up the glorious wide **beach** ❺.

If you wish to double the length of the walk, continue for another 1.5 miles (2.5 km) from Lough Naparka to the outflow from **Lough Gill** ❻, and follow it inland to reach the lough—a famous place for bird-watching, especially when black swans come from Siberia to overwinter.

From Lough Gill continue to the west side of the spit for a 2-mile (3 km) beach walk back to Fahamore. ∎

Lough Gur

SCATTERED IN A LOOSE RING AROUND THE SMALL C-shaped Lough Gur is a multitude of stone structures, evidence of occupation of this site for the past 5,000 years. An interpretive center helps pull the known facts together around the sites. Of these the Grange Stone Circle is truly breathtaking.

Thatched roofs of the Lough Gur Interpretive Centre face down the lough, around which lie the remains of buildings that span 5,000 years of human occupation in this quiet corner of County Limerick.

Since many of the ancient sites are on private land and therefore out of bounds to visitors, the short video in the thatched interpretive center is necessary viewing. It describes how the shores of the lake hold hut circles, field systems, circles of standing stones, wedge tombs, crannogs (artificial fortified islands), stone and earth forts, and a couple of medieval castles. This is a tremendous archaeological record, going back to 3000 B.C.

The importance of Lough Gur was first noticed when the lake level was lowered during the 19th century and thousands of artifacts came to light. They included the Lough Gur shield, a beautiful bronze ceremonial shield dating from about 700 B.C. and decorated with six concentric rings of raised studs. The original is now in the National Museum in Dublin (see pp. 58–61), and many other Lough Gur finds can be seen in the Hunt Museum

dense with trees. Just 100 feet (30 m) in diameter, the crannog can only have held one family at a time during its occupation between A.D. 500 and 1000. It was made by encircling a mound of small stones with larger boulders, then constructing a platform of earth and brushwood layers which held a house and sheds, safe inside a protective palisade.

Two castles stand nearby—the 15th-century **Bourchier's Castle** with slit windows and four boxy corners turrets (there are plans to open it to the public and site a restaurant in its basement), and the foliage-entangled **Black Castle,** which the Earls of Desmond used periodically from the 13th century onward.

The two remaining main archaeological attractions of Lough Gur are a short car ride away. The first is the huge **Giant's Grave** megalithic wedge tomb (named because of its wedge-shaped ground plan), on the left 1 mile (1.6 km) toward the Limerick–Bruff road from Lough Gur Cross. The bones of eight adults and four children, along with some cremation remains, were found in the tomb during excavations in 1938. The Giant's Grave was constructed about 2500 B.C. with a curb of upright stones around a central grave of massive boulders, topped by four huge side-by-side capstones. In the 19th century it was still covered by its original mound of stones, and was the home of an old woman.

As for the 4,000-year-old **Grange Stone Circle,** a mile (1.6 km) up the Limerick road, this is a place of grandeur and mystery, the largest and most impressive stone circle in Ireland. Some hundred stones guard a sunken circle under ancient trees, undoubtedly the scene of Bronze Age spiritual rituals. ■

in Limerick's Custom House (see p. 164). The interpretive center has copies and genuine items—axes, tools, weapons, pottery, arrow heads, and a metalworker's furnace.

Once outside, you are within a 100 yards (100 m) or so of the **spectacles,** the circular and rectangular foundations of a farmstead of about 900, its tiny fields separated by stone walls. Bones of cattle, sheep, pigs, and dogs have been found on site, along with knives, bone combs, and pins of bronze, together with neolithic or late Stone Age pottery and flint scrapers—so occupation must have stretched over 4,000 years at least.

Down on the lake shore it's a five-minute clockwise walk to the reed bed where you can stare across at **Bolin Island crannog,** now

Lough Gur
▲ 131 E4

Lough Gur interpretive center
✉ Bruff Rd., Holycross, Co. Limerick
☎ 061 385186
🕐 Closed Oct.–April
💲 $$

More places to visit in Southwest Ireland

ADARE

Limerick's prettiest, immaculately kept village exudes charm from every thatched cottage and flowery garden. The Earl of Dunraven laid it out in Victorian times as an estate village, in a pronounced English style.

🗺 131 D4 ✉ On the N21, 10 miles (16 km) SW of Limerick city, Co. Limerick **Visitor information** ☎ 061 396255 🕒 Closed Jan.

ARDFERT CATHEDRAL & BANNA STRAND

Beautiful tall lancet windows grace the gray-stone 13th-century cathedral at Ardfert. Next door are the shells of two chapels, one with lovely south window carvings, the other with two intertwined wyverns (heraldic winged dragons) on the northeast window.

Nearby, **Banna Strand** offers a 5-mile (8 km) stretch of glorious beach; a monument here shows where Sir Roger Casement was arrested on Good Friday 1916, having just stepped ashore from a German submarine to assist the Easter Rising.

🗺 130 B4 ✉ On the R551 Ballyheige road, 4 miles (6 km) N of Tralee, Co. Kerry **Visitor information** ☎ 066 713 4711 🕒 Closed Oct.–April 💲 $

BÉAL NA BLÁTH (THE HOLLOW OF THE FLOWERS)

A Celtic cross marks the spot where the Commander of the Irish Free State Army, Michael Collins—still a hero to many in Ireland—was ambushed and shot dead by anti-Treaty gunmen on August 22, 1922, during the Irish Civil War.

🗺 131 D2 ✉ On the R585, 3 miles (5 km) SW of Crookstown, Co. Cork **Macroom visitor information** ☎ 026 43280

CARRIGAFOYLE CASTLE

This 15th-century stronghold has a wonderful location on the Shannon. Climb the 95-foot (29 m) tower for memorable views along the estuary.

🗺 131 C4 ✉ On the Shannon Estuary; signed (2.5 miles/4 km) off the R551 at Ballylongford, 8 miles (13 km) N of Listowel by the R552, Co. Kerry

FOTA WILDLIFE PARK & ARBORETUM

Fota Wildlife Park has free-running zebra, giraffe, antelope, kangaroo, oryx, and more—also caged cheetah, its breeding specialty. The arboretum possesses rare and beautiful trees from South America, Australasia, the Himalaya, China, and Japan.

🗺 131 E2 ✉ Carrigtwohill, Co. Cork, signed on the R624 Cobh road, off the N25 7 miles (11 km) E of Cork city ☎ 021 481 2678 💲 $$$

JAMESON'S OLD MIDLETON DISTILLERY

See the world's biggest copper still and a huge old waterwheel—then sample Jameson's golden, nectarous whiskey.

www.irish-whiskey-trail.com 🗺 131 E2 ✉ Midleton, off the N25, 10 miles (16 km) E of Cork city, Co. Cork ☎ 021 461 3594 🕒 1-hour guided tours 9 a.m.–6 p.m., last tour 4:30 p.m. 💲 $$

LIMERICK CITY

Stroll the quays of Limerick to admire **King John's Castle** (*Kings Island, tel 061 411201, $$*), a massive 13th-century fortification on the River Shannon, juxtaposed with the ultramodern glass building of the City Hall. **St. Mary's Cathedral,** just south of these, has extraordinary 15th-century misericord carvings of mythical and demonic beasts.

South again you'll find the old Custom House, now the home of the **Hunt Museum** (*Custom House, Rutland St., tel 061 312833),* a wonderful collection of Irish archaeological finds and medieval processional crosses, bishops' crosiers, illustrations, and other artifacts.

As for why the five-line type of verse is called after the city, opinions differ. But there was a popular drinking song, "Will you come up to Limerick," which followed the five-line form and was all the rage in the 19th century around the time limericks became popular.

🗺 131 E5 **Visitor information** ✉ Arthur's Quay, Limerick, Co. Limerick ☎ 061 317522 ■

est Ireland breathes romance—the flow-ery Burren hills and musical pubs of gentle County Clare, the Connemara Mountains and sea-battered coasts of Galway, and the ancient beauty and mystery of Mayo.

West Ireland

Malachy Kearns, Conne-mara's mastermaker of traditional *bodrháns* (goatskin drums)

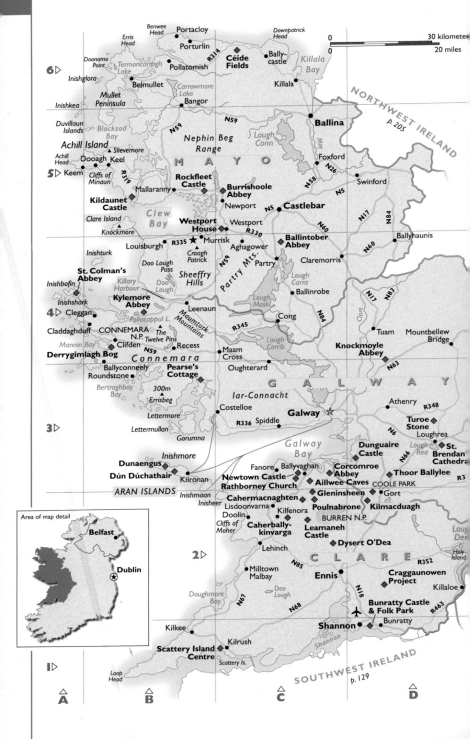

Benwee Head
Portacloy
Porturlin
Pollatomish
Céide Fields
Ballycastle
Killala Bay
Killala

Erris Head
Doonamo Point
Inishglora
Termoncarragh Lake
R314
Belmullet
Carrowmore Lake
Bangor
Mullet Peninsula

NORTHWEST IRELAND
p. 205

Inishkea
Duvillaun Islands
Blacksod Bay
N59
Nephin Beg Range
Lough Conn
Ballina
Moy

Achill Island
Slievemore
Dooagh Keel
Achill Head
Keem
Cliffs of Minaun
R319
Mallaranny
Rockfleet Castle
Burrishoole Abbey
Newport
Foxford
N26
Swinford
N58
N5

Clare Island
Knockmore
Clew Bay
Westport House
Westport
Castlebar
Ballintober Abbey
N60
N17
N84
Ballyhaunis

MAYO

Kildaunet Castle

Louisburgh
R335
Murrisk
R330
Aghagower
Claremorris
N60

Doo Lough Pass
Croagh Patrick
N59
Partry Mts.
Partry
Lough Carra
Ballinrobe
N17
N83

Inishturk
Killary Harbour
Sheeffry Hills
Leenaun
Lough Mask
Cong
N84
Clare
Tuam
Mountbellew Bridge

St. Colman's Abbey
Inishbofin
Inishshark
Kylemore Abbey
Doo Lough
Pollacappul L.
Maumturk Mountains
R345
Lough Corrib
N63

Cleggan
Claddaghduff
CONNEMARA N.P.
The Twelve Pins
Recess
Maam Cross
Oughterard
Knockmoyle Abbey

Mannin Bay
Clifden
N59
CONNEMARA

Derrygimlagh Bog
Ballyconneely
Roundstone
Pearse's Cottage
GALWAY

Bertraghboy Bay
300m
Errisbeg
Iar-Connacht
Athenry
R348

Lettermore
Costelloe
Turoe Stone
Loughrea

Lettermullan
Gorumna
R336
Spiddle
Galway
N6
Lough Rea

Galway Bay
Dunguaire Castle
N66
St. Brendan Cathedral

Inishmore
Dunaengus
Dún Dúchathair
Kilronan
Fanore
Ballyvaghan
Newtown Castle
Rathborney Church
Corcomroe Abbey
Aillwee Caves
COOLE PARK
Thoor Ballylee
Gleninsheen
Gort
R3

ARAN ISLANDS
Inishmaan
Inisheer
Cahermacnaghten
Lisdoonvarna
Kilfenora
Poulnabrone
Kilmacduagh

Doolin
Cliffs of Moher
Caherbally-kinvarga
BURREN N.P.

Leamaneh Castle
Dysert O'Dea
Lough Derg
Holy Island

Lehinch
CLARE

Milltown Malbay
Doo Lough
N85
Ennis
R352
Craggaunowen Project
Killaloe

Doughmore Bay
N67
N68
N18
Bunratty Castle & Folk Park
R463

Kilkee
Shannon
Bunratty

Kilrush
Scattery Island Centre
Scattery Is.
Shannon

Loop Head
SOUTHWEST IRELAND
p. 129

Area of map detail
Belfast
Dublin

0   30 kilometers
0   20 miles

6
5
4
3
2
1

A   B   C   D

Laid-back western Ireland is best appreciated at a slow pace, by bicycle or on foot.

West Ireland

OF THOSE VISITORS TO IRELAND WHO INTEND TO GET ANY FARTHER than Dublin, the majority head out west. Anyone who has heard anything about the character of the different regions of Ireland will have been told that west is best, whether you want wild traditional music, spectacular coast and small island scenery, vast open tracts of ruggedly beautiful landscape, or the most laid-back approach to life in this admirably relaxed country.

The west presents an Atlantic-facing seaboard, but its peninsulas and bays are not elongated or clearly defined as those of Kerry and Cork. Here the coast is fractured and battered by the sea into ragged lumps and gashes, all dotted with fragments ranging from well-populated islands to tiny scraps of offshore rock.

Three great inlets shape the coastline—the mouth of the Shannon running in under the avocet's-bill of southwest Clare, the squarish indentation of Galway Bay with the three Aran Islands at the entrance, and the islet-spattered Clew Bay in southern Mayo. With the domed hills of Clare, the all but uninhabited mountains, and the lakes and boglands of Galway and Mayo, it adds up to a memorably untamed mingling of land and sea.

County Clare is the greenest, mildest, and gentlest of the West's three counties. Down in the southwest are old seaside towns such as Kilrush and Kilkee, while farther north you come into the strange, haunting landscape of the Burren region—naked gray limestone hills where an incredibly rich flora flourishes.

Galway has a lively county capital in Galway city, and the rugged beauty of the mountains and boglands of Connemara, the westernmost part of the county; also the great fishing lakes based around mighty Lough Corrib, and a cluster of Irish-speaking islands.

As for County Mayo, discerning explorers are beginning to wake up to the wild beauty of this boggy and mountainous northern corner of the west, with its holy mountain of Croagh Patrick, its buzzing music town of Westport, and its empty, glorious beaches. ∎

CENTRAL IRELAND
p. 235

Suck

Ballinasloe
N6

Clontuskert
Abbey   Clonfert
             Cathedral

N65

Portumna

Shannon

Southwest Clare

THE SOUTHWEST CORNER OF COUNTY CLARE IS GENTLE, easy-going, and essentially rural—a long green peninsula where countryside or seaside are yours for the deciding.

The great arches of Bunratty Castle lead to medieval feasts of meat and mead.

Bunratty Castle & Folk Park

- ✉ Bunratty, Co. Clare
- ☎ 061 360788
- 💲 $$$

Craggaunowen Project

- ✉ 4 miles (6 km) SE of Quin
- ☎ 061 360788
- 🕐 Closed mid-Oct.–mid-April
- 💲 $$$

Bunratty Castle and the adjoining folk park, off the N18 Ennis–Limerick road, are certainly worth a stop if you don't mind sharing your enjoyment with a few thousand others. The well-restored castle, built by the MacNamaras around 1460, has a splendid keep where nightly "medieval banquets" are held. You can quaff mead and eat as much as you can (with your fingers), while minstrels serenade you and serving wenches bustle around with platters and jugs. If you're in a lively group, it can be great fun.

The same can be said of **Bunratty Folk Park,** a reconstructed 19th-century Irish village set on 25 acres (10 ha). To those who have already traveled among and appreciated real, living Irish villages, this can seem a theme park travesty; but if you come out of season to enjoy the cottages, shops, small businesses, and pub without the holiday crowds, you can catch an appealing atmosphere enhanced by the blacksmith, weavers, spinners, and buttermakers who bring a touch of life to the place.

Ten miles (16 km) north, off the road from Kilmurry to Moymore, you'll find the **Craggaunowen Project,** brainchild of formidable expert and collector of early Christian archaeology and art John Hunt (1900–1976). Craggaunowen, centered around a fortified tower house of 1550, offers an evocative telling by costumed guides of the story of the Irish Celts, their domestic lives, their warfare and religious practices, and the way they hunted and farmed. Specially constructed buildings and sites include a walled ring fort enclosing typical fifth- or sixth-century huts under conical thatched roofs; a causeway to a lake-bound crannog, or artificial fortified island, sheltering a wattle-and-daub house; burial sites; and a *fulacht fiadh* (hunter's cooking pit).

Also on display is the leather-hulled curragh, *Brendan,* in which explorer Tim Severin sailed to Newfoundland in 1976–77.

County Clare sweeps away southwest in a narrowing bird's-bill of a peninsula. The south coast of this 40-mile (60 km) promontory forms the northern shore of the widening Shannon Estuary, while the cliff-bound north coast, far more indented and battered, faces out into the Atlantic. The hinterland is gentle and green, the coast lined with long, sandy swimming beaches. There are a handful of old-style seaside resorts and some nice quiet country towns. Hereabouts you'll find a slow tempo to rural life and a splash of night-time gaiety very characteristic of County Clare.

North coast resorts with plenty of accommodations and sandy beaches are **Lehinch** (Lahinch) and **Kilkee,** the former with a beautiful golf course, the latter with some exciting natural rock-pool swimming in the Duggerna Rocks at the western end of the beach.

Between these two is **Milltown**

Malbay, normally a quiet enough town, where Willie Clancy Week *(information: tel 065 708 4148),* an annual music festival at the start of July, celebrates the life and skill of local piper Willie Clancy.

Loop Head at the southwestern point of the peninsula has fine cliff walks, while farther around into the mouth of the Shannon is the handsome town of **Kilrush,** with a strong riverside character and horse fairs in June and the fall.

Ask at the **Scattery Island Centre** *(tel 065 905 2139)* on Merchant's Quay about boats to **Scattery Island** a mile (1.6 km) offshore. Here you'll find several ruined medieval churches and a 110-foot-high (33 m) round tower. ■

The curragh *Brendan* may seem fragile, but in 1976–77 this replica of St. Brendan's boat crossed the Atlantic to prove that the saint could have sailed to Newfoundland 1,200 years before.

Southwest Clare
🅰 166 B1, C1, C2
Visitor information
✉ The Square, Kilrush, Co. Clare
☎ 065 905 1577
🕐 Closed mid-Sept.–late May

Burren National Park

MYSTERIOUS AND CONCEALING, YET LYING WHOLLY OPEN to view, the Burren region of north County Clare is a remarkable and haunting place. Among its bare gray hills lie hidden ancient tombs, churches, dwellings, and ring forts in a bleak setting jeweled with Ireland's richest flora. At the outer edge of the hills are villages that seem to run entirely on wonderful music. And the flanks of the hills themselves, solid though they look, conceal a heart of rock riddled with caves, passages, and seldom-seen underground rivers.

The Burren forms the whole of northwest Clare, some 200 square miles (500 sq km) bounded on the north and west by the sea and on the south and east by typical Clare grazing country, mild and green. But there is nothing either green, mild, or typical about the Burren. Boireann, its Gaelic name, means

rocky land. The region rises from a sharp-cut sea coast through a collar of meadows into a cluster of dome-shaped hills with their rounded tops and stepped flanks, their pale gray limestone seemingly naked of vegetation. It looks a dry, harsh landscape, drained of life; one in which nothing can have flourished

untuned eye it looks like rubbly, useless land. Gen. Edmund Ludlow reported to Oliver Cromwell in 1651 that the Burren region "had not any tree to hang a man, nor enough water to drown him, nor enough earth to bury him"— a telling remark, considering the Puritan leader's intentions for the Irish at that time. But Ludlow was observant enough to add: "Their cattle are very fat, for the grass growing in tufts of earth of two or three foot square that lie between the rocks, which are of limestone, is very nourishing."

It is the space "between the rocks," and the soil and rainwater trapped in the grykes, that allow such an extraordinarily varied range of plants to flourish in the Burren. These limestone crevices are sheltered from the salt wind, watered by the frequent rainfall of the area, and warmed by the Gulf Stream that moves just off the Clare coast and by sunlight reflected into their depths off the pale limestone. Plants that would not normally be found on the same continent, let alone on the same hillside, find the Burren conditions right for them. Some botanists think that certain Arctic-alpine plants are descendants of those that arrived in the Burren as seeds moving south in melting ice age glaciers 10,000 years ago.

Here you'll see plants of the north, such as the large creamy cups of mountain avens, coexisting with plants of the south like the yellow hoary rock-rose. In certain places streams bring acid bog peat to lodge in hollows of the alkaline limestone, so that acid-loving plants such as heather and saxifrage thrive side by side with milkwort or tormentil, lime-loving plants.

What this means in practical terms is a glorious flood of color across the gray hills and coastal shelves, and endless fascination

for a very long time. It is not until you get into the heart of the Burren, abandon your car, and walk out into this barren-looking world that you begin to appreciate just how much life and interest there is. And the fascination is not all above ground: The **Aillwee Caves** south of Ballyvaughan offer a glimpse of the stalactites and stalagmites, cavernous spaces, waterfalls, and passages at the heart of the hills.

LIMESTONE & FLOWERS

The Burren region is formed of rough, cracked limestone known as karst. The surface of the limestone is fractured into deep, narrow channels (*grykes*) a few inches wide but several feet long, with oblongs of rock (known as clints) of varying sizes islanded among them. To the

Burren National Park
166 C2
Visitor information
✉ Cliffs of Moher tourist information office, Liscannor, Co. Clare
☎ 065 708 1171

Aillwee Caves
www.aillweecave.ie
166 C3
✉ Ballyvaughan
☎ 065 707 7036
$ $$$

The Burren Way
This wonderful 20-mile (32 km) walk takes you southwest from Ballyvaughan across the roof of the Burren. It follows country roads, tracks, and an old walled lane down to Doolin (which makes a convenient overnight stopping point) and on to the Cliffs of Moher. ∎

hopping across the rocks with a flower book. You don't have to be an expert to appreciate the delicately marked orchids, the brilliant blue trumpets of spring gentians, or the extraordinary flush of magenta that stains the hills overnight to announce the dramatic June flowering of the bloody cranesbill.

PAST INHABITANTS

The Burren interior is completely devoid of settlements today, thanks to its shortage of water—the thirsty karst draws the rivers underground—and to what amounted to an ethnic cleansing policy by Cromwell, but there is plenty of evidence of a vigorous population in times gone past. The splendid portal dolmen of **Poulnabrone** and the nearby **Gleninsheen** wedge tomb show with what pomp and ceremony the prehistoric Burren-dwellers buried their chiefs. Stone-walled Celtic ring forts abound—**Cahermacnaghten** and **Caherballykinvarga** lie close to roads and can be explored. The law school run in medieval times by the O'Davorens at Cahermacnaghten was so well regarded that pupils came from all over Ireland to learn the tenets of ancient Brehon law (see p. 24). Nowadays it stands empty, a magnificent circular enclosure where cattle shelter. Graveyards, crosses, and ruined medieval churches dot the Burren. **Rathborney Church** was built inside a pre-Christian circular earthen rampart that must have been an object of superstitious awe, while the ruins of **Corcomroe Abbey** (fine stonework) in the northeast and of the church at **Dysert O'Dea** (magnificent high cross and a bizarre doorway of sculpted heads) in the south are notable examples.

Life in medieval Ireland being the risky business it was, there are also some fine fortified towers and houses in the Burren—**Newtown Castle** southwest of Ballyvaghan (Ballyvaughan) and **Leamaneh Castle** *(closed)* east of Kilfenora are worth a look.

Hundreds of such sites lie tucked away across the Burren, and to help find them you can't do better than buy Tim Robinson's hand-drawn *Folding Landscape* map of the Burren (ISBN 0-9504002 1-1)—by far the most informative guide you

could wish for, and widely available locally. It also features the many holy wells and "old faith" cures for headaches, sore backs, tooth trouble, and weak eyes to which Burren people still resort.

COAST & VILLAGES

The coastline of the Burren is a rocky one, relieved by fine if caravan-ridden dunes at **Fanore**, then trending southwest for another 15 miles (25 km) to culminate in the mighty **Cliffs of Moher**, at 665 feet (203 m) a magnificent piece of natural sculpture in layers of flagstone and shale. O'Brien's Tower, a Victorian viewpoint, tops them off. You can crawl up to the cliff edge and look over, if you dare—but watch out for unexpected gusts of wind! Seabirds

Below: According to the locals, their MP, Sir Cornelius O'Brien, built everything except the cliffs themselves. He scattered towers, columns, bridges, and schools across County Clare in the 1830s and '40s.

Newtown Castle
www.burrencollege.com
🗺 166 C3
✉ SW of Ballyvaghan
☎ 065 707 7200
🕐 Closed Nov.–March

Opposite: O'Brien's Tower, built in 1835, looms at the summit of the 665-foot (203 m) Cliffs of Moher that face into Galway Bay.

abound, and the view on a good day from the top of O'Brien's Tower takes in a circle of well over 100 miles (160 km) from the Kerry hills to the Aran Islands and the Twelve Bens of Connemara—even to a far glimpse of Croaghaun on Achill Island up in County Mayo.

Looped around the skirts of the uninhabited Burren hills is a string of villages that rely mainly on farming and tourism—all of them great places for conversation and music. **Ballyvaghan** (Ballyvaughan) is the northernmost settlement, looking out to Galway Bay. Monk's Bar is the place for music here. **Doolin,** however, is the music-lover's mecca (see pp. 176–177).

Sleepy **Lisdoonvarna** comes alive each September for its Matchmaking Festival (*tel 065 707 4696, www.matchmakerireland.com, held Sept.–early Oct.*), when spinsters and bachelors of the west converge on the village for a week of taking the spa waters, dancing, and making acquaintance. Part media circus, part revival of an old tradition, this is a good-time week that anyone can enjoy.

At **Kilfenora** there's a roofless 12th-century cathedral and four carved high crosses of the same date; also the **Burren Centre** (*tel 065 708 8030, closed Nov.–Feb., $$*), with excellent displays on the wildlife, geology, and archaeology of the Burren, and two great music pubs in Vaughan's and Linnane's. ■

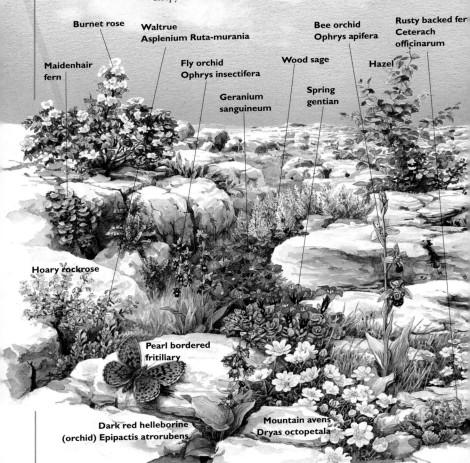

Burnet rose

Waltrue
Asplenium Ruta-murania

Bee orchid
Ophrys apifera

Rusty backed fern
Ceterach
officinarum

Maidenhair
fern

Fly orchid
Ophrys insectifera

Wood sage

Hazel

Geranium
sanguineum

Spring
gentian

Hoary rockrose

Pearl bordered
fritillary

Dark red helleborine
(orchid) Epipactis atrorubens

Mountain avens
Dryas octopetala

Right: At first glance, the naked limestone of the Burren may seem barren and lifeless, but this is an environment that offers plants exactly what they love—nutrition, shelter, warmth, and sunlight.

Below: The flora of the Burren

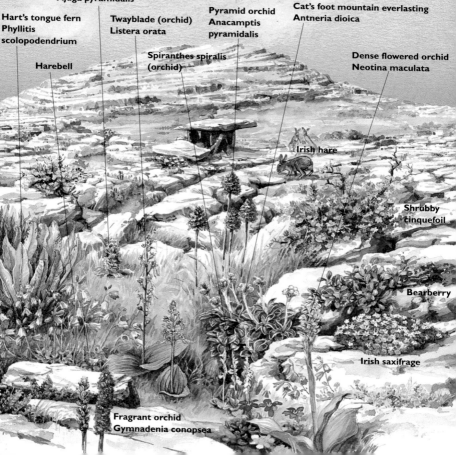

Ajuga pyramidalis

Hart's tongue fern
Phyllitis
scolopodendrium

Twayblade (orchid)
Listera orata

Pyramid orchid
Anacamptis
pyramidalis

Cat's foot mountain everlasting
Antneria dioica

Harebell

Spiranthes spiralis
(orchid)

Dense flowered orchid
Neotina maculata

Irish hare

Shrubby
cinquefoil

Bearberry

Irish saxifrage

Fragrant orchid
Gymnadenia conopsea

Pubs & music of west Ireland

Pub-going in the west of Ireland is an activity as natural as breathing. You'll find yourself gravitating naturally to the pub, because it's there that you'll meet local people and other visitors, join in the *craic* (crack), and hear the best music in Ireland. Note that information about sessions is given over the bar on the day—don't be afraid to ask.

Whatever it is about the west of Ireland—the lifestyle or the land, the peculiarly magical atmosphere woven by mountains, boglands, and sea coasts, or something in the water—it's a well-attested fact that the traditional music here is something special.

Some connoisseurs claim to detect a correlation between the character of the music and the shape and nature of the landscape it springs from—a smooth gentleness to the compositions and performances of Clare, for instance, or a melancholy wildness to those of Mayo. You can judge for yourself, either as a participant or an onlooker, in the numberless great music pubs of the west.

In southwest Clare try O'Mara's on O'Curry Street, Kilkee, where you'll get music of all sorts and great atmosphere; also Clancy's and Queeley's in Milltown Malbay for wonderful traditional sessions.

Around the Burren—famous music territory—you'll enjoy Linnane's in Kilfenora and the Roadside Tavern on the edge of Lisdoonvarna (great music here), while in the music-to-its-fingertips village of Doolin it's McGann's by the bridge for evening tune ses-

The crack

Even if you would never normally set foot in a bar, you should do so—regularly—in Ireland. The Irish pub is far more than a boozing den. In the city it is where that great Irish art, conversation, is practiced away from the roar and bright lights, while in small country towns and villages it is the focus of community activity. You get advice, make friends, and hear charming nonsense; the pub is where you pick up local news, hear of dog races and mountain walks, fix up a bed for the night, get a bite and a sip, and enjoy that wonderful tide of live music—traditional tunes, ballads, country, and rock music.

All this mixture of talk, fun, music, leg-pulling, and drink goes under the generic name of "the *craic*" (pronounced crack). You'll hear the crack talked of wherever you go—"You should have been in McGing's, the crack was mighty"; "We'll call in on Joe and have a bit of crack"; "Marie? Ah, she's great crack." You might run across the crack in a pub, a back kitchen, a corner shop, or a country lane—you never know your luck. But you'll know it when you find it. ■

Get out of the rain, in to the bar, up with the mood, and down to the beat at one of the exhilarating sessions of traditional music that enliven Irish pubs.

sions, and O'Connor's nearer the sea for rollicking ballads and showmanship, day and night. Ennistymon, too, is a famous town for music, in the Archway—beautifully placed by the River Cullenagh—and a dozen other pubs.

Galway city offers good impromptu music in Taafe's Bar on Shop Street, and more of the same in the wonderful old-fashioned Ti Neachtain on Cross Street, all cozy snugs and odd corners—there's a first-class restaurant here as well.

Out in Connemara there's a great pub round every corner; but for real character you could try the Irish-speaking Ost na nOilean down at the foot of Gorumna Island, or the even more remote and Gaelic pub on Inishmaan, the middle one of the three Aran Islands. The Strand Bar out at Claddaghduff in the far west (always known as Sweeney's)

does a great hot whiskey when the weather is biting back.

As for Mayo—head for Westport if you want music. Matt Molloy, flute player with the celebrated traditional music band The Chieftains, owns a bar on Bridge Street named Matt Molloy's, where the back bar sessions are regularly infiltrated by the great names of Irish music (including Matt himself when he's around). Hoban's and McHale's are two other marvelous pubs for music. For a quiet pint it has to be John McGing's little bar on the street above the clock tower (see p. 192).

In the country, westward, Owen Campbell's enormously friendly bar in Murrisk, the port of call for outward or incoming pilgrims walking up the holy mountain of Croagh Patrick (see p. 194–195), is often still humming at midnight. ∎

Galway city

A plate of Galway oysters—well-known for their aphrodisiac effect

GALWAY IS A LIVELY CITY, ONE OF THE LIVELIEST IN IRELAND, thanks to its university and colleges, and to a great revival in its economy and optimism over the past 20 years or so. At any time of year, but particularly in the summer, Galway's an exciting place to be. The *Tourist Trail of Old Galway* guidebook, available from the visitor information center, is excellent for sightseeing on foot.

The Anglo-Normans built Galway into an important castle town and port in the mid-13th century, and for 400 years it was an Anglicized enclave amid the Irish people and culture of Connemara. "From the fury of the O'Flaherties good Lord deliver us" was inscribed—not in jest—over the West Gate of the city that faced "native" territory.

The "Fourteen Tribes of Galway" were the Anglo-Norman families—or Welsh-Norman, as most of them were—who prospered on trade with Europe, notably with Spain. Spaniards were often seen in the city, and they forged a close link. Cromwell put an end to this golden age when he sacked Galway in 1652, and King William III completed the job in 1691. It took Galway 300 years to rise again, but it did, thanks to high-tech industries and the economic boom of the 1990s (see p. 10).

As it runs south from the tree-shaded gardens of **Eyre Square,** Galway's main street changes name, from Williamsgate to William Street, then Shop Street, High Street, and finally Quay Street as it reaches the River Corrib. There are curious carved stones set high on the walls of shops and houses—heraldic shields, beasts, foliage, and human faces, mostly dated to show when eminent persons married or took possession of the premises. After a while you develop quite a talent for spotting them.

At the Four Corners, where William Street becomes Shop Street, stands **Lynch's Castle,** a very fine late 15th-century fortified stronghold tower with a bank on its ground level. On the walls are coats of arms, elaborate roundels, several lions with human faces, and a row of gargoyles supporting the top of the tower.

Galway city
- 166 C3
- **Visitor information**
- Áras Fáilte, Forster St., Galway, Co. Galway
- 091 537700

There's always time to stop for a chat in the easy-paced, old-fashioned streets of Galway city.

A sidestep up Church Lane leads to **St. Nicholas's Collegiate Church,** rich in this vigorous, expressive Galway carving. A seductively curly-tailed mermaid clings to the west window. Inside are some fine tombs and more examples of the mason's art—they include graveslabs carved with the symbols of their incumbents' trades. Another stone carving has a low-slung cur chasing a hare, bug-eyed with terror, over the arch of the belltower door.

North of the church stands the rebuilt Lynch memorial window. On this spot in 1493 the Chief Magistrate of Galway, James Lynch Fitzstephen, hanged his own son Walter for murder. "Stern and unbending justice" is how a plaque describes the father's action. Just across the way, No. 8 Bowling Green was where Nora Barnacle lived before James Joyce ran off with her in 1904. It is now the **Nora Barnacle House Museum.**

A very pleasant walk follows the River Corrib to the whitewater sluices beyond Salmon Weir Bridge, and a randomly arranged but neatly labeled jumble of exhibits in the enjoyable **Galway Museum** by the Spanish Arch. Here you'll find everything from fish spears and a sack-sewing contraption to badger traps, photos, and pikes from the 1867 Fenian Rising.

A great time to be in Galway is around the end of July, when the **Galway Arts Festival** (tel 091 509700, www.galwayartsfestival.ie) is immediately followed by the week-long jamboree of **Galway Races** (tel 091 753870). It's a hectically crowded but very enjoyable three-weeks, during which normal life is suspended as activities from classical music and literary lectures to the maddest of street theater and music keep the place buzzing day and night. No sooner have the final Arts Festival fireworks fizzled out than attention switches to **Ballybrit Racecourse** (tel 091 753870), just northeast of the city. There's a full card of racing each day—supported with passionate enthusiasm by locals and visitors alike—and the city puts on dances, pub music, and exhibitions for gamblers both lucky and unlucky. ■

You'll find plenty of Irish dancers in Galway, whether it's a formal performance on stage or just a few people enjoying the moment in a pub.

Nora Barnacle House Museum

✉ 8 Bowling Green, Galway, Co. Galway

☎ 091 564 743

🕐 Open mid-June–Aug.

💲 $

Galway Museum

✉ Spanish Arch, Galway, Co. Galway

☎ 091 567 641

💲 $

Aran Islands

THE ARAN ISLANDS ARE A BYWORD FOR HARSH, UNFOR-giving landscape, and their Irish-speaking people have always epitomized hardy self-reliance. Things are changing fast under the influence of tourism and modern amenities, yet there's a strong thread of a way of life long passed into history elsewhere in Ireland.

The three islands (not to be con-fused with County Donegal's Aran Island) resemble a family of sea beasts swimming northwest out of Galway Bay. The little procession is headed by the beak-headed and humpbacked shape of Inishmore, the largest island at 8.5 miles long (14.4 km); of the two following "babies," Inishmaan with its 3-mile (5 km) downward-pointing arrow-head shape is in the middle, and round-bodied Inisheer—the small-est island, being less than 2 miles (3 km) across—brings up the rear.

It is wind-scoured, sea-bitten limestone that gives the Aran Islands their extraordinary atmos-phere, more out-of-this-world than

any other landscape in Ireland. The dark gray limestone is scored with thousands of north–south frac-tures, giving each of the three islands the appearance of having been raked by a giant comb.

These are virtually treeless islands, where soil has had to be built up laboriously by hand out of sand, seaweed, compost, and manure, and shielded from blowing away in stone-walled fields. The stone walls of Aran are the islands' best-known feature. They are built of thousands of loosely stacked blades of unmortared limestone through which pours the light, so that on a sunny day they form a lacy mosaic of gray stone and blue sky. The walls are repositories for unwanted stone cleared off the fields as much as they are wind-breaks or property boundaries.

As the capital island, **Inish-more** has a defined port village, Kilronan, and gets almost all the visitors, many of whom leave with one of the trademark fishermen's sweaters still made on the islands. Minibuses offer whistlestop tours of the island; pony traps do the same thing at a more leisurely pace. It's best to rent a bicycle or set out on foot, however, if you want to catch the spirit of the place.

The chief attraction is undoubt-edly **Dunaengus** (tel 099 61010, $), the Fort of King Aengus, which stands two-thirds of the way up the south coast of Inishmore—a mighty semicircular stone strong-hold some 2,000 years old, breath-takingly sited on the brink of a

Aran Islands

🗺 166 B2, B3

Visitor information

✉ Kilronan tourist information, Inishmore, Aran Islands, Co. Galway

☎ 099 61263

Left: Impassioned Gaelic singing, straight from the heart, in the bar of an Aran Island pub

300-foot (91 m) cliff. A cunning chevaux-de-frise (belt of upright stone blades) was set up to guard it from onrushing enemies.

But if you want an Inishmore fort more or less to yourself, make for **Dún Dúchathair,** the Black Fort, a couple of miles (3 km) down the cliffs from Dunaengus. The Black Fort is less well preserved than its better-known neighbor, but here you are more likely to have elbow room in which to admire the crumbling stairs and walkways in its 20-foot (6 m) walls of dark stone, and the enigmatic little labyrinth at its heart.

Other Inishmore sites well worth seeking out with the help of your *Folding Landscape* map by Tim Robinson, available in Kilronan, Rossaveal, and Galway, are the

ruined but beautiful churches that are scattered across the island.

Emigration of youngsters and the influence of incomers and holidaymakers have brought Inishmore further into line with mainland thinking and attitudes than the two smaller Aran Islands.

Inisheer, cheerful and relaxed in atmosphere, makes a memorable day trip from Doolin on the Clare coast. But it is on the middle island, **Inishmaan,** that you are most likely to hear Irish spoken and see old folk still wearing homespun clothes. Life goes on with fewer concessions (although not less courtesy) to visitors. The south end of Inishmaan, with its spouting blowholes and stony coast, is as wildly bleak and beautiful a spot as you'll find in Ireland. ■

The magnificent 2,000-year-old sea forts of Inishmore stand in breathtakingly dramatic locations at the very brink of the cliffs.

Connemara

FEW PLACE-NAMES IN IRELAND ARE MORE EVOCATIVE than Connemara, and no region more steeped in the romance of harshly beautiful, remote, and alluring country. Irish city-dwellers in search of their roots find inspiration and a confirmation of their Irishness in this wild western half of County Galway; and you can expect the same magic as you wander among Connemara's mountains, bogs, lakes, and along ragged coasts.

Connemara

166 B4

Visitor information

Clifden tourist office, Station House Complex, Clifden, Co. Galway

095 21163

Closed Nov.–Feb.

LAY OF THE LAND

Connemara is the region of west Galway bounded on the north by the narrow fjord of Killary Harbour that forms a border with County Mayo, on the east by Lough Corrib, on the south by Galway Bay, and on the west by the Atlantic. In the center rise the neighboring quartzite-capped mountain ranges of the Twelve Bens and the Maumturks. From the feet of the mountains, untamed boglands riddled with lakes and spattered with granite boulders stretch to a coast cut by the sea into rags and tatters of inlets, coves, headlands, and hundreds of islands.

This is an uncompromising landscape that has always demand-

ed backbreaking labor from its small-time farmers and fishermen in return for a meager living. Sour land of rock and bog, allied to geographical isolation and poor communications by land and sea, spelled hardship and poverty for Connemara inhabitants until very recently; and even today there are plenty eking out a thin livelihood from the soil and sea. "You can't eat scenery," is an oft-heard local reaction to a compliment on Connemara's untamed landscape. But tourism, the bread-and-butter of the region these days, is turning the truism on its head. Not packaged, bus-borne tourism for the most part, but a stream of independent visitors enjoying the lonely white sand beaches, the tiny towns with their musical pubs, the offshore islands, and the mountain paths.

The long upper coast of Galway Bay, the southern border of Connemara, runs due west from Galway city past the resort of Spiddal on its sandy swimming beach. After some 20 miles (30 km), this straight westward line shatters into an explosion of islands linked by causeways—Lettermore, Lettermullan, Gorumna, Furnace, Dinish, and their offshoot islets and rocks. If you enjoy strange, hard-edged country, windswept and weatherbeaten, turn south at Casla along the road through these Irish-speaking islands. Hungry locals built the causeways that link them for the Congested Districts Board, at a time late in the 19th century when this area was the poorest and most overpopulated in Ireland. Life

The archetypal Connemara view—a line of craggy granite mountains forming the horizon between wide waters and vast cloudscape skies

is still hard here, as witness the stone walls separating the tiny fields. These are carried on over granite boulders and through rushy bogs to mark out exactly which morsel of poor land belongs to whom. Rainstorms off Galway Bay are fierce and frequent here, double rainbows commonplace, sunsets magnificent, visitors few and far between. If you hit Ost na nOilean, the Hotel of the Isles at the toe-tip of Gorumna, on the right Saturday night, you may be lucky enough to take part in a ceilidh that you'll never forget.

Inland of the islands, a vast apron of granite-studded bogland, terraced and crenellated with turf beds cut by hand for domestic fuel, stretches north to the southern skirts of the Maumturk Mountains.

LANDMARKS

On the shores of Lough Oiriúlach near Gortmore stands **Padraic Pearse's Cottage,** whitewashed under a thatched roof and plainly furnished with hard beds and simple furniture. It was to this peasant house and landscape that Padraic

Pearse brought groups of students in the early 20th century to learn their native language and culture. The cottage and its Connemara backdrop were a source of refreshment and inspiration for the dreamy Dublin schoolmaster and poet who would become the symbol of Ireland's struggle for independence, proclaimer of the fledgling Republic from the steps of Dublin's GPO on Easter Monday 1916, and patriotic martyr a few days later when he was shot for treason in the yard of Kilmainham Gaol (see pp. 30–32 and 76–81).

The coast road twists on from Costelloe (Casla in this Irish speaking area) and the islands to skirt the wildly indented shores of Bertraghboy Bay. At **Roundstone** on the west side—a beautifully placed village with the shapely and easily climbable 987-foot (300 m) mountain of Errisbeg at its back— lives and works Malachy Kearns of Roundstone Musical Instruments *(tel 095 35808, www.musweb.com/ kearns.htm).* He has gained his nickname, Malachy Bodhrán, through nearly 30 years of hard

Padraic Pearse's Cottage

🗺 166 B3

✉ Rosmuc, near Gortmore, Co. Galway

☎ 091 574292

🕐 Closed mid-Sept.–late May

💲 $

Above left: In Roundstone listen hard: The peaceful sound of lapping waves might be joined by the muted thunder of Malachy Kearns' celebrated *bodrháns* (drums).

labor over his handcrafted *bodhráns*. These goatskin drums provide the *rum-a-dum, rum-a-dum* beat behind Irish jigs and reels, and the great names of Irish traditional music trust Malachy to choose the right goatskin to stretch and pin over an oiled circle of beech or birch wood.

Continue by the white shell sands of Gorteen Bay and Dog's Bay and the strands of Ballyconneely and Mannin Bay with their "coral" made of the calcareous seaweed lithothamnion. You will pass the hillside memorial to Sir John Alcock and Sir Arthur Whitten Brown, who completed the first nonstop transatlantic flight in June 1919 by landing their Vickers Vimy bomber plane nose-down in Derrygimlagh bog.

And so to **Clifden**, Connemara's one and only town, a handsome and lively bayside resort planned in the early 19th century in the classic layout: oval in shape, with three main streets, a market square, and a jail, courthouse, and harbor. Its two 19th-century churches are worth visiting: **St. Joseph's RC Church,** built in 1879 with emigrant money in post-famine times; and **Christ Church,** built in 1853 and offering superior views over town. Nowadays Clifden is mostly known for its summertime Connemara Pony Show. For this, sturdy little Connemara ponies, bred for hard work in the boglands, are gathered for judging and sale in an atmosphere of fun and celebration. This mid-August show brings together many of the best attributes

Above: There's only one town of any size in Connemara—the elegant resort of Clifden.

Below: Musicians share their love of music in an Inishbofin pub.

of Connemara—west Galway people in festive mood in a beautiful setting backed by the Twelve Bens, with a touch of sharp reality in the deals struck and judgments delivered.

In Clifden, the scenic Sky Road forks off to encircle the Kingstown Peninsula, while another narrow road continues along the north shore of Streamstown Bay to **Claddaghduff** at the western tip of Connemara. Here you could

wait for low tide over a drink in Sweeney's bar before crossing the sand causeway to visit the ancient graveyard and St. Fechin's Well on tidal **Omey Island.** If you do get caught on the island by an incoming tide, you'll have an enforced stay of six hours before the causeway is dry again, but this will give you plenty of time to explore. The low cliffs of Omey Island hold remnants of medieval cooking sites

Inishbofin

One of the most enjoyable of Connemara expeditions is the short ferry cruise from Cleggan out to Inishbofin. The island, 4 by 3 miles (6 by 5 km), has a small and friendly population, and a landscape that is low-lying, boggy, and wildly beautiful. You can find the ruins of the 13th-century St. Colman's Abbey on the site of the seventh-century monastery founded by Colman (there are two very early Christian slabs inscribed with crosses, too), a star-shaped fort built

by Cromwellian soldiers who imprisoned and killed Catholic priests on the island, and the outlines of Stone Age and Bronze Age field systems, huts, and cooking pits. A paperback guide, *Inis Bó Finne: A Guide to the Natural History and Archaeology* by David Hogan and Michael Gibbons (available at Connemara Walking Centre, *Market St., Clifden, tel 095 21379*), is the companion to take—along with your binoculars, and your singing boots if you intend to spend the night. ■

(look for the burned red stones), and locals in search of a cure or help from St. Fechin still leave offerings all around the holy well on the reverse slope of the island.

From Claddaghduff it's only a few miles to the harbor of **Cleggan** for the ferry to Inishbofin. The N59 would then take you east again through Letterfrack to pass the giant mock-Tudor pile of **Kylemore Abbey** on Pollacappul Lough, deservedly one of Ireland's most photographed buildings. A mile (1.6 km) or so farther east, the view across Kylemore Lough to the Twelve Bens mountain group is stunning.

THROUGH THE MOUNTAINS

The N59 is the main highway through Connemara, the choice of those who want to avoid the tortuous coast road. Travel west from Galway city to Clifden via Maam Cross and Recess, with superb views along the way of the mountains at the heart of Connemara—the **Twelve Bens** (often marked on maps as the Twelve Pins) and the **Maumturks.**

Just west of Recess, the R344 leaves the N59 to follow the spectacular Inagh Valley northward as it squeezes between the two ranges. These are real mountains, although the Twelve Bens only rise to 2,395 feet (730 m) and the Maumturks to 2,300 feet (701 m). The Twelve Bens cluster close around their summit peak of Benbaun, while across the Inagh Valley the Maumturks swing southeast in a long curved ridge. Capped with quartzite that glitters white in sunlight, they look majestic.

The waymarked **Western Way** offers a low-level walk along the flanks of the Maumturks to the east of the Inagh Valley. If you're after something tougher, seek advice at Ben Lettery hostel on the N59 5 miles (8 km) west of Recess.

A great but very demanding circuit of six of the Twelve Bens can be made from the north end of the side road that leaves the N59 a mile (1.6 km) back toward Recess from the hostel. But you don't have to hike—this road also offers stunning views as the rugged mountains come right up close. ■

A glorious view: The great pile of Kylemore Abbey, dwarfed by the wooded mountain slope behind

Kylemore Abbey
www.kylemoreabbey.com
166 B4
Kylemore, Connemara, Co. Galway
095 41146
Abbey: $$, garden: $$; joint ticket available

Cong Abbey is a picturesque ruin amid wooded hillsides on the north shore of Lough Corrib.

Drive: Shores of Lough Corrib

Sprawling for some 27 miles (44 km) northwest of Galway city, Lough Corrib is a vast sheet of water that hides itself cunningly in a low-lying landscape. This drive seeks out its hidden delights.

Start out of Galway on the N59 Clifden road. In Moycullen, turn right (Tullokyne, Knockferry sign) between stone-walled fields and thick hedges for a few miles to **Carrowmoreknock** ❶ (or is it Collinamuck, or even Callownamuck? The signs seem unsure!), where there is a peaceful jetty with boats and a view over Lough Corrib to the mountains.

At the next T-junction turn left to the N59, then right to resume your drive. In 2 miles (3 km) a sign on the right leads to **Aughnanure Castle** ❷ (*Oughterard, tel 091 552214, closed Nov.–mid-April & weekdays mid-Sept.–end Oct., $*), a fine six-story O'Flaherty castle bristling with murder holes, secret rooms, and bartizan side turrets, enclosed in a walled ward with its own pic-

turesque lookout tower. The floral carvings on the window of the old banqueting hall are best seen from the external walkway.

Back on the N59, continue to the little town of Oughterard. Keep an eye out for the sign on the right that points to the **Lakeshore Road** ❸, a beautiful, meandering 5-mile (8 km) drive through intensely green and lush backcountry of rhododendrons and woodland to the shores of the lake at Currain with fine hilly scenery all around—another excellent picnic spot.

Return to Oughterard by the same route and follow the N59 northwest to **Maam Cross** ❹, which lies bleak and exposed in the bogland. Here a signed turning on the right leads over wild moors to Maam (aka Maum), where you turn right on the R345 for

Cong. Soon **Lough Corrib** ⑤ appears on your right, offering superb lake views and opportunities for bird-watching.

Continue on the R345 to **Cong** ⑥ (*visitor information, tel 094 46542*), a beautifully kept village. At the far end you'll come to **Cong Abbey**, a handsome gray-stone monastery founded in 1128. Carved flowers, leaves, and tendrils decorate the pillar capitals, and tiny staring heads peep out among the leaves.

From Cong follow the R346 to Cross, then the R334 southeast to Headford, where you'll see signs to the glorious monastic ensemble of **Ross Errilly** ⑦ out in the fields by the sullen Black River. Under the slim church tower, the 14th- and 15th-century buildings stand simple and perfect—the best-preserved Franciscan friary in Ireland. Elaborate tombs abound, such as that of Hugh O'Flaherty under the east window; there are huge fireplaces, spouts, chutes, and bread ovens, giving an eerie feeling of monkish presence.

Five miles (8 km) south of Headford,

another detour from the N84 brings you to Annaghdown. Turn right immediately past the graveyard (Annaghdown Pier sign) to find the blunt and undecorated ruins of **Annaghdown Priory** ⑧, a complete contrast to the elegance of Ross Errilly. St. Brendan died here in 577, nursed by his sister Brigid, in the nunnery he had founded.

Return to the N84 and turn right for your journey back to Galway. ■

- ⓜ See area map p. 166
- ► Galway city
- ↔ 115 miles (185 km)
- ⊕ 4–5 hours, depending on stops
- ► Galway city

NOT TO BE MISSED

- Aughnanure Castle
- Lakeshore detour in Oughterard
- Cong Abbey
- Annaghdown Priory

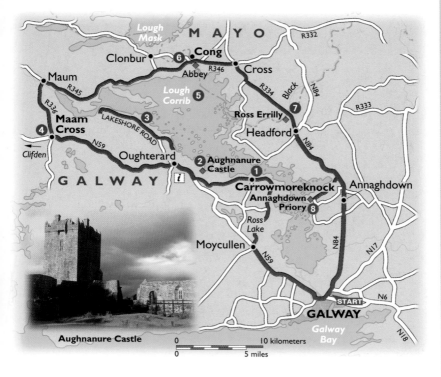

Aughnanure Castle

0   10 kilometers

0   5 miles

East Galway

MOST VISITORS TRAVELING WEST IGNORE THE EASTERN
region of County Galway, intent as they are on immersing themselves
in the dramatic beauty of Connemara as quickly as possible. But the
quiet, low-lying landscape of east Galway—an area larger than
Connemara—holds some enjoyable places, too.

The city of **Tuam,** 20 miles (30
km) northeast of Galway city, has
two cathedrals. The Protestant
Cathedral of St. Mary under
its 200-foot (61 m) spire is mostly
Victorian neo-Gothic work, but the
red sandstone chancel is a relic
of the 12th-century cathedral
founded here and has a splendid
Romanesque arch of six elaborate
orders. The **Roman Catholic
Cathedral of the Assumption**
has some notable 20th-century
windows by one of Ireland's best-
known exponents of stained-glass
work, the symbolist artist Harry
Clarke (1889–1931).

More memorable church
art is on show at 12th-century
Knockmoyle Abbey, 8 miles
(13 km) southeast of Tuam on
the River Abbert—although this is
medieval work. A rare early 15th-
century fresco shows three kings
out hawking, while three other
dead kings admonish them: "We

have been as you are; you will be as we are." Knockmoyle is a beautiful building with some fine carving in the chancel. It was founded by Cathal "Red Hand" O'Connor in 1189 to celebrate a great victory over the invading Normans and takes its ominous name from the battlefield—Cnoc Muaidhe, the Hill of the Slaughter.

Athenry (pronounced a-then-RYE), 14 miles (22 km) east of Galway city, preserves the North Gate and some other sections of the defensive walls built to encircle the town in 1211; also its Norman castle keep, and the ruins of a 13th-century Dominican friary.

From here the R348/R349 will take you 12 miles (19 km) southeast to Loughrea, where **St. Brendan's Cathedral,** built between 1897 and 1903, is a treasure-house of Celtic Revival craftsmanship—textiles, wood, stone carving, metalwork, and wonderful windows by Michael Healy, Sarah Purser, and Evie Hone, leading lights of the hugely influential 20th-century collective of stained-glass artists, An Túr Gloine, the Glass Tower.

Take the R350 north from Loughrea for a couple of miles (3 km) to Bullaun. Just outside the village, off the left turn signed Kiltullagh, you'll find the extraordinary **Turoe Stone** standing 3 feet (1 m) tall in a field. A phallic granite pillar heavily carved with swirling and zigzag patterns, the outline of a bird's head, and a four-pointed St. Brigid's Cross, the stone is dated from the late Iron Age period 300 B.C.–A.D. 100 and was brought here from a nearby earth-banked hill fort known as the Rath of Fearmore, the Big Man's Fort.

Near the eastern border where the counties of Galway, Offaly, and Longford meet, two notable monastic sites lie not far apart. The

diminutive **Clonfert Cathedral,** built around 1160 on the site of a monastery founded in 563 by St. Brendan the navigator, possesses a masterpiece of Irish Romanesque art in its wonderful west doorway of red sandstone. Six recessed orders of round arches frame the door, each heavily and humorously carved with animal heads and flowers, while above rises a tall triangular tympanum filled with alternating triangular darts and human heads, some grinning, others gazing morosely or blankly out.

Off the R355 Portumna–Ballinasloe road, 10 miles (16 km) northwest of Clonfert, stand the ruins of the Augustinian **Clontuskert Abbey,** founded during the 12th century in the flat meadows by the River Suck. Most of what you see is 15th-century work. The east window and rood screen are fine, and guardians—Saints Michael, Katherine, and John—along with more allegorical figures of a pelican, a curly-haired mermaid, and others flank the west doorway of 1471. ■

One of the wonderful stained-glass windows in St. Brendan's Cathedral, depicting the saint as a boy

Athenry

🅰 166 D3

Visitor information

✉ Athenry Arts and Heritage Centre, The Square, Athenry, Co. Galway

☎ 091 844661

💲 $

Westport & Clew Bay

WESTPORT IS THE MOST AGREEABLE TOWN IN COUNTY Mayo, a lively place full of music and talk. To the west of the town opens one of the most beautiful bays in Ireland, Clew Bay, spattered with a reputed 365 islands and dominated on the south by the cone of Croagh Patrick (see pp. 194–195).

Westport was a planned town, laid out in 1780 by the English architect James Wyatt (1746–1813). These orderly beginnings bequeathed the town an air of elegance, especially strong along the tree-shaded mall that flanks the sparkling Carrowbeg River through the middle of town. From here Westport's two parallel main streets run uphill—Bridge Street to the Clock Tower, and James Street to the Octagon with its tall column crowned by a statue of St. Patrick. Shops in Westport are friendly, chatty places—so are the pubs, many of which are the venues for fine traditional music in the evenings (see pp. 176–177). John McGing's little pub (opening hours: when John chooses), on High Street just above the Clock Tower, is a gem—unadorned, friendly, warm, and full of good conversation (John's wit is slow-burning and as dry as a bone) and even better Guinness. Don't miss this one.

Settlers have been attracted to Westport from all over the world. They come for the agreeable atmosphere of the trim town, for the glorious scenery, and the energetic friendliness of the locals. Their presence has given the town an arty, liberal-minded flavor, best seen during the **Westport Arts Festival** *(tel 098 66502)* toward the end of August.

Westport House, out on the western edge of town, is a Georgian country house whose construction started in about 1730; celebrated architect James Wyatt completed the job half a century later. Inside you can admire family portraits (and a beautiful "Holy Family" by Rubens), Georgian silver and glassware, and some fine furniture made of mahogany. The wood was brought back to Westport from the Jamaican sugar plantations owned by the wife of the 2nd Marquess of Sligo, who lived here during the early 19th century. Dungeons (complete with ghosts) from an earlier castle that stood on the site, horsedrawn caravan rides, a zoo, and a slot-machine arcade all conspire to cheer and cheapen the tone.

On **Westport Quay,** west of the town, stand handsome 18th-century stone warehouses. From here you look out across Westport Bay, itself only a corner of the great seaward opening of **Clew Bay.** Eight miles (13 km) across from north to south, 13 miles (21 km) from its inner eastern shore to its mouth in the west, Clew Bay is a mighty chunk bitten out of the Mayo coast. Scattered across the eastern half of the bay are 365 green humpbacked islands (count them); they originated as drumlins or hillocks of glacial rubble. Their seaward sides have been eaten by the prevailing western winds and storms into low cliffs of pebbly clay, so that they resemble a shoal of green sea-creatures baring their yellow teeth as they set off into the Atlantic.

Spectacularly beautiful at evening when the westering sun

Westport
🅼 166 C5
Visitor information
✉ James St., Westport, Co. Mayo
☎ 098 25711

Westport House
www.westporthouse.ie
✉ Westport Estate, Westport, Co. Mayo
☎ 098 27766 or 098 25430
🕐 Closed late Sept.–April (open Easter week)
💲 $$

lays their black shadows before them on silvered water, the islands were once productive, too, supporting a population of thousands. These days there are just a few hardy folk who live and work on the islands—fishermen on **Inishlyre,** a sailing school on **Collan More,** a couple tending an organic garden on **Island More** out at the western edge of the archipelago.

Back when the Beatles had more money than sense, John Lennon bought **Dorinish,** one of the Clew Bay islands, on a whim. Lennon hardly set foot on Dorinish, but for a few years it became a miserably uncomfortable hippy hangout, to the bemusement of locals.

You'll find wonderful sandy beaches between **Louisburgh** and **Murrisk** on the south shore of Clew Bay, and at **Mallaranny** on the north side.

Sporty souls can sail (Mayo Sailing Club, Rosmoney Quay; *contact Westport visitor information)* or fish (Sea Angling Centre, Westport) in Clew Bay, while lovers of wild local history should seek out **Burrishoole Abbey and Rockfleet Castle** near Newport on the north shore of the bay (see sidebar p. 204). The 15th-century tower and arches of **Burrishoole Abbey,** founded by sea-raider Grace O'Malley's second husband, "Iron Dick," stand right at the edge of the bay. **Rockfleet Castle,** just along the coast, is another fine building right on the water, a late medieval tower house of wonderfully grim aspect, where Grace got the better of "Iron Dick" in 1567. ■

The sparkling **Carrowbeg River** tumbles under a series of old stone bridges through the heart of **Westport.**

Croagh Patrick

TALL, GRACEFUL, AND IMPRESSIVE, CROAGH (MEANING "hill") Patrick rises on the southern shore of Clew Bay, dominating land and sea. Around its cone-shaped head, legends have gathered over millennia. An object of reverence to all manner of religious believers, it is the destination of one of the world's great Christian pilgrimages—and a stunningly beautiful mountain in its own right.

Croagh Patrick

⚠ 166 B4

It was in 441 that St. Patrick, traveling through Ireland on his great missionary expedition, came to County Mayo and climbed the 2,510-foot (764 m) peak of Cruachan Aigil on the first Saturday in Lent. The pagan Irish of the region already feared and venerated the mountain that would soon become known as Croagh Patrick ("The Reek" to locals), and Patrick, a canny operator with an excellent understanding of his fellowman, was not about to turn his back on a place with such spiritual resonance for thousands of potential converts. Instead he fasted 40 days and 40 nights at the summit, a feat that must have seemed tremendously brave to minds that had peopled the peak with demons, and made them more receptive to his message of baptism and salvation.

What happened at the peak quickly became the stuff of stories, making bedfellows of truth, myth, and symbolism. Patrick secured assurances from God that the Irish would never lose their faith, and that they would be saved on Judgment Day—in fact, that Patrick himself would be their judge, a favor which God only conceded after the saint had threatened to keep arguing on the summit until he died. Patrick also cleared Ireland of all its poisonous and offensive beasts by repeatedly ringing his Cloigin Dubh or Black Bell and then hurling it over the precipice of Lugnanarrib, sweeping masses of

A pilgrim staff, hewn ready for use from a nearby bog

snakes, toads, and other nasties to their doom with every throw. Helpful angels retrieved the bell and returned it to the saint after each consignment. The Cloigin Dubh also came in handy for dealing with a cloud of evil spirits in the form of black birds. They dispersed soon enough when Patrick slung his bell through their ranks.

THE HOLY MOUNTAIN

Within a short time the mountain peak became a place of pilgrimage for Christian Ireland. Over the following 1,500 years neither storms, lightning strikes, nor penal laws prohibitions halted the flow of pilgrims climbing Croagh Patrick. A 23-mile (37 km) pilgrim path, **Tóchar Phádraig** (see p. 197), was established from Ballintober Abbey along an ancient pagan route to the sacred mountain. Garland Sunday, the last Sunday in July, became the "official" day to climb Croagh Patrick—maybe because of its proximity to August 1, the date of a wild festival of fire and dancing that celebrated the Celtic harvest feast of Lughnasa.

In the late 20th century, a spate of accidents put a stop to the traditional night climb on the eve of Garland Sunday—an unforgettable spectacle as thousands of torches wrapped a glowing chain of light around the mountain. But the pilgrimage itself remains as popular as ever, with up to 50,000 climbing the mountain on Garland Sunday, many of them barefoot, to

attend Mass in and around the summit chapel. Nonbelievers can climb Croagh Patrick, too—it is one of the world's classic "anyone-can-do-it" ascents (see p. 196–197).

When gold was discovered on Croagh Patrick in 1988, and a working license applied for, there was international consternation. However much the poor and emigration-hit county of Mayo might need the money and jobs, Croagh Patrick was not to be mined. So numerous and passionate were the protests—and they came in from all over the world—that the scheme was rejected. The Reek still carries the scar of the road cut by the mining company, a slowly fading mirror image of the pilgrim path kept fresh by countless feet each year. ■

Croagh Patrick, Ireland's Holy Mountain, rises above the rocky wastes of the surrounding bog.

St. Patrick stands in statue form at the foot of the Pilgrim Path, overlooking Clew Bay.

Walk: To the top of Croagh Patrick

A hike up the holy mountain of Croagh Patrick is one of the classic activities for locals and visitors alike in the west of Ireland. It's demanding and tiring, but good for body and spirit, and when you finally reach the summit you will be rewarded with a stunning view. Whether you opt for the short but challenging route from Murrisk or the 23-mile (37 km) pilgrimage route from Ballintober Abbey, go prepared and do not attempt the trip in thick mist or heavy rain.

The three most helpful items you need for tackling Croagh Patrick are a good pair of walking boots, a stick, and plenty of determination. The route is very clear and you need no mountaineering expertise, but you will find it impossible to get all the way to the top if you are very out of condition. Don't be surprised—or put off—if you see the summit wrapped in clouds; often they part when you are up there.

SHORT CLIMB

Set off west from **Murrisk ❶,** beside Owen Campbell's pub—where you can admire the collection of pilgrimage photographs and memorabilia—and then head due south along the signposted lane. In about 200 yards (183 m), you will pass the statue of St. Patrick, thoughtfully blessing your start.

Follow the path southward, ascending to a **saddle of ground ❷** at 1,650 feet (500 m). It is at this point that the pilgrimage route from Ballintober Abbey (see p. 197) joins the path. You might want to take a rest here, because your next task is arduous. The summit awaits at the end of a very steep and boulder-strewn ascent of 860 feet (264 m).

At the top you'll spot **St. Patrick's Church ❸.** And the view from here, at 2,510 feet (764 m), is magnificent and far-reaching, encompassing the Connemara Mountains, the Nephin Beg range, the whole of Clew Bay and its islands, Achill Island, and Clare Island. You will even get a glimpse of the Slieve League cliffs some 80 miles (128 km) to the northeast on the coast of County Donegal.

From the summit, return back down to the pub the way you came.

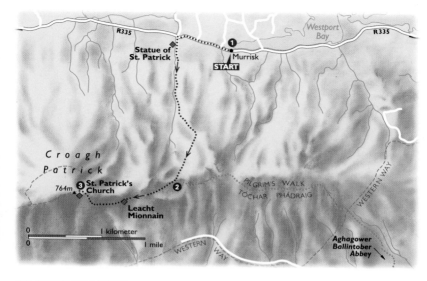

PILGRIMAGE ROUTE

Every year on Garland Sunday, the last Sunday in July, up to 50,000 people, many of them barefoot, climb Croagh Patrick to offer prayers to St. Patrick in the little church on the summit. It's a long and tiring journey, and unless you are very fit and determined, you will need two days to complete the walk, with an overnight stop. Anyone who intends to take this walk must register with Ballintober Abbey *(tel 094 30934)* before setting out.

To follow the ancient pilgrim route, start at **Ballintober Abbey** and take the route westward, guided by marker stones incised with crosses and numbered stiles. A guidebook, *Tóchar Phádraig, A Pilgrim's Progress*, is available at the abbey and adds enormously to the interest of the walk. It points out the holy wells, standing stones, inscribed rocks, enchanted woods, and fairy hillocks that you will pass along the way. It also contains detailed information on flora and fauna, the history of each field you go through, and plenty of stories both credible and incredible.

The best place to break your two-day journey is at the halfway village of **Aghagower,** where there is an ancient church and a round tower. From here you can order a cab to Westport (a ten-minute ride away) to get a good meal and a bed for the night.

On day two return to Aghagower and continue your journey west, following the track up the south flank of Croagh Patrick to the saddle (see ❷ opposite), where the path from Murrisk merges. Follow the directions for the Short Climb to reach the summit. ■

- ⋏ See area map p. 166 B4
- ➤ Owen Campbell's pub, Murrisk. Pilgrimage route: Ballintober Abbey, signed off the N84 Castlebar–Ballinrobe road, 7 miles (11 km) S of Castlebar
- ↔ 5 miles (8 km) up and down. Pilgrimage route: 23 miles (37 km)
- ⊕ Depending on fitness, allow 4–5 hours. For the pilgrimage route: allow 2 days
- ➤ Owen Campbell's pub

NOT TO BE MISSED
- Owen Campbell's pub
- Statue of St. Patrick
- Leacht Mionnain cairn or "station" at the foot of the summit cone
- St. Patrick's Church at summit
- Five-star view from summit

Northwest Mayo

ONE OF THE LEAST VISITED PARTS OF IRELAND, NORTHWEST Mayo is about as rugged, lonely, and beautiful as you can get. Islands, peninsulas, cliffs, and bays indent the coastline, while the interior is mountain and bog … interspersed with bog and mountain. If you love wild places, this is the region for you.

Northwest Mayo

⚠ 166 B5, B6, C5

Visitor information

✉ James St., Westport, Co. Mayo

☎ 098 25711

Achill Island

⚠ 166 B5

Visitor information

✉ On road between Achill Sound and Keel, Co. Mayo

☎ 098 47353

From Westport it's an hour's leisurely drive via Mallaranny (aka Mulrany) to Achill Sound, with the mountainous profile of **Achill Island** growing ever more prominent ahead. Achill is Ireland's largest off-island, at roughly 14 by 12 miles (22 by 19 km) a strikingly irregular sea-monster outline in a great mountainous inverted "L" shape. **Knockmore** (1,119 feet/340 m) and **Minaun** (1,320 feet/403 m) command the view as you cross the bridge over Achill Sound. Their loftier sister mountains of **Croaghaun** (2,195 feet/668 m) and **Slievemore** (2,204 feet/672 m) rise in the north of the island. Achill is very rarely crowded, though tourism has begun to infiltrate—welcomed by most of the islanders, who until

only a few years ago were generally eking out hard lives buttressed with money sent home by emigrant family members.

Drop in to Sweeney's supermarket at the island end of the bridge to catch the current buzz of the island before heading south on the narrow and winding coastal road labeled **"Atlantic Drive."**

Many islanders still farm in traditional ways, and in season you'll see ricks of cut turf and hay weatherproofed with little vividly colored canvas "headscarves." Monbretia and fuchsia brighten the roadsides, and the rocky bays are filled either with silver sand or orange seaweed.

At the southern tip of the island, the tall, grim 15th-century **Kildaunet Castle**—once a base for the famed Mayo "pirate queen"

Grace O'Malley (see p. 204)—stands near the ruined **Kildaunet church.** There are many poignant graves in the cemetery here, and a brackish holy well on the shore.

The character of Achill changes as soon as you swing north up the west side of the island, with a tremendous coastline of wave-battered rocks and cliffs. There's a beautiful view down over **Ashleam Bay**—can you spot the long-haired "Lady of the West" playing her harp in the sea?

At **Keel** you will find a fine Blue Flag beach (conforming to EU standards of cleanliness and safety; there are others at Keem and Doogort) and a spectacular prospect of the towering **Cliffs of Minaun.**

Dooagh village has attractive whitewashed cottages under thatch or tiles, and a pub (The Pub) where you can look through a book of photographs recording the arrival of Don Allum. He reached the shore here on September 4, 1987, after 77 days at sea—he had just completed the first there-and-back rowing of the Atlantic.

Keem Strand, a couple of miles (3 km) beyond Dooagh, is a perfect beach in a pincer-shaped bay under the slopes of Croaghaun. Amethysts are found on this southern part of the mountain.

Back in Keel, continue straight at Minaun View, and in a mile (1.6 km) steer straight ahead again where Atlantic Drive bends to the right. Just in front, on the slope of Slievemore, you'll see an abandoned village of roofless houses—booley houses or summer pasture dwellings, depopulated when famine struck Achill in the mid-19th century. You can walk the streets, peer at the cold fireplaces and empty stone cupboards, and ponder on the harshness and simplicity of island life back then. Then it's back across the bridge to the Mayo mainland.

The country between Achill Island and the Mullet Peninsula is harsh, wide-rolling brown bogland patched with somber green forestry. Just inland rise the **Nephin Beg Mountains,** Ireland's loneliest and most remote range. One footpath threads them: the **Bangor Trail,** a demanding and boggy but extremely rewarding 22-mile (35

The dark, dramatic ramparts of the Minaun Cliffs loom beyond Keel Bay on Achill Island.

Hand-raked haycocks, some capped with tarpaulin squares against the rain, stand in the village fields at Dooagh, Achill Island.

km) hike. For the fit and determined only! A ringed guidebook, *The Bangor Trail* by Joe MacDermott, is widely available locally.

Bangor is a village isolated in the bog, and **Belmullet** 12 miles (19 km) to the northwest is equally easy-paced and local in flavor. Belmullet is the gateway to the **Mullet Peninsula,** a little-visited but beautiful finger of land that runs south for some 20 miles (32 km). Very deeply indented, the peninsula shelters Blacksod Bay on its east, and looks out west from a treeless and weathered coast to a scatter of Atlantic islands a couple of miles (3 km) offshore. Like Achill Island, the Mullet is a Gaeltacht or Irish-speaking area where locals are paid grants to preserve traditional speech, culture, and ways of life.

Belmullet stands on an isthmus connecting the peninsula to the mainland. North and northwest of

Children of Lir

Inisglora, the scrap of an island off Cross Strand just west of Binghamstown, is the setting for the poignant conclusion of one of Ireland's best-known legends, the story of the Children of Lir.

Turned into swans (but retaining their beautiful voices) at the hand of their jealous stepmother's magical powers, the four children of the powerful chief Lir are condemned to spend 900 years in exile from their home. The final 300 years are spent on Inisglora, and it is here that the coming of Christianity finally releases them from their enchantment. But the shapes they resume are those of 900-year-old human beings.

A holy man (is it St. Brendan? He built a church on Inisglora in the sixth century) baptizes the Children of Lir before they crumble into death, and buries them on the island as they have directed—standing upright, with their arms supportively around each other in death as in life. ■

**Céide Fields
visitor center**

🅰 166 C6

✉ Ballycastle, Co. Mayo

☎ 096 43325

🕐 Closed Dec.–mid-
March, except by
appointment

💲 $

Right: Ireland's
notorious pirate
queen, Grace
O'Malley,
conducted some
of her raids
against English
settlers from this
gaunt Achill
Island tower.

the isthmus, the Mullet Peninsula
coast fractures into innumerable
rocky headlands—**Doonamo
(Doonamore) Point,** segregated
beyond an ancient wall, contains
house foundations and fortifications of pre-Christian date.

Termoncarragh Lake, a
reedy shallow water, supports rare
red-necked phalarope and other
bird species. Houses are widely
scattered down the peninsula, with
only Binghamstown calling itself a
village. There are several superb
beaches—the west-facing ones such
as Belderra, Cross, Portacarn, and
Carricklahan, reached by bumpy
little roads, are wilder and more
weed-strewn. Cattle walk the
strands and feed on the flowery
shell-sand meadows or *machair*.

The offshore **Iniskea** and
Duvillaun islands, and little
Inisglora (see sidebar p. 200), are
uninhabited these days. Their low
green curves enhance already sublime Atlantic views.

The country and coast northeast
of Belmullet is as wild as can be.
This is quintessential Mayo bogland, across which switchback roads
lead to pretty little **Pollatomish,**
tiny **Portacloy** on its slip of sandy
beach, and the equally small fishing
harbor of **Porturlin** between
mighty cliffs.

A little farther east is the astonishing archaeological site of **Céide
Fields**—astonishing not so much
for what you can see as for the
tweak your imagination receives. It
was in the 1930s that local schoolteacher Patrick Caulfield began to
investigate the ancient stone walls
that turf-cutters were unearthing in
the boglands between Belderrig and
Ballycastle. His son Dr. Séamus
Caulfield put archaeological students to work in the 1970s, and
they traced the patterns of a farming landscape 5,000 years old hidden in the bog.

These days there's a visitor center where you can learn how blanket bog crept in to smother the
Stone Age farmers' green fields with
up to 15 feet (5 m) of turf. The climate certainly became wetter
around 3000 B.C., and the early
farmers probably contributed to the
growth of the wet bog by felling
trees so that rain soaked the ground
instead of evaporating off the forest
leaves. It was this smothering of the
fields and settlements by the creep-
ing bog that kept the ancient landscape intact; almost all other such
sites were destroyed by the later
generations that took over the land.

Guided tours show you what
there is to be seen on the ground—
mostly lengths of crude stone
walling, which don't look too exciting to the nonexpert.

Just east of Céide Fields, the
promontory of **Downpatrick
Head** makes a stimulating walk.
There's a giant rock stack just off
the head and a couple of blow
holes that can drench you. ∎

The calm surface of **Killary Harbour** conceals Ireland's deepest sea inlet.

More places to visit in West Ireland

CLARE ISLAND

Out beyond the mouth of Clew Bay lies Clare
Island (population 150), accessible by ferry
from **Roonah Quay** *(tel 098 28288 or 098
26307)*. This is a beautiful green island, its harbor guarded by a castle that was the home of
Grace O'Malley (see sidebar p. 204). Stories
say that she had the mooring ropes of her
privateer fleet run through her bedroom
window in the castle and tied to her big toe,
so that she would wake if anyone tried to
steal her ships while she slept.

Clare Island has a sandy beach near the
harbor, fantastic music in the pub (island
work rhythms of fishing and farming mean it
can open at midnight and close the following
noon, if then), and the shapely and steep hill
of Knockmore (1,529 feet/461 m) for a

literally breathtaking climb and view.
🄰 166 B5 ✉ Mouth of Clew Bay, Co. Mayo

COOLE PARK

The home of Lady Augusta Gregory, friend
and patron of W. B. Yeats, no longer stands,
but the beautiful grounds continue as a
national park. You can view the **Autograph
Tree** where literary luminaries such as J. M.
Synge, George Bernard Shaw (flamboyant ini-
tials), Sean O'Casey, John Masefield the
English Poet Laureate, and many others carved
their names, and follow a waymarked walk
leading through woods to Coole Lake.
🄰 166 D2 ✉ Signed off the N18 Galway–
Ennis road, 2 miles (3 km) N of Gort, Co.
Galway ☎ 091 631804 🕓 Closed Oct.–
Easter 💲 $

Above: Dunguaire Castle on Kinvarra Bay was built by 16th-century descendants of a 7th-century king of Connaught.

Carvings on the tombs in the 13th-century Franciscan friary are particularly fine.

 166 C2 **Visitor information** ✉ Arthur's Row, Ennis, Co. Clare ☎ 065 682 8366

DUNGUAIRE CASTLE

Occupying a beautiful spot on Kinvarra Bay, Dunguaire is a four-story tower house complete with bawn (defensive wall). It was built by the O'Hynes around 1520 and restored during the 20th century by the poet-surgeon Oliver St. John Gogarty. "Medieval" banquets are held here daily.

📍 166 D3 ✉ Kinvarra, on the N67 Ballyvaughan–Galway road, Co. Galway ☎ 091 637108 or 091 361511 🕐 Closed Nov.–April 💲 $ **Medieval banquet** ☎ 061 360 788 🕐 Banquets held daily 5:45 p.m. & 8:45 p.m. 💲 $$

ENNIS

The county town of Clare, Ennis is a characterful place of long, narrow streets packed with little pubs. There's a tall column with a statue of "Swaggering" Daniel O'Connell, elected in 1828 to represent Ennis in the British Parliament as the first Catholic MP.

IAR-CONNACHT

This is the loneliest, wildest, most extensive bogland in County Galway, crossed by a single winding road. It is sheer bliss for solitude-seekers and lovers of bleak, beautiful landscapes.

📍 166 C3 ✉ Bounded by the road triangle of the R336 Galway–Ballynahown–Maam Cross and the N59 Maam Cross–Galway, Co. Galway **Visitor information** ☎ 091 537700

KILLARY HARBOUR

The splendid fjord of Killary Harbour forms the western Galway/Mayo border. It runs in from the west for 10 miles (16 km) in an upward-curving saber shape, in places more than 150 feet deep (45 m). Tremendous mountains sweep up from its shores—the Maumturks on the south, and opposite them the massive bulks of Mweelrea (2,699 feet/819 m) near the western entrance and Ben Gorm

(2,303 feet/750 m) toward the eastern head of the inlet. Their flanks are scarred with the corduroy stripes of lazybeds, the raised potato ridges tended by peasants of not so long ago.

From **Leenane,** the impossibly photogenic one-street village at the inland end of Killary Harbour, the R335 passes north through the narrow, dramatic defile of Doolough. **Doo Lough** itself, the Black Lake, is a moody stretch of water 2 miles long (3 km), hugged by the road that weaves through Doolough Pass between Mweelrea and the 2,500 feet (750 m) bulk of the Sheeffry Hills. This pass, like the Pass of Glencoe in Scotland, seems darkened as much by its own history as by the crowding mountain slopes, for it was along here that 600 men, women, and children struggled to Delphi Lodge to beg for food during the Great Famine of 1845–49. Having been turned away empty handed, 400 died on the return journey through the pass.
◪ 166 B4 ✉ 20 miles (30 km) SW of Westport (N59), Co. Mayo

KILMACDUAGH MONASTIC SITE
Backed by the layered gray hills of the Burren, here are the ruins of four churches (some tenth-century or earlier), a beautiful roofless cathedral, a medieval tower house, and a 115-foot (34 m) round tower leaning out of perpendicular.
◪ 166 D2 ✉ On the R460 Gort–Corofin road, 3 miles (5 km) SW of Gort (N18 Galway–Ennis road), Co. Galway **Galway visitor information** ☎ 091 537700

LOUGH DERG
This long, ragged-edged lake, a great favorite with boaters and fishermen, is handsomely backed by mountains and dotted with pretty villages. **Killaloe,** the main town at the south end, has the 12th-century St. Flannan's Cathedral and Oratory. From Mountshannon a boat *(tel 086 2601173 or 086 8749710, closed Oct.–May, $$$)* will land you on **Holy Island** to explore the remains of four churches (including a 16th-century cathedral and some fine Romanesque stonework), an 80-foot (24 m) round tower, elaborately carved medieval tomb slabs, and the holed Bargaining Stone of the monks.
◪ 166 D2 ✉ From Killaloe, Co. Clare, NE for 20 miles (30 km) to Portumna, Co. Clare
Killaloe visitor information ☎ 061 376866 (seasonal)

THOOR BALLYLEE
W. B. Yeats bought the neglected 14th-century tower house of Ballylee Castle in 1916 for £35. Restored, simply but stylishly, and renamed, it became his much-loved country retreat, and inspired his 1928 collection, *The Tower* and *The Winding Stair.* Recordings of the poet reading his own verse accompany your trip round the exhibition of Yeats memorabilia and first editions.
◪ 166 D3 ✉ Signed off the N66 Gort–Loughrea road, 3 miles (5 km) NE of Gort, Co. Galway ☎ 091 631436 (April–Sept.), 091 537700 (Oct.–March) 🕐 Closed Oct.–May 💲 $$ ∎

Grace O'Malley

Daughter of a Connacht chief, Grace O'Malley (ca 1530–1603) ran her own army and fleet of privateers from her island and coastal strongholds with dashing skill, exacting pilotage charges and cargo levies from passing shipping until she controlled the entire sea trade between the west of Ireland and the Continent.

Grace was 16 when she married her first husband, Donal O'Flaherty. In 1566, two years after he was murdered, she married Anglo-Irish lord "Iron Dick" Burke on the understanding that, after a year, either could divorce the

other. This she duly did, slamming the door of Rockfleet Castle against him—having first secured all of Iron Dick's castles by putting her own people in charge.

Calling in on Howth Castle to claim hospitality and break her journey near Dublin in 1575, Grace was incensed to find herself shut out and asked to wait because Lord Howth was at dinner. So she kidnapped her host's son, restoring him to his family only when they assured her that their doors would henceforth be kept open at meal times—a tradition still kept up at Howth Castle. ∎

The beautiful northwest contains some of the most striking landscapes in Ireland— the Sligo Mountains and coasts immortalized by poet W. B. Yeats and his painter brother Jack, and the wild hills and peninsulas of Donegal.

Northwest Ireland

Northwest Ireland, Stronghold of the Stone Age

p. 279

p. 235

p. 165

p. 235

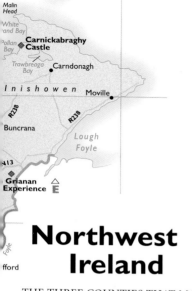

Northwest Ireland

THE THREE COUNTIES THAT MAKE up northwest Ireland are very different from each other in shape and atmosphere. Sligo, to the southwest, has a sandy coastline based around the complicated inlets of Sligo Bay and a lake-filled southern border, while Donegal to the north bursts out westward into a vast number of peninsulas and islets. Little Leitrim, squeezed between its two sister counties, has a minute coastline only 3 miles long (5 km), and a wooded, hilly interior with Lough Allen as its main water feature.

Sligo is forever associated with the Yeats brothers, poet William and painter Jack, who spent much of their childhood around Sligo town. The town itself is one of Ireland's most enjoyable, a lively but relaxed place of narrow streets and musical pubs. Weathering and glacial scraping on the limestone of the surrounding hills has produced striking table mountains with flat tops and shiplike prows. This is Yeats Country—there is a signed drive around many sites connected with William's poetry, while the settings for many of Jack's paintings can easily be identified.

Some of Ireland's most impressive prehistoric monuments lie in County Sligo—examples range from dozens of megalithic tombs in the cemeteries of Carrowmore and Carrowkeel to great prehistoric tombs such as the Labby Rock portal dolmen near Lough Arrow and the court tomb at Creevykeel.

Leitrim, sandwiched between the literary and artistic resonance of Sligo and the grand wildness of Donegal, lacks the glamour of these neighboring counties. For spectacles, Leitrim claims the Glencar Waterfall and Parke's Castle on Lough Gill; but this is mostly a county for watery pleasures, boating on the Shannon–Erne Waterway around Carrick-on-Shannon, fishing in Lough Allen and dozens of smaller lakes.

"It's different up here" is the Donegal tourism slogan—a fair summing-up. Donegal feels remote; the county is all but detached from the Republic, with only a 5-mile (8 km) border connecting it to Leitrim. Much of the west of the county is Gaeltacht (Irish-speaking); in the south rise the spectacular cliffs of the Slieve League, while up in the diamond-shaped Inishowen Peninsula at the top of Donegal you reach the wild, northernmost tip of Ireland. ∎

The landscape around Gortahork is typical of the wide wilderness that forms so much of County Donegal.

Sligo town

Sligo town

📍 206 C2

Visitor information

✉ Áras Reddan, Temple St., Sligo, Co. Sligo

☎ 071 9161201

THE ATMOSPHERE IN SLIGO TOWN IS DISTINCTLY LAID back. Little happens in a hurry here—but plenty does happen, particularly in the fields of the arts, music, and conversational drinking. Sligo has hung onto its Georgian and Victorian central streets, narrow and appealingly lined with old-fashioned shop fronts and pub facades. The broad and shallow Garravogue River rushes under a succession of bridges through the middle of the town, its noise and foamy shallows adding a dash of life to what can seem a staid and sleepy place. But Sligo is, after all, the social and commercial center of the northwest of Ireland. At night there's great music in the pubs; by day the streets are usually packed with gossiping shoppers. There is a May arts festival, in August the town's main jamboree, the Yeats Summer School, and music festivals in the autumn.

Verses in Bronze: The willowy statue of W. B. Yeats in Sligo town incorporates lines from his poems.

Sligo owes its place on the tourist map to the Yeats connection. The Yeats brothers (see pp. 210–211), poet William Butler (1865–1939), widely known as W. B., and painter Jack (1871–1957), spent their childhood holidays in Sligo with their Pollexfen cousins, and the town has several Yeats sites. At the **Model Arts and Niland Gallery,** the Niland Collection contains some 50 of Jack Yeats's paintings. There are a number of W. B. Yeats's manuscripts—including several first drafts of poems on old envelopes and sheets of hotel stationery—in the **County Library** *(tel 071 9147190)* on Bridge Street. The **Sligo County Museum** on Stephen Street has some W. B. Yeats memorabilia, but the majority of it is in the **Yeats Memorial Museum** *(tel 071 9142693)* on Hyde Bridge, crammed full of manuscripts, letters, and photographs of W. B. and his 1923 Nobel Prize.

On Stephen Street is Rowan Gillespie's impressionistic statue of the poet (erected in 1989), all spindly legs and billowing cloak overprinted with lines from Yeats's poetry. Just across Hyde Bridge is the dark red **Yeats Memorial Building** *(Hyde Bridge, Sligo town, tel 071 9142693, www.yeats-sligo.com),* headquarters of the annual Yeats Summer School and source of the most recondite Yeats information imaginable.

But Sligo is not all Yeats, by any means. A poignant sculpture on Quay Street of a ragged, skinny man, woman, and child is a reminder of how badly the town suffered during the Great Famine of 1845–49, when about a third of Sligo's population disappeared through death or emigration. Bad times had hit the town before: Vikings raided it in the ninth century, local clans fought over possession of Sligo Castle (later completely destroyed) in medieval times, and in 1641 Sir Frederick Hamilton took and burned the 13th-century Dominican Friary, killing many of the monks. The roofless ruins of the friary church on Abbey Street—Sligo's only surviving medieval building—contain some beautifully carved tombs and stonework, and a fine set of cloisters.

You can follow the Garravogue River through town, passing color-washed houses old and new along the various parades and quays. Local fishermen brave the slippery rocks in hopes of a catch—maybe a salmon. Another good wander is along Abbey Street, turning left up Teeling Street to find the famed engraved window of (now defunct) solicitors Argue and Phibbs.

Return to Abbey Street and continue along Castle Street and Grattan Street (Cosgrove's Delicatessen, where Market Street cuts in, is the place to buy the makings of a picnic lunch), before turning right along O'Connell Street to find **Hargadon's pub.**

Hargadon's is a Sligo institution, one of the rare, genuine "talking pubs" where music is not allowed to interfere with the day-long (and sometimes night-long) pleasures of rambling conversation. The front part of the pub remains unchanged, a dark den of partitioned snugs with sagging apothecary's drawers and shelves of old jars. Back rooms ramify into recently constructed bar and eating areas, but these have somehow taken on the general Hargadon's ease of atmosphere.

If you are after an evening of superb traditional music, head for **Furey's pub** on Bridge Street. It's owned by Sligo band Dervish, who have made their name playing breakneck traditional music on the concert stages of the world. But they have not forgotten where they came from, and band members take part in the fast and furious sessions here whenever they are in town. ■

The Yeats Society is headquartered in this redbrick building above the Garravogue River's rushing waters.

Model Arts & Niland Gallery
✉ The Mall, Sligo, Co. Sligo
☎ 071 9141405

Sligo County Museum
✉ Heritage Centre, Stephen St., Sligo, Co. Sligo
☎ 071 9147190

Sligo & the Yeats brothers

In spite of the worldwide experience and fame they gained as, respectively, Nobel Laureate poet and celebrated Postimpressionist painter, William Butler Yeats and his younger brother Jack looked on this small corner of Ireland as the source of their inspiration. Their mother, Susan Pollexfen, was a Sligo woman; their father, John Butler Yeats, was a lawyer turned not-too-successful artist. When money got tight, as it frequently did, Susan would take the boys and their sisters from their home in Dublin to stay for weeks and months at a time with her parents in Sligo. Both William and Jack responded passionately to the dramatic mountains and the coasts, the swirling Atlantic skies, and the life of the harbor town and its countryside— horse races, market days, country fairs; sailors, jockeys, and ballad singers.

William Butler Yeats, portrayed here in a 1907 etching by Augustus John, was inspired by the Sligo countryside.

Tales, legends, and other yarns he heard in and around Sligo stirred William's poetical imagination. His beloved Uncle George Pollexfen had a servant, Mary Battle, who would regale the young poet-in-the-making with tales of fairies, goblins, and wee folk. Mary had the "second sight," a door of spiritual imagination that opened at times, fascinating young Willie. The boy learned tales of Queen Maeve, or Medb, whose "tomb" he could see from his grandparent's house in profile on top of the hill of Knocknarea, and the story of Fionn MacCumhaill's final reckoning with his cuck-older Diarmuid on the slopes of Benbulben Mountain—also in full view from the house. These stories from Ireland's deep mythical past were generally regarded in the 1870s and '80s as superstitious nonsense fit only for peasant nursemaids and children. But the Yeats brothers continued to holiday regularly around Sligo when they were in their thirties

and forties, steeping themselves in this highly distinctive and seductive local landscape and culture. It was at the root of William's passionate championing of a specifically Irish literature enriched by tradition—what would become the Gaelic Revival, from the 1890s onward, intertwining with republican politics in the years leading up to the Easter Rising and the War of Independence. And Sligo drew the poet back at the end of his life to lie under a self-penned epitaph, "under bare Ben Bulben's head," in the graveyard at Drumcliff where his great-grandfather had been rector.

Susan Pollexfen's father, William, was a grim, solid businessman, disapproving of his feckless son-in-law and silently stern with his Yeats grandchildren. Grandmother Elizabeth was warm and loving to the Yeats children, but grandfather William was forbidding with all— except young Jack, with whom he struck up a very close relationship. Between the ages of 8 and 16 Jack came to live with his grandparents, an immersion in the Sligo scene that influenced him all his life. In adulthood he continued to visit whenever possible, staying in his Uncle George's seaside house out at Rosses Point and sketching local characters and scenes. "Sligo was my school, and the sky above it," he wrote later. From 1910 on, Jack was painting in oils, increasingly blurry and mystical in style and subject matter.

Sligo town has finally paid its adoptive artist son the honor he deserves with a gallery dedicated to his work (see pp. 208–209). Donating his painting of Uncle George, himself, and his wife, "Leaving The Far Point," to Sligo Corporation in 1954, Jack wrote, "From the beginning of my painting life every painting which I have made has somewhere in it a thought of Sligo." ■

Jack Yeats's desire to capture the fast-disappearing way of life he so loved in the west of Ireland is evident in both of his paintings, *A Lift on the Long Car* (above; 1914) and *Off the Donegal Coast* (below; 1922).

Yeats Country

THE LONELY, SANDY COASTS OF SLIGO BAY, DRUMCLIFF BAY, and Ballysadare Bay, the flat-topped mountains of the Benbulben range north and east of Sligo town, and the deeply indented shores of Lough Gill to the southeast—these contain the haunts of William and Jack Yeats, and the landscape that influenced them from childhood onward. An established Yeats Country Drive, marked with brown-and-white quill-and-inkstand signs, runs a meandering course for about 100 miles (160 km) around the area.

WEST OF SLIGO

A good place to start the Yeats circular route (*details from Sligo visitor information*) is at the 1,074-foot (328 m) summit of **Knocknaree (Knocknarea).** Shaped like an upturned dish with a round button on top, it towers over the landscape west of Sligo town. You can reach it by leaving the town along Castle Street—passing en route the house of Thornhill where the Yeats boys often visited their uncle, George Pollexfen (see pp. 210–211).

In 3 miles (5 km) a turn on the left (signed "Meascán Meadhbha") leads to a parking lot, from where a 45-minute hike reaches the summit. The "button" is in fact the huge Stone Age monument of **"Queen**

reach the tidal causeway to **Coney Island,** still the home of a few inhabitants, much beloved of Jack Yeats in his day. He set his late painting "The Sea and the Lighthouse" (1947) here, with a wind-torn figure staring out into a dark blue sky lit by a piercing beam from the Oyster Island lighthouse. You can see the painting in the Model Arts and Niland Gallery in Sligo (see p. 208). The great swath of sand enclosed in the bay is Cummeen Strand, often whipped by storm winds out of the west.

Across the bay is the shark-tooth peninsula of **Rosses Point,** scene of so much childhood freedom for the Yeatses, as children and well into adulthood, when they stayed at their Uncle George's summer house near the village. Rosses Point is a neat, compact little place with fine sandy beach walks. A metal effigy of a sailor stands in mid-tide pointing to the safest shipping channel, and on foggy days the bell buoy tolls dolefully. William loved the muted, often melancholic attractions of Rosses Point, from where he could see Knocknarea and Benbulben.

Rosses Point came to stand at the heart of Jack's art, and many of his best paintings were set here: "Shruna Meala, Rosses Point" of 1923, an early watercolor of "The Metal Man," "The Old Pilot House, Rosses Point," in which two capped figures stare seaward out of one of the pilot house's round windows. Other pictures such as "White Shower" (1928) and "The Graveyard Wall" (1945) are clearly set on a seabound landscape such as this. Most ethereal and suffused with spirituality is "Leaving The Far Point." Jack in a dark hat and his wife Cottie—a young woman in the painting, with one hand steadying her hat against the sea wind—are walking the wet gray strand at Rosses Point under a

Medb's cairn," a mini-hill of boulders (estimated at 40,000 tons of stone) that covers a passage grave. It was Queen Medb ("Maeve" to W. B. Yeats), the mythical (probably) first-century warrior queen of Connacht, who initiated the famous Cattle Raid of Cooley (see pp. 338–339). Her tomb reflects the size of her reputation: It stands 80 feet (24 m) high and measures 630 feet (192 m) around the base.

The extensive view from the summit is foregrounded by the tidal channels and sandbanks of Sligo Bay and Ballysadare Bay. Due west of the mountain lies the stony shore at **Strandhill,** backed by huge sand dunes. Ulster hero Cúchulainn fought the sea here.

Farther around the blunt-headed Strandhill Peninsula you

Yeats Country
🔺 206 C3
Visitor information
✉ Aras Reddan, Temple St., Sligo, Co. Sligo
☎ 071 9161201

wild, cloud-streaked sky. With them is the otherworldly figure of Uncle George Pollexfen, opaque to the point of transparency. He had died in 1910, so this painting is a study on past happiness and the presence of loved ones long gone. Cottie Yeats died soon after the painting was finished, adding poignancy to its effect.

LISADELL HOUSE
From the northerly tip of the Rosses Point sand spit, one looks across Drumcliff Bay to the estate of Lisadell (Lissadell), 2 miles (3 km) away. It would have been a clear view in the Yeats's day, but now conifers and tangled woodland make it hard to see the Gore-Booth family mansion of Lissadell.

Lisadell House, having fallen into decay, is now restored and open to the public. W. B. Yeats first visited in 1894 as a sensitive poet of nearly 30, fully into his "Celtic Twilight" phase of romantic nostalgia and soft-focus nationalism. He became friends with the two Gore-Booth girls, Constance and Eva, who provided plenty of hard-edged

realism as a counterbalance—especially Constance, who was to gain notoriety as Countess Markiewicz at the Easter Rising and during the run-up to the 1919–1922 War of Independence. A fervent Irish nationalist, she was an active participant in the fighting, and was given a death sentence (immediately commuted) for her part in the Dublin fighting on Easter 1916. She was soon imprisoned again for making speeches in support of the outlawed Sinn Fein. W. B. Yeats wrote of her at that time, in *On a Political Prisoner,* as "Blind and leader of the blind/Drinking the foul ditch where they lie."

William had gone through an intensely nationalistic phase. After the Easter Rising he became more conservative, but both he and Jack still supported nationalism—Jack expressing this in his 1924 painting "Communicating With Prisoners." In 1927, in *In Memory of Eva Gore-Booth and Con Markiewicz,* William remembered: "The light of evening, Lissadell/ Great windows open to the south/ Two girls in silk kimonos both/ Beautiful, one a gazelle."

Above left: Informal mural portraits of the Gore-Booth family, friends, and servants adorn the walls of the dining room at Lisadell House.

Lisadell House
🗺 206 B3
✉ Ballinfull, signposted from the N15 at Drumcliff
☎ 071 9163150
🕐 Closed mid-Sept.–May
💲 $

Above: The tower of Drumcliff Church rises among its trees, a landmark for miles around. W. B. Yeats lies buried in the churchyard.

In the house you can see photographs and portraits of the Gore-Booth sisters, along with elongated caricatures of male family members, the butler, the game-keeper, the woodman, and the dog, painted on the walls of the dining room by Constance's husband, Count Markiewicz.

DRUMCLIFF & BENBULBEN

Back on the N15 Sligo–Bundoran road, at **Drumcliff** is the austere gray **Church of St. Columba,** the stump of a round tower, and an ancient cross carved with biblical scenes, including Cain axing Abel in the head, and Adam and Eve shield-ing their private parts under the branches of the Tree of Knowledge. The church incorporates a visitor center with poetry readings, guided tours, and an interactive Yeats-related computer suite.

Next to the northwest angle of the church tower is the grave of W. B. Yeats and his wife, Georgie Hyde-Lees (1892–1968). The view from the graveside, through a thin screen of churchyard trees to the great bare-headed bulk of Benbulben, is as simple as it is majestic.

Benbulben (Benbulbin) is a noble-looking mountain, dominant in the landscape for 50 miles (80 km). It is table-topped, with sheer, deeply furrowed cliffs dropping from the summit to the upper rim of a great skirt of green that slants down to the agricultural lands below. From Benbulben Farm, reached via a country lane north from the N15, close under the mountain 3 miles (5 km) west of

Drumcliff church & visitor center

🏛 206 B2
✉ Drumcliff, Co. Sligo
☎ 071 9144956
💲 $

Drumcliff, you can climb a rough zigzag track to the saddle and bear north onto the grassy brow of Benbulben. Views are wonderful across the Dartry Mountains and down to diminutive farms and striped boglands some 1,700 feet (500 m) below. The Yeats boys roamed all over the mountain, fishing for trout in the pools and streams. In *The Tower* (1926), W. B. looked back nostalgically to "… boyhood, when with rod and fly/ Or the humbler worm, I/ climbed Ben Bulben's back/ And had the livelong summer day to spend …"

Jack slipped the distinctive dreadnought-prow shape of the mountain into his 1946 painting "The Mountain Window," as a silhouette seen in a cottage window, crowned with a cloud through which a gold sun is bursting.

Legends abound on Benbulben, the best-known being the saga of Diarmuid and Gráinne, with the final face-off between the elderly Fionn MacCumhaill and Diarmuid, who had run off with Fionn's betrothed, beautiful Gráinne. It was on the slopes of Benbulben that Fionn's warriors, the Fianna, drove a savage boar toward Diarmuid. In the act of killing it Diarmuid was gored. Twice Fionn went to the sacred spring for healing water; remembered Diarmuid's treachery and let the water trickle through his fingers. The third time he relented and brought the water, but it was too late—Diarmuid was dead. The bed where Diarmuid and Gráinne made love is suitably heroic in size, a huge rock arch 40 feet high (12 m) and 60 feet wide (18 m), standing above the inner end of Gleniff 3 miles (5 km) east of Benbulben summit. You can admire it during a circuit of the spectacular **Gleniff Horseshoe,** signposted from Ballintrillick Bridge (reached via Cliffony on the N15).

The road at the foot of Benbulben curves southeast around the mountain's flank to reach beautiful **Glencar Lough** and its waterfall. Diarmuid built a crannog in the lake to hide Gráinne from the Fianna. The waterfall is signposted from the road—a paved path leads up through mossy trees to where the stream plunges over a sill into a pool. In *Towards Break of Day* W. B. Yeats described it as "a waterfall/ Upon Ben Bulben side/ That all my childhood counted dear."

LOUGH GILL

One of the Yeats brothers' favorite Sligo places was the large, beautiful Lough Gill, east of Sligo town, with a 24-mile (38 km) scenic drive around much of its deeply indented shoreline. The southern shore road (R287 Sligo–Dromahair) passes a parking place at **Dooney Rock,** where marked paths lead up to the top of the rock—a well-known beauty spot and lookout point. W. B. had his "Fiddler of Dooney" rejoicing: "When I play on my fiddle at Dooney, Folk dance like a wave of the sea."

Farther on around the lake, the road skirts **Slish Wood** (Sleuth Wood to Yeats), where the young poet once trespassed and spent a sleepless night in fear of the wood-ranger—the subject of much saucy teasing by the servants. Close to the shore here lies **Innisfree,** the tiny wooded islet that W. B. made the subject of his best-known poem. You can reach the "Lake Isle of Innisfree" by boat from Parke's Castle (see p. 232) on the north shore and wander where Yeats longed to live in dreamy seclusion: "I will arise and go now, and go to Innisfree, And a small cabin build there, of clay and wattles made: Nine bean-rows will I have there, a hive for the honey-bee, And live alone in the bee-loud glade …" ∎

Opposite: The romantic name and location of the tiny islet of Innisfree in Lough Gill inspired Yeats's most widely known and best-loved poems.

Prehistoric Sligo

SLIGO IS A COUNTY RICH IN PREHISTORIC MONUMENTS, and its various ancient burial sites are atmospheric places to visit. Court tombs, cairns, portal dolmens, or whole cemeteries, most have far-ranging views. Wandering the hilltops and field slopes puts one's imagination to work on the nature and motivation of the people who labored so hard to build these monuments to the dead.

In the north Sligo country around Sligo town several sites are well worth exploring. Out to the west of the town (brown sign) lies **Carrowmore megalithic cemetery** *(tel 071 9161534),* the largest and oldest such site in Ireland. About 30 monuments remain in the fields, some mere scatters of stones, others complete with lintels and interior walling.

Cremated bones, stone and bone ornaments, and flint arrowheads have been found here, the artifacts of burials covering some two or even three thousand years. The oldest passage tombs at Carrowmore may date as far back as 5000 B.C.

A couple of miles (3 km) away is **Meascán Meadhbha** or **Queen Medb's Cairn,** the giant mound of stones on the top of Knocknaree

(see p. 212). The cairn is still unexcavated (it is bad luck to remove any stone), but it probably covers a 5,000-year-old passage tomb.

East of the N15 Sligo–Bundoran road lie two remarkable court tombs, each built some time between 3000 and 4000 B.C. There are many examples in Ireland of this style of tomb, in which a ceremonial open-air court (presumably for rituals) gives access to a number of burial chambers arranged in galleries inside the covered part of the tomb. But Deerpark and Creevykeel are two of the finest. **Deerpark court tomb** is reached by turning right ("Giant's Grave" sign) off the road to the north of Colgagh Lough (via the R287 Sligo–Dromahair road), then walking uphill for 30 minutes from the parking lot. The whole structure, on an open ridge-top above woods, is about 100 feet (30 m) long, with a central court, twin galleries on the east and a simple gallery on the west.

Deerpark is rugged, while **Creevykeel court tomb** (signed off the N15 just north of Cliffony) seems more artistic—trapezoid, with a pincer-shaped court, its rectangular chambers placed centrally and let into the sides of the huge pebbly monument. One of the lintels is still held up by massive jambs.

There is a cluster of three monuments around Lough Arrow in south Sligo. Among the hilltops of the Bricklieve Mountains to the west of the lake are the scattered passage tombs of **Carrowkeel neolithic cemetery,** signposted from Castlebaldwin on the N4 Collooney–Boyle road. Superbly sited to catch all the best views (and to be seen from far off), they vary in type—some have corbeled roofs like beehives and three central chambers, others fall between court and passage tombs. They date from

circa 3800–3300 B.C. Surveying the grand panorama with binoculars, you can spot many more cairns on neighboring hilltops.

Just north of Lough Arrow stands **Heapstown Cairn** (follow "Cromlech Lodge" signs from Castlebaldwin to the Bow and

Arrow pub at the crossroads—the entrance is some 100 yards/90 m north of the pub), a huge, unexcavated 5,000-year-old cairn. Two miles (3 km) southeast ("Cromlech Lodge" signs from Castlebaldwin—park at the lodge and follow the marked path) stands the magnificent **Labby Rock** portal dolmen. These are burial chambers with a capstone and entrance jambs, built between 4000 B.C. and 2500 B.C. The Labby Rock's capstone, a single block of limestone 14.5 feet (4 m) long and up to 6 feet (2 m) thick, is estimated to weigh 70 tons (70 tonnes). How the tomb-builders raised it is anyone's guess.

To find out more about the archaeology of Sligo, contact the Sligo visitor information office (*tel 071 9161201*). ■

Right: This stone-built chamber and passage of a neolithic tomb is one of many in the vast, scattered cemetery on the Carrowkeel hilltops.

Southwest Donegal

COUNTY DONEGAL, NORTHERNMOST AND REMOTEST OF
the Irish Republic's counties, throws dozens of peninsulas west and
north into the Atlantic. The southwest corner of this ragged coastline bulges out the farthest, leading at its tip to Europe's highest sea
cliffs and the beautifully enfolded sacred site of Glencolumbkille.

South of Donegal town is where
Donegal makes its tenuous connection with the rest of the Republic, a
5-mile (8 km) border shared with
the most northerly part of County
Leitrim. **Bundoran** is a first-class
little seaside resort between the
cliffs here, with a Blue Flag beach
(conforming to EU standards of
cleanliness and safety) and all the
holiday trimmings.

A little farther north comes
Ballyshannon, where myth sites
the first invasion of Ireland—a
landing by Parthelanus, a descen-
dant of Noah. Parthelanus built
a house on a rock in the mouth
of Ballyshannon Harbour and
named the islet Inis Sainer after a
favorite dog belonging to his wife,
Dealgnait. It was a remorseful nam-
ing—Parthelanus had killed Sainer
the hound with his own hands,
smashing its head on the flagstones
in a blind rage, believing that it had
treacherously allowed Dealgnait to
carry on an affair with a family
servant. You can look out on Inis
Sainer, and the winding sandbanks
and grassy dunes of the River Erne's
estuary, from Ballyshannon
Harbour, where a beautiful memorial commemorates three drowned
fishermen, showing the men transformed into gamboling dolphins.

On the way north to Donegal
town it is worth turning east to
Lough Derg, where **Station
Island,** long a place of retreat to
restore the soul, is smothered in
early 20th-century buildings of
functional design. They cater to
the many thousands of Roman

Catholics who come to the island
each May on pilgrimage *(tel 071
9861518, www.loughderg.org),*
enduring three days and nights of
barefoot perambulation and prayer
while fasting.

Donegal town is an enjoyable place to idle for a day. The
central square is known as The
Diamond, as are the squares of
plantation towns all across the
ancient province of Ulster.
County Donegal was one of the
disputed "three counties" where
Catholics were in the majority—
the others were Cavan and
Monaghan—arbitrarily separated
from Ulster by the Government of
Ireland Act of 1920 that created
Northern Ireland.

The accents you'll hear in
County Donegal seem harder and
more rapid than those in the rest
of the Republic—closer, in fact, to
the speech of Northern Ireland.
The celebrated Donegal style of
playing traditional music is notice-
ably quick and staccato, too, as if
patterns of speech were channeling
themselves out of the player's mind
through the instrument. Donegal
town has plenty of excellent music
pubs where you can catch the brisk
style for yourself.

It is worth taking a whole day
over the 75-mile (120 km) clockwise drive from Donegal town
around the roundish bulge of
County Donegal's most southwesterly peninsula. There are so many
places to stop, stare, and explore,
and the roads are twisty and
humpbacked. Glencolumbkille in

**Southwest
Donegal**
◪ 206
Visitor information
✉ The Quay, Donegal,
Co. Donegal
☎ 074 9721148

Bundoran
◪ 206 C3
Visitor information
✉ The Bridge,
Bundoran, Co.
Donegal
☎ 071 9841350
⊕ Closed Nov.–March

particular is not a place you'll want to hurry through.

A few miles west of Donegal town, a thin 8-mile (13 km) peninsula runs southwest from the village of Dunkineely to **St. John's Point.** Out toward the tip of the peninsula you pass through a wild landscape of limestone pavement rich in flowers, with fine views from the lighthouse at the tip that extend—with the help of binoculars—on a clear day from the north Mayo coast through Sligo and Leitrim to the cliffs just east of Slieve League.

AROUND THE GLENCOLUMBKILLE PENINSULA

Northwest of Donegal town, on the Glencolumbkille Peninsula, the mountains begin to rise around **Killybegs,** Donegal's premier fishing town. The harbor is lined with tough-looking, salt-rusted trawlers painted red and blue, and a fishy aroma wafts from the big fish-processing factory. West of Killybegs the coastal landscape becomes wild, a broken region of heathery headlands and small green fields sloping up to the feet of the mountains. The Coast Road detour (marked with brown signs off the R263) shows you the best of this wild landscape where trees are windblown and farmhouses are built of rough stone under slate roofs. You are into the Gaeltacht now, Irish-speaking country.

At Carrick a left turn ("Teelin Pier") leads off the main road. Soon signs to **Bunglass: The Cliffs** point up a steeply winding road

Trawlers lie up in the fishing harbor at Killybegs, a working Donegal town with a friendly, fishy atmosphere.

that climbs through gates and round rocky shoulders to a windy parking place and viewpoint above a ruined Napoleonic watchtower in a most precarious position. A few steps from the car brings you to a stunning view of the **cliffs of Slieve League,** reputedly the tallest in Europe, towering some 2,000 feet (600 m) out of the sea in a wall of black, yellow, orange, and brown. Brave scramblers with a head for heights can attempt the **One Man's Path** (or Pass), a fly-walk 2 feet wide (0.6 m) in places that teeters between the sheer cliff top and the sloping rock above to reach the summit. Do not attempt this path in wet or gusty weather.

An expanse of wild bogland, ramparted by the workings of many generations of turf-cutters, leads from Slieve League to the suddenly revealed, beautiful green valley of **Glencolumbkille.** This is one of Ireland's "special places" whose magical atmosphere far transcends the merely picturesque. Glencolumbkille runs due west, a long, sheltered valley that reaches the sea between rugged headlands.

There is a smallish amount of tourist traffic based around the **Folk Village Museum,** with its reconstructed thatched cottages and heritage displays. This manages to escape the tweeness that so often attends such heritage centers, partly because it was set up in the 1960s as a cooperative self-help scheme by the villagers of Glencolumbkille themselves, rather than being imposed from outside on a wave of EU grant money. If you fancy a bottle of seaweed or fuchsia wine, the Shebeen is the place to buy one.

But the real magic of Glencolumbkille has most to do with its connections with St. Columba, the Donegal-born saint from whom the valley takes its name. Columba, born in 521 at Gartan Lough, established monasteries and places of retreat in several Donegal locations, and was drawn by the loneliness of Glencolumbkille as well as by its reputation among pagan locals as a center of spirituality—witness the many standing stones and pre-Christian burial sites in the valley. **An Turas Cholmcille, Columba's Journey,** is a 3-mile (5 km) circuit of 15 stations or sacred sites, followed barefoot at midnight by pilgrims every year on Columba's Saint's Day, June 9.

You can seek out these sites and follow the Turas at your own pace from Station One, a court tomb in the churchyard, via standing stones

Glencolumbkille Folk Village Museum
www.infowing.ie/donegal/ad/fr.htm
🅰 206 B4
☎ 074 9730017
🕐 Closed Oct.–Good Friday
💲 $

Left: Harsh rock and smooth, falling water— contrasts that are typical of the rugged, elemental landscape of Donegal

and slabs incised with crosses, and a cluster of stations around **St. Columba's Chapel, Bed and Well** on the north slope of the glen. The ancient chapel is a sturdy box of chest-high walls on a knoll among incised cross slabs, and his highly uncomfortable bed in one corner of the chapel is a low-lying arrangement of two stone slabs boxed in by flanking stones.

From Glencolumbkille the road ribbons on eastward across stark bogland toward Ardara. A detour that's worth taking leaves the main route at a turning on the left in 2 miles (3 km). The narrow road becomes progressively bumpier after 5 miles (8 km) as it forks left and runs down to the abandoned fishing village of **Port**. This is a wonderful spot for lazing on the hillside above the ruins of the old houses and one or two restored buildings, looking out over a white pebbly beach to blue sea and sky. Only occasional do any fisherman come down to Port, so the little settlement is a perfect place for seekers of solitude.

Ardara (pronounced ar-DAR-a) is a friendly little town, that grew prosperous in times past through the tweed-weaving industry. Visitors can see demonstrations of handloom-weaving at the **Ardara Heritage Centre,** located beside the bridge in the town center, and half of the shops in town seem to sell Aran sweaters and Donegal tweed garments. **Nancy's,** halfway up the hill, and **Peter Oliver's** around the corner, are great pubs for music. ■

In southern County Donegal's Lough Derg, grandiose buildings weigh down the tiny Station Island— otherwise known as St. Patrick's Purgatory, for it is here that penitents come to spend three barefoot days of prayerful fasting.

West & northwest Donegal

DOZENS OF GRANITE-SCABBED, LAKE-STREWN PENINSULAS great and small make up the spectacular coastline of west and northwest Donegal. Together with the mountainous interior they form a landscape wild, harsh, and extraordinarily compelling. Hereabouts you'll find Irish spoken, tall tales told, and breakneck music made.

West & northwest Donegal

⛰ 206

Visitor information

✉ Blaney Rd.,
Letterkenny,
Co. Donegal

☎ 074 9121160

The **Dawros Peninsula** sticks jaggedly out across the bay of Loughros More, with views across to the mountains around Glencolumbkille. The low hills of the peninsula hide numerous lakes. In Lough Doon, between Kilclooney and Rossbeg, you'll find a fine specimen of an island ring fort perhaps 2,000 years old, with walls standing up to 15 feet tall (5 m). You can row yourself over to the island in a rented boat (signposted).

The peninsula has flat coasts of sand dunes and sandy beaches—especially around sheltered Narin, looking north into Gweebarra Bay. There are sandbanks and shining mudflats in the tidal creeks, too, attracting large numbers of over-wintering geese.

North of Dawros juts **Dooey Point Peninsula,** with more fine beaches and dunes. The **Crohy Head Peninsula,** north again, is rougher country with a meandering coast road good for walking or driving on the seaward slopes of a more mountainous interior. To get further into the mountain mood, try the 40-mile (64 km) drive from Lettermacaward northeast up the ever narrowing Owenwee Valley into the skirts of the Derryveagh Mountains, then down the Owenbeg and back by Fintown and Lough Finn.

The Rosses stand north of Crohy, for most people the quintessential Gaeltacht area. Donegal has more Irish speakers than any other county in Ireland, and the indigenous Irish language and culture are maintained most strongly in The Rosses. Grants and concessions have certainly helped—the population is on the rise, and new houses have been built along the lonely roads. The landscape here is as harsh as in the causeway islands of Galway Bay (see p. 183)—pieces of granite pushing through bog, uncountable numbers of loughs and lakelets, and a deeply cut and broken coastline.

Donegal's little airport (tel 074 9548284 or 074 9548232) is at Carrickfinn, on the flat grassy coast north of Annagry.

Tough little **Burtonport** has a pungent kelp works and a harbor full of trawlers to support its thriving fishing and kelp industry. You can get a sea angling trip from here (tel 074 9548403), or catch the ferry to Aran (Arranmore) Island (see pp. 230–231).

A more visitor-orientated village is **Dungloe** on the south side of The Rosses, with its annual "Mary From Dungloe" charm and beauty contest (tel 074 9521254)—an excuse for a few weeks of moneymaking and drinking in late July/early August, and none the worse for that.

Two further enjoyable Rosses venues are **Cruit Island,** a spit of an island a couple of miles (3 km)

north of Burtonport with some fine beaches and bird-haunted reed beds, and far-famed **Leo's Tavern** at Meenaleck near Crolly in the north of the region. Barbara and Leo Brennan, the owners, have raised a bunch of fine musicians for children—most perform together under the well-known group name of Clannad, while their internationally known sister Enya is queen of ambient Celtic synthesizer lullabies.

North again from The Rosses is **Gweedore,** an area of sandy coasts hardening to the red cliffs of **Bloody Foreland.** Inland stands Tievealehid, at 1,413 feet (430 m) a bulky backdrop in every corner of Gweedore. This is lonely country of twisty lanes on hillsides yellow with gorse (purple with heather in season), with marvelous sea views from Bloody Foreland—notably the low block of **Tory Island** (see pp. 230–231) some 7 miles (11 km) to the north. Meenlaragh, 5 miles (8 km) east of the Foreland, is the port of embarkation for the island.

Southeast of these peninsulas the **Derryveagh Mountains** raise bare quartzite tops and rolling heathery shoulders. The highest peak is **Errigal** (see pp. 226–227)—in fact the highest mountain in Donegal at 2,466 feet (750 m). A series of long, narrow glens runs southwest–northeast through the heart of the mountains, some with beautiful long lakes such as **Lough Beagh** and **Gartan Lough.** Overlooking the west shore of Gartan Lough is a huge cross marking the place of St. Columba's birth in 521 (signposted from the road).

A collapsed Bronze Age tomb lies nearby, its capstone covered in copper coins slipped into the cupmarks gouged into the stone. This is the **Flagstone of Loneliness,** where emigrants would come to lie in penance before setting out for America. ∎

The majestic simplicity of the Donegal coast near Gweedore—sand, sea, sky, and wild, heathery hills

Dungloe visitor information

✉ The Quay, Dungloe, Co. Donegal

☎ 074 9521297

🕓 Closed Oct.–May

Walk: To the top of Errigal Mountain

At 2,466 feet (751 m), Errigal Mountain is the highest in Donegal. It may look formidable from down below, but the hike presents no technical difficulty and the 150-mile (240 km) view from the top is reward enough for the long, upward slog.

Approaching Errigal Mountain along the R251 from the northwest (the Bunbeg direction), you view the mountain at its most formidable. It rises ahead, a sharp-peaked cone apparently covered in snow. As Errigal approaches and grows ever larger, you see that the dazzling whiteness of the mountain is in fact naked quartzite. Corries (circular hollows) scoop shadowed chasms in its southern flanks, and whitened curtains of scree cover its shoulders. By the time you reach Dunlewy on the shore of Dunlewy Lough, directly under the mountain, you may be thinking that it all looks a bit much for an ordinary walker to tackle.

But take courage! You can get information and reassurance at **Dunlewy Lakeside Centre** *(tel 074 9531699, closed Nov.–mid-March, $–$$$)*; they will direct you the 3 miles (5 km) along the road to the start of the climb, and tell you, "Sure, there's nothing to it."

However, there is quite a lot of upward effort to it, you will find. This is not a hike to attempt if you are unfit, or when low cloud, mist, or rain are obscuring the peak. Yet in normal conditions it's a climb that anyone who is reasonably fit and wearing a good pair of ankle-supporting boots can manage.

From the **lay-by and "walking man" sign** on the R251 the track is obvious, rising steadily up the long southeast shoulder of the mountain. In clear weather you cannot mistake the way. At first you climb among grass and heather; then, as you get higher up the mountain, rough scree of slippery stone shards and boulders takes over. Now you are into the quartzite zone—in sunshine you may see these upper slopes of the mountain sparkle with a million diamond winks of light. Nearing the top the stones become more fractured and slablike, and the path weaves round and over shelves and outcrops of bare quartzite as it steepens and zigzags.

The ridge curves round to the right above and ahead of you, with antlike figures moving slowly along it. The first **summit** is reached, and then the trick of Errigal becomes clear—

> ⛰ See area map p. 206
> ► "Walking man" sign from layby on the R251, 3 miles (5 km) east of Dunlewy
> ↔ 1.5 miles (2.5 km) each way and about 1,750 feet (532 m) of ascent
> 🕐 Allow 2.5–3 hours round-trip, depending on fitness
> ► "Walking man" sign
>
> **NOT TO BE MISSED**
> - Views of Errigal Mountain from the northwest
> - Dunlewy Lakeside Centre for information
> - Exhilarating narrow ridge path at the summit
> - Glorious views from the "far" summit

for there is a second, narrower peak beyond, connected to the first peak by a short ridge only 2 feet wide (0.6 m) in places. Vertigo-suffers could have difficulty here, since the slopes descend sharply on the right side. It's worth attaining the second (lower) peak, though, for the 360-degree view. This is a stunning prospect, with a foreground of scree dropping 2,000 feet (608 m) to lakes (Altan to the right, Dunlewy and Nacung to the left), and a magnificent far-flung backdrop of mountains and coasts. These generally extend to about 50 miles (80 km), and in exceptionally clear weather might be three times that—150 miles (240 km) from the Connemara Mountains in the southwest to Antrim and even across to Scotland in the northwest.

Return to the layby by the same path. ∎

Above right: **The reward for your effort is the breathtaking view toward Lough Altan when you stop for a rest on the summit of Errigal Mountain.**

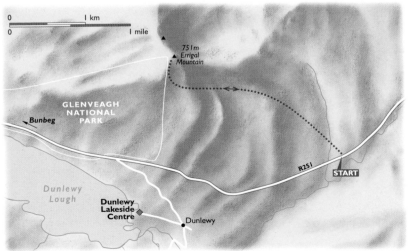

**GLENVEAGH
NATIONAL
PARK**

Bunbeg ◄

751m
▲ Errigal
Mountain

R251

START

*Dunlewy
Lough*

**Dunlewy
Lakeside
Centre**

● Dunlewy

0   1 km
0   1 mile

Inishowen & the northeast peninsulas

THE NORTHEAST OF DONEGAL IS A WONDERFULLY WILD region of bog, heather, and rocky slopes, cut into tatters by the sea. It's worth taking the time to skirt these coasts at leisure, savouring the loneliness, the seabirds, and the untamed scenery.

Inishowen & the northeast peninsulas

⌖ 207 E6

Visitor information

✉ Blaney Rd., Letterkenny, Co. Donegal

☎ 074 9121160

The Workhouse

www.theirishfamine.com

✉ Dunfanaghy, Co. Donegal

☎ 074 9136540

🕐 Closed Nov.–Feb.

💲 $$

Three peninsulas of very different character lead east to Donegal's largest and least-visited peninsula, Inishowen. The most westerly of these smaller three is the **Horn Head Peninsula.** Dunfanaghy, a smart plantation village, stands among dunes, and its former workhouse, built in 1845 at the start of the famine, has been reopened as a museum called The Workhouse, telling the story of the Great Hunger and demonstrating the grimness of workhouse life.

North of Dunfanaghy the peninsula bulges out to a mountainous tip where the 600-foot (183 m) cliffs of Horn Head plunge to the sea, their ledges lined with guillemots and puffins. Eastward is **Rosguill,** less dramatic but even more beautiful, with an 8-mile (13 km) Atlantic Drive that corkscrews up steep lanes to superb coast views.

East again lies **Fanad,** a fractured mass of land split almost in two by the narrow and tortuous inlet of Mulroy Bay. This is a flatter peninsula of lovely beaches—the best at **Ballymacstocker Bay** on the east or Lough Swilly side.

Rathmullan, farther south, has a Blue Flag beach. On September 14, 1607, this was the embarkation point for the Flight of the Earls when Hugh O'Neill, Rory O'Donnell, and Cuchonnacht Maguire, Ulster chiefs who could not accept British crown rule, sailed into exile on the Continent. It was the final nail in the coffin of Gaelic Irish autonomy.

Most easterly of all Donegal's peninsulas, the largest and the most northerly, is the great diamond-shaped mass of **Inishowen.** From a southern neck near Londonderry city only 8 miles (13 km) wide, the head of Inishowen broadens to three times that width before narrowing again toward its tip at Malin Head.

Inland, Inishowen features barren uplands above fertile valleys and long sea coasts—especially to the southeast, where a string of resorts faces Lough Foyle. Few visitors trouble to explore the beautiful, if bleak, northern and western parts, but the peninsula is well worth a day of back-road motoring.

Up at **Malin Head** there's not much to see except an old signaling tower and a fine vista. But this is where most visitors come, to stand on Ireland's most northerly point and, strangely, look south into Northern Ireland.

Both coasts of Inishowen make enjoyable drives, detouring often onto the little country lanes that bring you near the sea. The western or Lough Swilly coast is the more dramatic, with three wonderful beaches in its northern section—**White Strand Bay** near Malin Head, **Pollan Bay** on the dune-covered Doagh Isle Peninsula, and the estuary of **Trawbreaga Bay** near trim little Malin village. Doagh Isle also offers the multi-colored stonework of 16th-century **Carnickabraghy Castle,** a dolefully beautiful ruin, on its northwest tip. A mountainous coast

runs south to **Inch Island** and its bird-haunted slobs, or mudflats.

The greatest archaeological treasure of Inishowen is undoubtedly the cashel or circular stone fort of **Grianan of Aileach,** set commandingly on an 800-foot (245 m) hill northwest of Londonderry. Dr. Walter Bernard reconstructed it in the 1870s, restoring it to how it must have looked when built around 1700 B.C.—a mighty ring fortress, rising in three tiers to a narrow rampart 18 feet (5 m) tall. The O'Neill chiefs of Ulster made it their stronghold during their heyday from the 5th to the 12th centuries. St. Patrick preached here in 450, blessing the site as he did so. From the wall-top rampart the views extend across Londonderry city and over Lough Foyle and Lough Swilly. ■

These rugged pinnacles of rock mark the northernmost point of Ireland— Malin Head— at the top of the Inishowen Peninsula in County Donegal.

Aran Island & Tory Island

DONEGAL'S TWO MAIN INHABITED ISLANDS, ARAN AND
Tory, differ tremendously in topography, history, and character. Each
has accommodations, or you can visit on day trips—though in the
case of the more remote Tory be prepared for an overnight stay due
to a sudden worsening in the weather. You should not leave Donegal
without experiencing one or other of these idiosyncratic outposts.

**Aran Island & Tory
Island**
🅰 206 B5, C6

Aran (locally called Arranmore to
avoid confusion with Aran Island in
County Galway; see pp. 180–181),
lies a couple of miles (3 km) west of
Burtonport in The Rosses area.
Close to 1,000 people live on this
hilly island, very roughly circular,
that rises to 750 feet (228 m) in the
center and measures around 3 miles
wide (5 km) by 4 miles (6 km) from
north to south. August is a good
time to be here—the island's festival sees everyone letting their hair
down. But with half a dozen pubs
holding fishing port licenses, you
may find music and conversation
at any hour, day or night, in the
island's village of **Leabgarrow.**

A long morning or afternoon would suffice for a walk around the rugged coast. Roads and boreens (narrow lanes) climb from the low-lying and fertile eastern shore into the wild, boggy interior, but with a good pair of boots you can strike across the heather, rock, and rough grass. There's tremendous bird activity around **Green Island,** off the southwest tip of the island.

Aran is conveniently close to the mainland and sees a fair number of day visitors, but you have to be more adventurous—and a better sailor—for **Tory Island,** 7 miles (11 km) off the northern coast of Bloody Foreland. In contrast to Aran, Tory lies low, a slim bar measuring about 2.5 miles long (4 km) and less than a mile wide (1.6 km). Wind is a constant factor, whipping up the intervening seas, often driving salt-laden spray across the island. Anything that is grown here has to be protected in little stone-walled fields. Fishing is good enough, but hazardous. For the tiny Irish-speaking community, times have always been tough—they were nearly evacuated during a particularly bad winter in the 1970s. It took a tremendous publicity campaign by the priest of Tory to gain a sheltered harbor and regular ferry service for the island, along with proper sanitation and electricity.

Tourism has supplied a lifeline for Tory Island, which has archaeological treasures such as the ancient **Tau Cross** (now displayed at the pier in West Town, Tory's main village), and visitors enjoy the strong flavor of the life of this proudly independent island that has been (and still is) ruled by its own king since St. Columba first appointed a Tory islander in the sixth century.

Crack can be mighty in the pubs, especially during the festival in July, but the islanders do not put on an act for the visitors—they are as frank and outspoken about the difficulties of island life as they are willing to pass on Tory Island legends and beliefs. The island was the lair of the ferocious Fomorian brigands who attacked the mainland in the mythical era under their chief Balor of the Evil Eye, whose single eye was in the back of his head.

Painting for pleasure was almost unknown on Tory Island until 1968, when local fisherman James Dixon chanced upon English artist Derek Hill painting a Tory landscape and suggested that he could do a better job. He proved his point, and other islanders became interested, until a Tory Island school of naïve art was flourishing. Examples are on view (and on sale) in the **James Dixon Gallery,** in the late fisherman-painter's former home. ■

Ferries
Aran Island
20 minutes from Burtonport by Arranmore Island Ferry Service
☎ 074 9520532
💲 $$$

Tory Island
1–2 hours, depending on weather, from Bunbeg
☎ 074 9731991
45 minutes–1 hour from Magheroarty by Turasmara Teo
☎ 074 9535061
💲 $$$

James Dixon Gallery
✉ Near the school
🕐 Closed mid-Sept.–May

County Leitrim

LEITRIM IS CERTAINLY THE MOST OVERLOOKED AND undervisited county in the west of Ireland. It has no glamour, but an understated charm that well repays a day or two, especially if you are fond of fishing, boating, or hill walking.

Leitrim lies squeezed by Donegal and Fermanagh on the northeast, Cavan on the east, Longford to the south, and Roscommon and Sligo to the west. Its coastline is a strip only 3 miles wide (5 km), which explains why it is not more popular with visitors. But only a few miles inland rise the beautiful heartlands of the **Dartry Mountains,** bookended by beautiful lakes. **Lough Melvin,** on the Fermanagh border, has a spatter of islands and some fine hill slopes on the south. County Sligo to the southwest has the lion's share of **Lough Gill** (along with W. B. Yeats's "Lake Isle of Innisfree"), but Leitrim's eastern quarter of the lake boasts **Parke's Castle,** a handsome fortified house with a turreted bawn (tower)

CAROLAN
1670-1738

built in 1609 for Captain Robert Parke on a lakeside knoll, the site of an earlier five-story O'Rourke tower. The castle was abandoned by the Parkes in 1691 and stood in ruins until the mid-20th century. Now it has been restored using Irish oak for the roofs—held together with wooden dowels in the traditional manner.

Just to the south of the lake head is the village of **Dromahair,** scene of an abduction (or perhaps seduction and elopement) that dramatically changed Irish history. The 17th-century Old Hall stands on the site of Breffni Castle, a stronghold of Tiernan O'Rourke in 1152 when his wife, Dervorgilla, made off with O'Rourke's bitter rival Dermot MacMurrough, King of Leinster. O'Rourke got his own back in 1166, when he and his ally King Rory O'Connor drove MacMurrough out of Ireland. But it was a Pyrrhic victory. Dermot MacMurrough rallied support from Richard "Strongbow" de Clare, Earl of Pembroke, with the backing of King Henry II of England. Strongbow landed in Ireland in 1169, obtaining a foothold for the Anglo-Normans that eventually became an island-wide conquest.

Northeast of Dromahair is **Manorhamilton,** standing in hilly country. A well-marked long-distance footpath, the **Leitrim Way,** reaches Manorhamilton at the end of a 30-mile (48 km) northward course from Drumshanbo. Walking the path (Irish

County Leitrim

▲ 206 C2

Visitor information

✉ Old Barrel Store, Carrick-on-Shannon, Co. Leitrim

☎ 071 9620170

🕐 Closed Oct.–May

Left: Statue of harper Turlough O'Carolan (1670– 1738), in Movill, County Leitrim

Ordnance Survey 1:50,000 sheet No. 26) is the best way to get a feeling for this rolling countryside, especially as the first section runs up the east bank of **Lough Allen.**

On emerging at the foot of the lough some 8 miles (13 km) south, the Leitrim Way winds past the neat village of **Drumshanbo** to reach **Leitrim town** (another modest village) at the start of the **Shannon-Erne Waterway.** Reopened in 1994 after 125 years of dereliction, this meandering 40-mile (65 km) waterway provides the final link in a chain of lakes and rivers that can be navigated from Belleek (see pp. 322–323) on Lough Erne in County Fermanagh all the way south to Limerick and the Shannon Estuary, a total distance of 239 miles (382 km).

The canal began life as the Ballyconnell and Ballinamore Canal in 1860, but soon fell victim to competition by the Sligo, Leitrim & Northern Counties Railway (known locally as the Slow, Late, and Never Completely Reliable). It winds eastward to Upper Lough Erne through attractive green countryside of rounded drumlin hills, lakes, and small farms—the setting for many of the subtle novels and short stories of Leitrim's master storyteller, John McGahern.

This is prime fishing country, with plenty of well-stocked rivers and lakes. It's boating country, too, especially downriver at **Carrick-on-Shannon.** Here you can hire boats for cruising or angling, or sit back and enjoy a river cruise with a humorous local commentary. ∎

Leitrim's rolling green agricultural countryside holds plenty of low-key delights for walkers on the long-distance Leitrim Way.

Parke's Castle

✉ Dromahair, Lough Gill, near Sligo, Co. Leitrim
☎ 071 9164149
🕐 Closed Nov.– mid-March
💲 $

More places to visit in Northwest Ireland

BALLYSADARE

At Ballysadare (Baile Easa Daire, the "town of the waterfall of the oak tree"), the Ballysadare River runs through town over a series of weirs, with the remains of mills standing along its banks. A jungly graveyard surrounds the shell of a medieval church on the site of a seventh-century monastery. W. B. Yeats rode and rambled in the fields around here during his boyhood holidays: his Pollexfen relations, well-to-do millers in Sligo town, owned the Ballysadare mills as well.

🗺 206 B2 ✉ Junction of the N59 (Ballina) and the N4 (Boyle) roads, 3 miles (5 km) S of Sligo town, Co. Sligo **Sligo visitor information** ☎ 071 9161201

DOON WELL & ROCK OF DOON

A couple of bushes at the approach to Doon Well are laden with strips of rag, pairs of spectacles, and tiny holy statues, a clear message that the purportedly healing water of this famous well still exerts its curative magic on large numbers of pilgrims. Steps lead up from the well parking lot to Carraig a' Duin, the bald Rock of Doon, whose summit is imprinted with the shape of a human foot.

From the turn of the 13th century up until the Flight of the Earls in 1607, each O'Donnell King of Tyrconnell was crowned here, standing in the footprint to face his people.

🗺 206 D5 ✉ Signposted off the N56 between Kilmacrenan and Termon, 9 miles (14 km) N of Letterkenny, Co. Donegal **Letterkenny visitor information** ☎ 074 9121160

GLEBE HOUSE

Glebe House was built as a rectory in 1828 and bought by the English artist Derek Hill in 1953. The house itself has an Arts and Crafts feel, with William Morris wallpaper in several rooms and a kitchen hung with the colorful naïve paintings of Tory Islanders, including their doyen James Dixon (see p. 231).

The **Derek Hill Gallery,** opened in 1982, displays work by Picasso and Augustus John, as well as Irish artists such as Jack Yeats (see pp. 210–211).

🗺 206 D5 ✉ Churchhill, Gartan Lough, on the R251, 10 miles (16 km) NW of Letterkenny (R250), Co. Donegal ☎ 074 9137071 🕐 Closed Oct.–late May and Fri. 💲 $

GLENVEAGH NATIONAL PARK

Based around Lough Beagh and its surrounding moors, woods, and mountains, Glenveagh National Park covers 23,887 acres (9,650 ha) of superb hilly country. At the heart of the park is Glenveagh Castle, built of granite in Scottish baronial style in a fabulous position beside Lough Beagh. The castle was built and its parkland created by John George Adair, who notoriously evicted 244 tenants in the harsh winter of 1861 so that he could incorporate their land. His wife, Cornelia, laid out the rhododendron gardens and introduced the red deer that have become Ireland's largest herd.

🗺 206 D5 ✉ Entrance on the R251, 10 miles (16 km) E of Dunlewy and Errigal Mountain, Co. Donegal **Glenveagh visitor information** ☎ 074 9137088 🕐 Closed Nov.–mid-March

SLIGO FOLK PARK

Many aspects of life in Sligo can be explored at this splendid folk park in northern County Sligo. In the 19th-century **Millview House,** filled with restored artifacts and frequent demonstrations of old skills, visitors can experience how a well-off family would have lived 100 years ago. Another highlight is **Mrs. Buckley's Cottage,** surrounded by a lovely garden. The house was actually transported to New York in the mid-1980s for a special exhibiton, and then returned to its site here. An exhibition hall, built in the style of a traditional residence, features an excellent display of rural history and agricultural heritage, along with special events and temporary exhibitions. The park also has a craft center with quality items, many made locally, and there's a coffee shop serving homemade food and snacks.

✉ Millview House, Riverstown, Co Sligo ☎ 071 9165001 🕐 Nov.–April (but call for information regarding renovation work) 💲 $$ ∎

The central region is the heartland of Ireland, with green farming country, great lakes, and swaths of bog, dotted with medieval abbeys and ancient sites. It's the least well known part of the country—a secret waiting to be discovered.

Central Ireland

Monasterboice: Faith and art in the great stone crosses

Central Ireland

FROM THE AIR, THE IRISH MIDLANDS APPEAR AS A VAST GREEN flatland, patched brown with bog and winking with lakes. Driving through this same Irish heartland, the impression is of endless miles of farming country where the lakes are well hidden behind trees. The bogs, glimpsed from the main roads, look sterile and barren. There is little of the heightened expectation that travelers feel when they see the grand mountains and coasts of the west. Central Ireland, in fact, tends to be dismissed as somewhere to drive through on the way to somewhere better.

Water is an ever present feature of Central Ireland, its rivers and lakes linked by canals that represent great engineering skill.

Once you have caught on to the easy-paced, unruffled tempo of life in the nine midland counties, however, and have got your eye in for the subtle beauty of their round drumlin hills, their secretive lakes, and great sullen boglands, you'll be hooked.

This is uncrowded land, owing as much to water as it does to earth, a place to have a leisurely go at country pursuits—canoeing along the River Shannon, angling for pike in the Cavan lakes, tramping the Slieve Bloom Mountains, riding a horse along byways and green lanes, cruising up the Grand Canal in a narrowboat.

The counties of the central region fall loosely into three groups. Up at the top Monaghan and Cavan are neighbors on the borders with Northern Ireland. Like Donegal,

they were part of ancient Ulster and still have a plantation feel to their neat, well laid out towns. They are drumlin counties par excellence, pimpled with small hills and trenched with hundreds of valleys. A lake is never far away.

The five most central counties—Roscommon, Longford, Westmeath, Offaly, and Laois—are archetypal midlands counties, dairying regions with old-fashioned market towns and hedged, gently rolling landscapes.

The River Shannon flows on the borders of all but Laois, draining immense boglands that have recently begun to be conserved after decades of exploitation. Clonmacnoise, Fore and Boyle Abbeys, Strokestown Park House, and Birr Castle are prime attractions. ■

Map labels:
Shann
NORTHWEST IRELAND p. 205
Lough Allen
Lough Key
Lough Gara
Boyle
Boyle Abbey
N4
N5
Ballaghaderreen
ROSCOMMON
Strokestown Park House
Castlerea
Strokesto
N5
N61
Lanesborough
Shann
N60
△ A
Roscommon
Lough Ree
L
N63
Lough Funshinagh
Suck
N61
WEST IRELAND p. 165
Athlon
N6
Clonmacnois
Little Bro
Bi
EAST IRELAND p. 89
△ B

NORTHERN IRELAND
p. 279

Cuilcagh Mountains

NORTHERN IRELAND
p. 279

⊲6

30 kilometers
20 miles

Monaghan

Clones

M O N A G H A N

Ballybay

Castleblayney

N54

N2

Ballyconnell

Belturbet

Redhills Equestrian Centre

Butlers Bridge

Carrickmacross

Inishkeen

R180

Slieve Foye

Carlingford

N53

R173 Cooley Peninsula

⊲5

Shannon-Erne Waterway

Lough Oughter

KILLYKEEN FOREST PARK

Cavan

Crossdoney

C A V A N

Kingscourt

Dundalk

Dundalk Bay

Irish Sea

R198

Erne

N55

R165

L O U T H

Ardee

R166

R154

Virginia

Lough Sheelin

Lough Ramor

Dunleer

M1

Granard

N4

Oldcastle

Kells

Monasterboice

Mellifont Abbey

Dowth

N52

⊲4

Longford

Seven Wonders of Fore

Loughcrew Passage Graves

Knowth

Drogheda

N63

Fore

Fore Abbey

Lough Lene

Blackwater

Newgrange

Brú na Bóinne

N1

GFORD

Inny

Lough Derravaragh

N51

Navan

M E A T H

N2

N4

Lough Owel

N52

Bective Abbey

Hill of Tara

DUBLIN
p. 49

Mullingar

Boyne

Trim

R125

N3

Royal Canal

R392

R390

Lough Ennell

N6

N4

W E S T M E A T H

⊲3

N55

N6

Kilbeggan

△
E

△
F

R400

Grand Canal

Edenderry

R402

Tullamore

Brosna

N80

O F F A L Y

As for Meath and Louth, coastal counties north of Dublin, they are rich in historical sites, from the remarkable Stone Age necropolis at Brú na Bóinne to Monasterboice and the abbeys at Bective and Mellifont. ■

N52

Rosenallis

R422

R420

Barrow

Mountmellick

N7

⊲2

EAST IRELAND p. 89

rr astle

R421

R423

N80

Emo Court

Slieve Bloom Mountains

Portlaoise

Rock of Dunamase

M7

Area of map detail

Belfast

Dublin

Nore

L A O I S

Abbeyleix

N7

N78

N80

⊲1

△
C

△
D

N8

Strokestown Park House & the Irish National Famine Museum

UNLIKE ALMOST EVERY OTHER ASCENDANCY HOUSE IN Ireland, Strokestown Park House retains the effects accumulated by one family over 300 years. The Irish National Famine Museum explores the disaster that befell rural Ireland in the 1840s. After seeing the style in which a Big House family lived, the high-handed attitudes of so many landlords in the time of the Great Famine fall into perspective.

Left: Rakish Paddy and his colleen caper across the bogs— stereotypes in an old cartoon on display at the Irish National Famine Museum.

The last of the Pakenham-Mahon family to live at Strokestown was Olive, born here in 1894—she sold it in 1978 to local garage owner Jim Callery, whose company still owns and runs the estate. Looking to buy 5 acres (2 ha) of land to park his fleet of trucks, he actually purchased the entire estate at auction!

The **drawing room** where Olive and her husband ended up living, eating, and sleeping in the 1970s, selling pictures off the walls in order to keep solvent, contains family photos that include one of Olive's mother, her waist corseted to an incredible 16 inches (40 cm).

The **library** has more photos, including a poignant one of Olive's first husband, Edward Stafford-King-Harman—he was killed during World War I only four months after their marriage, while Olive was carrying their child. To lighten the mood, the guide sets the wind-up gramophone to play a 78 rpm record of Margaret Burke-Sheridan singing "Galway Bay" in the fruitiest of operatic voices—a verse about the Irish digging "prrraties" and talking "in a tongue we English do not understand."

Upstairs you view the **Lady's and Gentleman's bedrooms,** with their four-poster beds; the children's **schoolroom,** where their 1930s copybooks lie on their desks; and a wonderful **playroom** full of evocative old toys, dressing-up clothes, and a dolls' tea party.

The **kitchen** downstairs lay forgotten behind false walls until Jim Callery rediscovered it after he had bought the house, complete

Strokestown Park House and the Irish National Famine Museum

🅐 236 B4

✉ Strokestown, Co. Roscommon

☎ 071 9633013

💲 House: $$. Garden: $$. Museum: $$

with a huge black range and an 18th-century gallery from which the lady of the house could inspect the domestics at work without having to come into contact with them.

How those domestics' families and relations suffered during the Great Famine of 1845–49 (see pp. 27–28) is vividly, though even-handedly, told in the **Irish National Famine Museum** housed in the old stable block. Original Strokestown documents and well-mounted reproductions of contemporary cartoons and lithographs lead you through the story of what happened after the fungus *Phytophthora infestans* reduced the Irish potato crop to black slime during the Great Famine years.

The English government—and the English in general—thought of the Irish poor as "indolent, idle, inclined to do evil, and beyond the pale of civilization." Relief was ineffective, insufficient, and callously withdrawn when it was most needed. The peasants in their utter poverty depended entirely on the potato, and literally starved. Responsibility for helping the destitute people was thrown on landlords and rent-payers unwilling or unable to play their part. Evictions for non-payment of rent were widespread, enforced emigration commonplace.

At Strokestown, Major Denis Mahon, in process of evicting two-thirds of his tenants (about 5,000 people), was shot dead in 1847, one of seven landlords or agents murdered that year. Anguish and resentment flooded the Irish poor, and went with them on the disease-ridden coffin ships to England, North America, and Australia.

Blaming the landlords alone, though, is too simplistic. Major Denis Mahon received no worthwhile government help, had no resources to help those depending on him, and was forced to choose between watching them starve or paying for them to emigrate. More culpable was the mindset displayed by English politicians who could come out with such statements as: "The great evil with which we have to contend is not the physical evil of famine, but the moral evil of the selfish, perverse and turbulent character of the people." ∎

Above: Severely classical architecture was chosen by the Mahon family in the 1730s when they extended Strokestown Park House.

Boyle Abbey

BOYLE ABBEY, NEAR COUNTY ROSCOMMON'S BORDER with County Sligo, is a rare survival in Ireland—a remarkably complete, very early Cistercian monastery. Equally remarkable is the fact that Boyle owes its survival to the military. Instead of following their usual pattern of destroying what they found, they took over the buildings and converted them into a barracks. Taking the guided tour around the site is an atmospheric experience.

Boyle Abbey

- 236 B5
- Boyle, Co. Roscommon
- 071 9662604
- Closed Nov.–March
- $

Imagination and a sense of history are kindled from the outset as you walk into the site through the arch of the **gatehouse,** notched by the sword cuts of the idle soldiery. The inner gate jambs are incised with graffiti cut by bored guards. In the gatehouse an exhibit sets the scene around a scale model of the abbey in its heyday.

Monks from Mellifont Abbey (see p. 278) came to Boyle in 1148, looking for a place to build a new abbey, and fired with enthusiasm for a Spartan but charitable way of life. Six years before, a group of them had returned to Ireland fresh from a visit to France, where they had been inspired by the discipline and self-denial of the monks at St. Bernard's Monastery. After founding the Cistercian abbey of Mellifont, they were keen to spread their influence. The MacDermot clan, sensing an opportunity to gain prestige, gave them 1,000 acres (400 ha) of land to build their abbey and community at Boyle.

At its height of prosperity, from the 13th to 15th centuries, Boyle Abbey ruled vast tracts of land and supported a community of more than 400, but, by the time of its dissolution in the mid-16th century, there was only a handful of monks in a range of decayed buildings. Queen Elizabeth I granted the monastic lands to the Cusack fami-

ly, and they allowed the monks to linger on in the abbey. Then, in 1603, the new Stewart king of England, James I, gave the estate to a Staffordshire adventurer, John King. He turned the abbey into a garrisoned fortress known as Boyle Castle, and it remained in use as a barracks for a century and a half. In 1788 the Connaught Rangers—a rough lot—moved on, and the old buildings began a period of decay not arrested until the 20th century.

In monastic times the gatehouse would have contained a 24-hour guard and quarters for unexpected guests. Stepping through the archway, you come into the wide, grassy **cloister garth,** or garden, with low walls. Around these rises the outer wall of the abbey complex, patched roughly where it was broken through for military gateways.

There are **kitchens** with enormous fireplaces on the south. The cooking, cleaning, and general spadework of the abbey was done by a large lay community—St. Benedict's original decree that monks attend eight services of prayer a day while remaining self-sufficient through their own hard work proved impossible to obey.

In the big **refectory** on the southeast, the monks ate in silence (not enforced by oath, but a custom common to most Cistercian abbeys) while edified by readings of scripture from a wall lectern. Between mid-September and Easter they ate only once a day—and since they rose at 2:30 a.m., those days must have seemed long indeed.

Farther along the east wall were **reading rooms, dormitories** with a calefactory, or hot room, to warm them, a **parlor** for occasional conversation, the **chapter house,** and the **abbot's house.**

A low arch leads into the splendid **abbey church**—austere Romanesque at the eastern end, more decorative Gothic toward the west. Capitals become floral, and the pillars more elaborate. The westernmost capital of the north wall (which slopes alarmingly outward) has 14 little grimacing men peeping out of foliage—the master mason's team, suggests the guide, caricatured by him as a signing-off gesture on completion of the church. ■

Very few monastic sites came through Ireland's bloody wars and repressions as unscathed as Boyle Abbey, where domestic and devotional buildings stand side by side.

County Cavan

IF YOU LIKE LAKES, YOU'LL LOVE COUNTY CAVAN. THE little border country is spattered with them so thickly that a Cavan view without a slip of water in it soon feels strange. Bring your fishing rods to Cavan; and you could do worse than to pack your walking boots, too. Out to the west sticks a long thin panhandle separating Leitrim from Fermanagh, where the Iron Mountains meld into the Cuilcagh range, and the land rises and becomes beautifully wild, ideal for hill tramping.

The lake-bespattered landscape is at its most fragmented to the north and west of the little county town of **Cavan.** This is a trim but not particularly visitor-orientated place, pleasant enough as a base for exploring the lakes—or you could try the villages of **Butlers Bridge** or **Belturbet,** a little nearer to the lakes. Upper Lough Erne wriggles down from Fermanagh and breaks up into hundreds of thin, winding watercourses. These lakes, lakelets, and threads of river make islands and peninsulas of the green, well-wooded land between Belturbet near the border and the point near Crossdoney where the River Erne emerges as a single entity from this mazy waterworld to flow on south.

Driving and walking here is a puzzling business for any outsider at first, with innumerable signs pointing to different pieces of water—Tirliffin Lake, Drumlane Lake, Dumb Lake, Tully Lake. Look for brown signs to **Lough Oughter**—leading to a meandering circuit through brackeny back lanes with **Killykeen Forest Park** (tel 049 433 1046) at its hub. The Cavan tourist office will give you information about the park, including directions to the **Killykeen Equestrian Centre** (7 miles/12 km NW of Cavan town, tel 049 436 1707) or **Redhills Equestrian Centre** (tel 047 55042), and to the best locations for fishing on Lough Oughter. Or you can follow one of the marked trails through the woods of the park.

Most of the country lanes hereabouts are boreens, anyway—grass-green tracks going nowhere as slowly as possible, which make for fine undemanding strolling. Beware, though: Every road twists and bends among the lakes and the woods of hazel and ash, and it's easy to get lost! Fishing is excellent at Belturbet and Butlers Bridge, and there are plenty of experts around to tell you where to try for that fat lake trout.

Farther west at **Ballyconnell** you reach the Ballyconnell and Ballinamore Canal, better known as the **Shannon-Erne Waterway.** It starts at Leitrim town and is navigable all the way to the south shore of Upper Lough Erne at

Left: Another fine fish is taken from a County Cavan lake.

Cavan visitor information

⚑ 237 D5

✉ 1 Farnham St., Cavan, Co. Cavan

☎ 049 433 1942

🕐 Seasonal

Above: Ice age glaciers in retreat dumped gravel and clay to form the hillocks and lakebeds that are so characteristic of County Cavan.

Fishing permits
Licenses are available from local visitor information offices and local fishing shops. For more information contact North West Tourism (tel 071 916 1201) or Northern Regional Fisheries Board (tel 071 985 1435).

Foalies Bridge. The 1994 reopening of this 40-mile (60 km) link between the Erne and Shannon river and lake systems gave Ballyconnell a tremendous shot in the arm, turning a formerly sleepy village into a lively and well-to-do boating center. You can rent a boat in Ballyconnell—self-drive or piloted— to cruise the waterway, either to Ballinamore in County Leitrim or up the canal to Fermanagh.

West of Ballyconnell, County Cavan's panhandle sticks up to the northwest. This is far bleaker and wilder country than the mild lake-and-drumlin country to the east and south of the county.

Dominant in the landscape are the **Cuilcagh Mountains,** which climb in a series of flattish peaks to the summit of the range

on Cuilcagh itself at 2,180 feet (663 m). The Fermanagh-Cavan border runs through the summit, which is best climbed along the route of the long-distance **Ulster Way** from Florence Court Forest Park in Fermanagh—about 10 miles (16 km) there and back with a climb of about 1,350 feet (410 m).

Hill walkers looking for a good long day out make for the **Cavan Way,** a well-marked long-distance path that runs from Blacklion on the Fermanagh border for 16 miles (26 km) south to Dowra. The path hops over the outlying northwest toe of the Cuilcagh range and runs by the **Shannon Pot,** where the 230-mile (368 km) river—the longest in the British Isles—has its birth; from here the path follows the infant Shannon down to Dowra. ■

Monaghan town & around

Monaghan town
www.monaghantourism.com
[A] 237 D6
Visitor information
[✉] Castle Meadow Court, Tirkeenan, Monaghan, Co. Monaghan
[☎] 047 81122

Monaghan County Museum
[✉] Hill St., Monaghan, Co. Monaghan
[☎] 047 82928
[⏱] Closed Sun., Mon., & L

COUNTY MONAGHAN AND COUNTY CAVAN ARE ALWAYS spoken of together, as if they were sisters. Perhaps this linkage is due to the fact that they mirror each other topographically. Cavan (see pp. 242–243) is full of lakes and Monaghan is full of hills—little ones, roundish drumlins of rubble and clay dumped by the retreating glaciers 10,000 years ago. The hills give the sprawling border country of Monaghan an intimate, enclosed character very different from the open landscapes of the southern midlands or the west.

The county town of **Monaghan,** stone-built and solid, epitomizes the virtues of hard work and respectability. Though County Monaghan has lain in the Republic since 1921, it formed part of the ancient kingdom of Ulster and was planted or colonized by non-Catholic Scottish settlers in the early 17th century.

Monaghan shared Ulster's rise to prosperity through the linen trade, reflected in the substantial architecture of the county town with its three squares, great Victorian rocket of a drinking fountain, and the huge **St. Macartan's Cathedral** (constructed 1861–1891), whose 250-foot (76 m) spire dominates the town.

The **Monaghan County Museum** is one of the best of its kind, with an archaeological overview covering 5,000 years. Chief prize is the 14th-century **Cross of Clogher,** a beautifully worked altar crucifix of bronze from the ancient bishopric of Clogher a few miles northwest.

CARRICKMACROSS & CLONES

South of Monaghan the two lace-making towns of Carrickmacross and Clones still ply their trade, though for the specialist collector market these days. You can see occasional demonstrations of the art in the **Carrickmacross Lace Gallery** on the Market Square.

In Clones it's also worth looking for the weathered but still striking tenth-century **high cross,** relocated on the Diamond from the ruins of St. Tiernach's Monastery on Abbey Street. Panels on the south side show Old Testament scenes, while on the north, New Testament miracles are depicted.

Right: Monaghan lacemakers need keen eyes and quick fingers

Carrickmacross Lace Gallery

 Market Sq., Carrickmacross, Co. Monaghan

☎ 042 966 2506

Inishkeen Folk Museum

www.patrickkavanagh country.com

✉ Inishkeen, Co. Monaghan

☎ 042 937 8560

🕐 Currently closed for renovation; call ahead

INISHKEEN

So to the eastern border of the county, and the countryside around Inishkeen—poor farming land, where small farms make the best of the steep drumlin sides and reedy valley bottoms. Ireland's greatest poet of the mid-20th century, Patrick Kavanagh (1904–1967), celebrated, excoriated, and revealed this hedged-in landscape in his wonderful poems, colorful or black according to mood. Kavanagh was a small-time farmer around Inishkeen until he left in his early thirties to live as a writer in London and Dublin. Drink and cancer took charge of him before he died.

Inishkeen was always the spur to his talent, from lyrical productions such as his autobiographical *The Green Fool* (1938) to the bitterly realistic poems such as *Stoney Grey Soil* (1940), in which he writes of how peasant life and work sapped his joy and restricted his range.

In Inishkeen, **Kavanagh's birthplace** *(not open to the public)* is signed off the road—a dour gray house on a ridge. The old church in

the village contains the excellent **Inishkeen Folk Museum,** which features a fascinating exhibition about the poet and his work. Kavanagh's grave lies outside, marked with a simple wooden cross and the words: "And pray for him who walked apart on the hills, loving life's miracles."

Just past the modern church on the road to Carrickmacross from Inishkeen, a brown sign marked "My Black Shanco" indicates a track that winds for a mile (1.6 km) toward Kavanagh's farm of **Shancoduff,** mentioned in many of his poems. "The sleety winds fondle the rushy beards of Shancoduff," he wrote in *Shancoduff,* and here you can walk the lane and the rushy fields that the poet loathed and loved. ∎

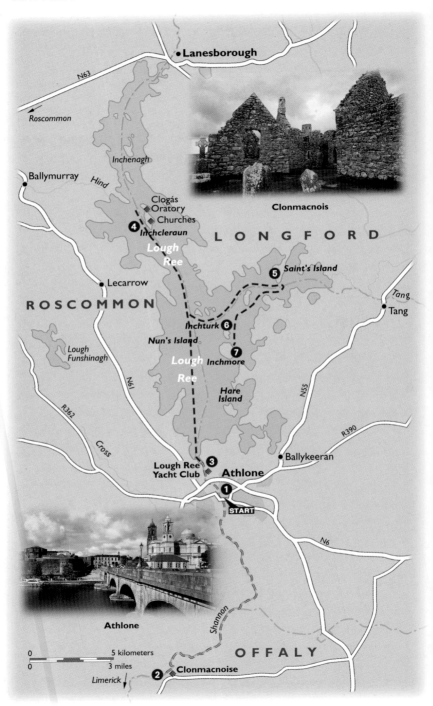

Lanesborough

N63

Roscommon

Inchenagh

Ballymurray

Hind

Clonmacnois

Clogás
Oratory
Churches
4 Inchcleraun

L O N G F O R D

Lough
Ree

Lecarrow

5 Saint's Island

R O S C O M M O N

Tang
Tang

Lough
Funshinagh

Inchturk 6
Nun's Island

7
Inchmore

N55

Lough
Ree

Hare
Island

N61

R362

Cross

R390

Ballykeeran

Lough Ree
Yacht Club
3
Athlone
1
START

N6

Athlone

Shannon

0   5 kilometers
0   3 miles

O F F A L Y

2 Clonmacnoise

Limerick

In the old town of Athlone, plenty of relaxing pubs offer good stout and music.

Cruise: River Shannon & Lough Ree from Athlone

The bustling if not exactly beautiful town of Athlone sits in the center of Ireland, and more or less at the midpoint of the Shannon, Ireland's longest river, as it makes its twisting journey of nearly 200 miles (320 km) from the Iron Mountains of County Cavan south to its estuary at Limerick. Athlone, plentifully supplied with cruise boats and self-drive hire craft, makes a great base for exploring the Shannon—southward to the monastic site of Clonmacnoise, northward among the wooded islands of Lough Ree.

You can hire your own cruiser, or you can travel onboard one of the excursion boats.

When you set off south from **Athlone ❶** *(visitor information, Athlone Castle, St. Peter's Sq., Athlone, tel 0902 94630)* for Clonmacnoise, you'll need to take account of Athlone's lock, through which you have to pass before reaching the Shannon below the town. It's best to be first in the line, early in the day—otherwise you may have to wait an hour or so for the lock to fill and empty several times. But it's a pleasant place, where freshwater admirals exchange yarns and boats bump companionably together. Once through and going downriver with the current, all you have to remember is to keep the black markers on your left and the red ones on your right.

The broad Shannon curves gently through grazing meadows; several of these are left

---

- 🗺 See area map p. 236 B3
- ▶ Jolly Mariner Marina, Coosan (tel 0902 72890 or 0902 72113, $$–$$$)
- ↔ Clonmacnoise and back, 19 miles (30 km); Lough Ree, 22 miles (36 km)
- 🕐 Half a day, either trip
- ▶ Clonmacnoise

NOT TO BE MISSED
- Athlone lock & waterfront
- Clonmacnoise
- Inchcleraun
- Fishing—bring a rod!

uncut till late in the summer to give shelter to the now very rare corncrake. You probably won't see this unassuming brown bird, but if lucky you may hear the male's loudly grating repetition of his Latin name, *crex crex,* before the towers of **Clonmacnoise ②** (see pp. 252–255) come in sight. A convenient jetty lies below the monastic site. Allow up to half an hour longer for the return journey to Athlone as you'll be sailing against the tide.

Cruising upriver from Athlone, it's only a mile or so (1.6 km) before you pass the **Lough Ree Yacht Club ③,** founded as far back as 1770, on your right. Don't forget that for upriver travelers the black markers are now on your right and the red on your left.

Beyond the yacht club, the waterway broadens out into the great expanse of **Lough Ree** at the heart of the Shannon. It is wise to heed the navigation advice given you at the Jolly Mariner Marina, Coosan, as the lake is shallow and has plenty of rocks and barely submerged reefs. The lough is 16 miles long (26 km), shaped like a pointy-headed leprechaun with one ragged sleeve extended to the east. Its shore lies flat and is mostly smothered with trees; low hills rise beyond, made to look taller by the flatness of the landscape.

If you wish to land on any of the islands, make sure that your boat has an anchor and a dinghy—complete with oars and rowlocks—attached. Ree is a great fishing lake, and you can take full advantage if you are in a rented craft.

Of the many islands and islets in Lough Ree, the most interesting in terms of its archaeological remains is **Inchcleraun ④,** sometimes known as the **Quaker's Island,** up in the northern part of the lake. If you want to explore the buildings of the island you'll need to anchor near the red lake-navigation marker No. 7 and row to the bouldery island waterline to scramble ashore. On haphazardly grazed grass in a smother of trees you'll find the tiny, ancient **Teampull Diarmuid Church,** the 13th-century **Teampull Mor** (Big Church), with its big gable and low door with a rugged lintel, and the little 12th-century **Chancel Church** and **Church of the Dead** near the shore. Toward the higher center of the island stands the dignified 12th-century **Clogás Oratory,** with its square bell tower. Harder to find is the

One of the most enjoyable and relaxing pastimes in Central Ireland is to explore the many islands of Lough Ree by boat.

ruin of **Fairbrother's House**—Fairbrother was the Quaker who lived on Inchcleraun early in the 19th century. While he was building the cottage, so stories say, he foolishly took the corner stones from the Clogás Oratory to use in his work. St. Diarmuid, sixth-century founder of the island's monastery, saw what was going on from his seat in heaven and was not amused. First the saint "smote the Quaker's horse with the bolt of his holy revenge, which caused it to run furiously, untamedly, terribly, outrageously, irresistibly mad." Then all the beasts on the island ran crazy, and were only restored to sanity when the Quaker vowed to touch no more of the holy stones of Inchcleraun.

It was only natural for reclusive early Christian hermits to choose the islands of

Lough Ree as their prayerful refuges. There are remains of churches on the **Saint's Island**  (in fact the tip of a peninsula) and on the **Nun's Island,** both now used as pasture.

Early in the 20th century, most of the islands supported resident families of eel-fishermen, who would hitch their boats to the back of passing Guinness barges for a free ride down to Athlone. Now many of the islands have become holiday retreats.

Some incumbents have found the realities of island life at odds with their fantasies, like the Dublin bookmaker who painstakingly built a beautiful retreat for his family on **Inchturk Island**  with wood interior, thatched roof, and local stone. The wife and son came over, spent one night, and pronounced it too quiet: The place was abandoned forthwith.

On **Inchmore Island** , the largest in the lake (private property), St. Liobán's Monastery shows a few remains. ■

Queen of Connacht

Lough Ree is not only full of fish—it's also full of legends. One of the best concerns the death of the mythical Queen of Connacht, the warlike and lecherous Medb (see pp. 338–339). Medb eventually received her comeuppance while bathing in Lough Ree. Forbaid, Prince of Ulster, from whose father the warrior Queen had stolen the Brown Bull of Cooley, had been hiding out on the shores of Lough Ree and planning to avenge his father's loss. He discovered where Medb loved to bathe, measured the distance from there to the shore, and practiced his slingshot skills at that exact range. When Medb came down to bathe on her day of doom, Prince Forbaid stove her head in with a well-aimed shot. Just why he chose to use a hard piece of cheese as the missile, though, has never been explained. ■

Seven Wonders of Fore

IN A QUIET WESTMEATH VALLEY 15 MILES (24 KM) NORTH-east of Mullingar, a remarkable group of monuments—some man-made, some works of nature—lies on the outskirts of the tiny village of Fore. On a fine day, you will have an experience to savor as you explore these curiosities, known as the Seven Wonders of Fore.

A Quaking Scraw is a bog, on which nothing can normally be built. The **Monastery in the Quaking Scraw**—a group of largely 15th-century Benedictine monastic ruins a couple of fields away from the road—certainly seems to be surrounded by sloppy wet bog; but it is in fact founded on an islet of solid ground within the marsh. The most extensive Benedictine ruins in Ireland, they have a full range of monastic buildings with huge fire-places and solid walls abutting a plain but lovely church. Restored cloister arches have discreet carvings of long-stemmed flowers. East stands the gatehouse, in use as a farm building; northeast are the circular remains of a dovecot.

Walking back down the path toward the minor road, you'll find an ash tree standing over a tumble of mossy stones beside the wall on your right. This is **St. Fechin's Bath** (not in fact one of the seven wonders, but curious all the same); it was St. Fechin who founded the first monastery at Fore in 630. The tree is usually hung with rags, and its trunk is literally crammed with thousands of coins pushed into the bark—the traditional offerings to leave at holy wells. The mossy stones are the remnants of the basin where the saint would kneel praying in cold water all night. Ailing children would be bathed here in expectation of a cure.

The **Mill Without a Race**—a jumble of broken walls—and the **Water That Flows Uphill** are on your left as you reach the road.

St. Fechin commissioned the original mill despite an absence of water, which he supplied by striking a hill at Lough Lene (south of Fore) with his staff. The water still flows—uphill, if you inspect it with rose-colored glasses.

Copper poisoning and the depredations of souvenir-hunters have reduced the **Tree That Won't Burn** to a stub. It might be breakable, but legend says it cannot be burned. It stands near the road beside St. Fechin's Well, which contains the **Water That Won't Boil**—a muddy puddle these days. Bad luck attends anyone rash enough to make the experiment.

Across the road you'll find the final two wonders. The **Stone Raised by St. Fechin's Prayers** forms the massive lintel of a church that mostly dates back to the 12th century. Look for the little seated monk carved on the chancel arch. The stone may be much older. On it is carved a Greek cross in a circle, a more Eastern than Western religious symbol. Up the bank from the church dwelt the hermit Patrick Begley, the **Anchorite in a Stone**, in the early 17th century. His humble cell was later incorporated into the grand church-shaped mausoleum of the Greville Nugent family. The cell is marked with a Latin inscription translated as: "I, Patrick Begley, hermit of the sacred retreat, hidden and buried in this hollow heap of stones …"

The key to the mausoleum is kept at the Seven Wonders pub in Fore, a friendly place for a drink. ■

Fore
🅜 237 D4
Visitor information
✉ Fore Abbey Coffee Shop, Fore, Castlepollard, Co. Westmeath
☎ 044 61780
🕒 Closed Mon.–Sat. Oct.–May

Mullingar
🅜 237 D3
Visitor information
✉ Market House, Mullingar, Co. Westmeath
☎ 044 48650

Seven Wonders
🅜 237 D4
✉ Head N from Mullingar on the R394 to Castlepollard, then NE on the R395 to Fore. The Stone raised by St. Fechin's Prayers and the Anchorite in a Stone lie to the south of the minor road through the Fore Valley, the other five wonders to the north.

Opposite: Looking across from the Tree That Won't Burn and the Water That Won't Boil toward the Monastery in the Quaking Scraw—three of the Seven Wonders of Fore

Clonmacnoise

BEAUTIFULLY SITUATED AMONG ISOLATED MEADOWS ON
a bend of the River Shannon, Clonmacnoise is the most complete and
evocative monastic site in the central region. With its exquisitely
carved high crosses, multitude of ancient churches, and splendid
round tower, many claim it as the best such site in all Ireland.

Clonmacnoise

⚑ 236 B3

✉ Shannonbridge,
Co. Offaly

☎ 0905 74195

$ $$

Clonmacnoise is well signposted
from Ballynahown on the N62,
7 miles (11 km) south of Athlone,
and you can reach the site equally
easily 5 miles (8 km) north of
Shannonbridge, on the R357
8 miles (13 km) southeast of
Ballinasloe. But there's only one
truly memorable way to arrive, and
that's by water from Athlone (see
pp. 246–249), seeing the round tower
and churches of the walled site out-
lined against the sky above their own
reflections in the Shannon.

The grandeur of the site lies
partly in its superb rural and river
location, partly in the variety and
splendor of its buildings. St. Ciarán
founded the first monastery here
circa 548, building it on Esker
Riada, the Kings' Highway—a
glacial ridge that ran west as a high
road through the kingdoms of
Leinster and Connacht.
Between its foundation and
the coming of the Normans
in the 12th century,
Clonmacnoise was
Ireland's most
important
center of
Christian
faith, litera-
ture, and art.

The kings of
Connacht and the High
Kings of Tara were brought
here for burial. In spite of
scores of assaults by Danes
and ill-disposed Irish—it
was attacked 27 times and
burned 12 times by the
native Irish between 720

and 1205—Clonmacnoise
remained a beacon of Christian
light whose influence extended over
northern Europe. But after the
Normans landed in Ireland the
monastery's power waned. In 1179
there were reported to be at least
100 houses and 13 churches in the
monastery precincts; 300 years later
the place had declined in status to
the seat of a minor bishop. In 1552
an English regiment marched down
from Athlone, wrecked the building,
and stole every treasure they could
shift—even the monastery books,
stained glass, and church bells.

The ruins of a 13th-century
Anglo-Norman **castle** totter
on a hillock overlooking the
Clonmacnoise jetty on the
Shannon. Entering the site, you
pass through a visitor center whose
exhibition is a must-see—it
contains the monastery's three
high crosses (replicas brave
wind and rain in their original
positions outside).

First of the
three is the
tenth-century
**Cross of the
Scriptures,**
with its stumpy
upward-tilted arms,
richly covered with panels.
The carved scenes include
a flute player summoning the
righteous to judgment, the
devil lying on his back with his
upraised feet providing a seat
for St. Anthony, and a bird
administering the kiss of life to
Christ, who wears a beaded

halo and lies in the tomb guarded by two Viking-looking warriors in peaked helmets. Also exhibited is a collection of inscribed graveslabs.

The walled site itself is roughly circular. The tenth-century round tower, some 65 feet (20 m) high, is a landmark for miles around. Known as **O'Rourke's Tower,** it is named after Fergal O'Rourke (died 964), King of Connacht. The top was shattered by a lightening strike in 1135 and never properly reconstructed.

East lies the cathedral, or **MacDermot's Church,** built in 904 and rebuilt during the 12th century. There is a side chapel full of carved stone fragments, and a Gothic west door of many recessed courses, decorated with dragons and foliage, overseen by Saints

Francis, Dominic, and Patrick in statue form. This doorway was erected, says the 15th-century Latin inscription, for the eternal glory of God. Press your ear to one side of the doorway and you can hear someone quietly whispering at the other side—priests used this to hear lepers' confessions in safety.

Scattered around the site are several smaller churches: **Teampull Doolin** and **Teampull Hurpan; Teampull Finghin** with a dogtooth chancel arch and round tower belfry. Some call this beautiful ruined chapel McCarthy's Church; built around 1160, it contains some really fine Romanesque carvings. The door of the diminutive round tower attached to the chapel is at ground level; by the time the church was

The mighty Shannon loops a protective arm around the great monastic site of Clonmacnoise.

built, the threat from Viking marauders had faded, so the tower was probably constructed as a belfry rather than for defense.

Just up the slope stands tiny **St. Ciarán's Chapel,** burial place of the saint. The floor of the chapel lies below ground level—generations of local farmers have scooped up handfuls of soil mixed with saintly dust to scatter in their fields, thereby ensuring a good crop. Most beautifully carved of all is the **Nun's Church,** 500 yards (455 m) east of the walled site, with heavy dogtooth arches, tiny faces, and, in the outer doorway, 11 beaked heads with bulging eyes. A penitent Dervorgilla, the Irish Helen of Troy (see p. 261), built the chapel in 1167. ■

Right: Superbly preserved examples of the early medieval stonemason's art adorn the shafts, arms, and bases of Clonmacnoise's wonderful high crosses.

Birr town & castle

THE FORTUNES OF BIRR HAVE BEEN BOUND UP SINCE 1620 with one talented and out-of-the-ordinary family—the Parsons clan, who became Earls of Rosse. They built a fine Georgian town in the farmlands of County Offaly, and at Birr Castle successive genera-tions were at the cutting edge of scientific enquiry all through the 19th century, the great age of the amateur gentleman scientist.

Birr

⬛ 236 B2

Visitor information

✉ Brendan St., Birr,
Co. Offaly

☎ 0509 20110

🕐 Closed mid-
Sept.–April

Birr Castle

www.birrcastle.com

☎ 0509 20336

🕐 Grounds only open

💲 $$$

**Handsome
Georgian houses
line Birr's streets.**

The way to get the best out of Birr is to follow the **Birr Town Trail** (leaflet guide available from the vis-itor information office). You start in John's Mall, one of the fine strolling streets laid out by the Parsons family. Another, farther along the trail, is Oxmantown Mall. John's Mall is shaded by well-grown Jerusalem plane trees, its small Georgian houses with their wide front door fanlights looking out on flowerbeds and neat white chain railings. The trail takes you past the Mercy Convent behind its high wall (English architect Augustus Pugin, 1812–1852, designed it), and along O'Connell Street and Main Street with their handsome old shop fronts. Many of these have carved wood surrounds. Keep an eye out for the druidic mistletoe-gatherers outside Mulholland's Pharmacy, and more examples at Guinan's Footwear, Owen's Fruit and Veg, and Barber the Watchmaker.

Birr Castle itself is still the residence of the Earl and Countess of Rosse, and it is not open to the public. But the estate (gardens and parkland) is open to all. These are some of the finest grounds in Ireland, and are in the long-drawn process of ongoing refurbishment and improvement. Paths crisscross the entire demesne, giving access to parkland and river and lake walks.

Particular features are the immense box hedges, more than 200 years old and up to 60 feet tall (18 m). Walking between these is a creepy but enjoyable experience. So, too, is searching for **"Sweeney,"** the wickerwork figure of the leg-endary Irish half-king, half-bird. With knees drawn up to a pointed beard, he sits in the fork of a holly tree near Lovers' Walk. Other delights are the roses, magnolias, and intricate formal gardens.

To appreciate the extent of the achievements of the Parsons family in the fields of science, it is worth spending an hour looking around **Ireland's Historic Science Centre** established in the castle stables. This is a very absorbing exhibition with plenty of original material—plans, letters, photographs, models, and instru-

ments. Charles Parsons (1859–1931) invented the steam turbine, spent $22,000 and 25 years trying to make diamonds, and got a steam-powered helicopter off the ground in 1897—six years before the Wright brothers' official first powered flight.

It was the 3rd Earl of Rosse, William Parsons (1800–1867), President of the British Association for the Advancement of Science, who planned and built the "Leviathan," a monstrous telescope with the largest cast-metal mirror ever made. It took four months to cool after casting, and four years (1841–44) to grind and polish it to a perfect parabolic curve. By the mid-19th century, the sky had been mapped into 7,000 areas of light, and the great puzzle was what exactly they were. When William Parsons first looked through his telescope in April 1845, he saw what he named a "whirlpool nebula"—another galaxy 40 million light years away.

William's wife, Mary, was a pioneer of photography, and thanks to her there are remarkable images of the great telescope in action. Even better—the instrument itself, beautifully restored, is still in its original position in the demesne, and is demonstrated three times a day. It is housed between two mock castle walls, a giant black barrel almost 70 feet long (21 m). Chains and weights clank as the telescope slowly rises along its immense curved rails and slides smoothly from side to side. You don't have to be a scientist to appreciate this extraordinary feat. ■

The Earl and Countess of Rosse welcome the public to the beautiful grounds of their home, Birr Castle, scene of many groundbreaking scientific inventions by members of the family.

Bogs beautiful

Fifty years ago, anyone who found beauty in the bogs would have been dismissed as a fool. But eco-awareness has brought a new understanding and appreciation of these magnificent, if moody, landscapes.

About one-seventh of Ireland is bog—three million acres (1,200,000 ha) of the stuff, either in the form of blanket bog or raised bog. Blanket bog tends to occur in the west, generally above 1,000 feet (304 m). It is undulating, grassy, and heathery, full of plants, and can smother archaeological sites to a depth of 6 to 10 feet (2–3 m), as at Creggan in County Tyrone (see pp. 320–321) and the Céide Fields of Mayo (see p. 201).

Raised bogs are the bogs of the midlands—acidic, waterlogged morasses of sphagnum moss up to 30 feet deep (9 m), with a level appearance and a scatter of plants such as beaked sedge, deergrass, starlike orange bog asphodel, and the insect-eating sundew.

Ireland is ideal for the growth of bog. The retreating ice age glaciers scraped hollows in the rock and plastered them with impermeable clay. In the rainy climate that followed, lakes developed and filled with vegetation that died but could not rot because of the underlying acidity. Peat formed, piling up into thick mattresses of bog fed by plentiful water supplies—sphagnum can hold up to 20 times its own weight of water in its maze of pores and cells.

Peat—"turf" in Ireland—burns hot and slow when dried, and for thousands of years was cut by hand for domestic use. But the

exploitation increased in a quantum leap in 1946 when Bord na Móna, the Peat Board, was set up to remove as much turf as possible for use in electricity-generating stations, as peat moss for gardeners, and as turf briquettes for domestic fireplaces. The bogs were seen as an almost endless resource—Bord na Móna owned over 200,000 acres (80,000 ha) of land perceived as otherwise valueless, which could yield several million tons of milled peat every year. For half a century the turf-cutting machines ripped up the bogs, with only the occasional pioneering conservationist voice raised now and again to oppose them.

But opinion changed. The bogs came to resemble World War I battlefields, sodden black wastelands so ugly that people began to mourn the destruction. Awareness has grown of their unique interdependent wildlife—the plants that thrive in these inhospitable places, the insects that are attracted by the plants, and the birds that live off the insects.

These young turf diggers traveled into the heart of the Blackwater Bog on Bord na Móna's former turf-workers' railroad, now the Clonmacnoise & West Offaly Railway.

Bord na Móna no longer purchases bog, and it is committed to cease exploitation by 2030. There are grand plans to turn the ruined bogs into wildlife reserves and outdoor recreation areas with lakes, fens, and forests.

Great bogs to visit include the Bog of Allen, 30 miles (48 km) west of Dublin, the Tyrone boglands, east of Omagh, and the Blackwater Bog—20,000 acres (8,000 ha) sprawling across the four counties of Offaly, Westmeath, Roscommon, and Galway.

Near Shannonbridge you can take one of Bord na Móna's Blackwater Bog Tours *(tel 090 96 74450, www.bnm.ie, $$)* aboard the Clonmacnoise & West Offaly Railway, and see for yourself a classic example of the destruction and conservation of bogs. ■

Rock of Dunamase

BROKEN WALLS, ARCHES, AND RUNS OF MASONRY, OUT-
lined against the sky, rise from flowery grass banks on the Rock of
Dunamase in County Laois. Two and a half thousand years of history can be read in these high and poignant remnants of fortifications.

as 500 B.C., it was a natural choice, given its eagle-eye command of 50 miles (80 km) of country. Iron Age men walled the summit round with stone. Whatever the fortification of Dunamase developed into, it was significant enough by 845 for the Vikings to plunder it. In the 12th century Dermot MacMurrough, King of Leinster, built a castle on the rock, which was strengthened by the formidably Anglo-Norman warlord Richard de Clare (better known as Strongbow) when he married MacMurrough's daughter Aoife. In 1650 Cromwell's forces blew it up and ended its active days.

What you see, looking up from the little parking lot, seems like a jumble of ages and stages beyond interpretation, but a quick glance at the explanatory board by the entrance gate will soon give you your bearings. Essentially the rock is divided by walls into **three wards** or defended enclosures through which you climb one by one to reach the summit. An **outer gate** pierces the first wall, and you climb to this across ditches and up banks shaggy with feathery grasses and bracken and spattered with wildflowers. Walk through the outer gate's tall arch and continue your climb up the steep, uneven slope of the **outer ward** or barbican, defended from above and below by stronghold gates. Soon you reach the curtain wall that encloses the top of the rock; its tremendously strong main gate has slit spyholes in each of its flanking towers so that the garrison could keep a watch on all incomers.

The landscape in the eastern half of County Laois, which borders County Kildare to the east and Counties Kilkenny and Carlow to the south, is generally either flat plain or rolling valleys. As a result, the abrupt limestone crag of the Rock of Dunamase, 3 miles (5 km) east of Portlaoise, draws the eye on its own account. The jagged ruins of the fortifications that cover the crag look doubly intriguing because of their elevation and the way they stand out of jungly banks of bracken and scrub. Towers and walls appear as natural extensions of the broken rock on which they are founded.

The Egyptian astrologer Ptolemy was probably referring to Dunamase when he reported on an Irish stronghold he called Dunum. If the rock was fortified as long ago

Left: Ruined drum towers still hold their 12th-century gateways on the Rock of Dunamase.

Portlaoise
🄰 237 D2
Visitor information
✉ Portlaoise, Co. Laois
☎ 0502 21178

Above: The Rock of Dunamase commands fine views: the middle ward, the ruin of the main gate, and the hilly landscape of County Laois.

Once through the main gate you are in the wide **middle ward.** To your right are the square foundations of an excavated gate; to the left a path curves up to a corner of the middle ward's upper wall, with the arched and offset remains of a sally port, from where defenders could rush out and surprise attackers.

If you prefer the direct approach, climb on up through nettles and scrub into the **inner ward** on the top of the rock. The separating wall has all but vanished; but three angles of Strongbow's Norman **keep** stand firm, with round-arched windows in plain, massive walls. The view is wonderful, to the Slieve Bloom Mountains in the west, 15 miles (24 km) away, to the peaks of the Wicklow Mountains 35 miles (56 km) off in the east. ■

Fatal attraction

It was Dermot MacMurrough, King of Leinster and builder of the castle on the Rock of Dunamase, who was responsible for bringing the English—or at any rate the Anglo-Normans—over to Ireland in 1169.

MacMurrough's affair with Dervorgilla, wife of Tiernan O'Rourke, had resulted in exile at the decree of O'Rourke's patron Rory O'Connor, High King of Ireland. England's King Henry II had obtained a Papal Bull in 1155 that authorized him to conquer and subjugate Ireland, and when the exiled MacMurrough approached him for help in his quarrel, Henry had exactly the excuse he needed. ■

Walks: Slieve Bloom Mountains

The Slieve Bloom Mountains rise from the level grassy plains of County Laois, a range of heathery hills with tremendous views from their windswept tops. Tucked into their flanks are secret valleys with waterfalls, woodlands, and plenty of sheltered paths. Here are two walks to introduce you to these splendid hills—one in a hidden valley, the other up on the crest.

WALK I—CLAMPHOLE FALLS

From the **Glenbarrow parking lot** walk down a track marked "Tinnahinch 3 km." In about 200 yards (183 m) bear left at a yellow arrow through the trees for 1 mile (1.6 km). This forest plantation is mainly of spruce and pine, and is a beautiful shady walk. Watch for red squirrels, which sadly have become extremely rare in Britain but are still quite widespread in Ireland.

After about 0.5 mile (1 km) you will reach an area of bare rock along the riverbed, an **old** quarry ❶ where the sandstone floor has been shaped into square flags. Shortly you will reach the **Clamphole Falls** ❷, a lovely stretch of water tumbling over sandstone boulders where locals come to picnic. In the sandstone of the river bed you'll be able to distinguish some rippling lines—marks hewn by the constant action of waves when the Slieve Bloom Mountains were a flat flood plain in ancient times.

From the falls, simply retrace your steps to the parking lot.

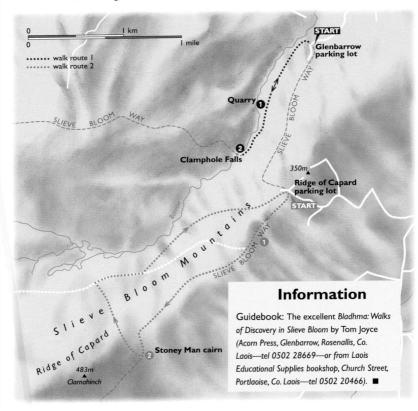

0   1 km
0   1 mile

• • • • • walk route 1
• • • • • walk route 2

START
Glenbarrow parking lot

SLIEVE BLOOM WAY

Quarry ❶

SLIEVE BLOOM WAY

❷
Clamphole Falls

350m
▲
Ridge of Capard parking lot

START

❶

SLIEVE BLOOM WAY

Slieve Bloom Mountains

SLIEVE BLOOM WAY

Slieve
Bloom
Ridge of Capard

483m
▲
Clarnahinch

❷ **Stoney Man cairn**

Information

Guidebook: The excellent *Bladhma: Walks of Discovery in Slieve Bloom* by Tom Joyce (Acorn Press, Glenbarrow, Rosenallis, Co. Laois—tel 0502 28669—or from Laois Educational Supplies bookshop, Church Street, Portlaoise, Co. Laois—tel 0502 20466). ■

The Slieve Bloom Mountains provide wonderful walks for strong and determined hikers.

WALK 2—RIDGE OF CAPARD

From the **Ridge of Capard parking lot,** pass the waymark for the **Slieve Bloom Way ❶**. This fine long-distance footpath makes a 31-mile (50 km) circuit of the peaks and ridges of Slieve Bloom. It's a tough but enjoyable hike.

Follow the Slieve Bloom Way, a moorland track labeled "Monicknew 8 km," through the heather for about 500 yards (450 m). Turn right along a graveled road for 100 yards (91 m) before bearing left across the heather, following pole markers southwest for 1.5 miles (2 km) to the **Stoney Man cairn ❷** seen ahead as you approach.

The Slieve Blooms swell out of a wild area of low-lying midlands country, and views from the Ridge of Capard are superb, extending over scores of miles out across the flat landscape of hayfields and woodland some 1,000 feet below (300 m). Don't spurn the wildlife of the heather: there are beautiful mosses and lichens of different types, described in Tom Joyce's book *(see information box)*. The tall cairn called the Stoney Man is a great place to picnic.

From the cairn, either retrace your steps to the parking lot, or bear right and descend over thick heather and through forestry trees to the forest road in the valley bottom. Turn right, and where the road divides take the left fork to return to the parking lot. ∎

WALK I

🅜 See area map p. 237 C2

➤ Glenbarrow parking lot (N7 to New Inn, 13 miles/21 km W of Kildare; R422 to Rosenallis; follow signs to Glenbarrow parking lot)

↔ 2 miles (3 km)

🕐 1–2 hours

➤ Glenbarrow parking lot

NOT TO BE MISSED
- Red squirrels in the plantations
- "Wave" lines in the rock of the riverbed
- A paddle in the pools at Clamphole Falls

WALK 2

🅜 See area map p. 237 C2

➤ Ridge of Capard parking lot (from Rosenallis—see above—take the Mountrath road and follow "Ridge of Capard" signs)

↔ 3.5 miles (5.5 km)

🕐 2 hours

➤ Ridge of Capard parking lot

NOT TO BE MISSED
- View from the Ridge of Capard
- Lichens and mosses of the heather
- View from the Stoney Man cairn

Kells & Trim

The giant keep of Trim Castle, guarded by curtain walls and D-shaped towers, stands above the River Boyne as an enduring expression of Norman power in Ireland.

THIS MODEST COUNTRY TOWN IN THE NORTHWEST OF County Meath is famous for just one thing: the Book of Kells, created in the monastery here about 807. Kells people are proud of the connection, so don't raise the possibility that the "World's Most Beautiful Book" might have been made in St. Columba's monastery on the Scottish island of Iona! Although the glorious book is kept in Trinity College, Dublin (see pp. 54–55), Kells is worth exploring for its magnificent high crosses and tiny oratory known as St. Columba's House.

Kells

🅰 237 D4

Visitor information

✉ Headfort Pl., Kells,
Co. Meath

☎ 046 9049336

Kells Heritage Centre

✉ Headfort Pl., Kells,
Co. Meath

☎ 046 9049336

🕐 Call ahead; days
vary year to year

💲 $$

St. Columba founded Kells Monastery in 559. A tenth-century **round tower** stands in a churchyard on the site now, a fine but capless cylinder 100 feet high (30 m).

Just up from the churchyard is **St. Columba's House,** a little oratory with a steep corbeled roof and a ladder to a tiny room under the roof space. It probably dates back to around the time that the round tower was built, but it might be contemporary with the arrival of the Iona monks at the turn of the ninth century.

The four ninth-century **high crosses** in the churchyard are worth close inspection. The **South**

Cross, or **"Cross of St. Patrick and St. Columba,"** is the finest, carved with scenes typical of high-cross art including the Burning Fiery Furnace, Doomsday, and the Crucifixion. The **North Cross** is only a stump; the **West Cross** is a shaft with Noah's ark and the Judgement of Solomon, while the **East Cross** displays a Crucifixion.

Kells's other high cross, the **Market Cross,** is a tenth-century sculpture; stories say that United Irish rebels were hanged from it in 1798. It stands outside the **Heritage Centre,** which houses monastic finds and replicas of the Market Cross and the Book of Kells.

TRIM

Set on the River Boyne some 15 miles (24 km) south of Kells, the historic town of Trim has two castles, two cathedrals, and enough monastic remains to keep you interested for a day.

The main sights at Trim are grouped north and south of the Boyne in the town center, with another group a mile (1.6 km) out to the east around the cemetery and St. Peter's Bridge.

Looming over the south side of the river is **Trim Castle,** the largest fortress in Ireland. It was built mostly in the early 13th century on the site of an earlier castle that was burned by Rory O'Connor, King of Connacht, in 1174, the year after it was built.

There was no such danger with the new castle, though, which by the mid-13th century had a curtain wall almost 500 yards long (457 m) that enclosed 3 acres (1.2 ha) of ground, a huge square keep 70 feet tall (21 m) with walls 11 feet thick (3 m), several sallyports, and ten D-shaped towers.

Opposite the castle on the north bank of the Boyne stands **Talbot's Castle,** a fine fortified manor built in 1415 by Sir John Talbot, battlefield opponent of St. Joan of Arc. Behind it the 14th-century **Yellow Steeple** is all that remains of St. Mary's Abbey.

Along the Boyne to the east of the town you come to **St. Peter's Bridge,** a handsome Norman span. South of the river here is the **Crutched Friary—**a fine 13th-century chapel and keep that belonged to the Crutched or Crossed Friars—they wore a red cross as a badge of honor, having assisted the crusaders.

North of the river and a little west is the ruined early 13th-century **Cathedral of St. Peter and St. Paul.** In the cemetery alongside lie the effigies of Sir Lucas Dillon (died 1593) and his wife, Jane, side by side, but separated by a sword. It symbolizes the rift caused when Jane had a fling with her brother-in-law. If you suffer from warts, prick them with a pin dipped in the pool of rainwater between the husband and wife— a certain cure, so locals say. ∎

Trim

🗺 237 E3

Visitor information

✉ Town Hall, Castle St., Trim, Co. Meath

☎ 046 9037111 or 046 9037227

🕐 Closed Thurs. Sept.–April

Hill of Tara

THE HILL OF TARA RISES FROM THE MEATH PLAINS
and commands 100 miles (160 km) of view. For a thousand years, all
through the first millennium, the High Kings of Ireland based themselves at Tara, and it became the symbol and seat of Irish government.
It is a powerfully moving place, soaked in history and heroic myth.

Hill of Tara site
 237 E3
Visitor information
✉ Off the N3, 7.5
   miles (12 km) S of
   Navan, Co. Meath
☎ 046 9025903
🕐 Closed Nov.–April;
   hill accessible at all
   times
💲 $

It was here that beautiful Gráinne
persuaded Diarmuid of the Fianna
to elope with her on the eve of her
wedding to Fionn MacCumhaill.
Tara was also the venue for the
great war council of Nuada the
Silver-handed, king of the magical
De Danaan, when defeat by the
fierce Fomorians looked inevitable.
The god Lugh the Long-handed
turned up providentially, and
proved his right to act as the De
Danaan's champion by slinging
heavy flagstones over the palace
wall and beating all comers at
fidchell, a kind of mythic chess.
When the time came for single
combat, Lugh felled the Fomorian
champion, Balor of the Evil Eye—
his own grandfather—with a well-
aimed *tathlun,* or magic stone.

Another tale tells of Conn of the
Hundred Battles standing on the
Lialh Fáil, the Stone of Destiny on
the Royal Seat, and causing it to let
out a great scream—the sign by
which the rightful High Kings of
Ireland could be identified.

In 435 St. Patrick lit an Easter
fire on the nearby Hill of Slane to
challenge the pagan fires on Tara;
then he came across to negotiate
with Laoghaire, the High King, for
the right to preach Christianity—
not in a spirit of confrontation, but
with a suggestion of partnership.

EXPLORING THE SITE

Archaeologically speaking, the Hill
of Tara was occupied for at least
3,000 years before its abandonment
in 1022. Entering the site from the
visitor center (a former church),

you are aware of multiple lumps
and bumps, and with the center's
booklet in hand your imagination
will quickly clothe them with both
fact and fancy. The northern part of
the hill contains the huge trenches
of a sunken entrance to Tara, 750
feet long (228 m), known as the
Banquet Hall—a thousand men
could feast in it together, say the
legends. Nearby is **Gráinne's
Fort,** a ditched mound, and the
circular **Sloping Trenches** where
Dúnlaing, King of Ulster, massacred
30 princesses of Tara in 222.

Going south along the hill, opposite the visitor center you pass the
three-ringed Iron Age hill fort called
the **Rath of the Synods,** where
two superb gold collars or torques
were found in 1810 (now in Dublin's
National Museum of Archaeology
and History; see pp. 58–61). The
largest embanked area, the **Royal
Enclosure,** comes next and encloses three sites. **Dumha na nGiall,**
the Mound of the Hostages, a grassy
hummock with a low doorway, is a
Stone Age passage grave where the
great High King Cormac MacArt
(A.D. 227–266) imprisoned captives
from Connacht until they died.

Side by side to the south are
Cormac's House, a Bronze Age
burial mound, and the ring fort
called the **Royal Seat** where the
Lialh Fáil or **Stone of Destiny**—
a fine pillar stone—stands alone.
Farther south from the Royal
Enclosure you reach another ring
fort, **Rath Laoghaire,** where King
Laoghaire is said to be buried standing upright in full battle gear. ■

**Opposite: In the
Royal Enclosure
on top of the Hill
of Tara, Cormac's
House stands to
the right of the
Royal Seat, with
the Stone of
Destiny at the
hub. Beyond lies
the smaller
Mound of the
Hostages.**

Brú na Bóinne

IN A LONG BEND OF THE RIVER BOYNE LIES BRÚ NA BÓINNE, the Palace by the Boyne—more than 50 ancient monuments that record the beliefs and religious practices of pre-Christian ancestors, in Europe's most concentrated site. Though most of that record is indecipherable, the sheer power of these tombs, henges, forts, and standing stones—especially the giant passage grave of Newgrange—is overwhelming.

Brú na Bóinne

- 237 E4
- Boyne Valley Archaeological Park, 7 miles (11 km) SW of Drogheda, Co. Meath
- 041 988 0300
- $

Most of the monuments of Brú na Bóinne stand on private land and are inaccessible to the public, and it is the three great passage graves of Newgrange, Knowth, and Dowth that attract all the attention. Of these, **Dowth** is open only to archaeological excavators for the foreseeable future, while **Knowth**—its stones richly carved

with circles, arcs, snake patterns, and one extraordinary "sundial" motif—can only be visited on an external tour.

So the kernel of a visit to Brú na Bóinne consists of the exhibition in the **visitor center,** followed by a tour to the heart of the Newgrange tomb. This tour is immensely popular, so it is wise to arrive early

in the day to secure a place.

Across Europe, the period between 4000 and 3000 B.C. saw the building of passage graves—tombs of stone, with a passage leading from the entrance to a burial chamber or complex of chambers at the heart of the structure. They varied from small tombs only a few feet long to vast mounds that took decades to complete.

Newgrange is one of the biggest, a man-made hill 280 feet (85 m) in diameter, 35 feet (11 m) high. The core of the mound consists of stones, 200,000 tons (200,000 tonnes) of them at least, layered with clay and shells from the Boyne, while a row of 97 massive stone blocks secures the circular external wall of the tomb. The small Stone Age farming community liv-

ing around this curve of the Boyne Valley 5,000 years ago—average life expectancy 30 years—would probably have taken between 40 and 80 years to erect the tomb.

But this was no haphazard mounding of material. The huge hill of stone is only a covering for the internal structure of the tomb—a stone-lined and stone-roofed passage 62 feet long (19 m) that leads from the doorway, with its threshold stone elaborately carved in spirals, to a corbeled **chamber** deep inside the mound. Off this chamber lie three recesses, holding two big shallow sandstone bowls or dishes. Passage and recesses are heavily carved with whorls, spirals, and wavy lines.

More remarkable still is the slit-shaped aperture above the door,

The great burial mound of Newgrange. On the winter solstice a shaft of the light of the newly risen sun pierces right into its heart.

known as the **roof-box.** The mound's doorway is precisely aligned with the position of the sun at dawn on December 21, the winter solstice, in such a way that on that day, and a couple of days either side of it, a ray of the rising sun penetrates the roof-box and pierces into the very heart of the tomb. For about a quarter of an hour the central chamber is flushed with golden light; then the finger of light withdraws along the passage. It is an intensely moving experience for those lucky few who are admitted just before the dawn of each winter solstice. So keen is the competition to witness the phenomenon that a ten-year waiting list has been closed until further notice.

What the tomb-builders intended is open to speculation.

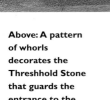

Mound of stones and turves

Above: A pattern of whorls decorates the Threshhold Stone that guards the entrance to the Newgrange tomb.

Front retaining wall of white quartzite stones

Remains of stone circle surrounding mound

The white stones that face the walls of the monument are of Wicklow quartz, and must have been brought by sea raft or coracle.

Standing stones guard the tomb in a loose ring. Evidently some irresistible imperative drove them to take on this huge task of planning, organizing, and building. A clue may lie in the cremation ashes found in the central recesses'

shallow dishes. They formed the remains of only half-a-dozen people, and it is surmised that the tomb may have been periodically cleared of remains to make way for the next few months' cremations. Perhaps the people believed that on the shortest day of the year the spirits of their dead rode the shaft of light out of the tomb, to help ensure the return of spring. ■

Below: Brú na Bóinne in its restored condition today

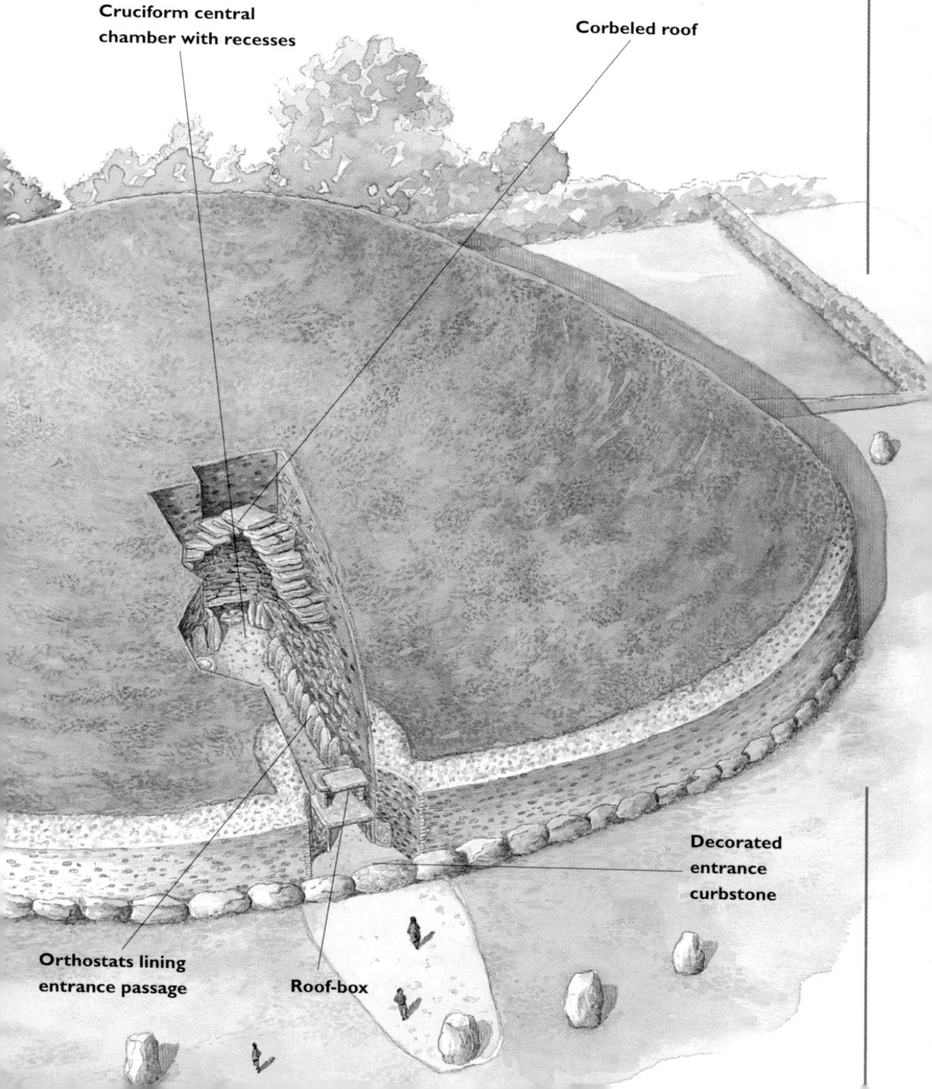

Cruciform central chamber with recesses

Corbeled roof

Decorated entrance curbstone

Orthostats lining entrance passage

Roof-box

The Irish Sea is not always calm off County Louth, so boats need strengthened storm decks.

Drive: Drogheda to Dundalk along the coast

You could zip from Drogheda to Dundalk in half an hour by way of the N1 highway, but the aim of following this meandering route northward up the coast of County Louth is to take your time, dipping in and out of the coastline and the little villages en route with neither time nor other visitors on your heels.

Drogheda ❶ *(visitor information, tel 041 983 7070 or 041 9845684, $)* is a historic town of gray stone built beside the River Boyne, with plenty to see and do. From **Millmount,** the ancient mound south of the river, you get a good panorama over Drogheda. Millmount is topped by a **Martello tower** built in 1808 as a defense against a possible invasion by the French under Napoleon Bonaparte. Below the tower is the fine **Millmount Museum** *(Mill-mount, Drogheda, Co. Louth, tel 041 983 3097),* whose display features the splendid 19th-century painted canvas banners of the Drogheda trades societies.

In the town itself, **St. Peter's Church** on West Street is notable for displaying the prison letters, the cell door, and the leathery brown severed head of St. Oliver Plunkett

(1629–1681), Archbishop of Armagh, who was hanged, drawn, and quartered for treason. He was canonized three centuries later.

From Drogheda take the N1 Belfast road and turn off to **Termonfeckin ❷** (signed on the right just uphill from the bridge in Drogheda). In the churchyard of St. Fechin's Church in Termonfeckin (entrance on the right some 150 yards/137 m past the bridge) stands a tenth-century **high cross,** blotched with lichens, with Christ in Glory on the west face and fine interlacing on the east. In front of the cross is set another ancient piece of sculpture—a much-weathered **Crucifixion** featuring a soldier piercing Christ with his spear.

Beyond the church (signed) stands the rugged three-storied **Termonfeckin Castle**

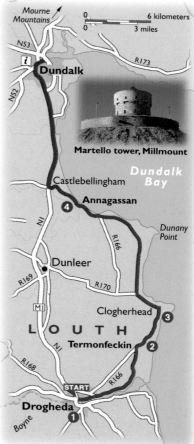

⚑ See area map p. 237 E4
► Drogheda
⇄ 27 miles (43 km)
⏱ 2–3 hours
► Dundalk

NOT TO BE MISSED
- Millmount Museum
- Relics of St. Oliver Plunkett, St. Peter's Church
- Termonfeckin high cross
- Coast views of the Mountains of Mourne
- Annagassan's harbor

Martello tower, Millmount

(key from the bungalow opposite), whose corbeled roofs still hold up. Previous owners (they included the Archbishop of Armagh) had the right to first choice of the local fishermen's catch.

From Termonfeckin, continue along the R166 to **Clogherhead ❸;** bear right in the village to reach the sandy **beach,** great for exploring rock pools and walking. Back on the road, a right turn (blue "Port Oriel" sign) leads in a mile (1.6 km) to the little **harbor** with its rusty trawlers. Here stands a roadside shrine to Mary, Queen of the Sea, built in memory of locals who lost their lives at sea.

Back on the R166, in 1.5 miles (2.5 km) a right turn (blue "scenic route" sign) leads to a beautiful lonely **scenic drive** by sandy beaches and through forgotten farmland where long straight tracks lead to houses hidden among trees.

Turn left on the R166 ("Annagassan 4" sign), with superb views of the Mourne Mountains ahead, to **Annagassan ❹,** with its friendly **Glyde Inn** next to **O'Neill's Bakery**—an instant indoor picnic. The little **harbor** is signed off the village street; creel boats on mud banks, an old ivy-covered kiln, and a huge iron anchor.

Continue to the N1 at Castlebellingham, and head north to Dundalk. ∎

The great round tower at Monasterboice was built late in the tenth century as a stronghold against the marauding Vikings.

Monasterboice

IN THIS COMPACT SITE IN COUNTY LOUTH NORTHWEST OF Drogheda, many superb early Christian monuments rub shoulders in close proximity. Muiredach's Cross, in particular, is the finest high cross in Ireland, a tenth-century masterpiece of the stonecarver's art.

Monasterboice

🅰 237 E4

✉ Collon, Co. Louth, 6 miles (10 km) NW of Drogheda. Turn left off the N1 from Drogheda near Monasterboice Inn

☎ 041 983 7070

Monasterboice stands in a beautiful rural location among rolling green fields, although trees mask the full glory of the site until you are right up close. Then you see the round tower, the high crosses, and the shells of the churches, and realize that this is one of Ireland's most striking collective monuments.

A disciple of St. Patrick, a hermit named Buite (or Buithe, Boethius or Boyce—even Boyne: It's claimed that the river was named after him) founded the

monastery sometime late in the fifth century. Buite died in 521; the angels lowered a ladder from the sky to enable him to climb straight into heaven. His monastery grew to exert great influence, becoming a famous center of learning.

Monasterboice survived a Viking occupation in 968, during which the marauders were driven out by a force from Tara led by the High King himself, Donal. After that, the 110-foot (33 m) **round tower** was constructed, a tremendously tall structure tapering toward the top, built with curved stones to make the cylindrical shape. The windows are no more than impenetrable defensive slits, and the door is 6 feet (2 m) off the ground. Entrance for the monks would have been via a ladder, which could be pulled up in times of attack. The interior of the tower burned in 1097, along with many of Monasterboice's valuables, and shortly afterward the monastery declined as the newly built Mellifont Abbey (see p. 278) prospered.

Ancient graveslabs, some perhaps from monastic times, surround the round tower and the two ruined churches in its shadow—**An Teampall Theas,** the South Church, and **An Teampall Thuaidh,** the North Church. In pride of place, though, are the three tenth-century high crosses. The **North Cross,** standing by itself beside the graveyard wall, has a weatherbeaten, whorly pattern to its head. The **West Cross,** beside An Teampall Thuaidh, is huge—21 feet tall (6 m)—and composed of separate shaft, wheelcross, and cap. Many of the carved panels are eroded beyond deciphering, but the Crucifixion in the center of the west-facing wheel is clear, and on the east face are scenes of Christ walking on the Sea of Galilee, the giant Goliath, and the children of Israel worshiping the golden calf.

The **South Cross** near the site entrance—otherwise known as **Muiredach's Cross**—stands 18 feet tall (5 m). Wheel and shaft were carved from the same piece of sandstone, with a cap shaped like a gabled house with a tiled roof on top and a base carved with the inscription "*Or do Muiredach Lasndernad Chros*"(A prayer for Muiredach, for whom this cross was made). Muiredach (died 923) was abbot of Monasterboice, and

the high cross would have been erected shortly after his death as a memorial and as a symbol of the wealth of Monasterboice.

All four sides of the cross, shaft, and wheel are heavily carved with biblical scenes. On the east face Christ sits in judgment in the central boss of the wheel. Beneath his feet St. Michael weighs souls, while the devil yanks down the scales. On the shaft below, four (not the conventional three) Wise Men worship the Infant Jesus; Moses knocks water miraculously out of a desert rock while ranks of Israelites look on; David readies a big slingshot for Goliath; and Eve offers Adam the fateful apple, while a beskirted Cain smacks Abel with a cudgel. On the west side is a central Crucifixion; then comes Christ presenting St. Peter with the keys of heaven; Doubting Thomas having his misgivings disproved by a rank of tablet-wielding apostles; and Judas delivering a betrayer's kiss in the Garden of Gethsemane. ∎

Right: Biblical preoccupations of the tenth century are depicted with stiff-limbed precision on the east face of Muiredach's Cross.

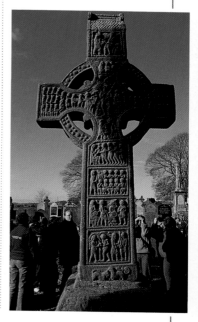

Walk the Cooley Peninsula: Táin Trail

This is a straightforward there-and-back walk with the most spectacular coastal and mountain views as reward for a little effort. The Cooley Peninsula in County Louth is a largely unfrequented corner of Ireland, so you are more than likely to have all this beauty to yourself.

Carlingford village ❶ *(visitor information tel 042 937 3033, closed Oct.–May)* looks out on Carlingford Lough, a superb wide inlet that separates County Louth in the Republic of Ireland from the Mourne Mountains in County Down, Northern Ireland.

Carlingford stands on the northern shore of the Cooley Peninsula, a glorious hump-backed piece of country with a mountainous spine and fertile green skirts. The village's neat, whitewashed streets stand under 1,930-foot (588 m) Slieve Foye, highest point of the knobbly ridge of Carlingford Mountain.

By the water's edge is the 12th-century **King John's Castle,** clinging romantically to its rock overlooking the fishing harbor. On the waterfront street stands **Taafe's Castle,** a 16th-century tower house of grim aspect.

Begin your walk at the **Village Hotel** on the square in Carlingford. Walk up the road that rises from the top of the square, and in about 300 yards (250 m) turn left for 0.5 mile (0.75 km). At a T-junction you'll see a "Táin Trail" marker post with its "walking man" logo. Turn right here, and follow the Táin Trail posts as they take you up onto a grassy path that bends back to the right above the village as it climbs the mountainside. This is a zigzag trail, steady but not steep!

Be sure to stop and look around frequently, because the views get better all the time. Across Carlingford Lough you will see the **Mourne Mountains** rise in ruggedly beautiful shapes, 1,600-foot (485 m) Slievemartin toward the left above the northern lough shore, the bulks of Eagle Mountain (2,090 feet/635 m) and Slieve Muck (2,210 feet/672 m) miles back in center frame, and over to

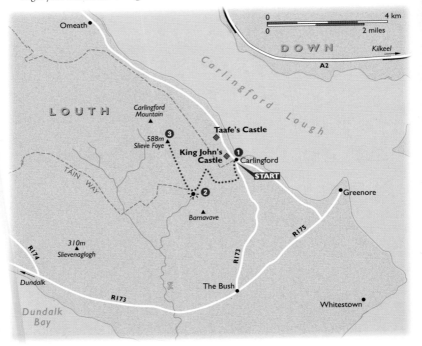

The wild moorland hills of the Cooley Peninsula offer superb, uncrowded walks.

the right the 2,450-foot (745 m) peak of Slieve Binnian. Up the lough the twin villages of Rostrevor and Warrenpoint lie by the water.

From the **saddle of the pass** ❷ at the top of the path this view is at its best, and another spectacular southwesterly view opens from this vantage point as well. The slopes of Carlingford Mountain rise away to your right, the lower shoulder of Barnavave to your left. In front the broad green valley of the Big River falls away toward Dundalk Bay, with a great sweep of coastline running away south for 15 miles (24 km) to Dunany Point.

You can retrace the Táin Trail down to Carlingford from here, but if you have enough energy it is worth bearing northeast for the steep but not difficult climb to the **summit of Slieve Foye** ❸ (around another 950-foot/300 m), where the views are even better.

From here, return the way you came. ■

🗺 See area map p. 237 F5
➤ Village Hotel, Carlingford, Cooley Peninsula
↔ 5 miles/8 km (7 miles/11 km with ascent of Slieve Foye)
🕐 2 hours (3 hours)
➤ Carlingford

NOT TO BE MISSED
- Carlingford village and its castles
- View of Carlingford Lough and the Mourne Mountains from the Táin Trail
- View to the southwest from the pass
- Slieve Foye—the climb and the view

More places to visit in Central Ireland

ABBEYLEIX

Viscount de Vesci, 18th-century Lord of Abbeyleix House, had a model village laid out at his gates—wide streets lined with trees, handsome buildings, and a very Georgian sense of order and calm. The **Abbeyleix Heritage House** in the former school gives a good runthrough of the place's history. When you have walked your fill around the village, take it easy over a pint in the self-consciously charming **Morrissey's** pub on Main Street, a stoutly unchanged old-fashioned bar dating from 1735, with grocer's shop attached.

🅰 237 D1 ✉ On the N8 Portlaoise–Kilkenny road, 9 miles (14 km) S of Portlaoise, Co. Laois **Abbeyleix Heritage House** ☎ 0502 31653 💲 $

BECTIVE ABBEY

In a glorious riverside setting by a bridge over the Knightsbrook River, Bective Abbey featured in the 1995 Mel Gibson blockbuster film *Braveheart*. The location is beautiful, and the ruins of the Cistercian abbey do full justice to their setting. Bective grew into being over the centuries; the cruciform church and the rib-vaulted chapter house are 13th-century work, while the cloisters date from the 15th century. After the abbey was suppressed in the 16th century a battlemented tower—incongruous but impressive-looking—was added to turn the abbey into a fortified house.

Huge de Lacy, Anglo-Norman Lord of Meath, was buried here in 1195. A man of ambition, he had the misfortune to be beheaded by an Offaly peasant, one O'Kearney, who objected to de Lacy demolishing Durrow Abbey to build a castle on the site.

🅰 237 E3 ✉ Signed off the R161, 4 miles (6 km) NE of Trim, Co. Meath **Trim visitor information** ☎ 046 9037111 or 046 9037227

EMO COURT

James Gandon, designer of Dublin's fabulous Custom House, made Emo Court his sole private commission. He designed it in 1792 for Lord Portarlington, creating a superb neo-classical house under a big dome. The main rooms, beautifully restored, form the focus of a tour round the house. The gardens are immaculate: classical statues stand among azaleas and rhododendrons, with paths leading down to a gorgeous lakeside walk.

☎ 237 D2 ✉ Off the N7 Kildare–Portlaoise road, at New Inn, 6 miles (10 km) NE of Portlaoise, Co. Laois ☎ 0502 26573 🕐 House closed mid-Sept.–mid-June; gardens remain open 💲 $

LOUGHCREW PASSAGE GRAVES

Up on the peaks of Sliabh na Caillighe, the Hill of the Witch, 32 passage cairns of 3000–2500 B.C. wait to be explored. Many have their stones incised with markings—mazy circles and zigzags, snaky lines, and what seem to be flowers. Take a flashlight, and be prepared for a 15-minute uphill climb.

🅰 237 D4 ✉ On Sliabh na Caillighe hill (parking lot), signed from the R154 5 miles (8 km) SE of Oldcastle (13 miles/21 km NW of Kells by the R163/R154), Co. Meath ☎ 049 8542009 or 041 9824488 🕐 Collect key from the Naper family nearby; it is essential to telephone in advance (049 8541922). 💲 Deposit required for key

MELLIFONT ABBEY

At the height of its medieval power, Mellifont Abbey supported a community of 400 and commanded more than 20 lesser houses. It was the nerve center and headquarters of the Cistercian order in Ireland, having been the order's pioneer house when established in 1142 by St. Malachy, Archbishop of Armagh, to put some discipline and rigor into Irish monastic life. By the 1550s it had been suppressed and turned into a fortified house; in 1727 it was abandoned; by the 19th century it was being used as a pigsty. So the mighty fell.

These days you can admire the big gatehouse, a gorgeous 14th-century vaulted chapter house, and something unique among Irish monastic remains—an octagonal 12th-century lavabo, or monks' washing place. Four sides remain, with beautifully carved Romanesque archways.

🅰 237 E4 ✉ 5 miles (8 km) NW of Drogheda, signed off the R168 and N2, Co. Louth ☎ 041 982 6459 🕐 Closed Nov.–April 💲 $ ■

The mordant wit of Belfast and Londonderry, the easy pace of conversations in the country towns, and humor wherever you go: The Northern Irish are extraordinarily welcoming, and extremely proud of their hills, lakelands, and coast.

Northern Ireland

**Bushmills Distillery—
there's liquid gold in them
thar barrels.**

Belfast

NO CAPITAL CITY IN WESTERN EUROPE HAS HAD A HIGHER NEWS PROFILE IN recent times than Belfast. Paradoxically, no city is more undervisited and misunderstood. Yet Belfast is one of the most interesting and, in its gritty way, enjoyable cities in either the Republic of Ireland or Northern Ireland for anyone prepared to spend a few days here with an open mind. The ordinary visitor is less likely to experience trouble or antagonism in Belfast, in fact, than in most other comparable European cities. Uncertain and halting as the peace process may be, Belfast people—like the people of every corner of Northern Ireland—are only too keen to show how greatly they appreciate visitors as symbols of the better times that are opening for the whole troubled province.

Belfast sits handsomely at the inner end of Belfast Lough, with a fine ridge of hills on the west—Black Hill, Black Mountain, Divis, Squire's Hill, and Cave Hill. The city is divided in two by the River Lagan, which winds its way

Victorian civic pride filled Belfast's center with splendid 19th-century buildings.

north into Belfast Lough. East of the river there's very little to see; the city center and almost all the other attractions are to the west of the Lagan.

If you are expecting a gleaming modern city you will be disappointed. Belfast was made prosperous by the textile and shipbuilding trades, and it has the appearance of a Victorian manufacturing city, one that could have been transplanted whole from the industrial north of England. There are grandiose 19th-century public buildings and churches, canyonlike shopping streets with big stores and warehouses, acres of redbrick terraced workers' housing, and tree-lined bourgeois avenues a little farther out.

Since 1998, marking the end of the 30-year Troubles, "peace money" has seen a certain amount of rebuilding and redesigning. The once stinking River Lagan in particular has been cleaned up and the riverfront now has a visitor center plus an array of new and refurbished buildings. Yet Belfast retains its old essential character—solid, busy, and rather shabby. The grandest buildings—the Town Hall, the Opera House, and St. Anne's Cathedral in particular—stand in the heart of the city, with the Botanic Gardens, that splendid symbol of Victorian philanthropic provision, to the south.

The best way to see all this is slowly. Be sure to talk to as many people as possible. Chat to the driver as you ride in a black taxi to see the sectarian murals, have a drink and a plate of champ (mashed potato and spring onions) in the ornate Crown Liquor Saloon, or stroll up on Cave Hill or out along the Lagan towpath. Belfast generosity and black humor make a potent tonic. ■

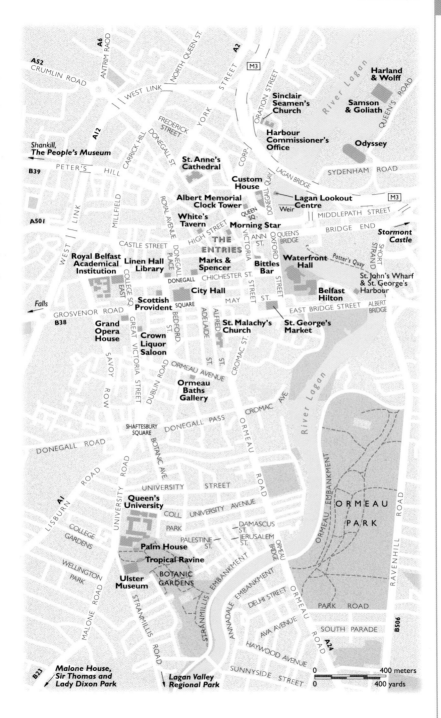

Center Belfast

BELFAST CITY CENTER HAS TWO VERY DISTINCT CHARACTERS.
There is the solemn grandeur of the great Victorian public
buildings—and there's the quickfire humor and friendliness of the
locals you'll meet on your strolls.

Belfast

⚑ 281

Visitor information

www.belfastcity.gov.uk

✉ Belfast Welcome
   Centre, 35 Donegall
   Pl., Belfast

☎ 028 9024 6609

DONEGALL SQUARE

Any stroll around the center of
Belfast should start in Donegall
Square, in the very heart of the city.
This fine wide plaza, with its central
lawns and gardens, contains many
of Belfast's best civic buildings.
Pride of place goes to the giant
City Hall (tel 028 9027 0456, public tours at variable times; call for
information and reserve in advance),
a great white wedding cake of a
building in pale Portland stone.
Begun in 1898 and opened in 1906,
its sheer size—a mighty portico in
a facade 300 feet long (90 m), a
verdigris-green central dome of
copper that rises 173 feet (53 m)—
and the elaborate confection of its
four corner turrets still breathe the
Edwardian confidence it was
designed to reflect. Queen Victoria
stares stolidly from her plinth in
front of the entrance; and there are
other fine monuments encircling
the City Hall, notably the memorial
to the crew of the Belfast-built
Titanic, and the splendid statue of
Frederick Temple, Lord Dufferin
and Ava (1826–1902).

Anyone who needs a reminder
of the intertwined histories of
Britain and Ireland should look at
Lord Dufferin's effigy. Imperious
but humorous-looking in his
breeches and waxed moustache,
he personifies the Empire-ruling
Briton of the Victorian era. He
was viceroy of India from 1884 to
1888 (a turbaned Sikh flanks him
with shield and saber), governor-
general of Canada (a woolly-
hatted and fur-coated Canadian
guards his other side, toting a
rifle and a caribou head), and
ambassador to Moscow, as well

as the catalyst for bringing Burma into the British Empire.

Walk below the huge pediment (where Hibernia presides over figures emblematic of Belfast's success in industry and the arts) and enter the great hall, highly decorated with three different kinds of Italian marble. Ornate plasterwork of swags and medallions decorates the walls and the interior of the great dome—this is viewed from below, crowning a cylinder of circular galleries and murals depicting the city's history.

The Council Chamber is the highlight of the daily **tours** of the City Hall. It is a sumptuous room, paneled in hand-carved Austrian oak, with red benches for the city councilors and a heavily carved throne for the Lord Mayor under stained-glass windows and a splendid crimson-and-white dome. Here you can also see the plain round wooden table at which Sir Edward Carson signed the Solemn League and Covenant against Home Rule on September 28, 1912, a document subsequently signed by thousands of Orangemen (see pp. 310–311), some in their own blood. The table was knocked together quickly out of rough wood especially for the signing ceremony.

In a nearby corridor hangs a vigorous and moving painting of Ulstermen in a conflict that united Irishmen across the political and religious divides. Thousands of Northern Irish Catholics and Protestants, unionists and nationalists, joined up to fight with British Crown forces during World War I. The picture shows 17-year-old 2nd Lieutenant Thornley and his men of the Ulster Division on July 1, 1916, the opening day of the Battle of the Somme, rushing forward from a captured trench with fresh blood gleaming on their bayonets.

Notable commercial and civic

buildings flank Donegall Square. The ornate, sculpture-encrusted **Scottish Provident** building on the west side of the square shows dolphins, queens, and lions, while the red sandstone **Marks & Spencer** building on the north side looks fabulously Italianate. At the northwest corner of the square stands the **Linen Hall Library,** housed in what was a Victorian linen warehouse—stone swaths of the stuff are bunched over the doorway. This is a real honest-to-goodness, old-fashioned library where hushed voices are in order and books stand on wooden shelves by the tens of thousands. In the Members' Room elderly Belfast folk quietly read the daily papers, and you can get an excellent cup of tea in the popular Tea Room. A fine curved wooden staircase leads to the upper floor and more labyrinthine shelving. There are crusty old books, both rare and curious, in the Governor's Room, and bound copies of the *Belfast Newsletter*—the oldest newspaper in the country—dating back to 1738. Any visitor is welcome to

Silence please: The timeless calm and sacred hush of massed books reign in the Linen Hall Library.

Linen Hall Library
- 281
- Donegall Sq. North, Belfast
- 028 9032 1707
- Closed Sun.

inside it is all crimson plush and huge gilt plasterwork elephants, cherubs, and thespians. The Opera House was restored in 1980, partially wrecked by bombs in 1991 and 1993, and restored to glory once more.

Opposite the Opera House is a Belfast drinking institution, the **Crown Liquor Saloon** *(tel 028 9027 9901),* such a remarkable example of extravagant late Victorian pub design that the National Trust now looks after it. Note the crown mosaic at the entrance. The story goes that during an 1895 refurbishment of what was then the Railway Tavern by the owners, Mr. and Mrs. Patrick Flanagan, the lady—a keen loyalist—demanded that the pub be renamed the "Crown" and that a crown image be created and installed. Patrick Flanagan, a dedicated nationalist as well as a wise husband, agreed to carry out his wife's wishes, but had the crown put on the floor so that everyone would wipe their feet on it. You can order a drink at the curved, tiled bar under the plaster foliage and scrollwork of the brown ceiling, and sip it in one of the carved wooden snugs with their frosted glass and handy metal matchstrikers. Try the Crown's famous "champ," a delicious mess of mashed potato and scallions (spring onions), maybe with a couple of pork and leek sausages.

On Ormeau Avenue (due south of Donegall Square by way of Linenhall Street), you'll find the **Ormeau Baths Gallery,** an imaginative conversion of an old swimming bathhouse into a gallery of contemporary art, strong on Irish artists. Just northeast of the gallery on Alfred Street is an early Victorian gem, Catholic **St. Malachy's Church.** An unpromising exterior of dark

trawl through the library's collections, and these include the Political Collection on the second floor, which documents the course of the contemporary Troubles through newspaper clippings, posters, tracts, and other material.

BEYOND DONEGALL SQUARE

A counterclockwise stroll from Donegall Square around the city center sights could start with a westward walk along Wellington Place to College Square, where the handsome brick-built **Royal Belfast Academical Institution** stands in a green setting. It was built in 1814 to a design by Sir John Soane, who also designed the Bank of England and many other London buildings. Going south from the "Inst" (as its pupils, and most of the rest of Belfast, call it), College Square East leads to Great Victoria Street and the wonderfully overblown **Grand Opera House** of 1894–95. "Smiley (comedy) and frowny (tragedy)" symbolic theatrical masks adorn the outside, while

Grand Opera House

- 281
- Great Victoria St., Belfast
- 028 9024 1919

brick and pink paint hides an exuberant interior with fanvaulting, plasterwork, and art nouveau stained-glass windows with tall purple lilies.

Northeast again where Oxford Street meets May Street stands the handsome redbrick **St. George's Market,** a late Victorian market hall where Belfast comes on Tuesdays and Fridays to shop for fresh flowers, fish, fruit, and vegetables under the glass-and-cast-iron roof. Arts events, exhibitions, and craft fairs take place here, too (*tel 028 9027 0386 for details*).

North and east of Donegall Square is another clutch of delights. **The Entries** is a tangled area of alleyways just south of High Street, the heart of old Belfast and full of characterful pubs (see pp. 290–291). At the top of High Street stands an unmistakable Belfast landmark, the 113-foot (35 m) **Albert Memorial Clock Tower,** built in 1865. The tower inclines 4 feet (1.25 m) out of perpendicular; it had to be founded on wooden piles because of the marshy ground, and these founda-

tions have shifted over the years. "Albert has the time and the inclination!" say locals.

The same stretch of boggy ground is responsible for the bumpy nave floor in the Protestant **St. Anne's Cathedral** (*tel 028 9032 8332*) on Donegall Street, west of the Albert Tower. Consecrated in 1904, it is founded on 80 feet (25 m) of log piling, which has moved around. The nave floor is beautiful, though, with Canadian maple and Irish marble, its shapeliness enhanced by the upward sweep of pillars that rise to capitals carved with scenes of the "Occupations of Mankind"—spinning flax, weaving, shipbuilding, seedsowing. Stone from each of Ireland's 32 counties was used in the construction of St. Anne's. There are three beautiful modern east windows full of Christian symbols—fish, vine, wheat, a lamb. Against the north wall you'll find a modest bronze memorial above the grave of Lord Carson (1854–1935), fierce opponent of Home Rule and the leader of Ulster from 1911 to 1921. ■

... then cross
the road to the
Crown Liquor
Saloon for more
imbibing amid
high Victorian
decor.

Ormeau Baths Gallery

www.obgonline.net

🅰 281

✉ 18a Ormeau Ave., Belfast

☎ 028 9032 1402

🕐 Closed Sun. & Mon.

City tours

A CITY LIKE BELFAST, WITH ITS TROUBLED AND EVER evolving history, is often best appreciated at the elbow of a native who can put what you are seeing into context. Embarking on a Black Taxi tour of the sectarian enclaves of West Belfast, a cruise-with-commentary up the River Lagan from the Belfast waterfront, or a guided pub crawl through the heart of the old city, you're bound to catch stories, opinions, and insiders' versions—especially related to the past Troubles in the city—that you would never get hold of by yourself. You needn't necessarily believe everything you are told, however!

Black Taxi to the Troubles enclaves—it's the best way to see the famous murals and learn what they mean.

BLACK TAXI TOURS

Depending on your mood and the chattiness of your driver, a Black Taxi tour of Belfast can be the best fun you'll have in the city. Given a gabby cabby (and almost all of them are), there's no better way to see Belfast from the insider's perspective. Whatever the political or religious affiliations of the driver, he or she will certainly not intrude them on you unless you want him to. You can of course use one of the regular service black taxis—sometimes known as People's Taxis—that ply routes around West Belfast. These started up in the 1970s when bus services were withdrawn from West Belfast because so many buses were being hijacked and used as barricades. The taxis undercut bus fares and operated a buslike service along regular routes. They still operate like buses, so you'll find them stopping to drop and pick up passengers frequently. But the presence of other passengers in the cab may inhibit you from asking questions, and you won't be able to stop when you like. It's better to go for the NITB-approved Black Taxi tours run by Michael Johnston.

You can discuss the route with your driver, who will be happy to tailor-make your tour. The standard route tends to take in some of the waterfront—generally the Lagan Weir, Lagan Lookout, and glimpses of the big Samson & Goliath cranes in Harland & Wolff's shipyard (see p. 299)—as well as city center sights such as the Crown Liquor Saloon, City Hall, and the Grand Opera House (see pp. 282–285). But the main interest of the tour comes

The Lagan Weir has transformed the river from a polluted drain to a pleasant strolling venue.

Black Taxi Tours

www.belfasttours.com

 Departs Belfast city center

☎ 028 9064 2264; Freephone 0800 052 3914

🕐 Tours at 10 a.m., noon, 2 p.m., 4 p.m., 6 p.m. (8 p.m., summer only)

💲 1-2 passengers: $$$$$; 3-6 passengers: $$$ per person

when you swing off toward the Shankill and Falls Roads and the "frontline" Troubles enclaves of West Belfast.

Protestant West Belfast starts on the **Crumlin Road,** with its heavily fenced-in Orange Hall where a statue of King William III rides high on the roof beside the inevitable Loyalist Union Jack flag. Curbstones are painted red, white, and blue (the colors of the flag) hereabouts. Unemployment is high, and many of the old Victorian side streets are slums—though they are being replaced by better housing.

The **Crumlin Road Courthouse** stands forbiddingly on the road, designed by Belfast's paramount Victorian architect Sir Charles Lanyon to personify the Dignity of the Law, with its massive portico and statue of Justice on top (someone stole her scales!).

Facing it is the even more oppressive dark brick **Crumlin Road Gaol;** a tunnel beneath the road connects the two. In the 1970s and '80s the Diplock Courts held their enclosed trials here; in some circumstances a prisoner on remand could find himself incarcerated for years before coming to trial. Now thankfully abandoned, the grim pair await refurbishment and a new life—no one seems to know in what capacity.

A block farther south, the **Shankill Road** runs parallel with the Crumlin Road. The Shankill is the main artery of Protestant West Belfast, essentially an old-fashioned suburban thoroughfare of small family-run shops, pubs, betting

Lights at night highlight the Waterfront Hall's bold design.

The People's Museum

🏛 281

✉ Fernhill House, Glencairn Rd., Belfast

☎ 028 9071 5599

shops, and sole proprietor businesses. You won't fail to notice the barbed wire and reinforced steel around the bookies' premises, though, nor the heavy steel shutters on some shops—tell-tale signs of a community that feels itself under siege. The fierce Loyalist sense of identity is expressed in the enormous murals that cover gable ends and whole house walls (see pp. 292–295). The Black Taxi driver is well aware that the murals, on both sides of the divide, are the main attraction, and is quite happy to stop while you photograph. He'll also tell you about what went on here—in garish detail if you want, but with thoughtful insight if he sees that you are prepared to listen.

If you carry on the whole length of the Shankill Road and continue to the end of Glencairn Road, you'll find **The People's Museum,** a run-through of the social history of the Shankill and also an abridged history of Unionism that will help you better understand the background and the mindset of these Protestant enclaves.

The area of sectarian violence in Belfast was astonishingly small. Barely 100 yards (91 m) separates the Shankill Road from the Catholic-dominated Falls Road and Springfield Road to the south. Here the **Peace Line** was built to keep both sides' extremists, and their fire-bombs, out of the opposing enclave. You can write your own peace message alongside thousands of others on this ugly, depressing, but necessary 20-foot (6 m) wall of concrete, wire, and corrugated tin.

which runs northwest off the Falls Road, the police station—a regular target for attacks at the height of the Troubles—is still hideously fortified. Your driver can tell you about it, also about the many republican dead who are buried in Milltown Cemetery a mile (1.6 km) farther along the Falls Road. It will be strange indeed if you don't finish your Black Taxi tour with a lot more understanding of the city and its problems than you started out with; also with a feeling of admiration for the stoicism and decency of ordinary Belfast people.

RIVER LAGAN CRUISE

The River Lagan cruise on MV *Joyce* shows you a side of Belfast that you won't discover any other way. You set off from Donegall Quay beside the **Lagan Lookout Centre** (see pp. 298–299), with the skipper's humorous and well-informed commentary putting you wise to the history and the current state of development of all you see along this river. The Lagan was a stinking, moribund open sewer until the building of the Lagan Weir in 1994. It's hard to believe nowadays, with salmon and sea trout coming upriver and anglers to be seen along the banks.

The boat goes under the **Queen's Bridge,** Sir Charles Lanyon's first major Belfast project, with its ornate triton lamp standards, and then passes the old **Custom House** (see p. 299) and the west bank developments that include the circular **Waterfront Hall** (1997) and the glassy **Belfast Hilton** (1998). On the opposite bank you catch a glimpse of the giant shipyard cranes **Samson and Goliath** over the long redbrick wall of the old Sirocco works that once made tea-drying machines. New trendy waterside apartments—St. John's Wharf, St.

In much of its appearance and atmosphere, the **Falls Road** mirrors the Shankill, though here the curbstones and flags are orange and green, the nationalist colors. You'll find the same small shops and businesses, the same kind of pubs, and a tremendous array of murals. Hereabouts you may see a sight vanished from almost every other industrial city in the British Isles—children playing on a lamppost swing, scooting and swinging round and round on homemade loops. Insights into Belfast's Catholic cultural heritage can be got in Sinn Fein's little center on the Falls Road, or in **Cultúrlann MacAdam O'Fiaich** a little farther out, an Irish cultural center where you can get lunch or a cup of tea.

Up on the Springfield Road,

River Lagan Cruise
www.loganboatcompany.com
✉ Lagan Boat Company, Donegall Quay, Belfast
☎ 028 9033 0844 or 07718 910423
🕐 Times of cruises: Mon.–Thurs. 12:30 p.m. (except Mon.), 2 p.m., 3:30 p.m.
💲 $$

Cultúrlann MacAdam O'Fiaich
✉ 216 Falls Rd.
☎ 028 9096 4180

Graduation Day at Queen's University

George's Harbour—and the old redbrick warehouses on Potter's Quay, now housing high-tech companies, give way to the big sheds of the Tennants textile company, one of the last of the old-fashioned industries along the river.

Things get more countrified past the big green trees of **Ormeau Park** and the redbrick terraces of the **"Holy Land"**—Damascus Street, Palestine Street, Jerusalem Street—around the Ormeau Road. Oystercatcher, sandpiper, and curlew can be seen on the gravelly river beaches, and the river supports eels, gray mullet, and even sea bass and baby plaice. Kingfishers flash electric blue across reedbeds planted by the Laganside Development Corporation. The overall impression is of a river, and a riverside environment, coming back to life.

GUIDED WALKS

If you like the idea of short guided walks around the city, the Belfast Tourism Development Office lays on an Old Town walk and a Belfast City Centre walk (tel 028 9024 6609). Perhaps the most agreeable form of guided city walk is the **Historical Pub Tour of Belfast** (tel 028 9268 3665) that leaves from Flannigan's upstairs at the Crown Liquor Saloon (see p. 284) on Tuesdays at 7 p.m. and Saturdays at 4 p.m. from May to the end of September. Each of these pleasant pub crawls takes in 6 out of 11 carefully chosen premises.

Particularly enjoyable are **White's Tavern** in Winecellar Entry off Lombard Street, Belfast's oldest pub (it dates back to 1630), a black-beamed, stone-floored drinking den with great character; the splendid peninsula wooden bar and railed-off snugs in the stylish old **Morning Star** in Pottinger's Entry; and **Bittles Bar** on Victoria Square, a sharp triangular building filled with paintings of celebrated literary figures by local artist Joe O'Kane. The best, hanging over the dais at the "sharp end" of the pub, shows W. B. Yeats, James Joyce, Brendan Behan, George Bernard Shaw, and Samuel Beckett drinking at a bar, with Oscar Wilde manning the beer pumps and Flann O'Brien looking on from a picture frame behind the bar.

If the center of Belfast is where the heart and soul of the city reside, then its stomach and liver have probably got lost somewhere along the **Golden Mile.** This loose triangle of the city south of the center between Great Victoria Street and Bedford Street, bulging out south of Shaftesbury Square as it nears **Queen's University,** is where most of the serious and fashionable eating, drinking, and late-night street partying takes place. Queen's University, another fine Lanyon building (1845–49) in the Tudor style, caters to nearly 10,000 students, which can make its colonnaded quad and the quietly elegant squares around the university pretty lively from time to time.

Beyond Queen's, on Stranmillis Road, you reach the splendid **Botanic Gardens,** beautiful to stroll in, and irresistible with their high Victorian iron-and-glass monsters of glasshouses. The hot and steamy **Palm House** of 1839–40, with its rounded prow and long wings, is superb; and so is the glassroofed **Tropical Ravine,** established in 1887 by curator Charles McKimm in an attempt to reproduce the sultry heat and fecundity of

a rain-forest gully. A raised balcony lets you wander at canopy level, or farther down, among ferns, orchids, dombeya, Dutchman's pipe, and guava, banana, and cinnamon trees.

Near the Tropical Ravine stands the absorbing **Ulster Museum,** one of Ireland's best city museums. The art collection is wonderful, ranging from Pissarro and Sickert through Stanley Spencer to Henry

Moore, with a superb collection of watercolors and drawings. Turner, Gainsborough, Reynolds, Stubbs, and Wilson are old-guard members, and there are plenty of examples of the work of Belfast-born artist Sir John Lavery (1856–1941).

Ancient artifacts include bronze crosses, brooches, and holy relic shrines. In the Technology Section you can wonder at the machines that brought textile prosperity to industrial revolution Belfast.

Most intriguing of all are the personal effects and the treasure of jewels, gold, and silver salvaged in 1967–69 from the wreck of the *Girona,* a Spanish warship that went aground near the Giant's Causeway (see pp. 306–307) with the loss of 260 lives during the fiasco of the 1588 Spanish Armada. ∎

Ulster Museum
www.ulstermuseum.org.uk
🅰 281
✉ Botanic Gardens, Belfast
☎ 028 9038 3000

The Palm House in the Botanic Gardens is a triumph of Victorian garden architecture in glass and cast iron.

Botanic Gardens
🅰 281
✉ Stranmillis Rd., Belfast
☎ 028 9032 4902

Gable-end art & the Troubles

One's first sight of the famed sectarian murals of Belfast can be a shock. They seem to pump anger and the threat of violence across the town, with their balaclava-clad gunmen and intolerant assertions—"Irish Out," "England's Genocide," "No Surrender"—blazoned house-high across gable ends and street walls. At the same time there is a kind of playground machismo about these paintings that robs them of some of their menace. As "political" murals—the

The republican heroes of the 1916 Easter Rising stride across a gable end—partisan expression in a contemporary art form.

euphemism employed by the tourist trade—many of them are way over the top, but as folk art expressing raw emotion they have great power. Murals come and go as buildings are demolished or new developments inspire fresh commentary, but the sites in Belfast remain roughly the same. Republican murals are thickest on the ground around the Falls Road and Springfield Road, the streets around the Ballymurphy estate and the Ardoyne farther north, and in the Short Strand district of East Belfast; Loyalist ones tend to be around the Shankill and Crumlin roads, and in East Belfast around Lower Newtownards Road.

The character of the murals reflects the nature of the 30-year confrontation known as the Troubles. Loyalists with their siege mentality and desire to keep the status quo tend to produce aggressive, die-hard images of bullyboy paramilitaries hefting guns, advertising a bewildering number of outlawed organizations: UDA (Ulster Defence Association), UVF (Ulster Volunteer Force), UFF (Ulster Freedom Fighters), LVF (Loyalist Volunteer Force), and many more. Republican murals are more aspirational, romantic, and imaginative.

Smiling hunger strikers exhort everyone to play a part, figures from Ireland's mythological past imperiously dispatch British soldiers back across the Irish Sea. The standard of execution varies from schoolboy crude to extremely skillful.

Protestant murals, generally of King Billy on his white horse at the Battle of the Boyne, were widespread in Belfast and Londonderry even before the Troubles began around 1968 with clashes between Protestants and Catholics. Discriminated against in housing, work, policing, and social services, and with local political representation fixed in favor of Protestants, the Catholic activists began a series of civil rights marches that soon turned into confrontations with the police and with Loyalists—especially around Londonderry's Bogside, an impoverished Catholic ghetto quickly renamed "Free Derry" in pioneer republican murals. British troops appeared on the streets of Londonderry on August 14, 1969, in Belfast two days later. At first Catholics saw the soldiers as protectors, but soon had them lumped in with the Royal Ulster Constabulary as oppressors—and foreign ones at that. In 1971 the IRA campaign of shooting and bombing to force a British withdrawal began. A government crackdown saw the imposition of internment without trial and direct rule from Westminster. On January 30, 1972—"Bloody Sunday"—13 people were shot dead in Londonderry by British paratroopers. In 1974 the IRA began a bombing campaign on the British mainland, killing 21 youngsters with pub bombs in Birmingham. Loyalists retaliated by activating their own paramilitary groups, and two bitter decades of tit-for-tat killings ensued. Loyalists wanted Northern Ireland to stay unchanged, within the United Kingdom; nationalists wanted civil justice, and to be part

Republican murals tend to vary from Emerald-Isle-style sentimental (above) to the righteous and self-mythologizing (below)

of a united Ireland. Neither would budge, nor listen to the other side. It was as simple, and as complicated, as that.

In 1975 internment without trial was suspended, but republican prisoners—hitherto accorded special status as "political" detainees—had their political status withdrawn. "Blanket protests" (refusal to wear prison clothes) and "dirty protests" (refusal to "slop out" the cell toilets, and the consequent

smearing of cells with excrement) followed. Prison protests escalated to their awful conclusion in 1981, when ten hunger strikers, led by Bobby Sands MP, starved themselves to death in the Maze prison south of Lisburn in an abortive attempt to force a return to political status. It is their faces, framed in 1981's long hair and big shirt collars, that stare or smile down from the Falls Road murals.

In the 1980s more extremist splinter groups

Above: Hunger-striker Bobby Sands MP smiles down on republican west Belfast.

split off from the main paramilitary organizations, making life harder for everyone. But political moves were still being made. A 1973 attempt to set up a power-sharing executive to govern Northern Ireland had been brought down the following year by a province-wide Protestant worker's strike. In 1982 a power-sharing Northern Ireland Assembly was established on a very limited basis. The year 1985 saw the signing of the Anglo-Irish Agreement, much hated by Unionists, which brought Dublin on board to some extent—the positive involvement of the Republic's government, for so long negatively anti-British and reiterative of its supposed claim to sovereignty over the North's six counties, being seen as vital to any conflict resolution.

In the 1990s signs of moderation began to grow. The 1993 Downing Street declaration saw the British government renounce any "selfish strategic or economic interest" in Northern Ireland, while Dublin accepted that any change in the constitutional status of the province would have to be subject of the agreement of a majority of the people. Then on August 31, 1994, the IRA declared a "complete cessation" of violence. Loyalist paramilitary groups followed suit. The British government responded with some troop withdrawals and the demolition of roadblocks and border crossings. Seeds of hope were sown. They were briefly frozen when the IRA resumed mainland bombing in 1996.

Then, in May 1997, a Labour government was elected in the United Kingdom, and the mood changed. The new government's majority was big enough to shrug off Unionist opposition and make strides. On April 10, 1998, the Good Friday Agreement was announced, a historic accommodation by all sides. It reasserted the points made in the Downing Street declaration, ended the Republic's claim over the six counties, promised the release of paramilitary prisoners, decommissioning of paramilitary weapons, and an independent commission on policing in Northern Ireland, and proposed a Northern Ireland Assembly elected by proportional representation. All signatories committed their parties to "exclusively democratic and peaceful means" of resolving political differences.

Huge problems remain for Northern Ireland. There have been bombings, beatings, and shootings since that Good Friday. The annual Orange marches continue to be flashpoints for violence. And decommissioning has yet to take place. But the mood of anger and despair reflected in these murals has lightened,

EOPLE'S SOLDIER'S

ster Division

and every visitor clicking a camera on the Shankill or Falls Road is a sign of normality returning. There is even a cross-community mural painted on a York Road wall, each arch decorated by a different community group— Protestant, Catholic, and couldn't-care-less. ■

Militaristic Loyalist artists credit their paramilitary heroes with the organization of a formal army (above), while a republican cartoonist makes his point rather more gently (below).

TIME FOR PEACE

TIME TO GO

The tremendous view over Belfast Lough is worth every step up Cave Hill.

Walk: Cave Hill

This fine walk, a favorite with Belfast folk, takes you up the mountain behind the city to visit prehistoric caves, to the promontory where United Irishmen pledged their lives in 1795, and to the heritage center in Belfast Castle.

Start from the parking lot on the south side of Belfast Castle. Follow the Blue Route footpath (blue arrows) and walk up to a T-junction and turn right. In 0.3 mile (0.5 km) bear left and then turn uphill under the great basalt cliff of **Napoleon's Nose ❶**. In about 300 yards (275 m), at a stone with two blue arrows and "McArt's Fort" sign, bear uphill through trees. Emerge from the wood, and in another 300 yards (275 m) or so turn left, aiming for a large **cave ❷** in the cliff face. With care you can scramble up the rock face into the cave.

Up here the view is tremendous—Belfast spread out along Belfast Lough, with the dark bulk of the Ards Peninsula hills rising beyond, crowned by the rocket shape of Scrabo Tower.

The cave itself is one of five neolithic excavations—Stone Age men found their essential material, flint, in the chalk under the basalt hill cap. Iron was mined here, too, opening up the delvings. "The Wages of Sin Is Death" warns a painted message on the cave wall. It may have been here, or at **McArt's Fort ❸** on the

summit, that Wolfe Tone, Henry Joy McCracken, Dr. William Drennan, and a small band of friends—mostly Presbyterians—met in 1795 to swear an oath that Irishmen of every creed should unite for independence. It was the birth of the United Irishmen, a rebel organization whose leaders would come to a bloody end at the conclusion of the rising they staged in 1798.

To reach McArt's Fort, bear right as you face the cave on a narrow path along the grass slopes under the cliff. It soon trends uphill. At the top of the slope cross a cattle grid, near a post with blue and yellow waymarks. Bear left uphill. In about 300 yards (275 m), cross a cattle grid and continue uphill with a fence on your right, bearing left to cross a depression and reach the fort at 1,182 feet (360 m). This old earthwork was named after Brian McArt O'Neill, one of the last Irish chieftains to die in the Tudor repressions—he was killed by Lord Mountjoy in 1601.

From the fort, retrace your steps and descend through the woods to the stone with two blue arrows. Bear left downhill here; in

about 150 yards (137 m) go straight ahead at a meeting of woodland tracks.

Follow the blue arrow on a stone at the **Volunteers' Well** ❹ to meet a road. Bear right along it; at a parking area bear right to reach **Belfast Castle** ❺, built in 1867–70 in baronial style for the Marquis of Donegall.

The **Cave Hill Heritage Centre** *(Belfast Castle, tel 028 9077 6925)* on the second floor gives fascinating insights into the wildlife, geology, and history of the area. ■

- See area map p. 301 F3
- ➤ Belfast Castle parking lot, Cave Hill Country Park—signed off the A6 Antrim road, 4 miles (6 km) N of city center. City bus 8, 9, 10, 45–51 from Donegall Square
- ↔ 2 miles (3.5 km)
- ⏱ 2 hours
- Free trail map and literature available from Cave Hill Heritage Centre
- ➤ Belfast Castle

NOT TO BE MISSED
- Napoleon's Nose
- Cave
- View from McArt's Fort
- Cave Hill Heritage Centre

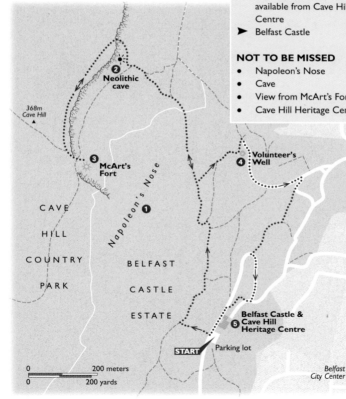

Sir Edward Carson (1854–1935), vehement Unionist, shakes a defiant fist outside Stormont.

More places to visit around Belfast

LAGAN TOWPATH

If you want to explore the Lagan on foot upriver from Belfast, there is an 11-mile (18 km) **Lagan Towpath Walk** (four brochure guides available from Belfast Welcome Centre) through the beautiful, wooded Lagan Valley Regional Park. The walk starts at Lockview Road parking lot—leaving the gates of the Botanic Gardens, turn left beside the Ulster Museum up Stranmillis Road, then right onto Lockview Road. The old towpath takes you through a 4,000-acre (1,600 ha) mixture of woodland and pasture, wetlands and forest, to its end at Union Locks in Lisburn.

In 3 miles (5 km) from the start of the Lagan towpath you can reach two of Belfast's most pleasant green oases. **Malone House** *(Barnett Park, Upper Malone Rd., Belfast, tel 028 9068 1246, city bus 70, 71),* south of the city center, is a fine restored late Georgian house with an excellent restaurant, standing on 100 acres (40 ha) of grounds ablaze with azaleas and rhododendrons in spring.

A mile (1.6 km) along the Upper Malone Road from Malone House you'll find **Sir Thomas and Lady Dixon Park** *(tel 028 9032 0202, city bus 71),* a varied mosaic of meadows, woodland, and water with the City of Belfast Inter-national Rose Gardens at its heart—11 acres (4 ha) of more than 30,000 shrub roses. These are spectacular beginning in mid-July, and in spring daffodils fill the park.
🚶 281

STORMONT

A great place for walks is around Stormont, 5 miles (8 km) east of Belfast city center. The 1928 Portland stone **Stormont Castle** *(tel 028 9076 0556, city bus 16, 17, 20),* seat of the Northern Ireland Assembly, is spectacularly sited at the crown of a mile-long (1.6 km) drive. The castle itself is only open to the public by appointment, but you are free to wander the 300 acres (120 ha) of parkland and woods.
🚶 301 F3

THE WATERFRONT

Belfast's waterfront areas have been revitalized since the 1994 building of the Lagan Weir's five steel sluice gates. The weir has stabilized river levels, eliminated offensive smells, and made Laganside a pleasant area to explore. The **Lagan Lookout Centre** *(Lagan Weir, Donegall Quay, tel 028 9031 5444),* has large windows overlooking the weir. Here there are displays on Belfast shipbuilding and the story of the River Lagan. You can look across to the giant twin cranes of Samson and Goliath in Harland & Wolff's shipyards, their gaunt yellow frames towering over 300 feet high (91 m) and 450 feet long (137 m). They symbolize a shipbuilding power that is all but gone from the yards where *Titanic* was built and launched in 1912. At their height the shipyards employed more than 25,000 men; today barely a couple of hundred work there.

Just behind the Lagan Lookout you'll see the Sir Charles Lanyon-designed **Custom House** of 1854–57, its pediment crowded with nautical statuary—Neptune, Britannia, dolphins, and anchors.

Across the river, playing Impudence to the Custom House's Dignity, stands **Odyssey** *(tel 028 9045 1055)*, a 150-million-dollar sports and culture venue of the most modern kind—testament to the confidence that the Laganside Development Corporation has engendered.

Walking seaward from the Lagan Lookout along Donegall Quay and under the motorway bridge, you round the corner to find two of Belfast's most interesting buildings side by side. The **Harbour Commissioner's Office** *(Corporation Sq., tel 028 9055 4422, e-mail info@belfast-harbour.co.uk, group visits by prior arrangement)* of 1854 has an interior rich in stained glass and elaborate plasterwork. Upstairs highlights include fine paintings of sailing ships in heavy seas, superb paintings of old Belfast harbor scenes by well-known turn-of-the-20th-century painter Eyre Macklin, and the Barnet Room, with its painted stucco barrel roof and stained-glass windows portraying the arms of Belfast's trading partners in days of the Empire—Australia, Canada, Russia, the United States, India, Italy, and the Cape Colony of South Africa.

Just along the street look for the **Sinclair Seamen's Church** *(Corporation Sq., tel 028 9071 5997, open Wed. 2–5 p.m. & Sun. for services at 11:30 a.m. & 7 p.m., and by appt.)*, designed by Sir Charles Lanyon and opened in 1857. Throughout the furnishings of this remarkable L-shaped Presbyterian church, with its separate Italianate tower, a nautical theme predominates, from the semaphore flags that spell out "Welcome" at each door to

the ship's binnacle used as a font. Fishing boats and tugs feature in the stained-glass windows, the collection boxes are miniature lifeboats, and the pulpit is shaped like a ship's prow. On the walls hang the mast of a Guinness barge, port and starboard ship lights, and a silver flashlight with which some shipwreck victims summoned help. Fifty seats are kept empty for visiting sailors every Sunday, and the start of the service to which they are welcomed is signaled by six strokes on the brass ship's bell of HMS *Hood,* sunk at the mouth of Portsmouth Harbour, England, in World War I to deny entry to enemy submarines.

⚠ 281 ■

Quite unique, the Sinclair Seamen's Church is furnished like a ship to make visiting sailors feel at home.

Northern Ireland counties

The counties of Northern Ireland fan out like segments of a wheel from the central hub of Lough Neagh, the biggest lake in the British Isles. Lough Neagh covers an astonishing 153 square miles (400 square km), and five of the six Northern Ireland counties—Armagh, Down, Antrim, Londonderry, and Tyrone—have a toehold on its flat shores. Only Fermanagh, out in the west, does not touch Lough Neagh. In spite of the possession of huge lakes such as this, as well as several fine hill ranges and a coastline that runs to the spectacular in places, rural Northern Ireland is still very little visited.

Dunluce Castle is just one of the spectacular attractions of the Antrim Coast.

County Antrim is the best known of the six counties, because of its glorious limestone, sandstone, and basalt coastline stretching north from Belfast—a succession of east-running glens ending in superb cliffs, with the 37,000 hexagonal basaltic columns of the Giant's Causeway as the icing on the cake.

County Londonderry (or Derry), western neighbor of Antrim, possesses Northern Ireland's second city, Londonderry (Derry), a lively and forward-looking town whose heart is enclosed within the best-preserved set of city walls anywhere in Ireland. On the cliffs of the north-facing Londonderry coast you'll find Downhill, the country estate of the eccentric 18th-century Bishop of

Londonderry, while inland are forests and the northern range of the Sperrin Mountains.

County Tyrone is the setting for the bulk of the Sperrins, glorious hills for striding over or for exploring by car. At the waist of Tyrone is a wide belt of bogland, in which lies a rich

p. 205

collection of archaeological sites.

Out to the west, County Fermanagh boasts Upper and Lower Lough Erne—a double lake 50 miles long (80 km) that offers superb cruising, fishing, and island-hopping.

County Armagh has the Lough Neagh Discovery Centre on Oxford Island, and the historic city of Armagh;

also the drumlin hills of south Armagh and volcanic Slieve Gullion. Northward toward Belfast is County Down, last of the six, with the beautiful Mourne Mountains in the south, St. Patrick's Country in the center, and the wildfowl paradise of Strangford Lough in the north. ■

County Antrim

THE PRIDE AND THE GLORY OF COUNTY ANTRIM RESIDES in its spectacular coast and green hinterland. Stretching 75 miles (120 km) from Carrickfergus to Portrush and forming the northeastern rim of Northern Ireland, this playground of basalt and sandstone is like a giant natural sculpture park. Driving the Antrim coast road is one of the great highlights of any trip to Ireland.

CARRICKFERGUS TO LARNE

Not that the topographical fireworks begin as soon as you leave Belfast. The A2 coast road, heading north out of the city, passes through the suburb of Newtownabbey to reach **Carrickfergus,** where the big and well-preserved Norman castle is worth a stop. **Carrickfergus Castle** stands on a rocky promontory by the harbor, a 90-foot (28 m) keep rising from gray battlemented walls. Sir John de Courcy built it in 1180 as a deterrent to any attacker thinking of advancing up Belfast Lough. It suffered various sieges and captures in its time, by Scots and French forces as well as the English—all owing to its vital strategic position at the lough entrance.

In the town center you can explore the 12th-century **Church of St. Nicholas** off the market place. The church contains notable late medieval glass, and the beautifully carved 17th-century tomb of Sir Arthur and Lady Chichester, 1st Earl and Countess of Belfast, and their poignantly tiny son.

Just north of the town you'll see the **Andrew Jackson Centre** signposted; though this thatched cottage offers a collection of Jackson-related material, fans and family of the former U.S. President (1767–1845) should be aware that his connection with the house itself is tenuous. Jackson's parents emigrated from the town two years before Andrew was born, but this house was not their home.

Beyond Carrickfergus, you can take a worthwhile detour around the 7-mile-long (11 km) **Island Magee Peninsula** (reached by the B150, off the A2 just north of Whitehead). The tidal inlet of Larne Lough, all but enclosed by the eastward arm of Island Magee, is good for bird-watching and boating, while the peninsula itself has the very fine cliffs of the Gobbins looking out east into the Irish Sea. Local people alive and dead were hurled off those cliffs by a party of soldiers from Carrickfergus garrison in 1641 as a payback for the killing of some of their number. Island Magee was known as a witchy kind of place—the last eight witches to be convicted at Carrickfergus court were Island Magee women tried in 1710.

A ferry connects Ballylumford at the northern end of the peninsula with **Larne,** a coastal ferry port with plenty of bustle but not much charm. But Larne is the gateway to the real delights of the Antrim coast, which you skirt all the way north on the A2—a notable road in its own right. It was designed in 1834 by Sir Charles Lanyon, chief architect of 19th-century Belfast, as a project to enable destitute locals to earn some money. Built by Scottish engineer William Bald, the coast road hugs the cliffs and passes the mouth of each of the nine Antrim Glens. Before the road was built the

Carrickfergus visitor information

✉ Knight Ride, Antrim St., Carrickfergus, Co. Antrim

☎ 028 9336 6455

Carrickfergus Castle

✉ Marine Hwy., Carrickfergus, Co. Antrim

☎ 028 9335 1273

💲 $

Andrew Jackson Centre

✉ Boneybefore, Larne Rd., 2 miles (3 km) N of Carrick-fergus on the A2

☎ 028 9336 6455

Larne visitor information

✉ Narrow Gauge Rd., Larne

☎ 028 2826 0088

inhabitants of the coast villages of Carnlough, Glenariff, Cushendall, and Cushendun had been all but cut off by intervening cliffs from each other and from Ballycastle to the north and Larne to the south. Trade in goods, and very soon in holidaymakers hungry for romantic scenery, quickly improved once the coast road was opened.

BALLYGALLEY TO CUSHENDALL

From Ballygalley the coast begins to rise to some fine limestone cliffs at **Carnlough,** a pretty fishing village and harbor around Carnlough Bay. But these cliffs are only the prelude to the drama of the Antrim coast and its contributory glens. There are many glens or valleys in Antrim, but nine in particular are recognized as the **Antrim Glens**—from south to north they are Glenarm, Glencloy, Glenariff, Glenballyeamon, Glenaan, Glencorp, Glendun, Glenshesk, and Glentaisie. Carved by rivers and shaped by ice age glaciers and meltwaters and by frosts and other weathering processes, the Antrim

Glens veer northeast as they bend and wriggle through limestone, sandstone, and basalt to the coast. There is something magical in their quiet depths, all well grown with woodlands, and in the moorland and bare rock that rims them. The glens are a very popular visitor destination; but almost all visitors rubberneck from their cars, so once you have parked and set out to explore these delectable valleys on foot you should have the landscape more or less to yourself.

Glenarm and **Glencloy** reach the sea at Carnlough Bay, from where the coast road curls on at the feet of the cliffs around Garron Point. Here the limestone hands over to dusky red sandstone as the cave-burrowed cliffs shoot up some 800 feet tall (250 m). Around the corner from Garron Point begins the most striking section of the Antrim coast as the coastal plain flattens into a green apron of land 3 miles long (5 km). **Glenariff, Glenballyeamon,** and **Glenaan** converge here, their mouths separated by the dominant, flat-topped 1,153-

Carnlough, created for Protestant settlers, displays all the neatness, order, and architectural harmony of a planned village.

Horse-racing through the streets is one of the thrills of the Ould Lammas Fair at Ballycastle.

Glenariff Forest Park
- 301 E4
- On A43 Ballymena—Waterfoot Rd.
- 028 2955 6000
- $

Ballycastle visitor information
- 301 E5
- 7 Mary St., Ballycastle
- 028 2076 2024

Kebble Cliffs National Nature Reserve
- 301 E5
- W end of Rathin Island
- 028 2076 3948. Call ahead.

foot (350 m) prow of Lurigethan.

Turn left inland from the coast village of **Waterfoot** on the aptly named Red Bay—its shore is still stained with the iron ore mined up in Glenariff until the turn of the 20th century.

Continue up Glenariff, widest and grandest of the glens, on a road that climbs under dark granite slabs, over which waterfalls pour after heavy rain. **Glenariff Forest Park** is signposted high up the glen, and you can leave your car in the parking lot here to enjoy a number of waymarked trails— short nature trails, a medium-sized scenic trail, and the 3-mile (5 km) **Waterfall Trail** around some of Glenariff's best falls.

CUSHENDALL TO BALLYCASTLE

Back on Red Bay, the road continues to the big village of **Cushendall;** there is another sidetrack here up Glenballyeamon by way of the B14. From Cushendall a country road leads past the golf course over the long hill of Cross Slieve, a short route to Cushendall's sister

village of Cushendun at the foot of Glendun. But if you bear inland with the A2 you can turn off in 1 mile (1.6 km) on a marked road to **Ossian's Grave.** It's best to leave your car at the foot of the steep farm track that climbs to the monument; the reward for 10 or 15 minutes of upward walking is a wonderful view over glens, mountains, and coasts from Ossian's Grave. This is a 4,000-year-old horned cairn, a court grave with pointed "horns" guarding its sacred enclosure; legend names it as the burial place of Fionn MacCumhaill's son Ossian.

A side road climbs unfrequented **Glenaan** to a junction of roads in wild moorland; bear right here to return seaward down the beautiful wooded **Glendun.** You pass the triple-arched red sandstone viaduct by which Sir Charles Lanyon brought the main coast road over the Glendun River, and then Craigogh Wood, where an 18th-century Mass rock—generally adorned with offerings—carries an incised Crucifixion scene.

Cushendun, just below, is a

charming model village (now cared for by the National Trust) created for Lord Cushendun in the early 20th century by the visionary architect Clough Williams-Ellis. Its rugged cottages feature plenty of whitewash and slate as they peep out of the trees.

The A2 now takes off inland for a 10-mile (16 km) moorland run to Ballycastle. A much more enjoyable alternative, however, is the rough, bumpy coast road (signed "Scenic Route"), which snakes and switchbacks through a high, rolling coastland of farms and sloping fields by way of **Torr Head** (a parking area here, and wonderful sea views to add spice to a picnic lunch) to rejoin the A2 at Ballyvoy.

From here it's a short run into **Ballycastle,** a handsome little seaside resort that comes alive at Lammastide, the last Monday and Tuesday of August. This is the date of **Ould Lammas Fair,** held here for the last 400 years, when lovers of seaweed, shellfish, and yellow-man toffee arrive for an orgy of tasting. The seaweed is dulse, picked off the rocks locally and dried—eaten au naturel, or lightly toasted according to taste. Yellowman toffee, available throughout the town, is a bright yellow, very hard toffee that has to be broken up with a hammer.

From Ballycastle a ferry leaves daily for **Rathlin Island,** a friendly and beautiful place that you certainly shouldn't miss. The L-shaped island, roughly 5 miles (8 km) from east to west and 3 miles (5 km) from north to south, is home to about 70 islanders who rely on tourism, farming, and fishing—in that order—for their survival. Chief attraction is the **Kebble Cliffs National Nature Reserve** out at the west end of the island, where 250,000

seabirds—fulmars, kittiwakes, puffins, razorbills, guillemots—whirl and shriek during the April to July nesting season. At the harbor village there's a pub, and an excellent island museum in the **Boathouse Centre.**

BALLINTOY TO PORTRUSH

Next come the three chief visitor attractions of the Antrim Coast—two man-made, and one the work of nature (or of a giant, depending on how you view these things). First is **Carrickarade (Carrick-a-rede) rope bridge** near Ballintoy, a scary cat's cradle of ropes and planking slung each salmon-fishing season by local fishermen between the mainland cliffs and a huge offshore rock—almost an island. The rock stands right in the path of salmon on their spawning run, forcing them to divert course into the nets cunningly set by the fishermen. The 60-foot (20 m) bridge, administered by the National Trust, is a great visitor attraction. Although it sways, bucks, and lurches as you

The swinging, swaying rope bridge at Carrickarade

Boathouse Centre Museum
- 🅰 301 E5
- ✉ Rathlin Island Harbor
- ☎ 028 2076 3951
- 🕐 Closed Sept.–April

Carrickarade rope bridge
- 🅰 301 E5
- ✉ 5 miles W of Ballycastle off B15
- ☎ 028 2073 1159
- 🕐 Closed Oct.–mid-March
- 💲 $ per car

Old Bushmills Distillery (see p. 306)
- 🅰 301 E5
- ✉ Distillery Rd., Bushmills, Co. Antrim
- ☎ 028 2073 1521
- 🕐 Call for tour times.

walk 80 feet (25 m) above the sea, it's quite safe.

Seven miles (11 km) beyond Carrickarade, and very well signposted, lies Northern Ireland's most celebrated tourist site, the **Giant's Causeway,** 37,000 hexagonal columns of cooled basalt, formed from lava flow after a volcanic eruption some 60 million years ago. The cooled lava flow can be seen in the form of dark columns remarkably like closely stacked pencils, up to 40 feet high (12 m), in the face of the 300-foot (92 m) cliffs. Victorian guides named the most striking of these formations the "Giant's Organ Pipes," a very apt title. The giant was—who else?—the mighty Fionn MacCumhaill; and the best-known part of the lava flow, the long shelf of tessellated columns that noses into the sea, is the causeway he laid down to reach his girlfriend on the Hebridean island of Staffa.

The mythology and geology of the Giant's Causeway is explained in the **visitor center** *(tel 028 2073 1855)* on the cliffs above. From here you can take a road train down to the causeway, or you can stroll down in 10 minutes. Walkers can continue from the causeway to the Organ Pipes, then turn back to the visitor center along a cliff path with excellent views down onto the causeway and back along the spectacular basalt cliffs.

Just inland of the Giant's Causeway is the village of Bushmills, where Northern Ireland's finest whiskey is made at the **Old Bushmills Distillery.** Bushmills is the world's oldest licensed distillery, first operating in 1608, its buildings graced by a pair of big pagoda-roofed towers. You can take a tour around the distillery and view the gleaming copper stills and the quaking brew in the giant mash tuns. The warehouse is a delightful

place, cool and dark, full of the sweet spirituous fragrance of the "angels' share"—whiskey vapor evaporating from the seams of the piled wooden butts. You get a sample or two, and the chance to buy a bottle of blended or single malt Bushmills.

Before reaching the resort of Portrush and the border with County Londonderry, turn aside for one of Ireland's most evocative sights: the extensive ruins of **Dunluce Castle** perched on the edge of the cliffs in a wonderfully romantic setting. In 1584 one of the turbulent years of Tudor repression, its gallant and bloody-handed owner Sorley Boy MacDonnell recaptured it from the English in a fantastically daring attack—his followers achieved complete surprise, having been hauled up the 200-foot (60 m) cliffs in baskets. Sorley Boy later fortified it with cannon from the wreck of the Spanish Armada galleon *Girona* (see p. 291; Ulster Museum). In 1639 tragedy struck during a storm when the castle kitchens fell into the sea. Dunluce was abandoned, and left in ruin. ■

Above: Clifftop turrets and pinnacles of Dunluce Castle

Dunluce Castle

⚑ 301 D5

✉ Port Ballintree, on the A2, 3 miles (4.8 km) E of Portrush

☎ 028 2073 1938

🕐 Closed Oct.–Dec.

💲 $

Opposite: Was it Mother Nature that formed the hexagonal columns of the Giant's Causeway from cooling basalt, or was it Fionn the Hero who flung them down in the sea? The answer depends on how much blarney you've absorbed.

Londonderry city

YOU WILL HEAR THE CITY CALLED LONDONDERRY— generally if the speaker is a Protestant or a mainland Briton. You will hear it called Derry—usually if the speaker is a Catholic, and/or a nationalist. Londonderry, or Derry, is Northern Ireland's "second city" after Belfast; a vibrant, lively, small city, very conscious of its past as a springboard to its future.

Maybe it's the more rural surroundings that make Londonderry conversation and humor seem lighter and less caustic than their Belfast counterparts. Or maybe it's just the effect of being a very small city that has moved on a long way from the dark days of the 1960s and early '70s. Whatever the cause, Londonderry breathes a most attractive energy and optimism. This is a great place to spend a day or two, and the locals are only too happy to bend your ear or lend an ear— whichever you choose.

Londonderry, meaning the "Place of the Oaks," stands on the River Foyle at the point where the river begins to widen into the great sea outlet of Lough Foyle. It's an obvious prime location for trade and defense; and in 1613–18, at the start of the plantation of Ulster with Protestant outsiders (see p. 26), the London trade guilds that had taken over the running of Londonderry built a tight lozenge of defensive walls around the heart of the city. These walls had their most testing trial toward the end of that century when, in April 1689, the deposed Catholic King of Britain, King James II, laid siege to the town. Londonderry had in fact been in a state of siege since the previous December, when 13 apprentice boys had locked the city gates against the Jacobite army. By the time the Great Siege had been broken in July 1689, 7,000 of the 30,000 defenders lay dead of disease, wounds, and starvation. It was an epic event—one destined to fuel centuries of provocation and bitterness. These flared in the 1960s as the city's Catholic majority, resentful of their lack of civil rights, found no redress from a city council dominated by supremacist Protestants. Bloody

Londonderry city
www.derrycity.gov.uk
🅰 300 C4
Visitor information
✉ 44 Foyle St.,
   Londonderry,
   Co. Londonderry
☎ 028 7126 7284

Guildhall
✉ Guildhall Sq.,
   Londonderry
☎ 028 7137 7335
🕐 Closed Sat. & Sun.

Left: Hope, despair, resignation, defiance—the many facets of emigration are caught in this Londonderry statue.

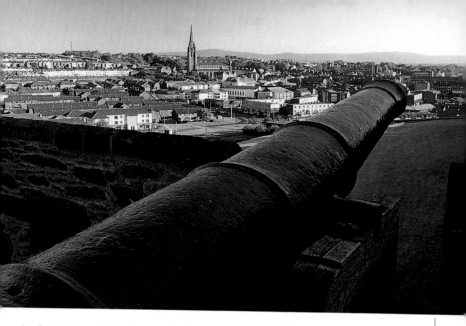

Sunday 1972 (see p. 292), when British paratroopers shot dead 13 civil rights marchers, was a Londonderry tragedy. Levels of violence soared, especially in the hard-line extramural Catholic ghetto of the Bogside. At one time three-quarters of all buildings outside the city walls had either been damaged or destroyed by fire, bombs, or neglect.

You'll be hard put to recognize any sign of such past miseries in today's Londonderry. The bars along **Waterloo Street,** just outside the walls to the west, are thronged at night. The **Craft Village** (tel 028 7137 0191) inside the northern angle of the walls is flourishing, with craft workshops, eateries, wine bars, and cafés around little paved squares.

There are exhibitions of Irish music and dance every summer weekday lunchtime in the thatched **Bridie's Cottage** (tel 028 7136 3448) here—not quite an authentic *ceilidh* house (see p. 388), but a sign of budding social life in the city.

The town's splendid 1890 **Guildhall,** built in local red sandstone under a monstrous clock tower, has the 1689 Siege of Derry depicted vividly in its stained-glass windows, and more stained glass in its Council Chamber and Main Hall.

The **Tower Museum** in Union Hall Place inside the walls, built in the 1970s, gives a balanced rundown of Londonderry over the centuries. The displays start with prehistoric times and continue through a series of brick-lined tunnels, replicas of those built under the city after the seige. You learn of 17th-century prosperity, 18th-century industrialization, and the Home Rule movement of Victorian times. Last comes an exploration of the Troubles.

By far the best way to appreciate Londonderry is to walk the **Walls of Derry** (tel 028 7126 7284), starting the 1-mile (1.6 km) circuit from the Tower Museum. Looking outward you'll see the slogan-painted Bogside, poor Protestant estates, new shopping areas, and a gorgeous view of the surrounding hills. Looking inward there are shiny new shops and restaurants and regenerated housing. Make time to look into **St. Columb's Cathedral** inside Bishop's Gate, a shrine to the Great Siege and to Protestant nostalgia. ∎

Londonderry's superbly preserved 17th-century city walls offer a circular walk with truly memorable views over the city and hills beyond.

Tower Museum
- ✉ Union Hall Pl., Londonderry, Co. Londonderry
- ☎ 028 7137 2411
- 🕐 Closed Sun.–Mon. Sept.–June

St. Columb's Cathedral
- ✉ London St., Londonderry, Co. Londonderry
- ☎ 028 7126 7313
- 🕐 Worshipers only on Sun.

The Orange & the Green

Every July 12 the city streets and country lanes of Northern Ireland resound with the thump of Lambeg drums (marching drums with a painted skin) and the squeal of flutes as the Orange Order men go marching. For outsiders it can be hard to understand the passionate commitment that these sober-faced, bowler-hatted Protestants in their orange sashes feel for this ritual, and the bitter resentment it provokes in Catholic onlookers. At Drumcree on the outskirts of Portadown, County Armagh, the July 12 marches have caused enormous anger and some bloodshed in recent years—so much so that successive Drumcree marches have been banned by the Parades

Other side of the coin on St. Patrick's Day

Commission set up to control such explosive situations. Other venues across the province have been flashpoints for trouble, too.

If you ask an Orangeman, he will tell you that he is marching (a) to commemorate the victory of the Protestant King William III over the deposed Roman Catholic King James II at the Battle of the Boyne on July 12, 1690, and (b) to uphold Protestant tradition. If a nationalist Catholic gives an opinion, it will be that the Orange marches are a show of triumphalism, a reinforcement of the traditional Protestant upper hand. There is truth in both assertions.

The Orange Order was formed in September

Orangemen on the march, the very picture of Unionist pride and defiance

1795 after a Protestant vigilante group, the Peep O'Day Boys, had repulsed a raid on Dan Winter's farm at Loughgall, County Armagh, by the Defenders, a Catholic group. An **Orange Order museum** has been established at the house *(Dan Winter's Cottage, 7 Derryloughan Rd., Loughgall, tel 028 3885 1344, weekends by arrangement)*. The first July 12 march took place the following year, 1796, and has continued as a Protestant tradition ever since. Plenty of salt has been rubbed in Catholic wounds along the way, especially with the making of offensive gestures and the playing of inflammatory sectarian tunes as the marchers pass through predominantly Catholic areas. Yet most Protestants deplore such provocation, and are greatly distressed at the image the outside world has of them as insensitive supremacists.

Other Orange marches have been used to taunt Catholics, too, particularly the parades round the walls of Londonderry on the Saturday nearest August 12 (the anniversary of the 1689 relief of the Great Siege) and the Saturday nearest December 18 (the date of the locking of the city gates by the 13 apprentice boys in 1688). Overlooking the Catholic enclave of the Bogside, these marches symbolized the Orangemen's possession of the political and economic as well as the physical high ground. But with the recent hope of better interdenominational relations, the Derry Walls parades have dwindled in size and contentiousness.

Meanwhile, the green-sashed Catholic marchers of the Ancient Order of Hibernians—founded in 1838, though originating way back in Tudor times—continue to mount their own marches on St. Patrick's Day, March 17, and on the Feast of the Assumption, or Lady's Day, August 15. But these are lower-key affairs, more rural and more church-based, and provoke little or no aggression and bad feeling. ■

County Londonderry

Did Frederick Hervey, Bishop of Londonderry, really keep one of his mistresses in the Mussenden Temple that he built on the cliffs at Downhill?

Downhill Castle and Mussenden Temple

🅰 301 D5

✉ Mussenden Rd., Castlerock, Co. Londonderry

☎ 028 7084 8728

🕐 Temple closed Nov.–Feb., & weekdays March–May & Sept.–Oct.

COUNTY LONDONDERRY (OR DERRY) FORMS THE NORTH-western segment of Northern Ireland. A stretch of coast less dramatic than that of neighboring Antrim, but with its own charm, leads along the east and south shore of Lough Foyle to Londonderry city; while inland the Sperrin Mountains spill over the border from County Tyrone, and a great stretch of hilly, forested country rises above the farmlands along Londonderry's eastern boundary of the River Bann.

DOWNHILL TO LIMAVADY

Five miles (8 km) west of Coleraine via the A2 on the northern Antrim border, a strange collection of buildings stands on the cliffs above the golfing resort of Castlerock. This is **Downhill Castle,** an estate that once belonged to Frederick Hervey, 4th Earl of Bristol and Protestant Bishop of Londonderry. In England he built himself a giant rotunda of a house at Ickworth in Suffolk; and here on the Derry cliffs he created in the 1780s the great palace of Downhill, complete with a vast gallery to accommodate his art collection. You can wander the sprawling ruins of the castle and its walled garden complete with ice house and dovecote. Then stroll to

the cliff edge to view the domed **Mussenden Temple** (1783–85), built by Hervey—some say—to accommodate one of his mistresses.

If you like flat, lonely, windswept coastal scenery, carry on west from Downhill to where the shark's-nose peninsula of **Magilligan Point** almost closes Lough Foyle—only a mile (1.6 km) of water separates it from the Inishowen shore in County Donegal. Side roads will give you access to this flat, fertile curve of coast, much of it reclaimed from the sea for agriculture.

Inland and due south of Magilligan Point sits **Limavady,** a neat little Georgian town on the River Roe—"roe" means red, and the river does run a dusky crimson-brown. You can see it at its most spectacular just south of Limavady in the **Roe Valley Country Park** (*tel 028 7772 2074*), a 3-mile (5 km) stretch of gorge and valley. Preserved remnants of Londonderry's prosperous linenmaking industry are scattered along the park—scutch mills where the flax fibers were separated for weaving, bleaching meadows in which the coarse woven cloth was spread to dry, and beetling mills where water-powered wooden hammers beat the linen to flatten and smooth it.

SOUTH TO MAGHERA

The B68 leads south from Roe Valley Country Park to **Dungiven.** Just south of the town, off the A6 Maghera road, the impressive ruins of the early 12th-century Augustinian **Dungiven Priory** perch on a bluff above the River Roe. In the church you'll find one of the best tombs in Ireland—that of "Cooey of the Foreigners," Cooey-na-Gal O'Cahan (died 1385), who lies ready for battle in his armor, guarded by carvings of six soldiers in kilts—"gallowglasses," or mercenaries, from Scotland, whose hire gave Cooey his nickname.

The A6 leads southeast to **Maghera,** where you can head north for 2 miles (3 km) on the A29 before turning left on the Grillagh road. In 1.5 miles (2.5 km), bear left after Rockfield Farm on a track to a parking lot, the entrance to **Drumlamph Wood.** This is one of Northern Ireland's few remaining pieces of ancient woodland—45 acres (18 ha) of hazel and oak, rustling with red squirrels, where walkways lead through a mosaic of bog, river, and rushy pasture.

MAGHERA TO BELLAGHY

Lovers of poetry will continue from Maghera by the A42 and the B182 to Bellaghy. The fortified farmhouse of **Bellaghy Bawn,** built in 1613, contains a display on the life and work of local boy Seamus Heaney, Ireland's greatest living poet and 1995 Nobel Prize winner, who was born in 1939 and brought up at nearby Mossbawn Farm. You can see first editions and manuscripts. ∎

Limavady visitor information

⚠ 301 D4
✉ 7 Connell St., Limavady, Co. Londonderry
☎ 028 7776 0307

Bellaghy Bawn

⚠ 301 E3
✉ Castle St., Bellaghy, Co. Londonderry
☎ 028 7938 6812
🕐 Closed Sun. Oct.–Easter
💲 $

Right: Splashing through the waves along the beach below Mussenden Temple

Ulster-American Folk Park

SOUTH ACROSS THE LONDONDERRY BORDER IN COUNTY Tyrone, this admirable collection of buildings was brought from all over Northern Ireland and reassembled. They give an authentic flavor of life in bygone rural Ulster, while exploring the poverty and insecurity of tenure that forced families to emigrate. Another area of the park shows the kinds of homemade houses that emigrants built for themselves in America, and the life they took up there.

**Ulster-American
Folk Park**

www.folkpark.com

⛰ 300 C3

✉ 2 Mellon Rd.,
Castletown, Omagh,
Co. Tyrone

☎ 028 8224 3292

🕐 Closed Sat. & Sun.
Oct.–Easter

💲 $$

Thomas Mellon was five years old when he emigrated with his family from the simple house at Camphill, just north of Omagh, around which the Ulster-American Folk Park has grown since its inauguration in 1976. It was Mellon family money that brought the Folk Park into being; the young emigrant grew up to be Judge Thomas Mellon, whose son Andrew founded the steel industry in Pittsburgh. His descendants wanted to create a memorial to him, and to millions like him, forced from their native land by poverty and lack of opportunity.

The main benefactor, Dr. Matthew T. Mellon, flew over for the opening of the Folk Park Visitor Centre in 1980. He delighted everyone by recounting the tales he had heard his great-grandfather, Judge

World collection were rescued from demolition and brought here to be resurrected. There's a dark, cobwebby **blacksmith's forge** piled with sods of turf, and a **weaver's cottage** where a costumed spinner sits outside the door, busy at her wheel. Inside is one of the big looms that made possible the cottage weaving that sustained Ulster's linen industry until industrial mechanization superseded the home workers.

Nearby is the **Hughes house,** birthplace of another poor emigrant who made it big—John Joseph Hughes, who emigrated in 1817 as a child from Augher in south Tyrone. Hughes rose to become the first Catholic Archbishop of New York, and he founded St. Patrick's Cathedral there in 1858.

The **National School from Castletown** is a great favorite with visiting school parties: Lessons are put on twice a day under the "firm but fair" schoolmarm, who

Above: History brought to life: Authentic costumes and props help re-create scenes from Irish history at the Ulster-American Folk Park near Omagh in County Tyrone.

Right: Buildings such as this old post office are carefully dismantled elsewhere, then reconstructed stone by stone in the Folk Park.

Thomas Mellon, tell of the Atlantic crossing he had made back in 1818, a dreadful three-month voyage.

Nucleus of the **Old World section** of the Folk Park, the **Mellon house** is typical of 19th-century peasant dwellings—dark and low with smoke-pickled yellow walls, creaky wooden beds, smelling of turf smoke and damp. Women in period costume bake and offer bread; ducks and hens are kept to quack and cluck round the door. It's a good introduction to this bucolic way of life, though the brisk waft of sanitization remains. An earlier house, of the kind lived in by most peasants in 18th-century penal law times, is a single-roomed cabin into which parents and their many children would have crammed.

Most of the buildings of the Old

instructs the children as they sit at cramped wooden desks.

A complete 19th-century **street** has been created with reconstructed small-town premises from all over Ulster—the poky little Mountjoy post office, a saddler's shop, a printer and stationer, Devlin the pawnbroker, Murray the draper, Hill the chemist (drug-store), and Reilly's Pub, transported from Newtownbutler.

The street leads to a dark and gloomy dockside with a ticket office, where at a cobbled quay awaits a full-size reproduction of the central section of an **emigrant sailing ship.** You pass down a gang-way into the ship's hold with its head-cracking beams, tables, and wooden box berths 4 feet wide (1.2 m) and 5 feet long (1.5 m) into which a whole family would have squeezed.

A mockup of a **New World dockside,** with tumbledown houses advertising "Cheap Logins" and plenty of cheats and sharpers ready to exploit the exhausted emi-grants, reinforces a sense of the struggle most of them had when they did get to the other side.

The **New World collection** shows the kinds of log cabin built by those emigrant settlers who went on to try their luck in the huge open spaces of the Midwest. ■

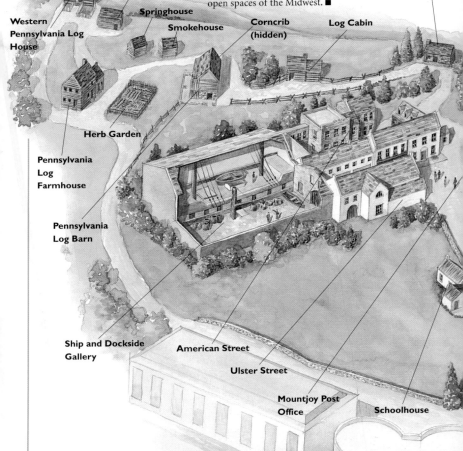

Cunningham Springhouse

Springhouse

Smokehouse

Western Pennsylvania Log House

Corncrib (hidden)

Log Cabin

Samuel Fulton Stone House

Herb Garden

Pennsylvania Log Farmhouse

Pennsylvania Log Barn

Ship and Dockside Gallery

American Street

Ulster Street

Mountjoy Post Office

Schoolhouse

Left: Reilly's Pub on the park's reconstructed Ulster street

Below: The Ulster-American Folk Park

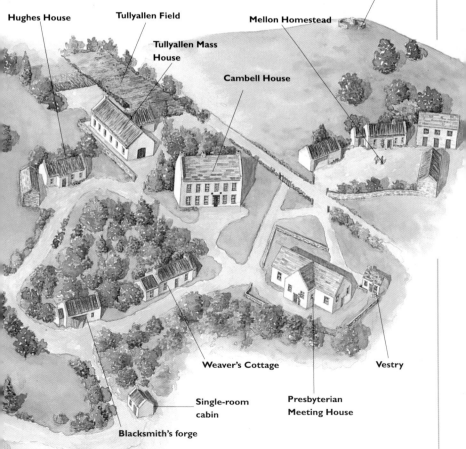

Viewpoint

Hughes House

Tullyallen Field

Mellon Homestead

Tullyallen Mass House

Cambell House

Weaver's Cottage

Vestry

Single-room cabin

Presbyterian Meeting House

Blacksmith's forge

Drive: Sperrin Mountains

The Sperrin Mountains are wild, lonely, and beautiful. They rise in a series of waves on the Tyrone/Londonderry border, seamed with the parallel east–west valleys of the Owenkillew and Glenelly Rivers. Settlements are tiny, views far and wide. This is the haunt of birds of prey, mountain hares, and the very occasional hiker.

The rolling landscape of County Tyrone's beautifully untamed Sperrin Mountains

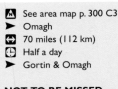

- See area map p. 300 C3
- Omagh
- 70 miles (112 km)
- Half a day
- Gortin & Omagh

NOT TO BE MISSED
- Gortin Glen Forest Park
- Aghascrebagh Ogham Stone
- Views from Barnes Gap
- Sperrin Heritage Centre
- Sawel Mountain—views from the summit

From Omagh take the B48 north toward Gortin. In 6 miles (10 km) the road enters the narrow defile of Gortin Glen between heavily wooded slopes. A 5-mile (8 km) side track along the marked scenic drive of the **Gortin Glen Forest Park ❶** *(tel 028 8167 0666)* will show you some beautiful corners of this coniferous forest.

There are splendid views ahead as the B48 dips down into **Gortin ❷,** a small village at the foot of the Owenkillew Valley. The **Badoney Tavern** is a walkers' hangout, and the owners can answer your questions about the locality.

From Gortin take the B46 eastward for 4 miles (6 km); a mile (1.6 km) beyond Drumlea Bridge bear left on a twisty mountain road along the south side of the valley. In 4.5 miles (7 km) at Monanameal, the road

bends right for Greencastle; keep straight here. After a mile (1.6 km) you'll pass a field on your left with two ancient stones; one is a fine standing stone, the other a pillar known as the **Aghascrebagh Ogham Stone ❸** with an inscription at least 1,500 years old in the ancient Irish writing called Ogham—the only specimen in County Tyrone.

At Crouck Bridge, 10 miles (16 km) from Gortin, bear left and left again onto the road that returns you up the Owenkillew Valley on the north side of the river. In 6 miles (11 km) bear right at Scotch Town on a road that wriggles up, over, and down through the spectacular viewpoint of **Barnes Gap ❹,** with fabulous views ahead across the Glenelly Valley to the highest Sperrin peaks—**Sawel Mountain** (2,225 feet/678 m) to the right with its satellite **Dart Mountain** (2,030 feet/619 m), and straight ahead the bulge of **Mullaghclogha** (2,080 feet/635 m).

Down in Glenelly Valley, turn right onto the road that keeps to the south side of the valley. In 3.5 extremely snaky miles (5.5 km) turn left to descend and cross the river at Oughtboy Bridge. Bear right on the B47 along the north side of Glenelly Valley.

In 1 mile (1.6 km) you'll pass the **Sperrin Heritage Centre ❺** *(tel 028 8164 8142,*

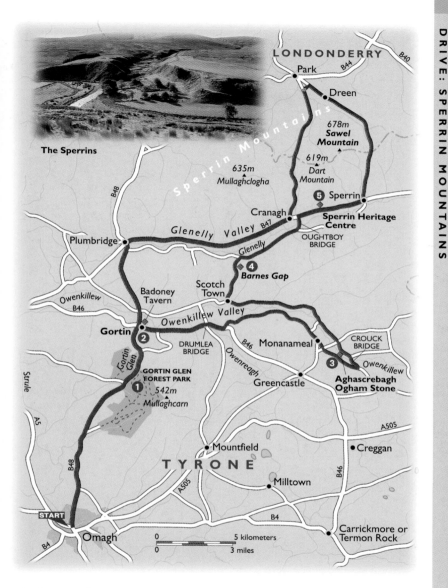

The Sperrins

LONDONDERRY

Park

Dreen

Sperrin Mountains

678m
*Sawel
Mountain*

635m
▲
Mullaghclogha

619m
▲
*Dart
Mountain*

⑤ Sperrin

Cranagh   B47

**Sperrin Heritage
Centre**

OUGHTBOY
BRIDGE

Plumbridge

Glenelly Valley

Glenelly

④
Barnes Gap

Scotch
Town

Badoney
Tavern

Owenkillew
B46

Owenkillew Valley

Gortin **②**

DRUMLEA
BRIDGE

B46   Monanameal

CROUCK
BRIDGE

Owenkillew

Owenreagh

③

**Aghascrebagh
Ogham Stone**

*Gortin
Glen*

**GORTIN GLEN
FOREST PARK**

542m
▲
Mullaghcarn

①

Greencastle

Strule

A5

B48

▲Mountfield

A505

●Creggan

T Y R O N E

A505

●Milltown

B46

B4

START

Omagh

B4

0   5 kilometers
0   3 miles

Carrickmore or
Termon Rock

---

closed Nov.–March, $), where the staff will fill you in on the folklore, wildlife, and geological history of these hills. It's all good priming for the next stage of the drive, for in another 1.5 miles (2.5 km) you turn left at Sperrin village and shoot up and over the moorland heart of the hills on a narrow road that takes you right under the eastern flank of **Sawel Mountain.**

On the far side of the hills the mountain road descends to meet the B44 at Park. Just before the B44, bear sharp left to return over the Sperrins into the **Glenelly Valley** once more. At Cranagh turn right along the B47 for the lovely 7-mile (11 km) run to Plumbridge, from where the B48 returns you south to Gortin and Omagh. ■

Enigma in the
Tyrone bogland:
The mysterious
stone circles and
avenue at
Beaghmore
represent only a
fraction of the
monumental
prehistoric
landscape that
lies around An
Creagan—most
of it still hidden
under the turf.

An Creagan & the Tyrone bogland

TO THE SOUTH OF THE SPERRIN MOUNTAINS, THE WAIST of County Tyrone wears a thick belt of blanket bog—a peat bog mostly composed of dead grasses and dependent on high rainfall. Hauntingly beautiful, it hides a marvelous archaeological treasure—a vast Stone Age and Bronze Age landscape, only now beginning to emerge.

The best place to start your wanderings around the blanket bogs of Tyrone is **An Creagan Visitor Centre** on the A505 road, midway between Omagh and Cookstown. The center gives an excellent overview of the area—its culture and traditions, the bogs themselves, the way they were formed and their great variety of wildlife, and the rare archaeological landscape that surrounds An Creagan. You can also get a meal here and pick up pamphlets that will direct you to the best sites within a 5-mile (8 km) radius of the center, some reachable on foot and others by recommended cycling routes. To rent bikes, enquire at the Omagh visitor information office (*tel 028 8224 7831*).

The blanket bogs began to develop during a cold and wet climatic phase around 1000 B.C. They crept in on a partly wooded landscape of birch, oak, hazel, and alder, much of it already cleared for farming thousands of years before. Those Stone Age farmers had erected standing stones, field walls, wedge tombs, and court tombs, and the Bronze Age people who followed them circa 2000 B.C. added stone circles, cist cairns, and artificial crannog islets in the bog lakes. The bog smothered all these and a moody landscape came into being: heathery and grassy bog and oily pools undulating to the horizon.

Farming ceased, for all practical purposes, until dispossessed Catholics were forced to make the best of the boglands during the 18th and 19th centuries. Their attempts to cultivate the peat can be seen in the ruins of lime kilns and telltale ridges of earth beneath which potatoes were stored. The bog turf proved more useful for fuel, and turf cutters began to unearth such treasures as the Beaghmore Stone Circles in the 1930s.

Beaghmore is the best known of the Tyrone archaeological sites, lying northeast of the center with wonderful views north to the Sperrins. The site contains an extraordinary number of stone align- ments set up some time between 2000 and 1200 B.C.—three pairs of circles formed of stones varying from craggy chest-high boulders to prone chunks of rock, one solo circle filled with more than 800 little stone lumps, a dozen or so round cairns, and several stone rows running off to various unfathomable destinations.

Due north of An Creagan lies **Peadar Joe Haughey's Cottage,** the restored home of one of Tyrone's last native Gaelic speak- ers, and the large patch of raised bog known as the **Black Bog.** Much deeper than the surrounding blanket bog, it formed over the remains of a deep lake. North again is **Dun Ruadh,** the Red Fort, a horseshoe- shaped cairn in which Bronze Age people buried 13 of their number.

South of the A505 lie several sites, pride of which are three remarkable tombs. Most westerly is **Loughmacross wedge tomb,** built around 2000 B.C. with great capstones perched on kerbstones. Southeast of An Creagan Centre, overlooking lonely Lough Mallon, **Creggandevesky court tomb** predates Loughmacross by at least 1,500 years, and is one of Ireland's finest examples of its type. About 60 feet long (18 m) and composed of countless tons of tiny stones, it has three chambers. The burned bones of 21 people were excavated here.

Two miles (3 km) east, up a grav- elly lane beyond a farmhouse, lies **Cregganconroe court tomb.** A giant capstone stands tilted to the sky among its kerbstones and the remains of two sizeable galleries and two small side chambers. ■

County Fermanagh

LEGEND HAS IT THAT A PAIR OF YOUNG LOVERS WAS responsible for flooding County Fermanagh with water. It seems that the whole county used to be a dry plain, with a fairy well in the middle that was always kept covered for fear of a curse the fairies had laid on it. One day this girl and her lover happened by. Feeling thirsty, they took the lid off the well and had a drink, but they forgot to put the lid back on. Next dawn, as the rising sun hit the well water, it over-flowed and would not stop. Soon much of Fermanagh was filled with water, and that's how things still stand today.

One-third of the county is under water, locals will tell you, almost all of it in the great twin lake system known as **Lower** and **Upper Lough Erne.** Together the two lakes stretch for some 50 miles (80 km), hinged together by the isthmus on which stands Fermanagh's county town of Enniskillen. Lower Lough Erne is all of a piece, one mighty sheet of water, while Upper Lough Erne is more like an immensely complicated system of small rivers winding between and

encircling innumerable tiny islands, peninsulas, and bulbous headlands.

From here via the Ballynamore and Ballyconnell Canal (renamed the Shannon-Erne Waterway; see p. 233), it is possible to cruise all the way south to the Shannon Estuary. As for the two lakes themselves, providing cruising and fishing for visitors is their economic lifeblood (see p. 233).

At the most westerly end of the Lower Lough sits **Belleek (Beleek),** a lively village right on the border between County Fermanagh in Northern Ireland and County Donegal in the Republic. Belleek is a pretty place, with cast-iron street furniture and renovated wooden shop fronts. Its claim to fame is the glittering white parian ware that has been turned out since the 1850s by **Belleek Pottery.** A tour around the factory shows you the process, in which a mixture of Cornish china clay and glass is beaten with wooden paddles to squeeze out air bubbles; then snakes of the stuff are made by the pottery craftsmen into various forms of artifact—basketware is the most popular—before being decorated, perhaps with minute birds or flowers. The craftsmen tend to use homemade tools; they say a humble 5-inch (13 cm) nail with one end flattened is the key to success. Naturally you

Tully Castle

- 300 B2
- Derrygonnelly, on Enniskillen–Belleek road, Co. Fermanagh
- 028 9023 5000
- Closed Oct.–March; Mon.–Tues. June–Aug.; weekdays April, May, & Sept.

Belleek Pottery

- Belleek, Co. Fermanagh
- 028 0865 8501
- Closed weekends
- $$

Left: Nothing but the finest craftmanship at Belleek Pottery

The Tudor water gate of Enniskillen Castle, looking out over the River Erne, is one of the classic sights of County Fermanagh's chief town.

ExplorErne Museum

✉ Erne Gateway Centre, Corry, Belleek, Co. Fermanagh

☎ 028 6865 8866

🕐 Closed Oct.–April

💲 $

can buy examples of Belleek ware in the pottery showroom, though your pockets will need to be deep to afford the best basketware. Some pieces are decorated with lucky shamrocks, although it's doubtful whether these will bring you the kind of good fortune that attended one of the men who helped build the pottery. During construction he slipped and fell from the roof to the ground, but somehow landed on his feet, unharmed. He was given a stiff tot of whiskey and a pat on the back, and sent straight back up again to carry on with the job.

At Belleek you can rent a cruiser for the Lower Lough and also visit the **ExplorErne Museum,** an excellent introduction to the world of the lakes.

TO THE SOUTH

A long ridge of hills crowned and collared by two big forests—Lough Navar Forest and Big Dog Forest—dominate the wide, hilly area south of Lower Lough Erne. **Lough Navar Forest** is well set out for forest driving and for waymarked walking. Most paths and tracks seem to lead eventually to the big panoramic map at **Lough Navar Forest viewpoint,** right on the dramatic bluffs of the **Cliffs of Magho,** where you can look across a vast vista of Lower Lough Erne, its islands and straggly peninsulas. Not only this: Benbulben stands out small but sharp in County Sligo, 25 miles (40 km) to the west, while the pale 2,467-foot (750 m) triangle of Mount Errigal rises northward like

Journey into the depths (if not the center) of the Earth—the wonders of Marble Arch Caves are viewed by boat.

Marble Arch Caves
- 🗺 300 B1
- ✉ 5 miles (8 km) W of Florence Court off A4 Enniskillen–Sligo road
- ☎ 028 6634 8855
- 🕐 Closed Oct.–mid-March
- 💲 $$$

Enniskillen
- 🗺 300 B2

Visitor information
- ✉ Wellington Rd., Enniskillen, Co. Fermanagh
- ☎ 028 6632 3110

a sail, 40 miles (60 km) away in northwest Donegal.

Two fine castles from the early 17th-century plantation days stand to the south: Tully Castle beside the lough shore, and Monea Castle on a rocky bluff farther inland. **Tully Castle** was built around 1610 by the incoming Scottish Hume family. In 1641 Roderick Maguire, whose Catholic clan had had all their Fermanagh land confiscated after Hugh O'Neill's disastrous 1601 rising (see p. 26), enthusiastically joined in a general rebellion and burned Tully. Its garrison perished, in spite of Maguire's assurances of safe conduct to Enniskillen. The tall, gaunt ruins still have the turreted walls of their bawn, or defensive enclosure, and a delightful herb garden with a clipped hedge has been laid out in early 17th-century style.

Monea Castle, with its tall, baronial drum towers, looks as if it has been transported from the Scottish Highlands. It, too, was burned in 1641, and again by Jacobite troops in 1689 during their abortive attempts to take and hold

Enniskillen. After another fire in 1750 it was finally left to decay.

The southern border of Fermanagh bulges into the panhandle of northwest County Cavan. Down here, south of lovely Lough Macnean Lower, the hills are riddled with caves. In the northern flank of Cuilcagh Mountain you can visit **Marble Arch Caves,** an exciting tour that starts with a boat ride on an underground river and ends with a walk among stalagmites, stalactites, and other weird calcite formations.

TO THE NORTH
The north side of Lower Lough Erne possesses two fine forest parks, both with extensive shorelines. **Castle Caldwell Forest** *(tel 028 6634 3032),* 4 miles (6 km) east of Belleek, has beautiful walks along two long wooded lake peninsulas. There's excellent bird-watching here. By the lodge at the park entrance on the A47 is a **memorial stone,** shaped like an outsize violin, to Denis McCabe, a fiddle player who drowned on August 13, 1779, after falling off Sir James Caldwell's barge into the lough while drunk.

Castle Archdale Forest Park, halfway down the lough, has a herd of red deer, a marina where boats can be rented, and more walks.

Five miles (8 km) south toward Enniskillen, it's worth turning aside into the village churchyard at Killadeas to look at the **Bishop's Stone.** This memorial stone, probably carved around the eighth century, commemorates an abbot with a profile portrait on one side; on the other a very pagan looking face stares out fixedly. It is as if the carver was reflecting the changeover (or maybe the early Celtic church's live-and-let-live policy) between paganism and Christianity.

ENNISKILLEN

Both north and south routes along the shores of Lower Lough Erne converge at **Enniskillen** on the narrow isthmus separating the lower from the upper lake. Fermanagh's chief town sits right at the heart of the county, socially and economically as well as geographically. There's an excellent tourist office here, several decent hotels, and all the main facilities of a sizeable town. The straggling main street—which changes name six times in its mile-long (1.6 km) course—contains a gem of a watering hole in the unreconstructed Victorian pub known as **Blake's of the Hollow** (tel 028 6632 2143). From the whiskey tuns and wood-paneled snugs to the excellent Guinness and frequent traditional music sessions, this is a treasure of a place.

Along the River Erne you'll find **Enniskillen Castle,** with its handsome twin-towered watergate; a regimental museum here deals with the history of the Inniskilling Fusiliers, and a good heritage center covers Fermanagh history. You can buy local crafts in the converted Buttermarket and watch Fermanagh dealers and farmers in the lively cattle market.

The town's **war memorial** commemorating World Wars I and II at the top of East Bridge Street gained worldwide notoriety as the scene of the murder of 11 people by the IRA in a bomb explosion on Remembrance Day, November 11, 1987.

North of the memorial is Forthill Park, where **Cole's Monument** rises from the center of a star-shaped 17th-century fort. The fluted column was erected in 1857 to honor General Sir Galbraith Lowry Cole (1772–1842), a brother of the 2nd Earl of Enniskillen and one of the Duke of

Wellington's fighting generals in the Napoleonic Wars. You can climb the 108 spiral steps inside the column for a wonderful view over Enniskillen and Lough Erne.

South of Enniskillen the landscape explodes into a crazed maze of water and land as the River Erne wriggles through the countless windings and backwaters of Upper Lough Erne.

Derrylin on the south side of the upper lough ("the friendliest place in Fermanagh") and **Lisnaskea** on the north side are two pleasant small towns where you can catch your breath.

Down in the south part of the lough near the Cavan border, 3 miles (5 km) west of Newtownbutler, the National Trust administers the **Crom Estate** on the east shore of the lake (note: New Crom Castle is a private residence). The old 1611 plantation castle is a picturesque ruin by the lakeshore, with two giant and gnarled 17th-century yews growing in the garden. There are woodland and lough shore walks, deer, and pine martens. ■

Bliss in Blake's of the Hollow, with the paper, a pint, and a perch by the fire

Enniskillen Castle
www.enniskillencastle.co.uk
- ✉ Castle Barracks, Enniskillen, Co. Fermanagh
- ☎ 028 6632 5000
- 🕐 Closed Sat.–Sun. Oct.–April; closed Sun. May–June & Sept.
- 💲 $

Crom Estate
- ✉ 3 miles (5 km) W of Newtownbutler off A34, Co. Fermanagh
- ☎ 028 6773 8118 or 028 6773 8174
- 🕐 Closed Oct.–mid-March
- 💲 $$

The round tower
and monastic
buildings on
Devenish Island
are one of the
chief attractions
for boaters on
Lough Erne.

Cruising Lough Erne

THOUGH YOU CAN CATCH MANY CHARMING GLIMPSES OF
the upper and lower loughs from the shore, you can only enjoy the
full picture by cruising their island-dotted waters. The two main
boating centers are Beleek and Enniskillen, in County Fermanagh.

There are reputed to be 93 islands
in Lower Lough Erne (or is it 97?),
and 152 (or is that 177?) in Upper
Lough Erne. No one's counting—
but there are plenty for all.

The lower lough's best-known
island is **Devenish,** just downstream of Enniskillen *(ferry from
Trory Point, signed off the A32,
closed Oct.–May & Mon., $),* with
its superb round tower, ruins of
monastic churches, and finely
carved high cross. In Caldragh
cemetery on **Boa Island** *(causeway*

bridges on the A47), you'll find the
enigmatic fifth- or sixth-century
Janus Figure, its two pagan faces
staring wildly in opposite directions.

On **White Island** *(ferry from
Castle Archdale Country Park, closed
Sept.–March & weekdays April–June,
$$)* stand seven stone carvings that
experts have puzzled over. Look for a
sheela-na-gig (the figure of a grinning
woman holding open her vulva), a
figure with a book, two probable
representations of Christ, along
with a bishop and someone who

may be King David, and a scowling head. They may date back to the sixth century, and seem both Christian and pagan in character.

In Upper Lough Erne three islands with ancient pagan or monastic carvings are easily reached by car or boat. **Inishkeen** *(causeway off the A4 just S of Enniskillen)* has strange carved stones in the cemetery of St. Fergus's Church—an antlered head, and someone in a vessel.

On **Cleenish,** reached by a bridge 2 miles (3 km) east of Bellanaleck, are several finely carved gravestones; while down in the south on **Galloon** *(causeway from Landbrock crossroads, 2 miles/ 3 km S of Newtownbutler)* are more macabre 18th-century graveslabs with skull-and-crossbones and hourglass motifs. ■

Boat rental & cruises on Lough Erne

Enniskillen

Guided cruises on Lower Lough Erne, and day boat rental: Erne Tours Ltd. *(tel 028 6632 2882)* Cruiser rental: Lochside Cruisers *(tel 028 6632 4368)*

Beleek (Belleek)

Day boat rental: Beleek Angling Centre *(tel 028 6865 8181)* Cruiser rental: Beleek Charter Cruising *(tel 028 6865 8027)*

Lisnaskea

Guided cruises on Upper Lough Erne: Share Centre *(tel 028 6772 2122)* ■

Florence Court stretches its arcaded wings wide, as if embracing its beautiful parkland.

Two great Fermanagh houses

THE 18TH CENTURY WAS THE GOLDEN AGE OF GRAND landscaping and domestic architecture in Ireland. If you were rich enough, you showed the world by commissioning the very biggest and best country house that your money could buy. County Fermanagh boasts two of the most enchanting.

Florence Court

📍 300 B1

✉ Signed off the
   A32 Enniskillen–
   Swanlinbar road,
   8 miles (13 km)
   SW of Enniskillen

☎ 028 6634 8249

🕐 House open
   May–Aug. Wed.–Mon.
   p.m., and April &
   Sept. Sun. p.m. and
   Bank Holidays. Estate
   open year-round.

💲 $$

FLORENCE COURT

Florence Court is a secluded 18th-century house, tucked away in beautiful wooded grounds looking southwest to the jagged ridge of Cuilcagh Mountain. The Cole family (later Earls of Enniskillen) built it in stages from the 1750s—first the three-story central block, and then the arcaded wings.

In the summer these grounds provide the setting for various out-door events, from Victorian garden parties and country fairs to a children's teddy bear's picnic. One interesting feature is the sawmill that was established by the 3rd Earl of Enniskillen during the Great Famine to give paid work to some of his destitute tenants.

Among various lovely woodland walks one leads toward Cuilcagh Mountain. It passes the Florence Court Yew, a tattered old thing shaped like a rocket that was found growing on Cuilcagh in the mid-

18th century. Its offspring cuttings have established a distinct species, the Irish yew.

The house interior had to be completely restored by the National Trust in 1955—only five years after it acquired the property—following a fire. Wonderful rococo plaster-work can be seen, particularly on the staircase walls and the dining ceiling, where puff-cheeked cherubs represent the Four Winds of Heaven, and a rosette of birds flies among flowers.

Upstairs, family prints, drawings, and photographs are displayed. In the bedside table beside the elegant four-poster in the countess's bed-room is a rare piece of Belleek Pottery (see pp. 322–323)—a chamberpot with a picture of 19th-century British Prime Minister William Gladstone strategically placed on the bottom. Gladstone forfeited the allegiance—indeed, inspired the hatred—of many Irish Ascendancy families (those with British backgrounds who lived and owned land in Ireland) with his support for the Home Rule Bill that threatened to destroy their comfort-able supremacy.

CASTLE COOLE

The Lowry-Corry family, Earls of Belmore, built Castle Coole at the end of the 18th century. A flock of greylag geese has been resident in the park for at least 300 years, and legend says that the Belmores will remain at Castle Coole as long as the geese do. At present the earl lives in another house on the estate.

Regency architectural supremo James Wyatt designed the great Palladian mansion. Completed in 1798, it is reckoned to be the finest neoclassic house in Ireland. It was commissioned by Armar Lowry-Corry, a country squire who got lucky in 1741 when he inherited the estate along with streams of money,

property, and lands throughout Fermanagh, Tyrone, and Donegal. The house was built as a grand statement of his capacity to exercise power and influence over the Irish political scene. He was created 1st Earl of Belmore in 1797, but vicissitudes of life brought him no joy—his dark-haired beauty of a wife ran off and left him miserable. He died in 1802, so much in debt that his son the 2nd Earl had to wait 20 years before finishing the decorations and furnishings.

The house with its portico of four immense columns stands on a ridge on 1,500 acres (600 ha) of beautiful parkland. Almost all the original furnishings are here, still in the rooms for which they were designed and built. The oval saloon, with its elaborate cast-iron stoves, the dining room, and the drawing room are floored with Irish oak and opulently furnished. The canopied bed in the State Bedroom was created for a visit by King George IV in 1821 (he never showed up, reportedly because he was dallying elsewhere with one of his mistresses). ■

Immaculate elegance at Castle Coole: It took the 2nd Earl of Belmore 20 years to raise the money to finish the furnishings, after his father died leaving nothing but debts.

Castle Coole

🅰 300 B2

✉ On the A4 Enniskillen—Belfast road, 1.5 miles (2.5 km) SE of Enniskillen

☎ 028 6632 2690

🕐 House open mid-March—May & Sept. Sat.—Sun. p.m., June Wed.—Mon. p.m., and July—Aug. daily p.m. Parkland open year-round.

 $$

County Armagh

COUNTY ARMAGH, WITH ITS OPPRESSIVE REPUBLICAN reputation, is few people's idea of a visitor destination. Yet historic houses and towns, landscape beauty, and local friendliness are to be found in plenty in this most-maligned of the six counties.

**Oxford Island–
Lough Neagh
Discovery Centre**
- 🗺 301 E2
- ✉ Oxford Island, Lough Neagh, Craigavon, Co. Armagh
- ☎ 028 3832 2205
- 🕐 Closed Mon.–Tues. Oct.–March
- 💲 $–$$

The Argory
- 🗺 301 D2
- ✉ Derrycaw Rd., Moy, Dungannon, Co. Armagh
- ☎ 028 8778 4753
- 🕐 House open mid-March–May & Sept. Sat.–Sun. p.m.; June–Aug. daily p.m.; grounds open daily year-round
- 💲 $$

The southern shore of Lough Neagh closes the northern boundary of County Armagh, and here at the **Oxford Island–Lough Neagh Discovery Centre** you can learn about the natural history and traditions of the biggest lake in the British Isles. From the bird-watching blinds you can enjoy the sight of dozens of bird species in their seasons.

Two enjoyable National Trust houses stand a little south of the M1 Dungannon–Belfast motorway. **The Argory,** signed from junctions 13 and 14, was built in 1820. This is a house whose atmosphere and furnishings have remained frozen in the year 1900. **Ardress House,** 3 miles (5 km) southeast of the Argory, is a 17th-century farmhouse swollen into an 18th-century mansion by adding a wing

at one side and a matching dummy wing at the other! Children love the working 18th-century farmyard attached to the house.

Armagh city is well worth a day's wander. This ancient capital of Ulster and seat of both Catholic and Anglican Bishops of Ireland has two cathedrals, one for each denomination, on opposite hills—symbolic, many think, of their intransigent positions during the recent Troubles. The building of the Gothic **Catholic Cathedral of St. Patrick** began in 1838, stopped during the famine, and was completed in 1873 thanks to money raised through raffles, appeals, and bazaars. Standing proud at the top of a long flight of steps, it's a marvel of ornate marble and mosaic, with gold-winged angels soaring high in the vaulted nave roof.

Across the valley the **Anglican Cathedral**—also dedicated to St. Patrick—is lower, smaller, and far older than its Catholic counterpart. Built in medieval times and restored in 1765, it holds some fine monuments, including the splendid Tandragee Idol, an Iron Age effigy grinning under his fat cheeks and clutching one arm. He might be a representation of Nuada the Silver-handed (see p. 266). Outside on the west wall of the north transept is a memorial to Brian Boroimhe or Boru, mightiest of all Ireland's High Kings, who died in 1014 at the Battle of Clontarf, the final victory over the Vikings. Brian lies buried "in the north side of the great church," according to contemporary accounts.

Armagh's **public library** (*tel 028 3752 3142*), on Abbey Street near the Anglican cathedral, is an antiquarian's dream of old leather books in a solemn and splendid room. The **County Museum** in the Mall East has a fabulous collection of artifacts, wooden drinking cups, Bronze Age jewelry, and tools. Just off the Mall the heritage center of **St. Patrick's Trian** (*tel 028 3752 1801*) has tableaus of monks and warriors, and a treat for children in its "Land of Lilliput."

Two miles (3 km) west of Armagh is **Navan hill fort,** the ancient Eamhain Mhacha, or Queen Mhacha's Palace. It was from this great mound that the Kings of Ulster ruled for 1,000 years. Many of the Ulster hero Cúchulainn's mighty deeds are set here.

Don't miss a swing through the tumbled drumlin-and-lake country of south Armagh. There is regular music and storytelling at the **Tí Chulainn Centre** (*tel 028 3088 8828*) in Mullaghbane.

The **Slieve Gullion Forest Park** is signed off the B113 between Meigh and Forkhill; from here you can drive or walk. The final scramble to the Bronze Age cairns on the summit of Slieve Gullion is short but steep, the view spectacular. ■

Armagh County Museum
- 🏛 301 D2
- ✉ The Mall East, Armagh, Co. Armagh
- ☎ 028 3752 3070
- 🕐 Closed Sun.

Navan Hill, for a thousand years the Red Branch Knights' fortress

Ardress House
- 🏛 301 E2
- ✉ Annaghmore, Co. Armagh, on B28, 7 miles (11 km) W of Portadown
- ☎ 028 3885 1236
- 🕐 Open mid-March–May & Sept. Sat.–Sun. p.m., June–Aug. Wed.–Mon. p.m.
- 💲 $

Slieve Gullion Forest Park
- 🏛 301 E1
- ✉ On B113, 5 miles (8 km) SW of Newry, Co. Armagh
- ☎ 028 3755 1277
- 🕐 Closed Sept.–Easter

Fionn MacCumhaill on Slieve Gullion

When you climb to the top of Slieve Gullion you'll find a dark little lake, the Calliagh Beara Lough, just by the north cairn. Don't touch the water ….

It was Fionn MacCumhaill who met Miluchra, an enchantress in the shape of a beautiful young woman, on the top of Slieve Gullion. She begged him to dive into the lake to retrieve her gold ring. Gallant Fionn did as the maiden asked; but on climbing out of the water the hero found himself transformed into a feeble old man. The damsel, meanwhile, had turned into a withered hag, the Calliagh Beara.

Some say it was Fionn's men who found the Calliagh Beara hiding in the summit cairn and forced her to undo the mischief. Others tell of how Fionn's dog Bran fetched the hero's grandson Oscar from Killarney, and Oscar caught a fairy man who gave Fionn a drink of youth to revitalize him. ■

Walk: Trassey Track to Hare's Gap, Mourne Mountains

The Mountains of Mourne sweep down to the sea at the southern extremity of County Down—beautifully shaped pink-gray granite peaks, 12 of them over 2,000 feet (610 m), all packed into an area measuring 15 by 8 miles (24 by 13 km). Lakes are hidden in the heart of the Mournes, and there are famous beauty spots such as the narrow and dramatic Spelga Pass. These are accessible by car; but the Mournes are above all walkers' country.

You need to dress in suitable hill-walking gear and take with you a map, a compass, and food and drink. Weather conditions can change quickly, and though the highest peak, Slieve Donard, is only 2,788 feet (850 m), these are proper mountains. Once on the peaks, though, it's hard to get lost, thanks to the Mourne Wall, a 22-mile (35 km) circuit of drystone wall that links the main inner summits. It was built between 1904 and 1922 to help poverty-stricken, hungry men earn enough to feed their families.

The walk to Hare's Gap starts from the little parking lot under the forest-covered Clonachullion Hill. From the entrance walk left along the road, and after about 70 yards (64 m) bear left over a stile and join the **Trassey Track,** a well-trodden path that climbs gradually up, keeping the large

forestry plantation ❶ on your left.

At the top edge of the trees the Ulster Way long-distance footpath bends away to the right; but you keep straight ahead, swinging a little to the left and then straightening to climb on steepening ground with the Trassey River on your right.

The section of the track you are on now is known as the **Brandy Pad** ❷, with good reason: It is part of an old smuggler's path by which contraband goods (including brandy) were brought by pack pony through the heart of the Mournes from the coast south of Newcastle. Once down in the lowlands on the inland side of the mountains they could be hidden around any number of farms before onward transportation.

Just after the track crosses the river by a footbridge, bear left away from paths going up

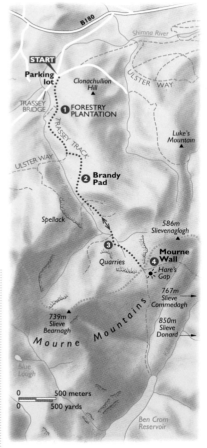

Glorious prospect: The spectacular views from the high places of the Mourne Mountains make the climb worthwhile.

to the old **quarries** ❸ behind the naked cliffs of Spellack. Soon you recross the river. From here it is a straightforward climb, aiming between converging rock cliffs to reach the **Mourne Wall** ❹ in Hare's Gap. Take plenty of time to walk forward and admire the stunning views over the end of Ben Crom Reservoir to the bulk of Slieve Commedagh (2,515 feet/767 m) and Slieve Donard.

From here, retrace your steps back down to

🅐 See area map p. 301 F1

▶ Parking lot just NE of Trassey Bridge, below Clonachullion Hill (1 mile/1.6 km off the B180, 4 miles/6 km W of Newcastle), Co. Down

↔ 4 miles (6 km), with 850 feet (260 m) of ascent

🕐 3 hours

▶ Parking lot just NE of Trassey Bridge

NOT TO BE MISSED
- Views back from the Trassey Track
- Views forward from Hare's Gap

Information

Map:
Ordnance Survey map of Northern Ireland 1:50,000 Discoverer Series No. 29 "The Mournes"

Guide Card:
Walk No. 10 in *Mourne Mountain Walks* pack available from bookstores, outdoor shops, Mourne Heritage Trust's Countryside Centre in Newcastle (*987 Central Promenade, tel 028 4372 4059*), or Newcastle Tourist Office (*10–14 Central Promenade, tel 028 4372 2222*).

St. Patrick's Country

THE SPIRIT OF IRELAND'S PATRON SAINT INFUSES THE region known as St. Patrick's Country; for it was in this lovely but rather overlooked corner of County Down between Strangford Lough and the Mourne Mountains that St. Patrick landed in 432 to begin his great mission of converting Ireland to Christianity.

Saul Church was built in 1932 on the 1,500th anniversary of St. Patrick's arrival.

Downpatrick
🅜 301 F2
Visitor information
✉ Saint Patrick Centre (see below)

Saint Patrick Centre
🅜 301 F2
✉ 53a Market St., Downpatrick, Co. Down
☎ 028 4461 9000
🕐 Closed Sun. Oct.–March
💲 $$

Did St. Patrick even exist? The answers to this question vary, depending on who you talk to, but it is most probable that he did. The best guess is that he was born in Scotland or Wales, perhaps the son of a Roman centurion at the end of the Roman Empire's tenure in the British Isles. At the age of about 16, he was captured by Irish marauders and taken to County Antrim, where he was put to work herding sheep on Slemish Mountain for six years or so. It seems that some pioneer missionary converted him to Christianity during this period of enslavement. Finally he escaped on a ship that was carrying a cargo of wolfhounds and made his way to Gaul (France). Perhaps a quarter of a century of wandering and preaching across the Continent followed;

then in 431 Patrick was appointed bishop, and the following year made his landing in County Down. He probably sailed up the estuary of the Slaney River and landed at Ringbane near Saul, just east of present-day **Downpatrick.**

Patrick, always a practical missionary, hastened to convert the local chief, Dichu, the man with the greatest on-the-spot influence, and Dichu gave Patrick use of a barn (*sabhal* in Irish, hence "Saul") as a temporary base. Though the saint was to move on and travel all through the north of Ireland, it was to Saul that he returned to die in 461, in the monastery he had founded there.

In 1932, the 1,500th anniversary of Patrick's arrival, a church and round tower in traditional Gaelic style were built on the spot. The **Saint Patrick Centre** contains a very good exhibition about the saint's life and work, with emphasis on local Patrick-related sites. You can climb the purgatorial Stations of the Cross path up the nearby hill of Slieve Patrick to the altar and 30-foot (10 m) cross on top. From the summit there are great views over Strangford Lough and the Lecale Peninsula.

In common with all early Christian missionaries, Patrick was a great mortifier of the flesh. At **Struell Wells** (*information from Downpatrick visitor information*), 2 miles (3 km) south of Saul (*signed off the Downpatrick–Ardglass road*), the saint tested his own fortitude by immersing himself in freezing water and spending "a great part of the night, stark naked, singing psalms and spiritual songs." The wells in their green valley gained a great reputation for healing powers, and were developed in the 18th century into a pilgrimage complex.

Today you can explore the roofless women's bathhouse and the men's bathhouse, with its benches and dark, cold bathing tank under a heavy stone roof. Look, too, for the well whose water cures eye disease, and the domed drinking well—long known as the Tub—in which St. Patrick spent his prayerful night of immersion.

Downpatrick Cathedral on its rise of ground is mostly 19th- and 20th-century work. In the shadow of its walls lies the vast slab of rock, inscribed "Patric," that was laid over St. Patrick's grave in 1901 to stop pilgrims removing the sacred earth. Late 12th-century Norman Lord Sir John de Courcy vowed he had reburied Patrick's bones here, along with those of St. Columba, who died on Iona in 597, and St. Brigid who died in Kildare

in 523. Whether all or any of them really lie under the great rock is open to question.

Two more ecclesiastical sites a little to the west of Downpatrick are well worth visiting. **Inch Abbey,** off the A7 just beyond the river bridge, is a Cistercian monastery with a fine triple-lancet east window, beautifully sited beside the River Quoile. At **Loughinisland** (*take the B2, then the Loughinisland road*) three old churches stand on a drumlin island in a lake cradled by hills. You can cross by causeway to explore the churches—notably MacCartan's Chapel with its tiny door, inscribed PMC (Phelim MacCartan) and dated 1636—a time when to build a Catholic church was to invite persecution, and maybe death. ∎

Each spring fresh daffodils are placed on the great incised graveslab of St. Patrick outside Downpatrick Cathedral.

Inch Abbey
- 301 F2
- Off A7 W of Downpatrick, Co. Down
- 028 9023 5000

Bangor
🅰 301 F3
Visitor information
✉ 34 Quay St., Bangor,
Co. Down
☎ 028 9127 0069

Strangford Lough
🅰 301 F3, G2
Strangford Lough Office
✉ 13 The Strand,
Portaferry, Co. Down
☎ 028 4272 8886

Mount Stewart
✉ 5 miles (8 km) SW
of Newtownards on
A20, Co. Down
☎ 028 4278 8387
🕐 House open mid-
March–April & Oct.
Sat.–Sun. p.m.; May–
June & Sept.
Wed.–Mon. p.m.;
July–Aug. daily p.m.;
grounds open year-
round
💲 $$

Strangford Lough & the Ards Peninsula

EAST OF BELFAST LIES ONE OF IRELAND'S MOST BEAUTIFUL and haunting landscapes—the long southward-curving arm of the Ards Peninsula, and the great bird-thronged sea inlet of Strangford Lough. Two fine National Trust houses, a spatter of islands, and some dramatic coastline complete the picture of County Down.

The Ards Peninsula begins at the seaside town of **Bangor** on the northernmost shoulder of County Down, and runs south for some 25 miles (40 km). Its east-facing coast looks onto the Irish Sea over splendid sandy beaches, often heaped with weed, and interspersed with rocky coves and fishing villages. At the southern tip, a glorious 5-mile (8 km) coastal walk leads around the hamlet of **Kearney** *(tel 028 4488 1411 or 028 4488 1668)*—both village and coast are maintained by the National Trust.

The inner coastline of Ards is entirely different; **Strangford Lough,** onto which it looks, has a muddy, mysterious, estuarine feel.

The lough is 19 miles (30 km) from innermost corner to the peninsula tip, a great tidal inlet full of drumlin islands, whose waters recede at low tide to expose mighty mud flats and sand banks. Bird-watching here is unequaled in Northern Ireland; some 12,000 light-bellied brent geese—10 percent of the world population—fly from Greenland to overwinter here, and regular gatherings occur of huge numbers of golden plover, lapwing, curlew, godwit, and redshank, as well as vast clouds of ducks such as wigeon, shelduck, and pintail.

The Stewarts had—and still have—their seat at **Mount Stewart,** a beautiful country

house on the east shore of the lough now in the care of the National Trust. There's a family feel to the house—original bird paintings by English artist and humorist Edward Lear casually stuck to a firescreen; copies of playwright Sean O'Casey's works dedicated in his own hand to Edith, wife of the 7th Marquis of Londonderry. Edith laid out the superb gardens and the Dodo Terrace, with freakish and funny animal statues dedicated to members of her informal "Ark Club" of politicians and soldiers.

Grey Abbey, 4 miles (6 km) farther south, is a fine 12th-century ruin by the shore. At Portaferry, an attractive little village along the water, you catch a ferry across the narrows to reach Strangford village and the southern and western shores of Strangford Lough. In a couple of miles (3 km), a signed turning on the right leads to the National Trust property of **Castle Ward,** beautifully set on wooded parkland at the southern end of the lough. The house is an architectural oddity, the front half being in sober Palladian style, while the back

half is all exuberant Gothic—the 18th-century owners, Bernard and Lady Anne Ward, disagreed bitterly over the design of the house, so took half each. Bernard's front half is a model of classical restraint on the outside and has wonderful plasterwork within (including a genuine fiddle, basket, and hat dipped in plaster and added to the ensemble); Lady Anne's rear half features pointed windows and doorframes, fan vaulting, and Moorish decorations.

There are fine river and wetland walks at **Quoile Countryside Centre** (*tel 028 4461 5520, closed weekdays Sept.–March*) just north of Downpatrick, and far up the western lough shore some excellent birdwatching at **Castle Espie Wildfowl and Wetlands Trust** (*tel 028 9187 4146*).

Between the two lies **Mahee Island** (*signed*), a lonely islet at the end of several causeways. St. Patrick preached here at the monastery of St. Mochaoi. Ancient stone walls, ruins of a round tower and church, and some rugged monastic graveslabs are all that remain. ∎

House and garden form a fine, harmonious composition at Mount Stewart on the shores of Strangford Lough.

Grey Abbey
- 301 G3
- Grey Abbey, Co. Down
- 028 9054 3033
- Closed weekdays Oct.–March; Mon. April–Sept.

Castle Ward
- 301 G2
- On A25, 1.25 miles (2 km) W of Strangford, Co. Down
- 028 4488 1204,
- Closed Nov.–mid-March; weekdays mid-March–April & Oct.; Tues. in May
- $$

Cúchulainn, Ulster's warrior hero

The ancient kingdom of Ulster, of which Northern Ireland comprises a major part, is steeped in colorful legend. Much of it revolves around the indomitable warrior Cúchulainn, the only hero who might have given that other Irish mythical daredevil, Fionn MacCumhaill (Finn McCool), a run for his money.

Cúchulainn, in his warrior glory, strides toward the Shadow Land.

Son of the god Lugh the Long-handed, Cúchulainn was given the birth name Setanta. At the age of seven he slew a ferocious hound that had attacked him on the slopes of Slieve Gullion by jamming his *sliotar* (hurling ball) into its jaws and then beating out its brains with his *camán* (hurley stick). The hound's owner, Culainn the Smith, was none too pleased; so Setanta offered to guard his house until he had trained up another dog. Thus he acquired his proper name: Cúchulainn, the Hound of Culainn.

Cúchulainn proved to be a handful. Haughty but beautiful Emer set him impossible tasks in order to win her hand: to leap the salmon leap, to slay eight men with a single blow—not once, but three times over—and to carry off two women along with their weight in gold and silver. Of course, he accomplished all with ease. Before battle, fearsome changes would come upon Cúchulainn. He would swell to giant stature and turn different colors, while one eye bulged to enormous size and his body burned so hot that snow melted, sparks showered from his mouth, and a mist of blood spurted from the crown of his head.

The ultimate warrior's finest hour came when treacherous, lecherous Queen Medb of Connacht launched the Cattle Raid of Cooley

upon Ulster. Envious of a fabulous bull, the White-horned One, that belonged to her husband King Ailill, she was determined to steal a beast that would match it—Ulster's famed Brown Bull of Cooley. The men of Ulster were under an enchantment that made them as weak as newly delivered mothers, so the 17-year-old Cúchulainn was obliged to defend Ulster single-handed. With sword, slingshot, and the dreaded many-barbed spear *Gae Bolga,* he dealt out so much death that Medb's armies were utterly defeated. The wicked Queen did manage to get back to Connacht with the Brown Bull of Cooley, only for her prize to kill the White-horned One and rampage through Ireland before dropping dead of sheer rage.

Queen Medb had the last laugh, though. Ten years after the Cattle Raid of Cooley, she enlisted three witches—their enchanter father had been killed by Cúchulainn—to put the warrior hero under a spell. Believing that Ulster was being attacked, Cúchulainn set out to defend his homeland.

Soon he met the sons of the Kings of Munster and Leinster. Unfortunately, Cúchulainn had killed those kings, too. In the ensuing battle the hero was mortally pierced with a spear thrust. Binding himself for support to a standing stone, he wielded his sword until he died. But even then the Hound of Chulainn was not quite finished. As young King Lughaidh of Munster stepped up and sliced off Cúchulainn's head, the sword fell from the hero's grasp and cut off his enemy's right hand. So passed Ulster's doughtiest champion, a mighty warrior to the last. ■

Top: Cúchulainn rides his war chariot into battle; above left: A druid warns Queen Medb to beware of Cúchulainn; above right: Cúchulainn carries his wounded foster-brother, Ferdia.

Wrinkled rocks of Ardglass overlook the uncrowded sands of the Lecale Peninsula.

More places to visit in Northern Ireland

CASTLEDERG

It's worth taking the B72 out to Castlederg in the west of County Tyrone because, while it has no spectacular visitor attractions, it's a good example of a friendly working village, dependent on agriculture. The Tuesday morning sheep sales in Forbes Livestock Mart out on the Killen road are a great gathering place for hill farmers, whose weatherbeaten faces ring the auctioneer with his machine-gun patter. West of Castlederg, County Tyrone makes a bulging salient into County Fermanagh. There's great walking and leisurely motoring here along lonely back roads and lanes around **Killeter Forest** on the border.

🔺 300 B3 **Castlederg visitor information** ✉ 26 Lower Strabane Rd., Castlederg, Co. Tyrone ☎ 028 8167 0795

KNOCKMANY CHAMBERED CAIRN

Southeast of Omagh, and not far from the border with County Monaghan, the Clogher Valley is a forested, secret glen. Signposted at the summit of a steep wooded hill here is Knockmany chambered cairn, a Bronze Age passage tomb whose pink stones are carved with wonderful whorls and spiral patterns, parallel lines like Ogham script, and mazy shapes. The view from here over miles of forest and hilly country is superb.

🔺 300 C2 **Omagh visitor information** (see p. 342)

LECALE PENINSULA

The blunt-nosed Lecale Peninsula, east of Downpatrick, has plenty of delights and

In 5 miles (8 km) you reach **Ardglass,** a lively fishing town that in its day was the most important fishing port in Ulster—hence the large number of towers, mini-castles, and other fortified buildings. **Killough,** 3 miles (5 km) on, was laid out neatly in the 18th century by Lord Bangor of Castle Ward as a port to ship out lead and farm produce from his estate. The rule-straight 8-mile (13 km) road he made to connect port and estate is still there. From Killough you can drive or walk the couple of miles (3 km) to the ruined tenth-century chapel on **St. John's Point.** From the tip of the point awaits a fabulous view of the Mourne Mountains.
301 G2 East of Downpatrick, Co. Down **Downpatrick visitor information** 53a Market St., Downpatrick, Co. Down 028 4461 2233

LOUGH NEAGH

Across on the eastern border of Tyrone, Lough Neagh stretches its vast, flat shore. Coarse fishing for lough eels, bream, roach, perch, and pike is superb: The Sperrin Tourism Partnership issues a pamphlet guide.

On the shores of Lough Neagh east of Cookstown stands **Ardboe High Cross,** a magnificently carved tenth-century cross 18.5 feet tall (5.5 m) featuring the Judgment of Solomon, Cain bashing Abel with a flail, and Daniel with two lions. Nearby stands a wishing tree, poisoned to death by thousands of votive coins pushed into its trunk.
301 E3 **Magherafelt visitor information** 6 Church St., Magherafelt, Co. Londonderrry 028 7963 1510

surprises. The 22-mile (35 km) coast drive, starting at Strangford village, turns south through **Kilclief,** where there is a fine 15th-century tower house. It was built by a naughty Bishop of Down, John Cely—he was defrocked in 1443 for living with Lettice Savage, a married woman, in the tower.

Ancient architecture

Ireland is particularly rich in the architecture of the ancients. Stone and Bronze Age peoples left us few artifacts to judge and understand them by, but their massive monuments in stone are markers that the passage of many millennia has failed to erase. Most notable are the court tombs from around 4000 B.C., with their partly enclosed courts or ritual spaces fronting the burial chambers. Wedge tombs, wedge-shaped court tombs, were built perhaps a thousand years later. Hard on their heels

came the passage graves, man-made mounds with a passage leading to central chambers; these could be any size, with the largest—such as Newgrange (see p. 269)—being as big as a small hill.

Stone circles were erected by both Stone Age and Bronze Age people, some as boundary markers around burial sites, others apparently to form enclosed spaces for rituals. Some possess much larger stones that seem to have had a guardian role. ■

Beautiful, secluded Murlough Bay lies in the midst of Co. Antrim's busier coastal attractions.

MURLOUGH BAY

This is a glorious bay, and though it lies between the popular Antrim Coast Road and the Giant's Causeway area, it remains unspoiled because of the absence of a major road along this northwest shoulder of the Antrim coast.

Rocks and silvery sand lie under cliffs and slopes clothed in silver birch and mountain ash. From the upper parking lot various walks are indicated; one of them goes along the cliffs to Fair Head and a wonderful view north to Rathlin Island. From the lower parking lot there is a choice of beautiful beach and hill slope rambles.

🅰 301 E5 ✉ 5 miles (8 km) E of Ballycastle, off the coast road between Fair Head and Torr Head, Co. Antrim **Ballycastle visitor information** ✉ 7 Mary St., Ballycastle, Co. Antrim ☎ 028 2076 2024

OMAGH

Tyrone's county town of Omagh was known only as a shopping and local business center until the infamous day of August 15, 1998. Then a republican splinter group opposed to the Good Friday Agreement (see pp. 294–295) and calling itself the "Real IRA" exploded a car bomb in a street crowded with Saturday shoppers; 29 people were killed. This appalling act brought condemnation across the board, and paradoxically sealed determination to make the peace process work.

🅰 300 C3 **Visitor information** ✉ 1 Market St., Omagh, Co. Tyrone ☎ 028 8224 7831

PRESIDENT WILSON ANCESTRAL HOME

In the northeast of County Tyrone, 2 miles (3 km) east of Strabane, the President Wilson Ancestral Home is well signposted. The white-washed cottage that Woodrow Wilson's grandfather James Wilson left in 1807 is kept by the curators, who are members of the Wilson family, still farming the ancestral land.

Inside are two rooms: a kitchen, and a living room with a press (storage cupboard) and fancy iron fireplace. A ladder leads through a hole in the ceiling to an upper room under the smoke-blackened thatch. In this little house with its tiny windows and thick stone walls, each generation of Wilson parents brought up swarms of children, often 12 or more. James Wilson married Annie Adams, a Sion Mills girl he met on the boat to America; his grandson Woodrow served as U.S. President from 1913 to 1921.

Colors, shapes, and sizes of plants blend and contrast at Rowallane Garden.

 300 C3 ✉ Spout Rd., Dergalt, 2 miles (3.2 km) SE of Strabane, Co. Tyrone ☎ 028 7138 2204 🕐 Open July & Aug. Tues.–Sun., at other times by arrangement

ROWALLANE GARDEN

This is a gorgeous, natural-looking garden on a 50-acre (20 ha) site with no artificial landscaping whatsoever. The Rowallane estate was bequeathed to Hugh Armytage Moore by his uncle, Reverend John Moore, in 1903, and he tended it for the next half century, planting specimens from all over the world.

You can wander through the walled garden full of azaleas—gorgeous in May—and down to the natural outcrop rock garden by way of the shallow glen of New Ground between banks of orange, scarlet, pink, yellow, purple, and white rhododendrons.

 301 F2 ✉ Signed off the A7 Belfast–Downpatrick road near Saintfield, 11 miles (18 km) from both Belfast and Downpatrick, Co. Down ☎ 028 9751 1031 💲 $$

SCRABO TOWER

An eye-catching landmark for many miles around, Scrabo Tower rises 135 feet (41 m) from the summit of Scrabo Hill, at the northern end of **Strangford Lough** (also see p. 336). It was erected in 1857 as a gesture of thanks to the 3rd Marquis of Londonderry for his efforts to relieve the suffering of his tenants during the Great Famine.

Nowadays, the tower houses an exhibition about the natural and social history of the area, including Strangford Lough, and if you have the energy to climb up the 122 steps to the top of the tower, it is definitely worth it. The view is wonderful, one of the most impressive in Northern Ireland, taking in the Mountains of Mourne, the hills of the Antrim Coast, Belfast, the great swath of Strangford Lough itself, and the Ards Peninsula. On particularly clear days, you might even be able to get a glimpse of the Isle of Man and the hills of Scotland across the Irish Sea.

The tower is at the heart of the Scrabo Hill Country Park, where woodland gives way to open areas where the dark volcanic rock that overlies the sandstone makes dramatic shapes of outcrops and quarry scars in the green surroundings.

 301 F3 ✉ Just over a mile (1.6 km) SW of Newtownards, Co. Down ☎ 028 9181 1491 🕐 Closed Oct.–Easter and Fri. Easter–Sept. Country Park open year-round

SPRINGHILL

Springhill is an excellent example of a plantation house. Built by the Conyngham family from Scotland around 1690, it was enlarged with two wings in the 18th century. Inside is a well-stocked 18th-century library; splendid 18th- and 19th-century furniture, from ladderback chairs to delicately crafted cabinets; a gun room with some historic weapons displayed (flintlock muskets used by defenders at the Siege of Derry, and some pikes captured at the Battle of Vinegar Hill, County Wexford, in 1798); and an exhibition of costume through the centuries. Outside is a walled garden, and well-marked walks through park and woodland.

🅰 301 D3 ✉ Signed on the B18 Moneymore–Coagh road, 5 miles (8 km) NE of Cookstown, Co. Londonderry ☎ 028 8674 8210 🕒 Closed Oct.–mid-March; weekdays mid-March–June & Sept. 🅢 $$

The circular Ulster Way is Northern Ireland's best known trail and its longest at some 560 miles (901 km), though one can just walk sections of it. Although largely waymarked, there are plenty of maps available to help you find your way around.

TOOMEBRIDGE EEL FISHERY

Call in on this fishery in the west of County Antrim, and enjoy the astonishing sight of eels in the millions. It's a commercial concern, but you are welcome to drop in. The fishery, at the point where the River Bann flows out of the northernmost point of Lough Neagh, is a prime site for eel catching—mostly for export, since Ulster people seem not too fond of these wriggly delicacies. Lough Neagh eel fishermen make their living from the trade, however, and lower along the Bann in summer eel-fishing for sport is very popular.

🅰 301 E3 ✉ Lough Neagh Fishermen's Co-operative Society, Toomebridge, Co. Antrim ☎ 028 7965 0618 🕒 Closed Sat. & Sun.

ULSTER HISTORY PARK

In Gortin Glen Forest Park on the B48 Omagh–Gortin road you'll find this collection of full-scale reconstructions of Irish buildings through the ages. Highlights include Stone Age houses, a Bronze Age *crannog* (lake dwelling), a pre-Norman monastic site, and a 17th-century plantation settlement.

If you want a glimpse of an authentic piece of Tyrone history, seek out the ruined sweat-lodge at Rouskey to the east of Gortin. A turf fire would be built up within, then fever sufferers and other sick people would be shut in for a session of steamy heat before being immersed in the nearest river.

🅰 300 C3 ✉ Off B48, Cullion, Lislap, Gortin, Co. Armagh ☎ 028 8164 8188 🕒 Closed Nov.–Feb. 🅢 $$

WELLBROOK BEETLING MILL

The mill was one of six built in this narrow valley from 1767 onward. Their function was to beat linen cloth to a fine sheen with water-powered wooden hammers. You can admire the noisy "beetles," or hammers; the water-wheel; and the rest of the original machinery, and learn about Ulster's once thriving linen industry in the drying loft display.

🅰 301 D3 ✉ Signed off the A505 Cookstown–Omagh road at Kildress, 4 miles (6.5 km) W of Cookstown, Co. Tyrone ☎ 028 8674 8210 or 028 8674 1735 🕒 Closed Oct.–mid-March; Mon.–Fri. mid-March–June and Sept. (except bank holiday Mon.) 🅢 $$ ∎

Travelwise

**Horse-drawn wagon
vacation: Romantic Ireland
encapsulated**

TRAVELWISE INFORMATION
PLANNING YOUR TRIP

WHEN TO GO

The best time of the year to visit Ireland is spring and early summer. April to June tend to be the sunniest and mildest months, the population are not yet suffering from tourist overload, and the countryside is green and fresh from the winter rain. Visitor numbers have not yet begun to build to their peak, so the roads are quiet, but most attractions have opened after the winter layoff.

However, if you want to enjoy the biggest concentration of the festivals for which Ireland is famous, you'll need to visit in high summer. Cork and Dingle Regattas, Galway Arts Festival and Races, the Dublin Horse Show and the Connemara Pony Show, the International Rose of Tralee Festival, and the Fleadh Cheoil na h'Éireann (All-Ireland Music Festival) all take place in July or August. Things are really buzzing in Ireland then, but prices are high, and the weather can be "soft" (Irish for mist and drizzle).

The months of September and October tend to see better weather and beautiful colors in woods and moors; prices are on the way down by October, too. Winter weather is generally mild, but can be dark and gloomy, though you may be lucky and encounter a succession of glorious sparkling days of cold blue skies. This is the season of low prices and indoor fun— many visitor attractions have closed, but fire-warmed pubs come into their own.

WHAT TO TAKE

Pack clothes that take account of the informal, mostly outdoor nature of a holiday in Ireland. It's certainly wise to take good waterproof clothing, a hat, and an umbrella. There's lot of lively weather out in the Atlantic, and nothing to halt its 3,000-mile (4,800 km) eastward build-up until it hits Ireland! The west in particular sees plenty of "soft" days at all times of the year. It's bound to rain at least some of the time during your visit.

Pack golf shoes, too—Ireland has lots of good golf courses—and a pair of walking boots if you want to take advantage of the 50 or so long-distance trails that have been established in all corners of the island. As for other clothing, the keynote is informality unless you intend to stay or dine at the very classiest 5-star places.

Take a pair of binoculars for bird-watching and admiring the scenery. Camera and camcorder film is widely available in the larger towns. If you want to join in with the music, a couple of harmonicas (keys G and D) will fit easily into your case—it's the best instrument for unobtrusively "faking it." And bring a couple of songs, too, in case someone invites you to oblige the company in the pub. There's no better ice-breaker, even if your voice is itself a rusty instrument.

A wide range of over-the-counter and prescription medicines is available in Irish pharmacies (sometimes called chemists); but you should consider bringing any very specialized medication with you.

INSURANCE

Medical and dental treatment are available on the Irish health service for nationals of EU countries and certain others on production of insurance form E111 (not necessary for United Kingdom nationals), but U.S. and most other nationals should arrange comprehensive health and travel insurance before traveling to Ireland.

ENTRY FORMALITIES

All non-EU nationals need a passport to enter Ireland. U.S. citizens do not need a visa. No ID is needed to cross between southern and Northern Ireland.

Customs: The usual prohibited goods, including illegal drugs, are forbidden in Ireland. Travelers within the EU can carry, duty-paid, 50 liters of beer, 25 liters of wine, and 800 cigarettes in and out of Ireland. Duty-free goods allowances (Republic only) include 200 cigarettes, 1 liter of spirits, and 2 liters of fortified wine.

Currency restrictions: You can bring as much money as you like into Ireland, but amounts of Irish or other currency taken out of the country are restricted. It is a good idea to complete a currency declaration on arrival.

HOW TO GET TO IRELAND

BY AIR

Flying time between the U.S. and Ireland is between six and nine hours. Scheduled flights link many North American airports to Dublin, Shannon, Cork, Knock (Co. Mayo), and Belfast. The Republic's national carrier (operating to Belfast, too) is Aer Lingus; call the New York office at 800/223-6537; Boston: 617/ 728-0060; rest of U.S.: 800/223-6537

Popular flights are:
Dublin from Atlanta, Baltimore, Boston, Chicago, Los Angeles, Newark, New York JFK, and Philadelphia
Shannon from Atlanta, Baltimore, Boston, Chicago, Los Angeles, New York JFK, Newark, and Philadelphia
Belfast from Boston and New York via Shannon

Arrival by air in the Irish Republic is most likely to be at either Dublin or Shannon airport; in Northern Ireland, either Belfast International or Belfast City airport.

All have foreign exchange bureaus, generally open by 7 a.m., the major car hire firms, and taxi ranks—fares are about five times the bus fares.

GETTING TO THE CITY CENTERS

(Journey times to city centers are all 0.5–1 hour, depending on traffic; from Belfast City airport allow 10–15 minutes).

DUBLIN AIRPORT TO DUBLIN

By car—take the M1 south
By bus—Airlink bus every 20 minutes (moderate fare, under 16s free) via central bus station and Connolly railway station to Heuston railway station
By taxi—expensive

SHANNON AIRPORT TO LIMERICK

By car—take the N18 east
By bus—Bus Eireann runs a frequent, inexpensive airport–Limerick service
By taxi—moderate/expensive

BELFAST INTERNATIONAL AIRPORT TO BELFAST

By car—take the A52 east
By bus—Airbus service (moderate fare, children free) runs to the city center every half hour
By taxi—expensive

BELFAST CITY AIRPORT TO CENTRAL BELFAST

By car—follow city-center signs
By taxi—moderate

GETTING AROUND

There are no subways in Ireland.

GETTING AROUND IN DUBLIN

BY BUS

Dublin Bus (tel 01 873 4222) runs bus services in Greater Dublin (extends to the outskirts of Counties Meath, Kildare, and Wicklow).

Tickets—cheaper pre-paid tickets can be bought en bloc

from the CIE information desk in Dublin Airport, from the Dublin Bus head office at 59 Upper O'Connell Street, and from several hundred ticket outlets across the city.

BY RAIL

DART is an efficient, moderately priced fast rail service connecting outer Dublin, north and south, with the city center. There are 25 stations—the three most central are Connolly (north of the river, a 10-minute walk to O'Connell Street), Tara Street, and Pearse Street (both south of the river, 5 minutes to Trinity College). Buy tickets at any DART station.

BY TAXI

Dublin taxis are not hailed or stopped in the street: you call them by telephone (numbers in the Golden Pages), or find a taxi rank. The main city-center taxi ranks are at St. Stephen's Green, College Green, O'Connell Street, and Westland Row to the east of the Trinity College grounds. Dublin taxis are mostly metered; agree fares in advance with drivers of those that are not.

LEAVING DUBLIN BY CAR

Dublin is ringed by the M50 motorway.
Main roads out of the city are:
M1 to Dublin Airport, Drogheda, Dundalk, and Belfast
N2 to Slane, Monaghan, and Derry
N3 to Navan, Cavan, Enniskillen. and Donegal
N4 to Kinnegad (where the N6 leaves for Galway), to Longford (where the N5 leaves for Westport), and on to Sligo
N7/M7 to Naas (where the N9 leaves for Waterford), Portlaoise (where the N8 branches off for Cork), and Kildare
N11 to Bray, Wicklow, Wexford, and Rosslare car ferry

TRAVELING AROUND THE REPUBLIC

BY AIR

Aer Lingus, the national airline (U.S. tel 800/474-7424; Ireland tel 01 844 4777) flies from

Dublin to airports at Cork and Shannon.
Aer Arann Express (01 814 1058) operates services to many regional airports.

BY CAR FERRY

Two short car ferry trips that save hours on the road are:

Across the Shannon (20-minute crossing, every hour) between Killimer, County Clare, and Tarbert, County Kerry (tel 065 90 53124).
Across Waterford Harbour (10-minute crossing, continuous operation) between Ballyhack, County Wexford, and Passage East, County Waterford (tel 051 382 488).

BY PUBLIC TRANSPORTATION

CIE is the company that runs bus and train services in the Republic of Ireland through its subsidiaries Irish Rail (Iarnród Eireann), Irish Bus (Bus Eireann), and Dublin Bus (Bus Átha Cliath).

By bus
Irish Bus (tel 01 836 6111), with its distinctive Red Setter logo, runs bus services to all towns and cities, and many rural villages. The daily express buses between Dublin and Belfast are good value, and can beat the train for time if traffic conditions permit.

By train
Irish Rail (tel 01 836 6222) runs the Republic's train services—efficient north and south of Dublin; slow and in need of investment farther west. Major cities are all connected by rail. The excellent Dublin–Belfast express (eight per day) takes two hours. Reserve in the peak holiday season, and for traveling on the very crowded last trains on Friday and Sunday nights.

Tickets
Buy them from any train or bus station. Under-16s and other concessions are up to half-price. There are various good ticket deals on offer, many of them

including bus and train, e.g.: Irish Explorer (5- or 8-day), valid on bus or trail Emerald Card, valid on Irish Rail, Irish Bus, Dublin Bus, Northern Irish Railways, and Ulsterbus.
Irish Rover for rail travel in the Republic and Northern Ireland.

STUDENT DISCOUNTS
The Student Travelsave Stamp gives good discounts on mainline rail, long-distance bus, and ferry tickets. Get it from USIT (19/21 Aston Quay, O'Connell Bridge, Dublin 2, tel 01 602 1600, open Mon.–Fri. 9 a.m.–6 p.m., Sat. 11 a.m.–4 p.m.) or Bus Eireann Travel Centre (Central Bus Station, Store Street, Dublin 1).

DRIVING

CAR RENTAL
You'll need a full valid driver's license from your home country, held for two years without endorsement. Age limit is generally 23–70. A deposit is payable before you drive away. Fly-drive or rail/sail-drive deals offer the best prices. Reserve for mid-July to mid-August, or you may not get a car. High-season rices are much higher than in low season; they usually include third party, fire, theft, and passenger indemnity insurance, unlimited mileage and VAT.

DRIVING IN THE IRISH REPUBLIC
Driving in the Republic, generally speaking, is still a pleasure. Out of the big towns the roads are uncrowded, and most drivers observe the courtesies. The farther west you go, the more roads get narrow, steep, and twisty. Distances on signposts take some getting used to—essentially, Irish Eurocrats have switched to kilometers (shown on green-and-white signs) and the other 99 percent of the population still operates on miles (black-and-white signs).

Drive on the left; overtake on the right.

Don't park illegally in Dublin; you'll be wheel clamped.

Drivers and front seat passengers must wear seat belts. Speed limits: 30 mph (48 kph) in towns, 60 mph (96 kph) on other roads, 70 mph (112 kph) on motorways.

Drink limit: 80 mg of alcohol per 100 ml of blood, i.e. one pint of Guinness.

MAPS
Ordnance Survey of Ireland 1:50,000 Discovery Series covers all of Ireland in 89 sheets, good for exploring and walking. Information offices and car hire firms supply general road maps.

GETTING AROUND IN BELFAST

BY BUS
Citybus (tel 028 9066 6630) operates buses within Belfast. Buy tickets on the bus or from Europa Bus Centre (Glengall Street) or Laganside Bus Centre (Oxford Street near Central Station). Cheap multiple tickets/concessions are available. Free bus connects the Central train station with the two main bus stations and the Youth Hostel; Rail-link bus connects Central and Yorkgate train stations.

By taxi
Black "London" cabs with yellow identifying discs are metered; others may not be. City-center taxi ranks are at Yorkgate and Central train stations, at bus stations, and at City Hall. Taxi firms are listed in Yellow Pages.

Leaving Belfast by Car
Main routes are:
A2—north up the coast to Antrim and the Giant's Causeway, east through Bangor and round the Ards Peninsula
M2/A6 to Derry
M1 to Dungannon/A4 to Enniskillen
M1 to Jct7/A1 to Dundalk and Dublin.

GETTING AROUND NORTHERN IRELAND

BY BUS
Ulsterbus (tel 028 9066 6630) operates to all towns and most villages across Northern Ireland. Buy tickets at bus stations or on board buses. Cheap day returns, unlimited travel tickets, bus/rail options, or child/student/OAP concessions are available.

BY RAIL
Northern Ireland Railways (tel 028 9066 6630) runs from Belfast to Larne (Yorkgate station, tel 028 9074 1700), and to Derry, Bangor, and Dublin (Central Station, tel 028 9089 9400). Buy tickets at train stations.

DRIVING

CAR RENTAL
Requirements are the same as for the Republic, except that the driver's license need only have been held for one year. If you plan to drive in both the Republic and Northern Ireland, ensure the insurance covers you.

Driving in Northern Ireland
Roads are uncrowded and drivers generally relaxed and courteous. Road surfaces are good, and signpost distances are given in miles. Rules and laws apply as in the Republic.

MAPS
Ordnance Survey of Northern Ireland 1:50,000 series of 18 sheets covers all of Northern Ireland (along with Donegal, and parts of Cavan, Leitrim, Louth Monaghan and Roscommon). Ireland North at 1:250,000 is a useful driving map, available from visitor information centers.

PRACTICAL ADVICE

CHILDREN

Well-behaved children are made welcome everywhere. In practice, pubs operate individual admittance policies—just ask.

Concessions on transport and entrance fees are usually available.

COMMUNICATIONS

POSTAL SERVICE
The Republic's mail boxes and post vans are green. You can buy stamps from a post office or machine. Letters take roughly two days to reach the United Kingdom, three to four days to get to the United States In the North the post boxes and vans are red; British stamps are used.

TELEPHONES
Phone booths in the Republic tend to be either gray, or green and white. You'll find them at train and bus stations, near post offices, and on street corners. Hotels, pubs, and larger shops usually have a payphone. You'll need plenty of coins, but about half the telephone booths use phonecards, sold by newsagents, post offices, and bigger shops such as supermarkets. You can phone anywhere in the world.

The international code for the Republic of Ireland is 353. Dial 10 for the domestic operator, 114 for the international operator.

To call Northern Ireland from the Republic, dial 048, then the local number.

Northern Ireland has red telephone boxes, along with a plethora of flimsy plastic ones. The international code for Northern Ireland is 44. Dial 100 for the domestic operator, 155 for the international operator.

CONVERSIONS

Distance multiply by
kilometers to miles	0.62
miles to kilometers	1.6

Length multiply by
centimeters to inches	0.39
inches to centimeters	2.54
meters to feet	3.28
feet to meters	0.30

meters to yards	1.09
yards to meters	0.91

Area multiply by
hectares to acres	2.47
acres to hectares	0.40

Weight multiply by
kilograms to pounds	2.21
pounds to kilograms	0.45
kilograms to U.S. tons	0.001
U.S. tons to kilograms	907

Volume multiply by
liters to U.S. gallons	0.26
U.S. gallons to liters	3.79

Temperature
°C to °F multiply by 1.8, add 32
°F to °C Subtract 32, multiply by 0.55

ELECTRICITY

Electricity is at a standard 230-volt AC (50 cycles). Wall sockets are for plugs with either three flat or two round pins. U.S. visitors will need a transformer/adaptor.

ETIQUETTE & LOCAL CUSTOMS

There are no formal rules of etiquette in Ireland. In pub, shop or street, it's most unlikely that you will be left out of the conversation. Irish people love to include strangers, and find out all about them. This isn't nosiness, just genuine warmth and curiosity. Such personal interest, understandably, may be less evident in crowded tourist spots in the high season. Pub and street musicians and raconteurs don't like to be crowded or interrupted while they are performing, even if it looks as if no one is paying them any mind. If you want to make a request to hear a favorite tune or song, it's as well to be sensitive to the kind of gathering you are in—a riproaring sing-along session is a better bet for such requests than a quiet gathering of specialist musicians. And if you want to join in with your own instrument, don't forget that it's good manners to ask first!

The old adage about not initiating conversations about sex, politics, and religion is a good one to have in mind, particularly in sensitive areas of the North. But nowadays many northerners are keen to talk about the past, present, and future of their troubled country to anyone who isinterested. It's perfectly acceptable to take a lively interest if ticklish subjects are raised by your hosts; but be wary of expressing your own opinions, however strong they may be.

HOLIDAYS

January 1 (New Year's Day)
March 17 (St. Patrick's Day)
March/April (Good Friday–Easter Monday)
First Monday in May (May Holiday)
Last Monday in May (Spring Holiday–Northern Ireland)
First Monday in June (June Holiday–Republic)
July 12 (Orangemen's Day—Northern Ireland; Nearest Monday is a holiday; parades take place on nearest Saturday)
First Monday in August (August Holiday—Republic)
Last Monday in August (Late Summer Holiday–Northern Ireland)
Last Monday in October (October Holiday—Republic)
December 25 (Christmas Day)
December 26 (Boxing Day/St. Stephen's Day)
Most businesses are closed on national holidays.

LIQUOR LAWS

Licensing hours are rapidly changing to reflect demand, and 24-hour drinking may be just around the corner. Already in Dublin and Belfast there are plenty of places with late licenses up to 1 a.m. or later. Technically, you can buy alcohol in the Republic between 10:30 a.m. and 11:30 p.m, Monday–Wednesday, 10:30 a.m.-12:30 a.m. Thursday to Saturday, and from 12:30–11 p.m. on Sunday.

In Northern Ireland the official hours are 11:30 a.m.–11 p.m.,

Monday–Saturday, and from
12:30–10 p.m. on Sunday. But
flexibility is Ireland's middle name.

MEDIA

Among the Republic's serious
national papers, two stand out:
the *Irish Times* and the *Irish
Independent.* There's one
authoritative regional paper, the
southwest's *Cork Examiner,* and
dozens of local papers.

RTE, the state broadcasting
corporation, has two television
channels in English and one in
Irish, and four radio stations—
RTE1 (news, current affairs,
magazine programs, drama), RTE2
(pop music), Lyric (classical music,
jazz, traditional, world music), and
Raidió na Gaeltachta (RnaG), worth
listening to for the beauty of
spoken Irish (even if you can't
understand a word) and wonderful
Irish traditional music and singing.

Northern Ireland receives some
of the Republic's transmissions,
and is served with mainland
British newspapers, television,
and radio as well as its own
regional varieties. It's instructive
to read the opposing views of
the two strongly aligned Belfast
daily papers, the pro-Unionist
Protestant News Letter and the
nationalist *Catholic Irish News.*

MONEY MATTERS

In the Republic on January 1,
2002, the euro replaced the punt
as the valid currency. There are
100 cents to 1 euro. Euro bills
are in different colors, with
designs representing periods of
architecture. Bills come in
denominations of 5, 10, 20, 50,
100, 200, and 500 euros.
The coins come in 1 and 2 euros
and 1, 2, 5, 10, 20, and 50 cents.

In Northern Ireland the British
pound is used, with 100 pence to
the pound. All major credit
cards are recognized.
The two currencies are not
interchangeable, although a
number of northern Ireland

attractions will accept euros for
admission fees.

OPENING TIMES

Republic Banks: are generally
open Monday–Friday, 10 a.m.–
4:30 p.m. In smaller towns they
may close for lunch. Bigger Dublin
banks are open till 5 p.m. on
Thursdays and on Saturday
mornings.
Shops are generally open
Monday to Saturday, 9 a.m.–6 p.m.;
in central Dublin many stay open
later. On Sundays supermarkets
and some big stores open from
noon to 5 or 6 p.m. Shopping
centers often stay open till 8 or
9 p.m. Shops in smaller towns
may close at 1 p.m. on
Wednesdays or Thursdays.

Northern Ireland: Banks are
generally open Monday–Friday
10 a.m.–3:30 p.m. Shops: as in
the Republic.

PHARMACIES

All large towns and many small
ones have pharmacies (sometimes
called chemists); they should all
display a notice on the door giving
directions to nearby chemists
scheduled to be open after hours.

PLACES OF WORSHIP/RELIGION

Church of Ireland (Protestant) and
Roman Catholic churches abound
in Ireland. Methodist, Baptist,
and other nonconformist
congregations are scarce, as are
Jewish, Sikh, Muslim, Hindu, and
other religious groupings and
places of worship. The local visitor
information office can advise.

SENIOR CITIZENS

Concessions on transport and
entrance fees are usually available.

TIME DIFFERENCES

Ireland is on Greenwich Mean
Time (e.g. at noon in Ireland it is
7 a.m. in New York and 4 a.m. in
Los Angeles). Clocks are set

forward 1 hour between late
March and late October.

TIPPING

This is very much a matter for
you to decide. Generally speaking,
the only people who will be
upset at the lack of a tip are
restaurant waiters/waitresses and
cab drivers. Ten percent of the
check/fare is reckoned as
acceptable, fifteen percent is
considered very handsome.

REST ROOMS

You'll find public rest rooms in
all the places you'd expect—
airports, train and bus stations,
and city centers. Some are free;
in others you gain entry with a
small coin. There are always
facilities in hotels and public
places. Rest rooms are generally
kept in a reasonable state—
though in more rural locations
things may be a bit spartan.

VISITORS WITH DISABILITIES

Increasing numbers of hotels and
other public buildings are being
adapted or built to cater to
travelers with disabilities. Helpful
booklets are *Guide For Disabled
Persons* and *Accommodation Guide
For Disabled Persons,* both available
from the National Disability
Authority, 25 Clyde Rd, Dublin 4,
tel 01 608 0400.

VISITOR INFORMATION

Bord Fáilte (The Welcome
Board) is the Irish Republic's
Tourist Board. Baggot St. Bridge,
Baggot St., Dublin 2, tel 01 602
4000, www.ireland.ie
Northern Ireland: 59, N. Main
St, Belfast BT1 1NB, tel 028
9023 1221, info@nitb.com
U.S.: 345 Park Ave, New York,
N.Y. 10154, tel 800/223-6470

**PRINCIPAL BORD FÁILTE
OFFICES**
Dublin: Dublin Tourism, Suffolk
St., tel 01 605 7700,

information@dublintourism.ie;
www.visitdublin.com
Kilkenny: Rose Inn St., tel 056
77 51500
Waterford: 41, The Quay, tel
051 387 5823
Cork: Tourist House, Grand
Parade, tel 021 425 5100
Killarney: Beech Road, tel 064
31633
Limerick: Arthur's Quay, tel
061 317522
Shannon Airport: Arrivals
Hall, tel 061 471664
Athlone: Athlone Castle, tel
090 649 4630
Galway: Aras Fáilte, Forster St.,
tel 091 537700
Westport: James St., tel 098
25711
Sligo: Áras Reddan, Temple St.,
tel 071 916 1201

NORTHERN IRELAND

**Northern Ireland Tourist
Board,** 59 North St., Belfast
BT1 1NB, tel 028 9023 1221,
info@ nitb.com,
www. discovernorthernireland
.com
Ireland: 16, Nassau St., Dublin
2, tel 01 679 1977, or 01 850
230230 if telephoning in Ireland
U.S.: 345 Park Ave., New York,
N.Y. 10154, tel 800/223-6470

PRINCIPAL NITB OFFICES
IN NORTHERN IRELAND

Belfast: see above
Antrim: Giant's Causeway, 44
Causeway Rd., tel 028 2073 1855
Armagh: Old Bank Building, 40
English St., tel 028 3752 1800
Derry: 44 Foyle St., tel 028
7126 7284
Down: 34 Quay St., Bangor, tel
028 9127 0069
Fermanagh: Wellington Rd.,
Enniskillen, tel 028 6632 3110
Tyrone: 1 Market St., Omagh,
tel 028 8224 7831

WOMEN

Women travelers are as safe in
Ireland as anywhere in the
world, provided sensible rules
are followed about not being
alone on public transportation

or in deserted city streets late at
night. Serious harassment is
extremely rare, and behavior
such as wolf-whistling has all but
died out.

EMERGENCIES

FOR ALL
EMERGENCIES,
TELEPHONE 999

CRIME AND POLICE

The kind of crime likely to affect
a holidaymaking visitor to
Ireland —petty theft, pocket-
picking, bag- snatching—is largely
confined to the more
disadvantaged areas of Dublin
and Belfast. Outside of these
enclaves, into which it's unlikely
you would stray, the usual
general precautions are all you
need to observe. If you do get
into trouble, help and support
are available from the Tourist
Victim Support Service,
Harcourt Sq., Harcourt Street,
Dublin 2, tel 01 478 5295.

As far as security in the North is
concerned—even in the worst
years of the Troubles, Northern
Ireland was seen as a safe place
for tourists. With the recent
change in attitudes north and
south of the border, the
atmosphere in central Belfast—
the only sign of tension that
most visitors would notice—has
become far more relaxed. You
should tour and explore
Northern Ireland freely and with
confidence. But it's as well to
bear in mind that here, as
anywhere, good manners suggest
that a guest in a foreign country
does well to listen and learn
rather than to voice opinionated
attitudes.

In the Republic, the police are
known as the *Gardai* (pronounced
"Gard-ee") or the "gards"; they
normally work unarmed. In
Northern Ireland the police
force, formerly the Royal Ulster
Constabulary, or the RUC, has
recently been renamed the Police
Service of Northern Ireland
(PSNI). They tend to be less

forbidding-looking in recent years
since shedding their semi-
automatic rifles and flak jackets.
Both sets of officers will do their
best to help any visitor in
trouble.

EMBASSIES &
CONSULATES

Canada: Fourth Floor, 65–68 St.
Stephen's Green, Dublin 2, tel 01
417 4100

United Kingdom: 29 Merrion
Rd., Dublin 4, tel 01 205 3700

United States: 42 Elgin Rd.,
Dublin 4, tel 01 668 8777 or
Queen's House, Queen's St.,
Belfast, BT1 6EQ, tel 028 9032
8239

**What to do in the event of
a car accident**
1. Dial 999 for fire, police, or
   ambulance services.
2. Remain at the scene.
3. Exchange names, addresses,
   and insurance details with
   anyone else involved.
4. Do not admit liability, whatever the circumstances.
5. Most car-hire firms detail in
   their documentation the steps
   they require. These may
   include a requirement to use
   a specified towing and repair
   service; use of another service may invalidate your insurance coverage, so check up.

LOST PROPERTY

If you lose something, make
your first inquiries in the last
place you can remember having
it. Someone will more than
likely be keeping it for you.
Otherwise, report the loss to
the nearest police station. Don't
forget to ask for a signed and
dated acknowledgment that you
have reported the loss, to show
your insurance company.

HEALTH

No inoculations are necessary.
Tap water is safe to drink. Take
the normal precautions against
sunburn. Insurance: see p 346.

HOTELS & RESTAURANTS

Time was—and not so long ago at that—when the traveler outside Dublin would need to look long and hard for a good place to stay. The norm, especially in country towns, was a run-down hotel with bad beds and worse (though always friendly) service. But things have changed, and today there is an enormous range of accommodations from magnificent castles on hundreds of acres of grounds to simple hostels, and standards rarely fall below what's acceptable.

HOTELS

In the Republic, tourist offices have lists of accommodations approved by Bord Fáilte (Irish Tourist Board); north of the border tourist offices have the same with establishments approved by the NITB (Northern Ireland Tourist Board). You can also book ahead (paying a small supplement): telephone 1800 668668 within the Republic, 0800 668668 66 within Northern Ireland.

Converted castles and stately homes can be very atmospheric and great fun, though the quality is variable and you may have to put up with some of the inconveniences (lack of elevators, odd-shaped rooms, steep staircases) that come with a rambling old building. Large, very well-organized country house and golf hotels are another option at the luxury end. The trend for staff to mouth "international welcome" phrases is on the increase in Ireland as it is all over the world—a regrettable tendency in a country whose people have such natural warmth. These pleasant traits are more evident in the growing number of small, owner-run hotels with very high standards of care and attention.

BED-AND-BREAKFAST

It is the famous Irish bed-and-breakfast (B&B), though, that for most visitors offers the most enjoyable accommodations you are welcomed with true Irish warmth. Generally the owners are only too pleased to share their insiders' knowledge about the best attractions, music pubs, and places to eat. Those approved by Bord Fáilte display a shamrock sign; you can expect very high standards at these places.

Another trustworthy organization is Town and Country Homes (tel 071 982 2222, www.townandcountry.ie), which has more than 1,600 properties, chosen for the friendly welcome. And there are thousands of non-affiliated B&Bs where standards are very high, and the village pub, shop, or post office is a good places to make enquiries.

One word of caution—many small businesses are closed in the winter, so it is always best to make a reservation. And one more word—the Irish breakfast (in the North known as the Ulster Fry) is an enormous, artery-unfriendly cholesterol blast, absolutely irresistibly bad for you. But you are on holiday, and, in any case, with one of those on board you won't want lunch.

EATING OUT

It used to be a thankless task trying to find a decent place to eat in Ireland but, as with hotels, things have changed. Demand has created supply, and now you'll find a huge range of really good restaurants in every corner.

Though menus and cooking styles vary from the terrifically trendy to the terminally traditional, the claims of the best Irish restaurants to be among the best in Europe have solid foundations—fresh produce from the land and sea. Meat has been the mainstay of Irish cooking for the past hundred years; Irish-reared beef, lamb, and pork are excellent, the art of the sausage flourishes, and there has been a cautious but now snowballing welcome of the organic meat movement.

Many places grow their own, or buy in, organic vegetables and herbs nowadays, too, and Irish cheeseboards, for long confined to soapy cheddar, have taken on

PRICES

HOTELS
An indication of the cost of a double room without breakfast is given by $ signs.

$$$$$	Over $280
$$$$	$200–$280
$$$	$120–$200
$$	$80–$120
$	Under $80

RESTAURANTS
An indication of the cost of a three-course dinner without drinks is given by $ signs.

$$$$$	Over $80
$$$$	$50–$80
$$$	$35–$50
$$	$20–$35
$	Under $20

a rapidly growing selection of delicious Irish cheeses. As for seafood, Ireland is, of course, an island, and there are any number of excellent fish and seafood specialists making diners happy from Kinsale to Portrush.

The Irish cellar has kept up with the improvements in the kitchen, though market town hotel restaurants can still serve up some pretty execrable plonk under the guise of "house wine."

Don't neglect the café at afternoon teatime for Irish baking. Don't spurn the pub for an inexpensive meal—many pubs now put on a range of dishes that can outclass the local restaurants. And don't forget that your B&B may offer a home-cooked evening meal that might well be more enjoyable than the fanciest restaurant in town.

ORGANIZATION & ABBREVIATIONS

All sites are listed first by price, then in alphabetical order.

The abbreviations used are:
L = lunch   D = dinner

AE = American Express DC = Diner's Club MC = MasterCard V = Visa

DUBLIN

HOTELS

🏨 BERKELEY COURT
$$$$$
LANSDOWNE RD., DUBLIN 4
TEL 01 665 3200
FAX 01 661 7238
E-MAIL berkeley-court@
jurysdoyle.com
This highly polished and
professional operation offers
the service and facilities
expected from a 5-star hotel.
🛏 188 🅿 120 ⭗ 🚭
🅫 All major cards

🏨 CLARENCE
$$$$$
6–8 WELLINGTON QUAY,
DUBLIN 2
TEL 01 407 0800
FAX 01 407 0820
E-MAIL reservations@
theclarence.ie
Owned by members of the
rock band U2, this beautifully
refurbished hotel looks out on
the River Liffey, with Temple
Bar at its back door.
🛏 49 ⭗ 🚭 🅫 All major
cards

🏨 FITZWILLIAM
$$$$$
ST. STEPHENS GREEN
DUBLIN 2
TEL 01 478 7000
FAX 01 478 7878
E-MAIL enq@fitzwilliamhotel.com
This luxurious hotel in
Dublin's most favored location
has elegant modern decor
and a notably helpful staff.
🛏 130 🅿 85 ⭗ 🚭
🅫 All major cards

🏨 THE MERRION
🍴 **$$$$$**
UPPER MERRION ST.
DUBLIN 2
TEL 01 603 0600
FAX 01 603 0700
E-MAIL info@merrionhotel.com
Deceptively modest, this
Georgian building surrounds a
garden. First-class cuisine,
immaculate service, and the
likelihood of rubbing

shoulders with stellar
personalities. The
Mornington's Brasserie is less
breathless, while Restaurant
Patrick Guilbaud provides a
grand setting for fine food
rooted in French tradition.
🛏 145 🅿 60 ⭗ 🚭 🚱
🅫 All major cards

🏨 RADISSON SAS
ST. HELEN'S HOTEL
$$$$$
STILLORGAN RD.
BLACKROCK, DUBLIN 4
TEL 01 218 6000
FAX 01 218 6010
An elegant, luxurious Georgian
out-of-town house,
overlooking terraced gardens,
which retains many 18th-
century features.
🛏 151 🅿 230 ⭗ 🚭
🅫 All major cards

🏨 HIBERNIAN
$$$$–$$$$$
EASTMORELAND PLACE
BALLSBRIDGE, DUBLIN 4
TEL 01 668 7666
FAX 01 660 2655
E-MAIL info@hibernianhotel.com
Located in a quiet residential
area south of the river, the
Hibernian is a particularly
hospitable hotel with efficient
staff. It occupies an imposing
building of magnificent
architectural style, and prides
itself on warmth of service,
real comfort, and extra
touches for the enjoyment of
guests.
🛏 40 🅿 18 🕐 Closed
Christmas ⭗ 🅫 All major
cards

**SOMETHING
SPECIAL**

🏨 LE MERIDIEN
SHELBOURNE
The Shelbourne, an elegant
Georgian on St. Stephen's
Green, oozes atmosphere, as
befits a hotel that played a part in
the Easter 1916 Rising (see pp.
30–31). At the heart of the Dublin scene for centuries, staying
here, you'll eat, drink, and sleep
with the shades of everyone who
was anyone in Ireland's historic

and literary life.
$$$$–$$$$$
27 ST. STEPHEN'S GREEN,
DUBLIN 2
TEL 01 663 4500
FAX 01 661 6006
E-MAIL shelbourneinfo@
lemeridien.com
🛏 190 🅿 45 ⭗ 🚱
🅫 All major cards

🏨 BROWNES BRASSERIE
& TOWNHOUSE
$$$$
22 ST. STEPHEN'S GREEN,
DUBLIN 2
TEL 01 638 3939
FAX 01 638 3900
E-MAIL info@brownesdublin.com
If you base yourself in this
well-appointed town house,
right on Dublin's most famous
square, you'll be right in the
thick of things for shopping,
sightseeing, and nightlife.
🛏 11 ⭗ 🚭
🅫 All major cards

🏨 BURLINGTON
$$$$
UPPER LEESON ST.
DUBLIN 4
TEL 01 660 5222
FAX 01 660 3172
A traditional, comfortable
hotel within a few minutes.
walk of St. Stephen's Green
and the city's main Southside
attractions.
🛏 506 🅿 600 ⭗ 🅫 All
major cards

🏨 BUSWELLS
$$$$
23–25 MOLESWORTH ST.
DUBLIN 2
TEL 01 614 6500
FAX 01 676 2090
E-MAIL buswells@quinn-hotels.com
Located very close to the
National Museum and the
Natural History Museum just
north of St. Stephen's Green,
this is an 18th-century town
house that has been stylishly
converted into a comfortable
hotel in a surprisingly peaceful
location.
🛏 69 🕐 Closed Christmas
⭗ 🅫 All major cards

⭗ Elevator 🚭 Nonsmoking 🚱 Air-conditioning 🚰 Indoor/🏊 Outdoor swimming pool 🅫 Credit cards **KEY**

CLARION STEPHEN'S HALL
$$$$
THE EARLSFORT CENTRE
LOWER LEESON ST., DUBLIN 2
TEL 01 638 1111
FAX 01 638 1122
E-MAIL stephens@premgroup .com
Near St. Stephen's Green in the heart of Southside, this is an interesting idea that works well—a hotel containing several types of accommodations ranging from penthouses and suites to studios, all very well appointed.
🛏 34 🅿 40 ⇄ 🚫 All major cards

SCHOOLHOUSE
$$$$
2–8 NORTHUMBERLAND RD.
DUBLIN 4
TEL 01 667 5014
FAX 01 667 5015
E-MAIL school@schoolhousehotel .iol.ie
School phobics have no cause to be alarmed! The enjoyably atmospheric decor does indeed reflect the building's original incarnation as a Victorian school, but there's nothing at all spartan about the well-appointed bedrooms,.
🛏 31 🕒 Closed Christmas 🅿 21 ⇄ 🚫 🚫 All major cards

TEMPLE BAR
$$$$
FLEET ST.
TEMPLE BAR, DUBLIN 2
TEL 01 677 3333
FAX 01 677 3088
E-MAIL reservations@tbh.ie
This cozy, centrally located hideaway shares its name and location with Dublin's trendiest quarter—right on the doorstep—for ambling around by day and living it up by night.
🛏 129 🕒 Closed Christmas ⇄ 🚫 All major cards

GRESHAM
$$$–$$$$$
23 UPPER O'CONNELL ST.
DUBLIN 1
TEL 01 874 6881

FAX 01 878 7175
E-MAIL ryan@indigo.ie
Just north of the River Liffey, the Gresham offers comfort and a high standard of service.
🛏 288 🅿 150 ⇄ 🚫
🚫 All major cards

JURYS BALLSBRIDGE HOTEL
$$$–$$$$$
PEMBROKE RD.
BALLSBRIDGE, DUBLIN 4
TEL 01 660 5000
FAX 01 660 5276
E-MAIL ballsbridge@ jurysdoyle.com
Comfort and friendly service are to be found at this flagship Jurys hotel. The Towers is the luxury accommodations wing for those with deep pockets. The hotel was purpose-built in the 1960s, and provide a modern couterpoint to the Georgian architecture that lines the surrounding streets.
🛏 403 🅿 280 ⇄ 🌊 🌊
🚫 All major cards

LONGFIELD'S
$$$–$$$$
FITZWILLIAM ST. LOWER
DUBLIN 2
TEL 01 676 1367
FAX 01 676 1542
E-MAIL info@longfields.ie
Longfield's offers Georgian elegance and a friendly, capable staff in a quiet location south of St. Stephen's Green.
🛏 26 🕒 Closed Christmas
⇄ 🚫 All major cards

MARINE
$$$–$$$$
SUTTON CROSS,
DUBLIN 13
TEL 01 839 0000
FAX 01 839 0442
E-MAIL sales@marinehotel.ie
A comfortable gabled hotel on the north side of Dublin Bay, built in a traditional seaside style and situated only a few minutes from central Dublin by DART railway.
🛏 48 🅿 150 🕒 Closed Christmas ⇄ 🌊 🚫 All major cards

MERCER
$$$–$$$$
MERCER ST. LOWER
DUBLIN 2
TEL 01 478 2179
FAX 01 478 0328
E-MAIL stay@mercerhotel.ie
You'll find nicely furnished guest rooms and capable staff at this centrally placed hotel near St. Stephen's Green.
🛏 41 🕒 Closed Christmas ⇄ 🚫 🚫 AE, MC, V

MOUNT HERBERT
$$$–$$$$
HERBERT RD.
LANSDOWNE RD., DUBLIN 4
TEL 01 668 4321
FAX 01 660 7077
E-MAIL info@mountherbert hotel.iol.ie
Located to the southeast of the city center, the Mount Herbert is a pleasant hotel a minute's walk from Lansdowne DART station.
🛏 185 🅿 90 ⇄ 🚫 All major cards

ABERDEEN LODGE
$$$
53 PARK AVE.
BALLSBRIDGE, DUBLIN 4
TEL 01 283 8155
FAX 01 283 7877
E-MAIL Aberdeen@iol.ie
A classy Edwardian building houses one of Dublin's best private hotels, where high standards of comfort and efficiency are not allowed to get in the way of friendly service.
🛏 16 🅿 16 🚫 All major cards

BLAKES TOWNHOUSE
$$$
50 MERRION RD.
BALLSBRIDGE, DUBLIN 4
TEL 01 668 8324
FAX 01 668 4280
E-MAIL blakestownhouse@iol.ie
Four-poster beds, garden balconies, air conditioning—the accommodations at Blakes are both luxurious and tasteful.
🛏 13 🅿 6 🚫 🚫 All major cards

JURYS TARA
$$$
MERRION RD.
DUBLIN 4
TEL 01 269 4666
FAX 01 269 1027
E-MAIL tara@jurysdoyle.com
Accommodations that are
smartly furnished and an easy
atmosphere are the hallmarks
of this modern hotel southeast
of the city center. It enjoys fine
views northward over Dublin
Bay to the spectacular
promontory of Howth Head.
🛏 113 🅿 100 ⬆ ⬧ All
major cards

ARIEL HOUSE
$$-$$$
50–54 LANSDOWNE RD.
BALLSBRIDGE, DUBLIN 4
TEL 01 668 5512
FAX 01 668 5845
E-MAIL reservations@
ariel-house.net
This beautifully kept period
Victorian house near Lans-
downe DART station is run to
very high standards.
🛏 37 🅿 30 🕐 Closed
Christmas ⬧ MC V

CHARLEVILLE LODGE
$$-$$$
268/272 NORTH CIRCULAR RD.
PHIBSBOROUGH, DUBLIN 7
TEL 01 838 6633
FAX 01 838 5854
E-MAIL charleville@indigo.ie
A short terrace of fine
Victorian houses has been
skillfully combined to create
this congenial bolt-hole near
the northern perimeter of
Phoenix Park.
🛏 30 🕐 Closed Christmas
🅿 18 ⬧ All major cards

MERRION HALL
$$-$$$
56 MERRION RD.
BALLSBRIDGE, DUBLIN 4
TEL 01 668 1426
FAX 01 668 4280
E-MAIL merrionhall@iol.ie
Edwardian elegance, modern
comforts, and fine food
combine in this award-winning
guesthouse next to the RDS
and close to the city center.

Four-poster beds and Jacuzzis
are just some of the features.
🛏 34 🅿 20 ❄
⬧ AE, M, V

BEWLEY'S HOTEL
$$
MERRION RD.
BALLSBRIDGE, DUBLIN 4
TEL 01 668 1111
FAX 01 668 1999
E-MAIL bb@bewleyshotels.com
Bewley's prides itself on its
relaxed ambience, with staff
striking a welcoming note
from the outset.
🛏 220 🅿 240 🕐 Closed
Christmas ⬆ ⬧ All major
cards

DONNYBROOK LODGE
$$
131 STILLORGAN RD.
DONNYBROOK, DUBLIN 4
TEL 01 283 7333
FAX 01 260 4770
E-MAIL info@donnybrook
lodge.com
In an exclusive area of Dublin,
this is a charming modern
home set in lovely gardens. It's
on direct bus routes from the
city center, airport and ferry
terminal. The proprietors are
friendly, and breakfast is
included in the room rate.
Vegetarian and special diet
options are available.
🛏 7 🅿 8 ⬧ MC, V

LYNCH GREEN ISLE
$-$$$
NAAS RD.
CLONDALKIN, DUBLIN 22
TEL 01 459 3406
FAX 01 459 2178
E-MAIL greenisle@jurysdoyle.com
A comfortable, relaxed hotel
on the southwestern outskirt of
Dublin, Green Isle is suitable for
visitors who want easy access
to southeast and southwest
Ireland as well as to the capital.
🛏 90 🅿 250 ⬆ ⬧ All
major cards

RESTAURANTS

🍴 RESTAURANT PATRICK
GUILBAUD
$$$$$

21 UPPER MERRION ST.
DUBLIN 2
TEL 01 676 4192
E-MAIL restaurantpatrick
guilbaud@eircom.net
Faultless French cuisine and
immaculate service have won
Patrick Guilbaud more
awards than any other
restaurant in the whole of
Ireland. Impeccable culinary
creations here include
succulent Connemara
Lobster ravioli and Sole and
Duck Confit. Housed in the
Merrion Hotel, with a fine
collection of original Irish art,
the restaurant is a classy,
upscale dining experience,
with considerable Irish charm.
🕐 Closed Sun., Mon. ⬧ All
major cards

🍴 THORNTON'S
$$$$$
FITZWILLIAM HOTEL,
ST. STEPHENS GREEN
DUBLIN 2
TEL 01 478 7008
E-MAIL enq@fitzwilliamhotel.com
Kevin Thornton is the chef
that everyone keeps on
raving about, year after year.
Here's your chance to see
why—if you manage to get a
table. It's worth making a
reservation before you leave
home, to sample the
wonderful combinations of
flavors and textures.
Perfectionism and flair, and
then some. Open pre-theater
by arrangement.
🕐 Closed Sun., Mon.
⬧ All major cards

🍴 KING SITRIC
$$$$
EAST PIER, HOWTH,
CO. DUBLIN
TEL 01 832 5235
E-MAIL info@kingsitric.ie
Right on the harbor, this
is a first-class fish restaurant,
with lobster and crab
caught by its own fishermen,
fresh fish landed daily on
Howth Pier, and oysters
and mussels rushed in from
the west coast. As well as
traditional Irish and French-

influenced dishes, there are Oriental touches.

♿ 🕐 Closed Sun., Oct.–April L, May–Sept. weekends
💳 All major cards

🍴 AYA
$$$
CLARENDON ST.
DUBLIN 2
TEL 01 677 1544
FAX 01 677 1546
E-MAIL mail@aya.ie

This is a wonderful Japanese restaurant, so there's sushi, sushi, sushi—but not just sushi. You can even get a full Irish bacon-and-sausage breakfast here, too. Eat in or takeout, order on-line or face to face from a charming attendant, gobble-and-go or take all the time in the world. It's a great concept, and it's all tacked on to one of Dublin's finest and most upscale stores, Brown Thomas—great news for hungry shoppers.
♿ 💳 All major cards

🍴 CAFÉ MAO
$$$
2/3 CHATHAM ROW
DUBLIN 2
TEL 01 670 4899
FAX 01 670 893

Bang in the heart of Dublin's shop-till-you-drop quarter, this is the place to rewire your flagging energy with delicious dishes from all over the Asian world.
💳 MC, V

🍴 EDEN
$$$
MEETING HOUSE SQ,
TEMPLE BAR, DUBLIN 2
TEL 01 670 5372
FAX 01 670 3330

Right at the hub of happening Temple Bar, Eden does throw its cap definitively into the modern cookery ring, but with no flim-flam. The flavors of quality ingredients sensitively handled speak for themselves. in spicy Thai soup, perhaps, or monkfish and peppers, or tangy balls of finely minced lamb.
💳 All major cards

🍴 JACOB'S LADDER
$$$
4/5 NASSAU ST.
DUBLIN 2
TEL 01 670 3865
FAX 01 670 3868

Very near Trinity College (with a view across the playing fields and gardens), this is a welcoming place patronized by Dubliners who appreciate the best modern Irish cooking.
🕐 Closed Sun., Mon. 💳 All major cards

🍴 KITES
$$$
15–17 BALLSBRIDGE TERRACE
DUBLIN 4
TEL 01 660 7415
FAX 01 660 5978

A very good Chinese restaurant with a pleasant, low-key atmosphere, serving a wide variety of dishes.
🕐 Closed Sat., Sun. L, Good Fri., Dec. 25–26 💳 All major cards

🍴 L'ECRIVAIN
$$$
109 LOWER BAGGOT ST.
DUBLIN 2
TEL 01 661 1919
FAX 01 661 0617
E-MAIL enquiries@lecrivain.com

A deservedly famous Dublin restaurant, full of good culinary ideas based on the best fresh ingredients, executed brilliantly but without bravado. Monkfish, oysters, prawns and scallops are all wonderful, and meat-lovers will … well, love the Irish lamb and beef. As a bonus, a particularly thoughtful and interesting wine list.
♿ 🕐 Closed Sat. L & Sun.
💳 All major cards

🍴 THE RED BANK
$$$
7 CHURCH ST.
SKERRIES, CO. DUBLIN
TEL 01 849 1005
FAX 01 849 1598
E-MAIL redbank@aircom.net

If you want to know what Dubliners will gladly venture out of town for, this is it—impeccably and excitingly

prepared seafood, straight out of the local boats, followed by deliciously gut-busting desserts that make you wish you were still a kid and could manage two.
♿ 🕐 Closed L (except Sun.), Sun. D 💳 All major cards

🍴 ROLY'S BISTRO
$$$
7 BALLSBRIDGE TERRACE
BALLSBRIDGE, DUBLIN 4
TEL 01 668 2611
FAX 01 660 8535

A tremendous atmosphere of Dubliners enjoying themselves, and an unfussy approach to food (notably the Dublin Bay prawns and the hearty "keep-out-the-cold" puddings) that lets basic flavors and textures speak for themselves.
💳 All major cards

🍴 SHANAHAN'S ON THE GREEN
$$$
119 ST. STEPHEN'S GREEN
DUBLIN 2
TEL 01 407 0939
FAX 01 407 0940
E-MAIL k.mularny@indigo.ie

Behind the very Irish name is very American cooking, huge steaks done to perfection—a rare art. There's something for everyone on the menu, but carnivores with heroic appetites will think they have died and gone to Dallas.
🕐 Closed Sat.–Thurs. L
💳 All major cards

🍴 THE TEA ROOM
$$$
THE CLARENCE HOTEL
ESSEX ST.
DUBLIN 2
TEL 01 407 0813
FAX 01 407 0826
E-MAIL fb@theclarence.ie

You can just drink tea here, if you must, but the Tea Rooms are really about fine dining in style. The modern cooking, including excellent fresh sea bass, or oysters in a crab sauce, for example, is enjoyed in a light and lively room that's paneled in pale wood, art deco fashion.

🕑 Closed Sat. & Sun. L
🖾 All major cards

BANGKOK CAFÉ

$$

106 PARNELL ST.
DUBLIN 1
TEL 01 878 6618

Surrounded by lots of bright chat from the clientele, you'll find there's a fizz about the whole place—not least because of the food, which represents spicy Thai cuisine at its most delicious.

🕑 Closed L 🖾 No credit cards accepted

BELLA CUBA

$$

11 BALLSBRIDGE TERRACE
DUBLIN 4
TEL 01 660 5539
FAX 01 660 5539
E-MAIL info@bella-cuba.com

Fabulous Cuban cuisine, meaty and fishy with bursts of flavor from combinations of spices and herbs.

🕑 Closed Sat.–Wed. L
🖾 AE, MC, V

CAVISTON'S SEAFOOD RESTAURANT

$$

58–59 GLASTHULE RD.
SANDYCOVE, CO. DUBLIN
TEL 01 280 9245
FAX 01 284 4054
E-MAIL info@cavistons.com

Quite simply, an unpretentious, family-run restaurant whose Irish-style seafood and other cooking is so superb that connoisseurs will visit Ireland specifically to eat here. Yet everyone feels welcome, and no one feels excluded. How do they do it?

🕑 Closed Sun., Mon. 🖾 All major cards

CHAPTER ONE

$$

PARNELL SQ.
DUBLIN 1
TEL 01 873 2266
FAX 01 873 3330
E-MAIL info@chapterone

restaurant.com

The Dublin Writers' Museum sits on top of this excellent north-of-the-Liffey eatery, which uses both French and Irish influences in its cooking to great effect.

🕑 Closed Sun., Mon. 🖾
🖾 AE, DC, V

DISH

$$

146 UPPER LEESON ST.
DUBLIN 4
TEL 01 664 2135
FAX 01 664 2719
E-MAIL info@tribeca.ie

Slices clean through the pretension and insubstantiality of many of Temple Bar's eateries, to do what matters—presenting food (for example organic meat, freshly caught fish, a potato tortilla) simply and temptingly, and making sure it tastes as fresh and clean as the tiptop ingredients that underpin everything.

🖾 All major cards

ELEPHANT & CASTLE

$$

18 TEMPLE BAR
DUBLIN 2
TEL 01 679 3121
FAX 01 679 1399

The Elephant & Castle opens early and closes late, so you could eat three (or four) square meals a day here. And why not, when the food's good from breakfast to dinner (enormous baskets of chicken wings, homemade hamburgers with an array of sauces, and a mighty Caesar salad to fill up any empty corners) and the atmosphere is so enjoyable?

🖾 🖾 All major cards

GALLAGHER'S BOXTY HOUSE

$$

20–21 TEMPLE BAR, DUBLIN 2
TEL 01 677 2762
E-MAIL info@boxtyhouse.ie

This is a world-famous temple of Irish cuisine, presenting wonderful "comfort food" in contemporary style. Boxty (potato pancakes) come with

a variety of imaginative fillings, and the menu also includes Irish Stew, Coddle, smoked salmon, and juicy Irish beef-steaks. There are vegetarian dishes too.

🖾 🖾 All major cards

GOOD WORLD

$$

18 S. GREAT GEORGE'S ST.
DUBLIN 2
TEL 01 677 5373
FAX 01 677 5373

Handy for Grafton Street shoppers or visitors to St. Patrick's Cathedral, this is the Chinese restaurant where the Dublin Chinese themselves prefer to eat. All the variations on noodles and beanshoots that you would expect, all beautifully cooked, plus Dublin's best and widest choice of Dim Sum.

🕑 Closed Dec. 25–26
🖾 All major cards

101 TALBOT

$$

100–102 TALBOT ST.
DUBLIN 1
TEL 01 874 5011
FAX 01 874 5011
E-MAIL pascalbradley@tinet.ie

Far East, East (Thai fishcakes), Middle East (North African chicken) and extremely Near East (Dublin Bay fish) collide to all-encompassing effect on the menu of this popular Northside restaurant where knowledgeable Southsiders collect. It's also very convenient for pre-theater fueling—both the Abbey and the Gate theaters are within strolling distance.

🕑 Closed Sun., Mon., L
🖾 All major cards

POPPADOM RESTAURANT

$$

11A RATHGAR RD.
DUBLIN 6
TEL 01 490 2383

Yes, the poppadoms are admirable—the real thing, properly made—but so is all the authentic Indian food.

Really good Indian restaurants are rarer than hen's teeth in Ireland, but here's one.

Closed L / All major cards

SOMETHING SPECIAL

O'CONNELL'S

What a great idea—this admirable place (downstairs at Bewley's Hotel) obtains all its food ingredients and its wine from top-class sources (organic, free-range, fresh almost goes without saying), and the menu lets you know exactly who and where it all came from. It adds a certain something to your enjoyment of salmon, for example, if you can visualize the cold blue waters off magical green Clare Island where the fish was raised. Why don't more restaurants do this?

$$
BEWLEY'S HOTEL,
MERRION RD., BALLSBRIDGE
DUBLIN 4
TEL 01 647 3304
FAX 647 3499
E-MAIL info@oconnellsballsbridge
.com
All major cards

BUTLER'S CHOCOLATE CAFÉ

$
9 CHATHAM STREET,
DUBLIN 2
TEL 01 671 0599
E-MAIL michelle@butlers.ie
Butler's has done for hot chocolate what Seattle did for coffee, and you can either drink it neat or add one of a variety of flavoured syrups. There's great coffee, too, along with freshly baked cakes and chocolate croissants, and it will be hard to leave without a selection of their handmade chocolates. If you have to have something savory, gourmet sandwiches are also available.
All major cards

EAST IRELAND

COUNTY KILDARE

ATHY

COURSETOWN COUNTRY HOUSE

$$
STRADBALLY RD.
TEL 059 863 1101
FAX 059 863 2740
This is a luxurious country-house hotel set on a 250-acre (100 ha) farm, which is also a wildlife sanctuary. The owners are only too happy to share their knowledge with their guests. Lovely walks.
5 22 Closed Nov.–Feb. MC, V

KILDARE

CURRAGH LODGE

$$
DUBLIN RD
TEL 045 522144 or 045 521136
FAX 045 521247
E-MAIL clhotel@iol.ie
This is a very comfortable hotel with efficient, friendly staff. Curragh Lodge is a handsome old house on the Dublin road coming into Kildare, and is excellently located within walking distance of the Irish National Stud, the Horse Museum, the Japanese Garden, and St. Fiachra's Garden.
21 30 All major cards

LEIXLIP

LEIXLIP HOUSE HOTEL

$$$–$$$$
CAPTAINS HILL
TEL 01 6242268
FAX 01 6244177
E-MAIL info@leixliphouse.com
In this fine Georgian house the enjoyable ambience is more than matched by the cooking, Irish style. With great attention to locally sourced seasonal produce, it sets the standard for other hotel restaurants in the area.

19 64 All major cards

STRAFFAN

THE KILDARE HOTEL & GOLF CLUB

$$$$$
STRAFFAN
TEL 01 6017200
FAX 01 6017299
E-MAIL resortsales@kclub.ie
A top-notch, 5-star hotel with its own Arnold Palmer-designed golf course—the 2005 Ryder Cup will be contested here. Efficient staff offers polished, attentive service. A luxury stopover for those who need not count the cents—nor the dollars.
69 plus 10 annex 205 All major cards

BALLYMORE EUSTACE

THE BALLYMORE INN

$$
BALLYMORE EUSTACE
TEL 045 864585
FAX 045 864747
E-MAIL theballymoreinn@hotmail
.com
From tempting starters to the excellent cheeseboard, this pub-style restaurant and bar offers top-quality fare, based on carefully selected ingredients—all served, of course, with a welcoming smile.
Closed Mon. D, MC, V

COUNTY WICKLOW

BLESSINGTON

DOWNSHIRE HOUSE

$$$
BLESSINGTON
TEL 045 865199
FAX 045 865335
E-MAIL info@downshirehouse .com
The beautiful scenery around Blessington, on the western edge of the Wicklow Mountains, sharpens the appetite for some solid country-house style cooking, with the emphasis on fresh ingredients.

🅿 30 🕐 Closed mid-Dec–early Jan. 🔷 MC, V

BRAY

🍽 TREE OF IDLENESS
$$$
SEA FRONT
TEL 01 286 3498
How to serve Greek Cypriot food—the dolmades, souvlaki, and moussaka, are sensational, and there's roast suckling pig for those who want to go whole hog, so to speak. The wonderful food is served to a cosmopolitan clientele. The Tree comes up triumphantly trumps.
🕐 Closed Mon. L 🔷 AE, MC, V

GLENDALOUGH

🏨 THE GLENDALOUGH
$$$
GLENDALOUGH
TEL 0404 45135
FAX 0404 45142
E-MAIL info@glendaloughhotel.ie
Right beside the captivating monastic site, the hotel offers comfortable accommodations and wonderful views in its setting deep in the wooded valley of Glendalough.
🛈 44 🅿 100 🕐 Closed Dec.–Jan. 🔄 🔷 All major cards

SOMETHING SPECIAL

🏨 TUDOR LODGE
An exceptionally hospitable house only a mile (1.6 km) from the beautiful valley and historic monastic site of Glendalough. The owners treat you as if you are a personal friend, rooms are very comfortable and well appointed, there's a cozy sitting room with a fire, and the breakfasts are so gargantuan that you can skip lunch and still wear a smile.
$
LARAGH
GLENDALOUGH
TEL/FAX 0404 45554
🛈 6 🅿 8 🔷 MC, V

KILMACANOGUE

🍽 AVOCA HANDWEAVERS
$
KILMACANOGUE
TEL 01 286 7466
FAX 01 286 2367
What real food is all about—fresh ingredients, combined into uncomplicated dishes, and served with the charm. The restaurant is attached to the famous knitwear store.
🕐 Closed D 🔷 🔷 All major cards

MACREDDIN VILLAGE

🍽 THE STRAWBERRY TREE
$$$$
THE BROOK LODGE INN
TEL 0402 36444
FAX 0402 36580
E-MAIL brooklodge@macreddin.ie
A wonderful place to enjoy the taste of beautifully cooked and presented food from purely organic sources—for example, lamb, wild rabbit with herby rice, and tangy local cheeses.
🔷 🕐 Closed Sun. D 🔷 All major cards

RATHNEW

🏨 TINAKILLY COUNTRY HOUSE & RESTAURANT
$$$$–$$$$$
RATHNEW
TEL 0404 69274
FAX 0404 67806
E-MAIL reservations@tinakilly.ie
A Victorian house in terraced gardens, with beautiful sea views on this unfrequented coast north of Wicklow town.
🛈 51 🅿 60 🕐 Closed Christmas 🔄 🔷 All major cards

WOODENBRIDGE

🏨 WOODENBRIDGE
$$–$$$
WOODENBRIDGE
TEL 0402 35146
FAX 0402 35573
E-MAIL wbhotel@iol.ie
A friendly hotel at the foot of the delectable Vale of Avoca in the south Wicklow Mountains. Some of the rooms date to the 17th century, others are new; all are very comfortable.
🛈 23 🅿 100 🔷 AE, MC, V

COUNTY CARLOW

CARLOW

🏨 BARROWVILLE TOWN HOUSE
$$
KILKENNY RD.
TEL 059 914 3324
FAX 059 914 1953
E-MAIL barrowvilletownhouse@eircom.net
A hospitable atmosphere pervades this Georgian hotel; tinkle on the grand piano, or relax in the gardens.
🛈 7 🅿 12 🔷 AE, MC, V

🏨 DOLMEN HOTEL
🍽 $$
KILKENNY RD.
TEL 059 914 2002
FAX 059 914 2375
E-MAIL reservations@dolmenhotel.ie
The Dolmen prides itself on re-creating the comfort and spaciousness of a bygone era, exemplified in its beautiful rooms. The hotel enjoys a riverside position; you can try coarse fishing, or stroll in 20 acres (8 ha) of landscaped grounds. You can eat in the formal Belmont Restaurant, the laid-back Barrow Grill, or lunchtime carvery.
🛈 40 plus 12 annex 🅿 300 🔷 🔷 All major cards

LEIGHLINBRIDGE

🏨 LORD BAGENAL INN
🍽 $$$
MAIN ST.
TEL 059 972 1668
FAX 059 972 2629
EMAIL info@lordbagenal.com
Famous for its fine food and wine, this upscale inn has luxurious accommodations and friendly hospitality. It is set in a heritage village, and has lovely gardens beside the River

Barrow—and its own marina for waterborne guests.
🛏 12   💳 All major cards

COUNTY KILKENNY

KILKENNY

🏨 BUTLER HOUSE
$$-$$$$
PATRICK ST.
TEL 056 776 5707
FAX 056 776 5626
E-MAIL res@butler.ie
The former Dower House of Kilkenny Castle provides elegant accommodations right in the heart of the town. It has magnificent plaster ceilings, marble fireplaces, and sweeping staircases, and the larger rooms have views over the peaceful garden and the castle. Breakfast is included in the price, either a Continental, served in the rooms, or a full hot breakfast provided at the Kilkenny Design Centre, just across the garden.
🛏 13   🅿 24   💳 All major cards

🏨 LANGTON HOUSE HOTEL
$$-$$$
69 JOHN ST.
TEL 056 776 5133
FAX 056 776 3693
E-MAIL langtons@oceanfree.net
Four times National pub of the year, Langton's now has a stylish hotel extension with the same high standards and attention to detail that won accolades for the bar and restaurant.
🛏 30   🅿 80   💳 All major cards

🏨 KILKENNY ORMONDE 🍴 HOTEL
$-$$$
ORMONDE ST.
TEL 056 772 3900
FAX 056 772 3977
E-MAIL info@kilkennyormonde.com
Consistently good food is on offer in both restaurants of this new, contemporary styled hotel with large lounge and reception areas.
🛏 118   💳 All major cards

🍴 CAFÉ SOL
$$
WILLIAM ST.
TEL 056 776 4987
The place to be at lunch time (or coffee time, or tea time, for that matter) for delicious food—freshly baked scones, Mediterranean salads, chicken stir-fry, local sausages—served with great charm.
🕐 Closed Sun., Mon. D   ♿
💳 MC, V

THOMASTOWN

🏨 MOUNT JULIET
$$$$-$$$$$
THOMASTOWN
TEL 056 777 3000
FAX 056 777 3019
E-MAIL info@mountjuliet.ie
Fine stucco, Adam fireplaces, 18th-century furniture, and *objets* d'art feature within this handsome Palladian mansion. Jack Nicklaus designed the hotel's golf course, and there are 1,500 acres (600 ha) of parkland to explore. Discreet luxury and attentive service are the keynotes.
🛏 32 plus 27 annex   🅿 200
🈁   💳 All major cards

COUNTY WEXFORD

ARTHURSTOWN

🏨 DUNBRODY COUNTRY 🍴 HOUSE HOTEL & RESTAURANT
$$$$-$$$$$
ARTHURSTOWN
TEL 051 389600
FAX 051 389601
E-MAIL dunbrody@indigo.ie
Individually styled bedrooms with marbled bathrooms in a Georgian country house set in parkland near the sea. Award-winning cuisine in the most beautiful surroundings on Waterford Harbour.
🛏 22   🅿 40   🕐 Closed Christmas   💳 All major cards

ENNISCORTHY

🏨 BALLINKEELE HOUSE
$-$$

ENNISCORTHY
TEL 053 38105
FAX 053 38468
E-MAIL info@ballinkeele.com
Bedrooms are extremely comfortable, the ambience relaxed at this upscale Victorian farmhouse at the heart of a working farm.
🛏 5   🅿 20   🕐 Closed Dec.–Jan.   💳 MC

GOREY

🏨 MARLFIELD HOUSE
$$$$$
GOREY
TEL 055 21124
FAX 055 21572
E-MAIL info@marlfieldhouse.ie
This luxurious hotel, once a fine Regency house, was home to the Earl of Courtown. The conservatory looks out on lovely gardens.
🛏 20   🅿 50   🕐 Closed mid-Dec.–Jan.   💳 All major cards

ROSSLARE

🍴 LA MARINE
🏨 **$**
KELLY'S RESORT HOTEL
TEL 053 32114
FAX 053 32222
E-MAIL kellyhot@iol.ie
A seafront hotel with a stylish modern approach, down to its imported French zinc bar. The same goes for the food, as superbly tasty as really direct contemporary cooking should be. The seafood chowder and the Wexford beef hot off the grill are outstanding.
🕐 Closed mid Dec.–late Feb.   💳 AE, MC, V

COUNTY TIPPERARY

BALLINDERRY

SOMETHING SPECIAL

🍴 BROCKA-ON-THE-WATER
Forget the whistles and bells of more pretentious restaurants. This one concentrates on the three things that matter—atmosphere, location … and, oh yes, food.

Brocka-on-the-Water is a relaxed and delightful place beside Lough Derg in northernmost County Tipperary. The freshest fish and meat are complemented by herbs and vegetables from the restaurant's own garden.

$$$
KILGARVAN QUAY
TEL 067 22038
🕐 Closed L, Sun. 🚫 No credit cards accepted

CASHEL

🏨 CASHEL PALACE HOTEL
$$$$-$$$$$
CASHEL
TEL 062 62707
FAX 062 61521
E-MAIL reception@cashel-palace.ie
This hotel really is a palace—the former palace of the Bishops of Cashel, with the spectacular backdrop of the Rock of Cashel (floodlit at night). Luxury bedrooms in the palace itself; family or group needs are catered for in mews accommodations alongside.
🛏 13 plus 10 annex 🅿 35 🕐 Closed 2 weeks Christmas/Jan. 🔁 🚫 All major cards

CLONMEL

🏨 MINELLA
$$$
CLONMEL
TEL 052 22388
FAX 052 24381
E-MAIL hotelminella@eircom.net
This is a cozy, family-run hotel with tastefully decorated bedrooms (some have Jacuzzis) in its own extensive grounds by the River Suir.
🛏 70 🅿 100 🕐 Closed Christmas 🏊 🚫 All major cards

COUNTY WATERFORD

ANNESTOWN

🏨 ANNESTOWN HOUSE
$$-$$$
ANNESTOWN

TEL 051 396160
FAX 051 396474
E-MAIL relax@annestown.com
Annestown House is a comfortable hotel occupying a superb position on the Waterford coast, with fine sea views and private access from the gardens to a sandy cove. The bedrooms are centrally heated and spacious.
🛏 5 🅿 10 🕐 Closed Nov.–Feb. 🚫 AE, MC, V

CAPPOQUIN

🏨 RICHMOND HOUSE
$$$-$$$$
CAPPOQUIN
TEL 058 54278
FAX 058 54988
E-MAIL info@richmondhouse.net
This is an elegant Georgian house on spacious grounds, with comfortable rooms and a renowned restaurant. Fresh fish and shellfish from local rivers and coastal waters and locally reared and dressed meat are featured.
🛏 10 🅿 40 🕐 Closed Tue. L (except high season), mid-Dec.–mid-Jan. 🚫 All major cards

DUNGARVAN

🏨 CASTLE FARM COUNTRY HOUSE
$$
MILL ST.
CAPPAGH
TEL 058 68049
FAX 058 68099
E-MAIL castlefm@iol.ie
Expect personal touches from the owners of this friendly, characterful farmhouse butted up to a medieval castle. The 18th-century rooms, spacious and beautifully furnished, have big sprawling beds.
🛏 5 🅿 7 🚫 MC, V

🍴 THE TANNERY
$$$
QUAY ST.
TEL 058 45420
FAX 058 45518
E-MAIL info@tannery.ie

An imaginative twist to everything from old favorites —tuna steaks, pork and noodles, bouillabaisse—to "go-on-give-it-a-try" innovations—special salt cod, saffron broth, Parmesan fritters—on the menu here.
🕐 Closed Sun., Mon. 🚫 All major cards

GLENCAIRN

🍴 BUGGY'S GLENCAIRN INN
$$
NEAR LISMORE
TEL/FAX 058 56232
E-MAIL buggysglencairninn@eircom.net
An Irish institution, where uncomplicated treatment of extremely fresh ingredients—notably the fish, which is caught locally—produces fabulously tasty dishes.
🕐 Closed L 🅱 🚫 MC, V

WATERFORD

🏨 WATERFORD CASTLE
$$$$-$$$$$
THE ISLAND
TEL 051 878203
FAX 051 879316
E-MAIL info@waterfordcastle.com
A chance to stay in a Norman castle, reached by ferry and set up to ensure the most romantic of sojourns. Realists will enjoy the 18-hole golf course, clay shooting, and other outdoor activities.
🛏 19 🅿 50 🔁 🚫 All major cards

🍴 THE WINE VAULT
$$
HIGH ST.
TEL 051 853444
FAX 051 853777
E-MAIL bacchus@eircom.net
The name of this friendly eatery tells you how high in the mix the owner sets his first-class wine list, which complements good cooking to perfection—gravadlax, fresh oysters and salmon, organic vegetables.

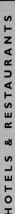

    Closed Mon. L, Sun.
AE, MC, V

SOUTHWEST IRELAND

CORK CITY

HOTELS

HAYFIELD MANOR
$$$$$
PERROTT AVE.
COLLEGE RD
TEL 021 484 5900
FAX 021 431 6839
E-MAIL enquiries@
hayfieldmanor.ie
A snug retreat where you can
shut the world away (and
work on your fitness in the
exclusive health club), Hayfield
Manor is a comfortable,
upscale hotel toward the
western outskirts of Cork city.
88 100
All major cards

AMBASSADOR
$$$
MILITARY HILL
ST. LUKES
TEL 021 455 1996
FAX 021 455 1997
E-MAIL reservations@
ambassadorhotel.ie
An imposing 19th-century
building houses this well-
equipped hotel that commands
fine views over the city from
its rise of ground.
60 60 Closed
Christmas All major
cards

THE KINGSLEY HOTEL
$$$
VICTORIA CROSS
TEL 021 480 0500
FAX 021 480 0527
E-MAIL resv@kingsleyhotel.com
A luxury hotel beside the
River Lee, with an agreeably
relaxed atmosphere. Big, airy
bedrooms have safes, trouser
presses, air conditioning,
interactive TVs with
messaging, —and there's a
same-day laundry service, too.
69 250
All major cards

IMPERIAL HOTEL
$$–$$$$
SOUTH MALL
TEL 021 427 4040
FAX 021 427 5375
E-MAIL sales@imperialhotelcork.ie
The individually styled ensuite
rooms of this chic hotel offer
comfort and a quiet
atmosphere in central Cork.
90 40 Closed
Christmas All major
cards

RESTAURANTS

CAFÉ PARADISO
$$$
16 LANCASTER QUAY
WESTERN RD.
TEL 021 427 7939
FAX 021 430 7469
If you like brilliant cooking of
vegetables rare and ordinary,
home-grown and exotic, this
restaurant on a loop of the
River Lee's South Channel is
the place to head for.
    Closed Sun. & Mon.
MC, V

JACOB'S ON THE MALL
$$$
30A SOUTH MALL
TEL 021 425 1530
FAX 021 125 1531
E-MAIL kingsley@tinet.com
Sophisticated cuisine that
doesn't require specialized
knowlege to appreciate it.
Dishes such as roast cod with
champ—mashed potato with
a touch of magic—or oysters
with shallots are served in a
relaxed atmosphere in the
heart of Cork city.
    Closed Sun. AE,
MC, V

JACQUES
$$$
PHOENIX ST.
TEL 021 427 7387
FAX 021 427 0634
E-MAIL jacquesrestaurant@
eircom.net
Dishes from around the
world, each treated with care
and attention to detail that
suggest a real understanding
of the various culinary

cultures—Spanish salads,
Mediterranean swordfish, Thai
green chicken curry, boeuf
Bordelaise, and many more.
Closed L, Sun. & Mon.
AE, MC, V

CRAWFORD GALLERY CAFÉ
$$
CRAWFORD GALLERY
EMMET PLACE
TEL 021 427 4415
FAX 021 465 2021
You wouldn't necessarily
expect to find a fabulous
eating experience in an art
gallery's café, but that's what
this is—largely because the
celebrated Ballymaloe House
kitchens, gardens, and bakery
supply most of what's on offer.
That could mean local lamb
and fish with intriguing herbs, a
vegetarian quiche with piquant
homemade chutney, or just a
pile of freshly baked bread and
some Cork farmhouse cheese.
Closed Christmas week
MC, V

ISAAC'S
$$
48 MACCURTAIN ST.
TEL 021 450 3805
FAX 021 455 1348
E-MAIL isaacs@iol.ie
Already a bit of a Cork
institution, this up-to-date
restaurant has a lively, friendly
approach and offers plenty of
fine international dishes—
though it really made its name
with traditional Irish recipes
given an imaginative shake-up.
    Closed Sun. L All
major cards

NAKON THAI
$$
TRAMWAY HOUSE
DOUGLAS
TEL 021 436 9900
FAX 021 488 8002
E-MAIL nakonthai@eircom.net
Superb Thai cooking, chosen
from either an à la carte menu
or from one of a number of
set menus, in which fresh
authentic ingredients are the
watchword.

🕐 Closed L, Christmas week
🚫 All major cards

COUNTY CORK

BALTIMORE

🍴 THE CUSTOMS HOUSE
$$$
BALTIMORE
TEL 028 20200
Specializing in the freshest of seafood and local produce, the Customs House closes in winter for the best of reasons—so that the welcoming and dedicated couple who run it can scour the world for more delightful ideas for the next season. Children under 12 are unlikely to feel comfortable.
🕐 Closed L, Nov.–April
🚫 None (foreign currency accepted)

BANTRY

🍴 BLAIR'S COVE RESTAURANT
$$$$
DURRUS
TEL 027 61041
FAX 027 61487
E-MAIL blairscove@eircom.net
A free-and-easy ambience allied to beautifully tasty but unfussy cooking.
🕐 Closed Nov.–March; Sun., Mon. 🚫 MC, V

🍴 O'CONNOR'S SEAFOOD RESTAURANT
$$$
THE SQUARE
TEL 027 50221
E-MAIL oconnorseafood @eircom.net
This was the first restaurant in Ireland to specialize in mussels, and all the seafood is excellent. The long, long menu includes starters such as seafood chowder or spicy fishcakes with chili and coriander jam, and main courses might include scallop and monkfish gratin or local mountain lamb. Good old fish and chips is enhanced by the use of stout in the batter.

Great bar snacks and light meals are also available.
🚻 🕐 Closed Christmas
🚫 V

FERMOY

🏨 BALLYVOLANE HOUSE
$$$
CASTLELYONS
TEL 025 36349
FAX 025 36781
E-MAIL ballyvol@iol.ie
You will enjoy an exceptionally warm welcome at this fine 18th-century Italianate country house, set in famous gardens within parkland. Stroll around the lakes; one has been stocked for fishing and might yield you a brown trout.
ℹ️ 6 🅿️ 25 🕐 Closed Christmas week 🚫 All major cards

🍴 LA BIGOUDENNE
$$
28 MCCURTAIN ST.
TEL 025 32832
Breton, Belgian, and northern French dishes served with imaginative flair in a very unfussy set-up. Vegetarians welcome with advance notice.
🚻 🕐 Closed Mon., L (except Thurs. & Sat.)
🚫 MC, V

KANTURK

🏨 ASSOLAS COUNTRY HOUSE
$$$$–$$$$$
KANTURK
TEL 029 50015
FAX 029 50795
E-MAIL assolas@eircom.net
An early Ascendancy house dating back over 300 years, delightfully set among attractive gardens, where the welcome is warm and the accommodation is both comfortable and characterful—you could opt for family-friendly rooms round the courtyard, or huge bedrooms overlooking the garden and the river.
ℹ️ 6 plus 3 annex 🅿️ 15
🕐 Closed Nov.–mid-March
🚫 DC, MC, V

KILBRITTAIN

🍴 CASINO HOUSE
$$$
COOLMAIN BAY
TEL 023 49944
FAX 023 49945
E-MAIL chouse@eircom.net
Stylish and innovative, Casino House is the place to eat if you are looking for a tinge of invention and a smack of originality (saddle of rabbit stuffed with pistachio nuts, monkfish with beetroot mousse) to spice up familiar staples of sophisticated cooking.
🕐 Closed Wed. & Sun. D, Jan.–mid-March 🚫 DC, MC, V

KINSALE

🏨 OLD BANK HOUSE
$$$–$$$$
11 PEARSE ST.
TEL 021 477 4075
FAX 021 477 4296
E-MAIL oldbank@indigo.ie
A hospitable Georgian house meticulously restored by the owners, who can arrange sea fishing, riding, and sailing for guests. Bedrooms are country house in character, furnished with fine antiques.
ℹ️ 17 🕐 Closed Christmas week 🔁 🚫 AE, MC, V

🍴 CRACKPOTS
$$$
3 CORK ST.
TEL 021 477 2847
FAX 021 477 3517
E-MAIL crackpots@iol.ie
A really enjoyable place in the heart of fish-worshipping country where carnivores can subversively enjoy Moroccan chicken and other beautifully cooked meat dishes (and—yes—fish as well, naturally, fresh off the local fishermen's lines) and then buy the plates their dinner was served on—like everything on the menu, these too are made on site. (early dinner; 6–8 p.m.)
🕐 Closed Mon.–Thurs. L, Nov. 🚫 AE, MC, V

🍴 KINSALE GOURMET STORE & FISHY FISHY CAFÉ

$$

GUARDWELL

TEL 021 477 4453

As you'd expect from the name, this is a modern place where the touch is light but the talent is truly heavy. Choose the fish you fancy from the wet fish slab and it will be cooked exactly to your liking; or go for fresh prawns, seafood chowder, crayfish, hake, or any of half a dozen other fishy fishy delights.

🕐 Closed D 🚫 🚭 MC, V

MALLOW

🏨 LONGUEVILLE HOUSE 🍴 HOTEL

$$$–$$$$$

MALLOW

TEL 022 47156

FAX 022 47459

E-MAIL info@longuevillehouse.ie

An elegant Georgian house with Italian stucco and other original features, providing upscale accommodations amid lovely secluded parkland. Bedrooms are huge, airy, and superbly decorated, in keeping with the style of the entire hotel. In the President's Restaurant you'll get superb food based on local sources—salmon in season from the Blackwater, lamb and pork from the estate farm, and fruit and greenstuff from the garden—not to mention Longueville's own white wine and its impeccable service. Unusually for Ireland, this is excellent for vegetarians. Booking essential.

🛏 20 🅿 30 🕐 Closed Christmas, limited service Nov.–Feb. 🚭 All major cards

MIDLETON

🏨 BALLYMALOE HOUSE 🍴 $$$$–$$$$$

SHANAGARRY

TEL 021 465 2531

FAX 021 465 2021

E-MAIL res@ballymaloe.ie

A 400-acre (160 ha) farm has

this charming and very comfortable country-house hotel at its heart. Rooms are in the main house or in buildings around the courtyard. In the restaurant, meticulous care over ingredients is the definitive Factor X. Home-made paté, Cobh smoked fish, local beef, fabulous Cork cheeses as a complement to the famous Ballymaloe bread—everything's fresh, everything is treated with care and attention, so everything is just exactly right in both presentation and taste. Hardly surprising, since this is where the famous Ballymaloe cookery school started.

🛏 22 plus 10 annex 🅿 30 🕐 Closed Dec. 23–26; restaurant closed for L.
🚟 🚭 All major cards

SCHULL

🍴 THE ALTAR RESTAURANT

$$$

TOORMORE, GOLEEN,

TEL 028 35254

Hidden out in the depths of West Cork, this excellent restaurant is quite a find. Named after the ancient stone altar sites in the area, it offers modern and traditional Irish cuisine, prepared from the finest ingredients, which has attracted the attention of all the top food guides. You can feast on local smoked salmon, Bantry Bay mussels, and such main courses as Skeaghanore Duckling with Plum Sauce or stuffed sea trout.

🕐 Closed Sun., Mon. L
🚭 AE, MC, V

🍴 LA COQUILLE

$$

MAIN ST.

TEL 028 28642

French-run, French in flavor—clear onion soup, country-style chicken with herbs, unfussily cooked fish—the repertoire in this reliable small restaurant in a characterful village.

🕐 Closed L 🚭 AE, DC, MC

SKIBBEREEN

🍴 ISLAND COTTAGE

A romantic boat ride to an island restaurant—sounds good? Island Cottage is entirely idiosyncratic, but in a good way. There's no choice of menu, because you don't need one with such out-of-this-world source material (all local, most organic) and beautiful, uncomplicated cooking. You'll eat what you're given and like it, d'you hear? And the setting is out-of-this-world, too—almost literally. Telephone well in advance though, and note there's a separate charge for the boat trip.

$$

HARE ISLAND,

TEL 028 38102

FAX 028 38102

E-MAIL ellmary@islandcottage.com

🕐 Closed L, Mon.–Tues. mid-Sept.–mid-May 🚭 No credit cards accepted

ROSSCARBERY

🍴 O'CALLAGHAN-WALSHE

$$$

THE SQUARE,

TEL 023 48125

FAX 023 48125

E-MAIL funfish@indigo.ie

Funfish—oysters, mussels, and lobster to turbot, cod, and Dover sole—all salty-fresh and served in a cozy environment. (No children under 12 after 7:30 pm during summer.)

🕐 Closed Mon., L 🚭 MC, V

YOUGHAL

🏨 AHERNES 🍴 $$$–$$$$

163 N. MAIN ST.

TEL 024 92424

FAX 024 93633

E-MAIL ahernes@eircom.net

Family run for several generations, this is a place that simply exudes traditional Irish hospitality, from the warm welcome to the fond farewell.

The restaurant is very strong on fresh seafood, fish, beef, and lamb.

🕐 13 ♿ 🅿 20 🕐 Closed Christmas 🚫 AE, DC, MC, V

COUNTY KERRY

BALLYDAVID

🍴 OLD PIER RESTAURANT
$$
FEOTHANACH
TEL 066 915 5242
E-MAIL info@oldpier.com
In a wonderful location on the north shore of the Dingle Peninsula, with a big bay window overlooking the sea, this is a stylish modern restaurant (and guesthouse). The extensive menu includes plenty of wonderfully fresh and tasty local seafood.
♿ 🕐 Closed L, mid-Nov.–mid-March, 🚫 MC, V

DINGLE

🏨 GREENMOUNT HOUSE
$–$$$
DINGLE
TEL 066 9151414
FAX 066 9151974
E-MAIL greenmounthouse@eircom.net
Greenmount House is set on beautiful Dingle Harbour, and offers warm hospitality and a relaxed, comfortable atmosphere.
🕐 9 🅿 12 🕐 Closed Christmas week 🚫 MC, V

🍴 DOYLE'S SEAFOOD RESTAURANT
$$$
JOHN ST.
TEL 066 915 1174
E-MAIL cdoyles@iol.ie
Famous worldwide for its superb seafood, which comes straight in from Dingle Bay, Doyle's is one of those places you should not miss. The restaurant is cozy, with old stone walls and an ancient stove. Lobster is the specialty here and the West Coast Platter is a great choice too. There are

delicious meat dishes too.
🚫 All major cards

KENMARE

🏨 PARK HOTEL KENMARE
$$$$$
KENMARE
TEL 064 41200
FAX 064 41402
E-MAIL info@parkkenmare.com
A smart and luxurious Victorian country-house hotel that is set in landscaped gardens, where strollers enjoy superb views over the Kenmare River's broad estuary. The staff combine competence and cheerfulness.
🕐 46 🅿 60 🛗 🚫 All major cards

SOMETHING SPECIAL

🏨 SHEEN FALLS LODGE

The Sheen Falls is an extremely comfortable hotel where standards of service and welcome are tiptop. The hotel used to be a fishing lodge, which accounts for its breathtaking position on a bay of the Kenmare River estuary. And what adds that touch of magic to the place is its backdrop, the spectacular falls of the Sheen River, which are floodlit at night.
$$$$$
KENMARE
TEL 064 41600
FAX 064 41386
E-MAIL info@sheenfallslodge.ie
🕐 66 🅿 76 🕐 Closed mid-Dec., and Jan.–early Feb. 🛗 🏊 🚫 All major cards

🍴 PACKIE'S
$$$
HENRY ST.
TEL 064 41508
FAX 064 42135
Desserts are rich and delicious here, particularly the home-made ice cream—but make sure you leave room for the main courses, which marry first-class ingredients to unpretentious (but perfect) cooking. The menu includes such dishes as potato cakes

with garlic butter.
🕐 Closed Nov.–Easter, Sun., L 🚫 MC, V

KILLARNEY

🏨 KILLARNEY PARK
$$$$–$$$$$
KENMARE PLACE
TEL 064 35555
FAX 064 35266
E-MAIL info@killarneyparkhotel.ie
Purpose-built for the luxury end of the Killarney visitor market, the Killarney Park gives you a soft landing and a stylish ride all the way.
🕐 71 🅿 70 🕐 Closed Christmas 🛗 ❄ 🏊 🚫 All major cards

🏨 AGHADOE HEIGHTS
$$$$$
KILLARNEY
TEL 064 31766
FAX 064 31345
E-MAIL Info@aghadoeheights.com
The AA's Hotel of the Year for Ireland 2001–2002 fully deserves all its accolades, and it has a superb location, with stunning views of the lakes and mountains of the Killarney National Park. The ambience is not at all stuffy—service is personal and very friendly, and the hotel is superbly appointed. The stylish bedrooms are air-conditioned, and many have their own sundecks for that magical every-now-and-then moment when the sun decides to reveal itself to Killarney.
🕐 56 🅿 120 🛗 🏊 🚫 All major cards

🍴 BEAUFORT BAR AND RESTAURANT
BEAUFORT
$$
TEL 064 44032
E-MAIL beaurest@eircom.net
This historic bar has been run by the O'Sullivan family since it opened in 1841, and from 1911–1914 it was the base of the American Kalem Film Company, who shot about 70 movies in the area (still

photographs hang on the walls here). The restaurant is a more recent addition, but soon acquired a reputation for excellent cuisine. Chef Timmy Brosnan has an impressive set of credentials, and pays meticulous attention to the creation of delicious dishes.

🕐 Closed Mon., L (except Sun), Sun. D, Nov.–April ⊗ All major cards

KILLORGLIN

🏨 CARAGH LODGE
🍴 $$$–$$$$$
CARAGH LAKE
TEL 066 9769115
FAX 066 9769316
E-MAIL caraghl@iol.ie
Tastefully furnished with antiques, and with beautiful gardens and spectacular mountain views, this is a very peaceful hideaway on Lough Caragh. Equally enjoyable as a venue for delicious local-produce dinners or for teas featuring plentiful home baking.
ℹ️ 15 🅿️ 22 🕐 Closed mid-Oct.–mid-April ⊗ All major cards

🍴 NICK'S SEAFOOD RESTAURANT & PIANO BAR
$$$
LOWER BRIDGE ST.
TEL 066 61219
A restaurant that would run a hundred miles rather than take itself too seriously, It fills your ears with music, your mouth with rollicking choruses, and your belly with good honest tucker. The menu leans cheerily on local meat and fish—Kerry-reared beef, say, or local shellfish such as mussels done in Nick's superb Franco-Irish style.
🕐 Closed L ⊗ All major cards

WATERVILLE

🏨 BUTLER ARMS
$$$–$$$$
WATERVILLE
TEL 066 9474144

FAX 066 9474520
E-MAIL reservations@ butlerarms.com
A spacious hotel that occupies a splendid location overlooking the sea. Most of the bedrooms have sea views, and all have en-suite marble bathrooms.
ℹ️ 40 🅿️ 50 🔁 ⊗ All major cards

COUNTY LIMERICK

ADARE

🏨 DUNRAVEN ARMS
$$$–$$$$
ADARE
TEL 061 396633
FAX 061 396541
E-MAIL dunraven@iol.ie
Relax in the easy-going atmosphere of this traditional country inn in Adare, one of Ireland's most attractive preserved estate villages.
ℹ️ 75 🅿️ 90 🔁 🖥️ ⊗ All major cards

🍴 THE WILD GEESE
$$$
ROSE COTTAGE
TEL 061 396451
FAX 061 396453
E-MAIL wildgeese@indigo.ie
A gorgeous cottage is the setting for this extremely well-regarded restaurant, where first-class ingredients are used to please a discerning and enthusiastic clientele. Light lunches only in summer.
🕐 Closed Mon. & Sun., L in low season ⊗ AE, MC, V

BALLINGARRY

🍴 THE MUSTARD SEED AT ECHO LODGE
$$$
BALLINGARRY
TEL 069 68508
FAX 069 68511
E-MAIL mustard@indigo.ie
Fine cooking based on local, organic, and seasonal produce for example pheasant and venison, or a rack of Irish mountain lamb—all done with a warmly hospitable touch.
♿ ⊗ All major cards

PRICES

HOTELS
An indication of the cost of a double room without breakfast is given by $ signs.
$$$$$ Over $280
$$$$ $200–$280
$$$ $120–$200
$$ $80–$120
$ Under $80

RESTAURANTS
An indication of the cost of a three-course dinner without drinks is given by $ signs.
$$$$$ Over $80
$$$$ $50–$80
$$$ $35–$50
$$ $20–$35
$ Under $2

CROOM

🍴 MILL RACE
$$
CROOM MILLS
TEL 061 397130
FAX 061 397199
E-MAIL croommills@eircom.net
Excellent home cooking, with roast rib of beef, bacon, and cabbage a particular favorite, served in the characterful environment of a corn mill with all the workings on show.
♿ 🕐 Closed D ⊗ AE, MC, V

KILMALLOCK

🏨 FLEMINGSTOWN HOUSE
$$
KILMALLOCK
TEL 063 98093
FAX 063 98546
E-MAIL flemingstown@keltec.ie
Just outside the country town of Killmallock, the Georgian farmhouse of Flemingstown House offers a winning combination of elegance and style—antiques in the drawing room, stained-glass windows in the dining room—together with the warmth and helpfulness of both the staff and the owner.

🍴5 🅿12 ⊕Closed
Nov.–Feb. 🚫MC, V

LIMERICK

🍴 GREEN ONION
$$$$$
THE OLD TOWN HALL
BUILDING, RUTLAND ST.
TEL 061 400710
Highly enjoyable, energetic
sort of place where you can
eat good food in good
company, or enjoy a modicum
of privacy (if you want it) in
one of their cozy little snugs.
⊕Closed Sun., Mon.
🚫AE, MC, V

🏨 GRESHAM ARDHU
$$$
ENNIS RD.
TEL 061 453922
FAX 061 326333
E-MAIL info@gresham-ardhu
hotel.com
Just outside Limerick city on
the road to County Clare, this
well-equipped hotel provides
modern family bedrooms.
🛈181 🅿180 🛗 🚫All
major cards

WEST IRELAND

COUNTY CLARE

BALLYVAUGHAN

🏨 GREGAN'S CASTLE
$$$$
BALLYVAUGHAN
TEL 065 7077005
FAX 065 7077111
E-MAIL res@gregans.ie
In a superb location in the
heart of Clare's Burren region,
the medieval tower house of
Gregan's Castle stands at the
foot of the famous Corkscrew
Hill. Accommodations are up
to date in character and
amenities, however. Each
bedroom individually furnished
in country house style – all
have wonderful countryside
views, and some have their
own private gardens. The
emphasis is very much on
peace and quiet—so much so

that bedroom televisions are
conspicuous by their absence.
🛈22 🅿25 ⊕Closed mid-
Dec.–mid-Feb. 🚫AE, MC, V

BUNRATTY

🏨 FITZPATRICK
BUNRATTY
$$$$
BUNRATTY
TEL 061 361177
FAX 061 471252
E-MAIL reservations@
bunratty.fitzpatricks.com
A modern, ranch-style hotel
with all modern facilities,
conveniently close to Shannon
Airport and to the castle and
folk park at Bunratty.
🛈119 🅿300 ⊕Closed
Christmas 🈴 🚫All major
cards

COROFIN

🏨 FERGUS VIEW
$
KILNABOY
TEL 065 6837606
FAX 065 6837192
E-MAIL deckell@indigo.ie
An excellent family-run
guesthouse, where Mary
Kelleher's cooking of local
meat and fish and home-grown
vegetables is scrumptiously set
off by her puddings (a dream
of cream in a tall glass!). Very
well positioned for exploring
the Burren or the coast.
🛈6 🅿8 ⊕Closed
Oct.–Easter

DOOLIN

🏨 ARAN VIEW HOUSE
HOTEL
$
COAST RD.
TEL 065 7074061
FAX 065 7074540
E-MAIL bookings@aranview.com
A friendly hotel. Each
bedroom is beautifully
furnished, equipped with TV,
ensuite bathrooms, and
direct-dial telephones, and
commands superb views out
across Galway Bay to the
Aran Islands from this snug

hotel. Traditional music is laid
on at the Aran View several
times a week.
🛈13 plus 6 annex 🅿40
⊕Closed Nov.–March
🚫All major cards

🍴 FLAGSHIP
RESTAURANT
$
DOOLIN CRAFTS GALLERY
TEL 065 707 4309
FAX 065 707 4511
An unpretentious place,
aiming to do well what comes
naturally—fabulously tasty
locally sourced food, for
example goat's cheese, salmon
smoked just up the road, and
home-made apple pie to die
for (well, to live for, actually).
⊕Closed Oct.–Easter

ENNIS

🏨 WOODSTOCK
$$$$
SHANAWAY RD.
TEL 065 684 6600
FAX 065 684 6611
E-MAIL info@woodstockhotel.com
A championship golf course,
jacuzzi, sauna, solarium,
swimming pool, steam room,
and gym are some of the
facilities available at this well-
equipped modern hotel set
in woodland. There are 67
luxury bedrooms, beautifully
furnished in restrained
good taste.
🛈67 ⊕Closed Christmas
🛗 ❄ 🈴 🚫All major
cards

KILFENORA

🍴 VAUGHAN'S
$
KILFENORA
TEL 065 708 8004
Vaughan's is a most delightful
pub where the Guinness is
great, the music is brilliant,
and the "plain Irish cooking"
uses the best local ingredients
for local dishes (bacon and
cabbage, beef and stout pie)
that locals eat with relish.
⊕Closed Good Fri.,
Christmas 🚫MC, V

KILLALOE

🍴 CHERRY TREE RESTAURANT
$$$
BALLINA ST.
TEL 061 375688
FAX 061 375689
On the shores of Lough Derg in southeasternmost Clare, you'll find expert cuisine that uses no culinary trickery to delight without overwhelming. Such dishes as Parma ham enwrapping asparagus with sage and wild mushroom, or local beef aged by drying and cooked exactly as you order, retain all the essential flavours of the ingredients.
♿ 🕐 Closed Mon. L
🃏 All major cards

KILRUSH

🏨 HILLCREST VIEW
$
DOONBEG RD. (OFF N67)
TEL 065 9051986
FAX 065 9051900
E-MAIL ethnahynes@eircom.net
This is a family house with a hospitable atmosphere and clean, comfortable rooms
🛏 6 🅿 7 🃏 AE, MC, V

LAHINCH

🍴 BARRTRÁ SEAFOOD RESTAURANT
$$
BARRTRÁ
TEL 065 7081280
E-MAIL barrtra@iol.ie
If the local boats have taken it out of the sea that day, the chances are it'll be on the table at Barrtrá, looking and tasting even better thanks to the fabulous sea views .
🕐 Closed Mon., Sun. except during July–Aug.
🃏 AE, MC, V

LISDOONVARNA

🏨 SHEEDY'S
🍴 RESTAURANT & HOTEL
$$$
LISDOONVARNA
TEL 065 7074026
FAX 065 7074555
E-MAIL info@sheedys.com
Comfortable and friendly, this small, family-run hotel is attached to an excellent restaurant (try the succulent casserole of local lamb with rosemary and organic vegetables) in one of Clare's most charerful towns.
🛏 11 🅿 40 🕐 Closed mid-Oct.–mid-March
🃏 AE, MC, V

🏨 DROMOLAND CASTLE
This is every multimillionaire's dream of a Gothic revival castle with turrets, irregular rooflines, and battlements. It may have been built many centuries after such defenses were actually necessary, but this fairy-tale pile is not about grim reality. It is about escapism, and about the pleasant reality of enjoying excellent modern facilities in a fantastical setting.
$$$$–$$$$$
NEWMARKET-ON-FERGUS
TEL 061 368144
FAX 061 363355
E-MAIL sales@dromoland.ie
🛏 100 🅿 120 🈺
🃏 All major cards

TULLA

🍴 FLAPPERS
$$
MAIN ST.
TEL 065 6835711
Excellent small restaurant, equally good for light-to-medium lunches or for full-blooded dinners. Even the simplest salads, fish pies, and breast of chicken are superb.
♿ 🕐 Closed Mon. D, Sun.
🃏 MC, V

COUNTY GALWAY

BALLYNAHINCH

🏨 BALLYNAHINCH
🍴 CASTLE
$$$–$$$$$

BALLYNAHINCH
TEL 095 31006
FAX 095 31085
E-MAIL bhinch@iol.ie
A cheery, outdoorsy place on the banks of a famous sporting river (most of the very comfortable bedrooms enjoy river views), with well-trained staff promoting a friendly atmosphere. You don't have to catch your own dinner here—though the chef will be only too delighted to cook anything you do bring in from lake, river, or sea. Otherwise, just settle back to enjoy the best of unfussy traditional cooking in one of Ireland's most agreeable castle settings.
🛏 40 🅿 55 🕐 Closed Feb., Christmas 🃏 All major cards

BUSHYPARK

🏨 GLENLO ABBEY
$$$$$
BUSHYPARK
TEL 091 526666
FAX 091 527800
E-MAIL glenlo@iol.ie
A hotel full of character, incorporating a restored church and early Georgian abbey buildings, on the shores of Lough Corrib. A modern wing houses the very comfortable bedrooms, many of which

have fabulous lough views.
[1] 46 [P] 150 [E] [S] All major cards

KILLEEN HOUSE
$$$
KILLEEN
TEL 091 524179
FAX 091 528065
E-MAIL killeenhouse@ireland.com
Antique furnishings, hand-woven carpets, and Irish linen and crystal all feature in this hospitable 19th-century house set in 25 acres (10 ha) on the south shore of Lough Corrib, a mile (1.6 km) or so north of Galway city.
[1] 5 [P] 6 [C] Closed Christmas [E] [S] All major cards

CASHEL

CASHEL HOUSE
$$$$–$$$$$
CASHEL
TEL 095 31001
FAX 095 31077
E-MAIL info@cashel-house-hotel.com
Stunningly set in 50 acres (20 ha) of superb gardens on one of Connemara's most beautiful bays, Cashel House offers elegant, stylish accommodation at the luxurious end of the market.
[1] 32 [P] 40 [C] Closed Jan.–early Feb. [S] All major cards

ZETLAND COUNTRY HOUSE
$$$
CASHEL BAY
TEL 095 31111
FAX 095 31117
E-MAIL zetland@iol.ie
Unpretentiously delicious cooking, appreciated in a beautifully appointed room with one of Connemara's classic sea and coastal views to aid digestion.
[C] Closed L, Dec.–Jan., [S] All major cards

CLARENBRIDGE

PADDY BURKE'S
$$

CLARENBRIDGE
TEL 091 796226
FAX 091 796016
Simply the most famous oyster house in Ireland, fons et origo of the Clarenbridge Oyster Festival, where the glitterati and the literati rub shoulders with denizens of the real world over excellent seafood and stout .
[C] Closed Good Fri., Christmas [S] AE, DC, MC, V

CLIFDEN

ABBEYGLEN CASTLE
$$$$
SKY RD.
TEL 095 21201
FAX 095 21797
E-MAIL info@abbeyglen.ie
Abbeyglen Castle is just west of Clifden on the fabulously scenic Sky Road. A highly dedicated family team runs the hotel with great professionalism, putting both comfort and cuisine in the top bracket, but also with antennae tuned to what might please the guests—hence the many a music session in the bar.
[1] 38 [P] 40 [C] Closed Jan. [S] All major cards

ARDAGH
$$$–$$$$
BALLYCONNEELY RD.
TEL 095 21384
FAX 095 21314
E-MAIL ardaghhotel@eircom.net
Beautifully located on Ardbear Bay near Clifden, this is a well-run family setup where guests' comfort and well-being come first. Well-furnished bedrooms with either sea or country views.
[1] 19 [P] 35 [S] All major cards

BYRNE'S MAL DUA HOUSE
$$–$$$
GALWAY RD.
TEL 095 21171
FAX 095 21739
E-MAIL info@maldua.com
Just outside Clifden, this is a very hospitable house with comfortable accommodations

and a real desire to please. There's a croquet lawn and bicycles for rent for exploring beautiful Connemara.
[1] 14 [P] 20 [S] AE, MC, V

ST. CLERANS
Break the bank and bust the wallet to stay here, if you relish a quirky streak in your deluxe accommodation. Film director John Huston once owned this Georgian pile in its 45 acres (18 ha) of secluded estate, and there's a filmic, larger-than-life quality to its huge bedrooms and spacious drawing rooms and dining room. Ride, putt, fish, or knock a croquet ball around in the grounds to your heart's content.
$$$$$
CRAUGHWELL,
NEAR LOUGHREA
TEL 091 846555
FAX 091 846600
E-MAIL stcleran@iol.ie
[1] 12 [P] 12 [S] AE, MC, V

OFF THE SQUARE RESTAURANT
$$
MAIN ST.
TEL 095 22281
E-MAIL info@offthesqaure restaurant.com
If you're hankering after pancakes with maple syrup, it's on the long breakfast menu here. The lunch menu includes old favorites like Irish Stew and fish and chips, then it all goes a bit more upscale in the evening, when you can choose from such dishes as roast duck with brandy and peach sauce and Atlantic salmon with asparagus and Bearnaise sauce.
[S] [S] All major cards

OUGHTERARD

ROSS LAKE HOUSE
$$$–$$$$$
ROSSCAHILL
TEL 091 550109
FAX 091 550184
E-MAIL info@rosslakehotel.com

HOTELS & RESTAURANTS

A handsome Georgian house in a quiet setting among the miles of beautiful woodland around Oughterard. Rooms are furnished in keeping with the elegant 18th-century ambience, including huge comfortable beds and big fireplaces. Rowing, sailing, and fishing on Ross Lake are easily arranged.
🛈 13   🅿 150   🚭 All major cards

RECESS

🏨 LOUGH INAGH LODGE
$$$–$$$$
INAGH VALLEY
TEL 095 34706
FAX 095 34708
E-MAIL inagh@iol.ie
A delightful lakeside retreat, formerly a 19th-century hunting lodge, set in a beautiful valley with the Twelve Bens rising mystically on one side and the Maumturk Mountains the other. All bedrooms with lovely views, and five are deluxe standard. In a nutshell: glorious mountain scenery, in comfortable surroundings.
🛈 12   🅿 16   🕒 Closed mid-Dec.–mid-March 🚭
🚭 All major cards

GALWAY CITY

🏨 HARBOUR HOTEL
$$$–$$$$$
THE HARBOUR
TEL 091 569466
FAX 091 569455
E-MAIL stay@harbour.ie
Forming part of development of Galway's harbor frontage, this hotel may be modern in design, but it offers all the traditional comfort of open fires and plush furnishings.
🛈 96   🅿 64   ♿   🚭 All major cards

🏨 ALMARA HOUSE
$–$$
2 MERLIN GATE
MERLIN PARK, DUBLIN RD.
TEL 091 755345
FAX 091 771585
E-MAIL matthewkiernan@eircom.net

The proprietors of Almara House also own a butcher's shop, so fresh bacon and sausages for breakfast are guaranteed. Cozy bedrooms and a warm welcome are assured, and there's a bus stop for city center services right outside.
🛈 4   🅿 8   🚭 All major cards

🍴 K. C. BLAKES BRASSERIE
$$$
10 QUAY ST.
TEL 091 561826
Dine royally in Blakes Castle, a restored 15th-century tower house, in Galway's "Latin Quarter". It's a beautiful medieval building that has been given a stylish modern décor, and the management promote a peaceful atmosphere. The menu combines global cuisine with classic French dishes.
🕒 Closed Christmas 🚭 AE, MC, V

🍴 THE ARCHWAY RESTAURANT
$$
3 VICTORIA PLACE
TEL 091 563693
FAX 091 563074
E-MAIL archway@indigo.ie
French is the flavor and style at this classy little place. Come hungry, as everything is tempting all the way down the menu.
🕒 Closed Sun. 🚭 All major cards

🍴 GOYA'S
$
2–3 KIRWANS LANE
TEL 091 567010
E-MAIL goyas@eircom.net
Stickies, slices, and sweet nothings to ruin your waistline and keep out the cold—even if it's a Galway heatwave.
🕒 Closed Sun., D 🚭 MC, V

COUNTY MAYO

ACHILL ISLAND

🏨 ACHILL CLIFF HOUSE
$$–$$$

KEEL
TEL 098 43400
FAX 098 43007
E-MAIL info@achillcliff.com
Breathtaking views of the mountains and sea coasts of Achill Island from this comfortable modern guesthouse, run by a warm and hospitable hostess who is full of good ideas and insider knowledge.
🛈 10   🅿 20   🕒 Closed Christmas 🚭 AE, MC, V

🍴 THE BEEHIVE
$
KEEL
TEL 098 43134
FAX 098 43018
Local produce—fresh salmon, oysters, crab, mussels, seafood chowder with home-made scones—offered with pleasure and eaten with a relish of the most spectacular cliff prospect on one of Ireland's most glorious and romantic islands.
🕒 Closed Nov.–Easter 🚭 AE, MC, V

CASTLEBAR

🏨 BREAFFY HOUSE
$$$$
CASTLEBAR
TEL 094 22033
FAX 094 683 3759
E-MAIL breaffyhotel@anu.ie
A 19th-century house among 100 acres (40 ha) of woods; old house public rooms, while a whole wing is given over to well-appointed bedrooms with modern amenities. Entertainment organized for guests during the summer.
🛈 62   🅿 300   🕒 Closed Christmas ♿ 🚭 AE, MC, V

CONG

SOMETHING SPECIAL

🍴 ASHFORD CASTLE
If you are really going to push the boat as far out as it'll go while in Cong, you can't do better than lie back and enjoy the Connaught Room's spot-on service and cuisine—one of a

handful of absolutely top-drawer Irish restaurants, set in the surroundings of the country's grandest castle. For those who want their boat to stay a little closer to shore, the George V Dining Room—the Connaught's brother restaurant at the castle—offers equally exalted standards in a slightly less rarified atmosphere.

$$$-$$$$$
CONG
TEL 092 46003
FAX 092 46260
E-MAIL ashford@ashford.ie
All major cards

BALLYWARREN HOUSE
$$$
BALLYMACGIBBON N.
CROSS
TEL 094 954 6989
FAX 094 954 6989
E-MAIL ballywarrenhouse@
eircom.net
Ballywarren House is located in an inland, rural area of County Mayo; an elegant house painstakingly converted into a stylish and welcoming country hotel. Some of the bedrooms boast four-poster beds, and all have luxurious bathrooms.
3 4 AE, MC, V

WESTPORT

HOTEL WESTPORT
$$$$
NEWPORT RD.
TEL 098 25122
FAX 098 26739
E-MAIL reservations@
hotelwestport.ie
A smart modern hotel with facilities that include a gym, sauna, and pool—and a staff that makes it all run efficiently.
129 220
All major cards

ARDMORE COUNTRY HOUSE
$$$-$$$$$
THE QUAY
TEL 098 25994
FAX 098 27795
E-MAIL ardmorehotel@
eircom.net

Superb views over Westport Quay, Clew Bay, and Croagh Patrick, the Holy Mountain, from the elevated position commanded by Ardmore Country House, a relaxed and enjoyable place to stay within an easy walk of the town centre.
13 40 Closed Jan.–Feb. AE, MC, V

THE LEMON PEEL
$$
THE OCTAGON
TEL 098 26929
FAX 098 26965
E-MAIL robbie@lemonpeel.ie
Everyone likes this friendly place, where the food comes served with a pleasant greeting. If you are a mashed potato connoisseur, look no further—though everything on the menu is delicious.
Closed Mon., Feb. MC, V

NORTHWEST IRELAND

SLIGO TOWN

SLIGO PARK
$$$
PEARSE RD.
TEL 071 91 6 0291
FAX 071 91 6 9556
E-MAIL sligopk@leehotels.com
Standing in 7 acres (3 ha) of beautiful parkland on the southern outskirt of Sligo town, the Sligo Park is well placed for exploring the countryside associated with the Yeats brothers, poet William and painter Jack. This is a well-appointed, smartly run hotel. with big ensuite bedrooms furnished in a straightforward, modern style.
110 200 All major cards

TOWER
$$$
QUAY ST.
TEL 071 91 44000
FAX 071 91 4 6888
E-MAIL towersl@iol.ie
This pleasantly relaxed hotel

is conveniently located on the old quays in the center of Sligo town. All of the bedrooms are comfortable and smartly furnished in a modern style; some are of luxury standard with plenty of space and huge beds; and some have been adapted to suit wheelchair users and other physically challenged guests.
58 20 Closed Christmas All major cards

CHESTNUT LAWN
$
CUMMEEN,
STRANDHILL RD.
TEL 071 91 6 2781
FAX 071 91 6 2781
A comfortable, carefully maintained house with modern, attractively furnished bedrooms. on the way out from Sligo town to Strandhill—within a very short distance of the Sligo Bay beaches, Knocknarea Mountain, and the remarkable megalithic cemetery at Carrowmore.
3 4 Closed Dec. 21–Jan.21 MC, V

HARGADON'S
$
O'CONNELL ST.
TEL 071 91 7 0993
The food in Hargadon's is fine, from good steaks to traditional bacon and cabbage—but this remarkable town-center pub, famous throughout the northwest, is really about relaxation and great conversation in one of the private snugs or up at the dark, characterful old bar.
Closed Good Fri., Dec. 25

MONTMARTRE
$$
MARKET YARD
TEL 071 91 6 9901
FAX 071 91 4 0065
E-MAIL montmartre@eircom.net
A dash of Gallic flair, zest, and ambience gives va-va-voom to dinner here; the accent's on all things French, but much of the

HOTELS & RESTAURANTS

menu (especially the shellfish) has only had to travel across the bay to the kitchen.
🕐 Closed Dec. 23–28, Mon., D 💳 AE, MC, V

COUNTY SLIGO

BALLYSADARE

🏨 SEASHORE HOUSE
$
LISDUFF
TEL 071 91 6 7827
FAX 071 91 6 7827
E-MAIL seashore@oceanfree.net
A bungalow guesthouse with a conservatory dining room looking out over sea and mountains, in a beautifully quiet spot on the seashore of tidal Ballysadare Bay.
🛏 5 🅿 6 💳 AE, MC, V

CASTLEBALDWIN

🍴 CROMLEACH LODGE COUNTRY HOUSE
$$$$
CASTLEBALDWIN, NEAR BOYLE
TEL 071 91 65155
FAX 071 91 65455
E-MAIL info@cromleach.com
Truly fabulous food that comes in interesting combinations,— pureed sweet potato around a slice or two of local beef, for instance. And there are some delectable deserts to round off the experience, such as poached pears or banana nougats.
🕐 Closed L 💳 All major cards

COLLOONEY

🏨 MARKREE CASTLE
$$$$
COLLOONEY
TEL 071 91 67800
FAX 071 91 67840
E-MAIL markree@iol.ie
You could probably eat a boiled boot and enjoy it in surroundings like these—a gorgeous old castle now turned into a fine hotel, with en-suite luxury rooms and its own riding stables. It's run by a family who has owned it since

Methuselah was a lad. But the food's great, too.
🛏 30 🅿 60 🕐 Closed Christmas 💱 💳 All major cards

GRANGE

🏨 ROWANVILLE LODGE
$
GRANGE
TEL 071 91 63958
E-MAIL rowanville@hotmail.com
Beautifully situated within full view of W. B. Yeats's magnificent mountain of Benbulben, this cheerful and very friendly house makes an excellent base for exploring the hills and coasts of Yeats Country (see pp. 212–217).
🛏 3 🅿 8 🕐 Closed Nov.–April 💳 MC, V

COUNTY DONEGAL

ARDARA

🏨 NESBITT ARMS
$–$$$$
Ardara
TEL 074 9541103
FAX 074 9541895
E-MAIL nesbitta@indigo.ie
A very characterful, central hotel offering comfortable en-suite accommodations, with friendly staff and some great musical sessions.
🛏 19 💳 MC, V

BALLYBOFEY

🏨 KEE'S
🍴 $$$
STRANORLAR
TEL 074 91 3 1018
FAX 074 91 3 1917
E-MAIL info@keeshotel.ie
A family-run hotel with a good reputation for solid, competent cooking. In spite of the fact that there's a mountain or two between Stranorlar and the sea, the fish is great—try Kee's pan-fried cod or smoked haddock chowder for a delicious smack of the briny.
🛏 53 🅿 90 💱 💳 All major cards

BALLYLIFFEN

🏨 OSTAN GWEEDORE
Right on the sea near Bunbeg, with fresh seafood daily on the menu and sea views come rain (from the big panorama windows) or shine (from the grounds), this is the place from which to get acquainted with Donegal's most far-out coasts. A haven of comfort in a truly wild region.
$$$
BUNBEG
TEL 074 953 1177 or 074 953 1188
FAX 074 953 1726
E-MAIL ostangweedore@ireland.com
🛏 69 🅿 80 🕐 Closed Dec.–Jan. 💱 💳 AE, MC, V

🏨 ROSSAOR HOUSE
$$
BALLYLIFFEN
TEL 074 9376498
FAX 074 9376498
E-MAIL rossaor@gofree.indigo.ie
Attractively set in gardens on the northwest side of the Inishowen Peninsula, Rossaor House looks out across Pollen Bay toward Malin Head. There are three ground-level bedrooms, and an upstairs family suite. A great base for exploring north Donegal.
🛏 4 🅿 10 🕐 Closed Dec.–Jan. 💳 MC, V

CARNDONAGH

🍴 THE CORNCRAKE
The word has got around, but so far the remoteness and un-chicness of Carndonagh—at the tip of the Inishowen Peninsula—has prevented crowds of foodies overwhelming this small, delightful restaurant where everything is just right.
$$
MALIN ST.
TEL 074 9374534
🕐 Closed L; Sun., Mon.
💳 No credit cards accepted

DONEGAL TOWN

HARVEY'S POINT COUNTRY HOTEL
$$$
LOUGH ESKE
TEL 074 9722208
FAX 074 9722352
E-MAIL reservations@
harveyspoint.com
Enjoying a very peaceful and beautiful location just outside Donegal town, by the sheltered shores of Lough Eske, Harvey's Point is a modern hotel with all the creature comforts. Bedrooms are furnished in Swiss mode, and big windows overlook the lake. Fairly formal dining, features classic cooking —baked salmon fillet, roast venison with truffle sauce.
🚹 20 🅿 300 🚫 All major cards

DUNFANAGHY

THE MILL RESTAURANT
$$$
FIGART
TEL 074 9136985
FAX 074 9136985
E-MAIL themillrestaurant@
oceanfree.net
A wonderful lakeside location for excellent, stylish, cooking based on the best of local ingredients—Donegal lamb, beef, and pork, locally caught fish and shellfish—and really decent artwork on the walls, too, all done by members of the owner's family.
🚫 🕒 Closed Mon., L except first Sun. of month 🚫 All major cards

GREENCASTLE

KEALYS SEAFOOD BAR
$$$
THE HARBOUR
TEL 074 9381010
FAX 074 9381010
E-MAIL kealys@iol.ie
This is a great restaurant for those who like a laid-back atmosphere in which to enjoy unfussy but perfectly cooked and presented food—not just

seafood, but that's what Kealy's particularly shines at.
🚫 🕒 Closed Mon. 🚫 All major cards

KILLYBEGS

THE FLEET INN
$$
KILLYBEGS
TEL 074 9731518
FAX 074 9731664
E-MAIL fleetinn@irishmarine.com
When you're in Killybegs, do what the locals do—go for the fish. And this upstairs eating spot is the ideal place to do it. You won't find fresher or tastier seafood.
🕒 Closed L, off season Sun. & Mon., mid-Feb.–mid-March 🚫 MC, V

LAGHEY

COXTOWN MANOR
$$$
DONEGAL
TEL 074 9734575
FAX 074 9734576
E-MAIL coxtownmanor@
oceanfree.net
If you're hungry in south Donegal, this is the place to go. Local produce combines with Belgian influences—rich-flavoured sausages, hearty soups, veal cutlets, fried fish—all in a very pleasant, warm atmosphere. The beer and the chocolate are both Belgian, too, hence irresistible…
🕒 Closed L, mid-Feb.–late March 🚫 MC, V

RATHMULLAN

FORT ROYAL
$$$–$$$$
FORT ROYAL
TEL 074 9158100
FAX 074 9158103
E-MAIL fortroyal@eircom.net
A country house with a fabulous position overlooking Lough Swilly from the Fanad Peninsula. Cooking is free of pretension, but has modern twists and turns. Abundant fresh produce from the hotel's garden goes into superb

vegetable and herb soups.
🚹 11 plus 4 annex 🅿 40 🕒 Closed Nov.–Easter 🚫 All major cards

ROSSNOWLAGH

SAND HOUSE
$$$–$$$$
ROSSNOWLAGH
TEL 071 9851777
FAX 071 9852100
E-MAIL info@sandhouse-hotel.ie
The welcoming, easy-paced Sand House commands one of southwest Donegal's best sea views, around the bay at Rossnowlagh. Bedrooms are in classical country house style, and some have four-poster beds and sea views.
🚹 55 🅿 40 🕒 Closed Dec.–Jan. 🚫 All major cards

COUNTY LEITRIM

CARRICK-ON-SHANNON

THE LANDMARK
$$$$
TEL 071 9622222
FAX 071 9622233
E-MAIL landmarkhotel@
eircom.net
A very luxurious and elegant hotel overlooking the River Shannon at the heart of this prime boating and angling area; cruising, fishing, riding, and golf can be arranged.
🚹 50 🅿 60 ↔ 🚫 AE, MC, V

CENTRAL IRELAND

COUNTY ROSCOMMON

BALLINLOUGH

WHITE HOUSE HOTEL
$$
BALLINLOUGH
TEL 094 9640112
FAX 094 9640993
E-MAIL info@white-house
-hotel.com
Situated near the Roscommon/Mayo border, this agreeable,

competently managed hotel is convenient for Knock shrine and airport, for the fishing lakes of the border country, and for Tuam and north Galway.
🛏 19 🕐 Closed Christmas 🔃 🚫 🚫 All major cards

ROSCOMMON TOWN

🏨 ABBEY HOTEL
🍴 $$$
GALWAY RD.
TEL 090 662 6240
FAX 090 662 6021
E-MAIL sales@abbeyhotel.ie
In this 19th-century house just outside the country town of Roscommon you can choose between bedrooms in contemporary-style in a modern wing or Victorian style in the original building. Locals out to enjoy a good dinner—dressed fillet of chicken, maybe, or sea bass— in a friendly atmosphere tend to gravitate to the restaurant.
🛏 50 🅿 150 🕐 Closed Christmas 🔃 🚫 🚫 All major cards

COUNTY LONGFORD

DRUMLISH

🏨 CUMISKEYS FARM
$
ENNYBEGS
TEL 043 23320
FAX 043 23516
E-MAIL kc@iol.ie
A large mock-Tudor house with several unusual features, including a spiral staircase from the parlor to the upstairs library, Cumiskeys Farm offers turf fires, pleasant rooms, and a warm welcome.
🛏 6 🅿 20 🚫 MC, V

GRANARD

🏨 TOBERPHELIM HOUSE
A very child-friendly set-up, with a separate family sitting room, private playground, and plenty of farm animals. The hotel

is in a Georgian country house, located in the lake country near Longford's border with counties Meath, Westmeath, and Cavan.
$–$$
GRANARD
TEL 043 86568
FAX 043 86568
E-MAIL tober2@eircom.net
🛏 3 🅿 10 🚫 AE, MC, V

COUNTY CAVAN

BALLYCONNELL

🏨 SLIEVE RUSSELL HOTEL GOLF & COUNTRY CLUB
$$$$
BALLYCONNELL
TEL 049 952 6444
FAX 049 952 6474
E-MAIL slieve-russell@quinn-hotels.com
A grand hotel with a championship golf course, attentive service and all the modern amenities. Includes ten luxury suites.
🛏 157 🅿 600 🔃 🚫 🚫 All major cards

🍴 POLO D
$$$
MAIN ST.
TEL 049 952 6228
A folksy feel to the decor here, and a friendly welcome—the setting for some really good, carefully cooked food. Seafood platters and crispy duck are proving very popular with discerning diners at Polo D.
🕐 Closed Sun. 🚫 MC, V

BLACKLION

🍴 MACNEAN BISTRO
In the MacNeans' small family run restaurant in a little village right on the North/South border, a 5-star, international culinary experience from the young maestro of the skillet, Irish master-chef Neven Maguire. Perish the day he moves on to bigger—though not necessarily better—surroundings.

$$
BLACKLION
TEL 071 9853022
FAX 071 9853404
🕐 Closed L (except Sun.), Mon., Tues., winter Mon.–Wed. 🚫 MC, V

KINGSCOURT

🏨 CABRA CASTLE
$$–$$$$
KINGSCOURT
TEL 042 9667030
FAX 042 9667039
E-MAIL sales@cabracastle.com
Fish, golf or practise your archery at this refurbished castle—or just relax amid 100 acres (40 ha) of parkland and let the friendly but well-drilled staff help you to enjoy a stylish few nights. Bedrooms are all decorated in keeping with the Georgian surroundings—chandeliers, luxurious furnishings, and all.
🛏 80 🅿 200 🕐 Closed Christmas 🚫 All major cards

COUNTY MONAGHAN

CARRICKMACROSS

🏨 NUREMORE HOTEL
🍴 $$$$–$$$$$
CARRICKMACROSS
TEL 042 9661438
FAX 042 9661853
E-MAIL nuremore@eircom.net
A large Victorian mansion skillfully brought up to date: deluxe demi-suites with separate sitting areas; extremely comfortable single bedrooms; or large family rooms. The ambience in the restaurant is rather formal, though perfectly friendly. Cooking is excellent throughout the menu (quails' eggs, duck, locally gathered mushrooms); nothing flashy or untoward, but plenty of style in the best sense of the word. There are plenty of sports facilities, including an 18-hole golf course, in a peaceful country setting.

🛏 72 🅿 200 ⬛ 🌀
🌀 All major cards

MONAGHAN

🏨 HILLGROVE
$$$–$$$$
OLD ARMAGH RD.
TEL 047 81288
FAX 047 84951
E-MAIL hillgrovegm@quinn-hotels.com

Just beside the cathedral and overlooking the town, the Hillgrove has a long-established reputation for comfort and a welcoming atmosphere.
🛏 44 🅿 430 ⬛ 🌀
🌀 All major cards

🍴 ANDY'S BAR
$$$
12 MARKET ST.
TEL 047 82277
FAX 047 84195

This is where the locals—and they should know—go to eat fine pub grub in the bar downstairs. The menu here might feature dishes such as sausages and mashed potato, or bacon and cabbage. There's also a decent middlebrow restaurant upstairs, where a more upscale selection could run to fish and steaks done in a range of sauces.
🕐 Closed Sun. L, Mon. D, early July, Good Fri., Christmas 🌀 MC, V

COUNTY WESTMEATH

ATHLONE

🏨 HODSON BAY HOTEL
$$$–$$$$
HODSON BAY
TEL 090 648 0500
FAX 090 648 0520
E-MAIL info@hodsonbayhotel.com

Commanding a wonderful panorama of Lough Ree, the Hodson Bay Hotel has been refurbished and extended to provide high levels of comfort and service. Some of the bedrooms overlook the lake, and the views from their big

picture windows are absolutely stunning. The hotel has its own golf course and lake marina.
🛏 133 🅿 300 ⬛ 🌀
🌀 All major cards

🏨 PRINCE OF WALES
$$
CHURCH ST.
TEL 0902 72626
FAX 0902 75658

An unpretentious family-run hotel with clean and comfortable bedrooms, conveniently positioned right in the center of Athlone.
🛏 73 🅿 35 🌀 All major cards

🍴 LEFT BANK BISTRO
$$
FRY PLACE
TEL 090 644446
FAX 090 6494509
E-MAIL leftbank@isite.ie

Veggies in Ireland have traditionally fared about as well as sun-worshippers, but here's one place where the art of the vegetable is understood. Not that meaties and fishies are left unsatisfied; sharp modern ideas based on sound techniques shine a light on every corner of the menu at the Left Bank. Children welcome before 7 p.m.
🕐 Closed Sun., Mon. ♿
🌀 🌀 AE, MC, V

🍴 WINEPORT RESTAURANT
$$$
GLASSON
TEL 090 6485466
FAX 090 6485471
E-MAIL restaurant@wineport.ie

One of the great restaurants of Ireland, in an area not exactly over-supplied with them. Wonderful lake views sharpen the appetite for a menu that's dictated by what's available locally, fresh and with regard to the season—think of all sorts of game, newly picked mushrooms and other local fungi, smoked eels; also Irish beef and delicious farmhouse cheeses. An infallible

route to success. Ask about local lakeside accommodations.
🕐 Closed L (except Sun.), Sun. D 🌀 All major cards

MULLINGAR

🏨 CROOKEDWOOD
🍴 HOUSE
$$$
CROOKEDWOOD
TEL 044 72165
FAX 044 72166
E-MAIL info@crookedwood house.com

Superb views over Lake Derravaragh on the outskirts of Crookedwood village are a feature of this fine old rectory beautifully converted to a comfortable guesthouse that prides itself on its friendliness and good food. Strong on flavor and the causes of flavor—the best of local meat, vegetables, and herbs, combined to stunning effect in roast lamb, for example—not fussily disguised, but brought to the fore and invited to lead the charge on your tastebuds. Delighted capitulation is inevitable.
🛏 8 🅿 10 🕐 Closed Christmas; Restaurant closed L (except Sun.) & Sun. D
🌀 AE, MC, V

COUNTY OFFALY

BIRR

🏨 COUNTY ARMS
$$$
BIRR
TEL 050 9720791
FAX 050 9721234
E-MAIL countyarmshotel @eircom.net

A charming, handsome Georgian house in the center of the historic town of Birr. The bedrooms look out onto the walled garden of the hotel, which supplies the fresh vegetables and herbs for the kitchen. The bedrooms are all individually furnished, and two have been specially converted to suit guests who are confined to a wheelchair.

🛈 24   🅿 150   ⊕ Closed Christmas.   🚫 All major cards

🍴 THE THATCH
$$
CRINKLE
TEL 050 9720682
FAX 050 9721847
A great pub, bursting with atmosphere, and very friendly, too. The menu here caters to those looking for a zest of the exotic (kangaroo steaks, anyone?), devotees of local game (rabbit, pigeon), and those who just want good traditional pub grub (steaks, pies).
⊕ Closed Good Fri., Christmas   🚫 DC, MC, V

COUNTY LAOIS

ABBEYLEIX

🏨 ABBEYLEIX MANOR HOTEL
$$
ABBEYLEIX
TEL 0502 30111
FAX 0502 30220
E-MAIL info@
abbeyleixmanorhotel.com
This pleasant hotel offers modern bedrooms that are decorated in warm colour schemes. It is located on the southern outskirts of one of the most attractive towns in the Irish midlands.
🛈 23   🅿 270   ⊕ Closed Christmas   🚫   🚫 All major cards

PORTLAOISE

🏨 IVYLEIGH HOUSE
$$
BANK PLACE, CHURCH ST.
TEL 0502 22081
FAX 0502 63343
E-MAIL dinah@ivyleigh.com
A friendly welcome awaits at this Georgian house, which is meticulously maintained and efficiently run, making it a very comfortable stopover in Portlaoise. The bedrooms are light and airy, with a striking decor of bright colour schemes.

🛈 6   🅿 6   ⊕ mid-Dec.– early Jan.   🚫 MC, V

🍴 KINGFISHER INDIAN RESTAURANT
$
PORTLAOISE
TEL 0502 62500
FAX 0502 62700
The Kingfisher does the things it does exceptionally well, employing fresh herbs and spices as well as high quality meat, fish, and vegetables. Creations on the menu include dozens of tasty Indian dishes, some old favorites, others to tempt the experimentally inclined.
⊕ Closed Sat.–Tues. L
🚫 AE, MC, V

COUNTY MEATH

BETTYSTOWN

🏨 NEPTUNE BEACH HOTEL & LEISURE CLUB
$$$
BETTYSTOWN
TEL 041 982 7107
FAX 041 982 7412
E-MAIL info@neptunebeach.ie
In the quiet resort town of Bettystown, the comfortable Neptune Beach Hotel offers its guests the year-round benefits of a sandy beach for warm weather, a Winter Garden to shelter in on chilly days, and splendid sea views whatever the weather.
🛈 38   🅿 60   ⊟   ⊠
🚫 AE, MC, V

🍴 BACCHUS AT THE COASTGUARD
$$$
BAYVIEW
TEL 041 982 8257
FAX 041 982 8236
This restaurant enjoys a wonderful setting, right on the bay, but it's not just the view that's the attraction. The excellent cooking features a menu with a wide range of choices, but fish is the thing here. Prawns, crab, fresh seasonal lobster, sea bass,

salmon, whitefish, and shellfish.
⊕ Closed Mon., and L (except Sun.), Sun. D

NAVAN

🏨 ARDBOYNE HOTEL
$$$
DUBLIN RD.
TEL 046 9023119
FAX 046 9022355
E-MAIL ardboyne@quinn-hotels.com
An efficiently run, well-equipped hotel on the edge of town, that offers comfort and good service in a relaxed atmosphere. The pleasantly upbeat bedrooms are well lit and have garden views.
🛈 29   🅿 186   ⊕ Closed Christmas   🚫 All major cards

🏨 KILLYON
$–$$
DUBLIN RD.
TEL 046 9071224
FAX 046 9072766
E-MAIL info@killyon guesthouse.com
Sit back on the balcony of this hospitable house and take in the view over the River Boyne, before enjoying some of Mrs. Fogarty's renowned home-cooked breakfasts—dishes such as feta cheese omelettes and smoked salmon eggs, with compotes of seasonal fruit and home-baked bread.
🛈 6   🅿 10   🚫 MC, V

COUNTY LOUTH

CARLINGFORD

🏨 JORDANS TOWNHOUSE
$–$$$
NEWRY ST.
TEL 042 937 3223
FAX 042 937 3875
E-MAIL info@jordans.ie
A row of 17th-century fishermen's cottages has been converted into a wonderfully characterful restaurant-with-rooms on the harbor, right in the middle of Carlingford. The standard of cooking in the restaurant is first class, and

there are fabulous views out across Carlingford Lough.
ⓘ 7 🅿 4 🅢 AE, MC, V

🍴 KINGFISHER BISTRO
$$$
DARCY MAGEE COURT
DUNDALK RD.
TEL 042 937 3716
This is a small restaurant that serves Carlingford Heritage Centre but its reputation has spread to a wider clientele, and people come from all over the place to eat here. The cooking is good—the fishcakes in particular are wonderful, and there are some spicy surprises from the Far East, too. Some enterprising choices find their way onto the wine list, and the service is both friendly and efficient.
🕘 Closed Mon., L 🅢 MC, V

🍴 OYSTERCATCHER
$$$
MARKET SQ.
TEL 042 937 3922
FAX 042 937 3987
E-MAIL bmckev@eircom.net
Help yourself to all the salad and vegetables you fancy to accompany the great entrées—majoring on seafood—in this pleasant restaurant.
🕘 Closed L, Mon.–Tues. Nov.– mid-Feb.; Christmas week 🅢 MC, V

DROGHEDA

🏨 BOYNE VALLEY HOTEL & COUNTRY CLUB
$$$
STAMEEN, DUBLIN RD.
TEL 041 983 7737
FAX 041 983 9188
E-MAIL reservations@boynevalleyhotel.ie
A leisure center, tennis court, gym, and putting green are just some of the attractions of this well-run hotel, with pleasant modern bedrooms.
ⓘ 73 🅿 200 🔀 🏊
🅢 All major cards

🍴 TRIPLE HOUSE
$$
TERMONFECKIN
TEL 041 982 2616
FAX 041 982 2616
If you're staying in Drogheda, head out to the village of Termonfeckin for dinner—this is a friendly house, with a neat hand with the local fish.
🕘 Closed L, Mon., Christmas week 🅢 MC, V

MONASTERBOICE

🏨 TULLYESKER COUNTRY HOUSE
$–$$
DROGHEDA/BELFAST RD.
TULLYESKER
TEL 041 983 0430
FAX 041 983 2624
E-MAIL mcdonnellfamily@ireland.com
A family-run country hotel in its own 3 acres (1.2 ha) of grounds. The smart bedrooms have fine countryside views.
ⓘ 5 🅿 20 🕘 Closed Dec.–Jan. 🅢 No credit cards

NORTHERN IRELAND

BELFAST

HOTELS

🏨 MALONE LODGE
$$$
60 EGLANTINE AVE.
BT9 6DY
TEL 028 9038 8000
FAX 028 9038 8088
E-MAIL info@malonelodgehotel.com
In a quiet, leafy street south of the city center, Malone Lodge offers a warm welcome, a friendly atmosphere, and very pleasant surroundings. This is one of the nicest hotels in the city, with extremely comfortable bedrooms.
ⓘ 51 🅿 35 🔀 🅢 All major cards

🏨 BALMORAL
$$–$$$
BLACKS RD., BT10 0NF
TEL 028 9030 1234

FAX 028 9060 1455
E-MAIL info@balmoralhotel belfast.co.uk
Just 4 miles (6 km) south of the city, this is a stylish modern hotel with a warm welcome and rooms equipped with TV, direct-dial phone and hospitality tray. There's a choice of spacious lounges, a restaurant, and bar.
ⓘ 43 🅿 300 🅢 All major cards

🏨 THE CRESCENT TOWNHOUSE
$$–$$$
13 LOWER CRESCENT
BT7 1NR
TEL 028 9032 3349
FAX 028 9032 0646
E-MAIL info@crescenttownhouse.com
A decent, comfortable hotel where the welcome is warm and staff are friendly and efficient. It's a stylish Regency townhouse next to the Botanic Gardens station; lively bars below, smart bedrooms above.
ⓘ 11 🕘 Closed part July, Christmas, 🅢 All major cards

🏨 CAMERA
$–$$
44 WELLINGTON PARK
BT9 6DP
TEL 028 9066 0026
FAX 028 9066 7856
E-MAIL pauldrumm@hotmail.com
A stylish guesthouse with bright, airy, modern rooms in the peaceful, well-maintained area close to the university.
ⓘ 9 🅢 All major cards

RESTAURANTS

🍴 RESTAURANT MICHAEL DEANE
$$$$
34–40 HOWARD ST.
BT1 6PD
TEL 028 90331134
FAX 028 90560001
E-MAIL deanesbelfast@deanesbelfast.com
If you are out to catch the real formal dining tiger by the tail there's only one place north of the border to go

hunting, and that's at Michael Deane's. Far and away the most accomplished cook in the North, who has set out every detail—room, service, wine list—to complement his marvelous skills at the stove. You can really blow out the walls on Michael's great 8-course Menu Prestige, or go for impeccable fish (monkfish, scallops) or meat (Irish mountain lamb, local beef). (Also see Dean's Brasserie, p. 378.)
Closed Sun.–Tues., Wed.–Thurs. & Sat. L, 1 week Jan., 2 weeks July
AE, MC, V

ALDEN'S
$$
229 UPPER
NEWTOWNARDS RD.
BT4 3JF
TEL 028 9065 0079
FAX 028 9065 00332
Alden's is one of Belfast's best and brightest; warm welcome, warm atmosphere, and a touch of southern warmth in the cooking. Southern Europe, that is.—roast sea bass, or for vegetarians some fritters of goat cheese with sweet red peppers. All on the unfashionable east side of the city, too.
Closed Sat. L, Sun.
All major cards

BEATRICE KENNEDY
$$
44 UNIVERSITY RD., BT7 1NJ
TEL 028 9020 2290
E-MAIL reservations@beatrice
-kennedy.co.uk
In an elegant 1920s row house right next to Queen's University, this stylish restaurant features modern, fusion dishes that are prepared with creative flair—chili salt squid with coriander salad, for instance, or seared scallops with Thai curry and sweet potato broth. Service is friendly and attentive.
Closed Mon., L (except Sun.), Christmas week, Easter
MC, V

CAYENNE
$$
7 ASCOT HOUSE,
SHAFTESBURY SQ,
BT2 7DB
TEL 028 90331532
FAX 028 90261575
E-MAIL reservations@
cayennerestaurant.com
A long, narrow dining room. run by celebrity chef Paul Rankin and his wife, Jeanne. Thai pork and crab, Mediterranean vegetable terrine, Japanese oysters, Far Eastern fishcakes shored up with the best of British cuisine. It's an animated environment, too—has to be, with so many wanting to eat here.
Closed Sat. L, Sun.
All major cards

DEANE'S BRASSERIE
$$
34–40 HOWARD ST.
BT1 6PD
TEL 028 9056 0000
FAX 028 9056 0001
If you like the sound of Michael Deane's (see p. 377), but the style or the price seem a little too up in the clouds, try the brasserie on the ground floor under the restaurant. It's generally a lively, bustling scene, and the food (overseen by Michael Deane) is as good as you'd expect.
Closed Sun., Mon.–Wed., and Sat. L, Christmas, 1 week Jan. & July AE, MC, V

NICK'S WAREHOUSE
$$$
35–39 HILL ST.
BT1 2LB
TEL 028 9043 9690
FAX 90230514
E-MAIL nicks@warehouse.dnet
.co.uk
An enthusiastic hand on the cooking and service tiller here ensures an enjoyable experience, for vegetarians as much as for carnivores, with more than a nod to Irish traditions of cuisine—local pork with red wine and delicious champ (mashed potatoes for

angels), a cheeseboard full of Irish produce.
Closed Sat. L, Mon. D, Sun.
All major cards

SHU
$$$
253 LISBURN RD.
BT9 7EN
TEL 028 9038 1655
FAX 028 9068 1632
E-MAIL eat@shu-restaurant.com
Excellent brasserie-style cooking, where traditional values of first-class ingredients and true flavors are what matter. Try their duck confit or a tasty dish of smoked hake with special chips. Service is efficient but friendly.
AE, MC, V

TATU BAR AND GRILL
$$
701 LISBURN RD., BT9 7GU
TEL 028 9038 0818
E-MAIL enquiries@ta-tu.com
Mingle with Belfast's young professionals and style gurus in this chic, modern grill bar and entertainment venue. The menu is as stylish as the surroundings, with international influences from Mexico to the Orient.
All major cards

THE CROWN LIQUOR SALOON
$
46 GREAT VICTORIA ST.
BT2 7BA
TEL 028 9027 9901
The Crown is a Belfast institution, and so firmly on the tourist trail that it must be superglued there. And it's no wonder—this fabulously ornate pub, impeccably cared for by the National Trust, is the best example anywhere in the city of an authentic Victorian imbibing emporium. The food is great, and most of it is traditional Irish cuisine—eat sausages and champ before you leave Ireland, and you'll pine and waste away until you're back in the Crown once more.
DC, MC, V

KEY   Hotel   Restaurant   No. of guest rooms   Disabled facilities   Parking   Closed

OLIVE TREE COMPANY

$

353 ORMEAU RD.

BT7 5GL

TEL 028 9064 8898

E-MAIL oliver@olivetreeco.fsnet
.co.uk

Eat hot (Irish fish stew) or cold (French pastry sweeties), lightly (cheese and olives) or substantially (duck salad), at this café, but always deliciously. And if you really like what you've had, you can buy the building blocks of the dish on site and try constructing it yourself at home—for the Olive Tree also shelters Belfast's finest delicatessen.

⊕ Closed Easter, Christmas week ⊗ No credit cards accepted

SOMETHING SPECIAL

SUN KEE

Do you like Chinese food? Real Chinese food, that tips no hat to enfeebled western tastebuds? Couldn't care less about pretentious decor, but care very much about a welcoming atmosphere? Come here. You'll absolutely love it. Bring your own wine.

$

28 DONEGAL PASS,

BT7 IBS

TEL 028 9031 2016

⊕ Closed Fri., L ⊗ No credit cards accepted

NORTHERN IREALND COUNTIES

COUNTY ANTRIM

BALLYMENA

GALGORM MANOR

$$$

BALLYMENA,

BT42 IEA

TEL 028 2588 1001

FAX 028 2588 0080

E-MAIL mail@galgorm.com

Horseback riding, water-skiing, and fishing are some of the activities you can enjoy at this handsome Victorian

manor-house hotel, set on 85 acres (35 ha) beside the River Maine—there are river views from comfortable bedrooms.

① 24 P 170 ⊗ All major cards

ADAIR ARMS

$$

I BALLYMONEY RD.

BALLYMENA,

BT43 5TS

TEL 028 2565 3674

FAX 028 2564 0436

E-MAIL reservations@adair
arms.com

A very pleasant hotel, with bright and spacious bedrooms and cheerful staff, located near the town center.

① 44 P 50 ⊕ Closed Christmas ⊛ ⊗ All major cards

BUSHMILLS

CRAIG PARK

$$

24 CARNBORE RD.

BT57 8YF

TEL 028 2073 2496

FAX 028 2073 2479

E-MAIL jan@craigpark.co.uk

This Georgian farmhouse has been refurbished to provide a comfortable experience. It is set in a stunning location, with views over Lough Foyle to the hills of Donegal—and on a clear day you can see right across the sea to Scotland.

① 3 P 8 ⊕ Closed mid-Dec.–early Jan. ⊗ MC, V

CARNLOUGH

LONDONDERRY ARMS

$$$

20 HARBOUR RD.

BT44 0EU

TEL 028 2888 5255

FAX 028 2888 5263

E-MAIL lda@glensofantrim.com

A comfortable old Georgian inn in a fishing village on the spectacular Antrim coast. Paintings of local scenes by well-known Ulster artists, antique furniture, and tasteful furnishings combine to make

this hotel—once owned by Sir Winston Churchill—a memorable place to stay. A relaxed approach allied to plenty of skill in the kitchen makes this a good place to stop for dinner (especially good locally-caught fish) on your way up the scenically stunning Antrim Coast Road.

① 35 P 50 ⊛ ⊗ All major cards

PORTRUSH

RAMORE WINE BAR

$$

THE HARBOUR,

BT56 8BN

TEL 028 7082 4313

FAX 028 7082 3194

E-MAIL jane@ramore.co.uk

The Ramore made its name as an upscale place for sophisticated dining. Don't expect that these days, and you won't be disappointed. It has turned into a cheap(ish) and very cheerful place serving superior grills, steaks, and pasta to a relatively young crowd.

⊗ MC, V

LONDONDERRY CITY

BEECH HILL COUNTRY HOUSE HOTEL

$$$

32 ARDMORE RD.

BT47 3QP

TEL 028 7134 9279

FAX 028 7134 5366

E-MAIL info@beech-hill.com

An early Georgian mansion in 32 acres (13 ha) of wooded grounds, gardens, and waterfalls, offering well furnished rooms and a stylish yet relaxed atmosphere.

① 17 plus 10 annex P 75 ⊕ Closed Christmas ⊛ ⊗ All major cards

BROWN'S

$–$$

I–2 BOND HILL,

DERRY, BT47 6DW

TEL 028 7134 5180

FAX 028 7134 5180

E-MAIL browns.tinvtee@aol.com

This is where discerning citizens

of Derry come to relax over great brasserie-style food. Examples from the menu include beans with Roquefort, and pork with roasted apples, and everything is based on the finest fresh ingredients, coupled with lots of experience behind the cooking pots.

🕐 Closed Sun., Mon., early Aug. 🚫 DC, MC, V

COUNTY LONDONDERRY

COLERAINE

🏨 GREENHILL HOUSE
$$
24 GREENHILL RD.
AGHADOWEY, BT51 4EU
TEL 028 7086 8241
FAX 028 7086 8365
E-MAIL greenhill.house@
btinternet.com
Comfort and a touch of elegance are provided to guests here, but not at the expense of its warmth of hospitality—and that's what brings people back to this handsome Georgian house in beautiful gardens in the valley of the River Bann.
🛏 6 🅿 10 🕐 Closed Nov.–Feb. 🚫 MC, V

🍴 CHARLY'S
$
34 NEWBRIDGE RD.
BT52 1TP
TEL 028 7035 2020
FAX 028 7035 5299
E-MAIL chatroom@charlys.com
If you can't be bothered to dress up and you don't have the patience for even a hint of swank this evening, get along to Charly's big, cheerful eating house and enjoy decent quick (as opposed to fast) food at very reasonable cost. This is a good place to take the children and their friends, too—Charly's will make them all welcome.
🚫 AE, MC, V

GARVAGH

🏨 GORTIN GLEN HOUSE
$

52 BALLYAGAN RD.
BT51 4ES
TEL 028 7086 8260
FAX 028 7086 8176
E-MAIL daphne@gortinglen.co.uk
Bedrooms are located in carefully converted outbuildings at Gortin Glen House, situated in the beautiful rolling countryside of east Derry.
🛏 3 🅿 6

LIMAVADY

🏨 RADISSON SASROE PARK RESORT
$$
LIMAVADY, BT49 9LB
TEL 028 7772 2222
FAX 028 7772 2313
E-MAIL reservations@
radissonroepark.com
A very well-appointed hotel in a beautiful location. Golfing fiends will find an 18-hole course, floodlit driving range, putting green, and a golf-training academy. Others will enjoy the wooded grounds, health and exercise facilities, and the chance to make the most of some excellent fishing.
🛏 118 🅿 300
🚫 All major cards

🍴 THE LIME TREE
$$
60 CATHERINE ST.
BT49 9DB
TEL 028 7776 4300
FAX 028 7776 4300
E-MAIL info@limetreerest.com
A hospitable house where the cooking is solidly spot-on. The menu might include lamb's kidneys in pastry, sirloin steaks in peppercorn sauce, or perhaps a plate of sensational crab cakes..
🕐 Closed Sat. L, Mon.–Tues., 1 week Nov. & July, 1 weekend Feb.–March
🚫 AE, MC, V

LONDONDERRY

🏨 TOWER HOTEL DERRY
$$-$$$
OFF THE DIAMOND, BT48 6HL

TEL 028 7137 1000
FAX 028 7137 1234
E-MAIL info@thd.ie
This is a new and very stylish hotel, with great views over the city from the upper floors. The public areas, which include a popular bistro and contemporary bar, are minimalistic, but there's no shortage of Irish hospitality from the staff.
🛏 93 🅿 25 🕐 Closed Christmas week 🚫 All major cards

PORTSTEWART

🍴 SMYTH'S
$$$
2–4 LEVER RD.
TEL 028 7083 3564
E-MAIL smythsrestaurant@
vevinternet.com
The service and the quality of the cooking here both won high praise at this restaurant, located opposite Agherton Parish Church at the Coleraine end of town. The menu majors on French and Mediterranean cuisine, and there are vegetarian choices. Children are welcome.
🕐 Closed Mon., Christmas week 🚫 MC, V

COUNTY TYRONE

DUNGANNON

SOMETHING SPECIAL

🏨 GRANGE LODGE
This is one of the friendliest and most comfortable guesthouses in Ireland. Nothing is too much trouble for the hospitable Browns, and the home cooking is superb.
$$
7 GRANGE RD.
BT71 7EJ
TEL 028 8778 4212
FAX 028 8778 4313
E-MAIL grangelodge@
nireland.com
🛏 5 🅿 12 🕐 Closed mid-Dec.–mid-Jan.
🚫 MC, V

GORTIN

🍴 BADONEY TAVERN
$

16 MAIN ST.
BT79 8PH
TEL 028 8164 8157
E-MAIL pksmckenna@aol.com
Very friendly pub where Peter
McKenna "will cook you
whatever you like, as long as
I *can* cook it …"

OMAGH

🏨 HAWTHORN HOUSE
🍴 $

72 OLD MOUNTFIELD RD.
BT79 7EN
TEL 028 8225 2005
FAX 028 8225 2005
E-MAIL info@hawthorn
house.co.uk
This handsome Victorian house
offers warm hospitality,
comfortable rooms, and a high
standard of cooking. Salmon,
sole, and steaks are all good,
and for vegetarians there are
such delights as mushrooms
with spinach and goat's cheese.
🛏 5 🅿 65 🅿 All major
cards

COUNTY FERMANAGH

ENNISKILLEN

🏨 KILLYHEVLIN
$$$

ENNISKILLEN, BT74 6RW
TEL 028 6632 3481
FAX 028 6632 4726
E-MAIL info@killyhevlin.com
A cozy modern hotel on the
outskirts of Fermanagh's
county town. Bedrooms are
furnished in the very best
up-to-date style.
🛏 43 🅿 500 🕐 Closed
Christmas 🅿 All major cards

🏨 DROMARD HOUSE
$

TAMLAGHT, BT74 4HR
TEL 028 6638 7250
E-MAIL dromardhouse@
yahoo.co.uk
Based in a beautiful old house,
with bedrooms in a converted

stable block. Dromard House
stands in extensive grounds,
and there are paths through
the woods down to Lough
Erne where you can fish.
🛏 4 🅿 4 🕐 Closed
Christmas 🅿 No credit cards

🏨 AGHNACARRA HOUSE
$

CARRYBRIDGE,
LISBELLAW, BT94 5HX
TEL 028 6638 7077
FAX 028 6638 5811
E-MAIL normaensor@talk21.com
Right on the shores of Upper
Lough Erne south of town,
this friendly guesthouse enjoys
a peaceful location and its
own lake fishing.
🛏 7 🅿 8 🕐 Closed
Nov.–March 🅿 MC, V

🍴 THE SHEELIN
$

BELLANALECK, BT92 2BA
TEL 028 6634 8232
FAX 028 6634 8232
E-MAIL malcolm.cathcart@
virgin.net
Innovative and traditional
dishes can be enjoyed in a
modest thatched cottage.
🕐 Closed Mon. 🅿 MC, V

IRVINESTOWN

🏨 MAHONS
$$

MILL ST., BT74 1GS
TEL 028 6862 1656
FAX 028 6862 8344
E-MAIL info@mahonshotel.co.uk
Handy for Enniskillen, the
islands of Lower Lough Erne,
and the beautiful hilly country
of southwest Tyrone, Mahon's
is a friendly family-run hotel
with comfortable, airy rooms.
🛏 18 🅿 40 🕐 Closed
Christmas 🅿 All major cards

COUNTY ARMAGH

ARMAGH CITY

🏨 DE AVERELL HOUSE
🍴 $$

NO. 3, THE SEVEN HOUSES,
47 UPPER ENGLISH ST.
BT61 7LA

TEL 028 3751 1213
FAX 028 3751 1221
E-MAIL tony@deaverellhouse.com
A fine listed 18th-century
building, De Averell House is
an excellent base for the
Georgian city of Armagh.
Bedrooms are in keeping with
the dignified character of the
house. The restaurant offers
a pleasant atmosphere and
good food.
🛏 5 🅿 5 🕐 Restaurant
closed Mon., also Tues.
Jan.–April & July 🅿 AE, MC,
V

KEADY

🏨 DUNDRUM HOUSE
HOTEL
$

116 DUNDRUM RD.
TASSAGH, BT60 2NG
TEL 028 3753 1257
FAX 028 3753 9821
E-MAIL liz@dundrumhouse.com
Surrounded by 80 acres (32
ha) of its own farmland, this is a
charming early 18th-century
farmhouse with some splendid
original features. It has been
creatively restored, and the
friendly hosts offer unlimited
choices for breakfast—at
whatever time you choose.
🛏 3 🅿 5 🅿 MC, V

NEWRY

🏨 CANAL COURT HOTEL
$$$–$$$$

MERCHANT'S QUAY, BT35 8HF
TEL 028 3025 1234
FAX 028 3025 1177
E-MAIL manager@canalcourt
hotel.com
With its imposing frontage and
dramatic lobby, this new hotel
announces to all its status as a
high-class place to stay. But
there's an intimacy about it, and
an emphasis on old-fashioned
hospitality. Rooms have classic
décor and king-size beds, the
restaurant offers fine dining,
and there's entertainment in
the Granary bar.
🛏 51 🅿 60 🕐 Closed
Christmas 🔄 🅿 All major
cards

HOTELS & RESTAURANTS

COUNTY DOWN

BANBRIDGE

🍴 ORIEL OF GILFORD
$$$
GILFORD, BT63 6HF
TEL 028 3883 1543
FAX 028 3883 1180
E-MAIL orielrestaurant@aol.com
The atmosphere is warm and
homey; the cooking is
international class, using
interesting combinations such
as duck and roast pepper
lasagne and fillet of beef with
leeks and horseradish butter.
🕐 Closed Tues.–Sat. L, Sun.
D, Mon. 🕭 All major cards

BANGOR

🍴 SHANKS
$$$
THE BLACKWOOD,
150 CRAWFORDSBURN RD.
CLANDEBOYE, BT19 1GB
TEL 028 9185 3313
FAX 028 9185 2493
Shanks sets the standard, with
imaginative cooking (hake with
artichokes, a fritto misto of
local seafood) complemented
by polished, attentive service.
Vegetarian menu.
🕐 Closed Sat. L, Sun., Mon.,
early–mid-July, Christmas,
Easter ♿ 🕭 AE, MC, V

CRAWFORDSBURN

🍴 OLD INN
$$$
15 MAIN ST.
BT19 1JH
TEL 028 9185 3255
FAX 028 9185 2775
E-MAIL info@theoldinn.com
Excellent fish dishes and others,
many jazzed up with reference
to Far Eastern trends.
🕐 Closed Christmas, Sun. D
🕭 MC, V

DOWNPATRICK

🏨 PHEASANTS HILL
COUNTRY HOUSE
$$
37 KILLYLEAGH RD.
BT30 9BL
TEL 028 4483 8707
FAX 028 4461 7246
E-MAIL info@pheasantshill.com
In a superb rural location north
of Downpatrick near Quoile
Pondage nature reserve, this is
an organic farm offering a
warm welcome and well-
appointed accommodations.
🛏 6 🅿 10 🕐 Closed Nov.
–Feb. 🕭 All major cards

🏨 DRUMGOOLAND
HOUSE &
EQUESTRIAN CENTRE
$
29 DUNNANEW RD.
SEAFORDE, BT30 8PJ
TEL 028 4481 1956
FAX 028 4481 1265
E-MAIL frank.mc_leigh@virgin.net
This comfortable Victorian
country-house hotel is set in
60 acres (25 ha) of woodland.
Bedrooms are large and well-
equipped and look out on
surrounding countryside. Riding,
based on the equestrian center,
is offered, as is lake trout fishing.
🛏 3 🅿 20 🕭 All major
cards

HOLYWOOD

🍴 FONTANA
$$
61A HIGH ST.
BT18 9AE
TEL 028 9080 9908
FAX 9080 9911
Bright decor and service
complement the beautifully
cooked and presented food in
this upstairs restaurant. The
fresh fish is particularly good.
🕐 Closed Sat. L, Sun. D,
Mon. 🕭 MC, V

NEWTOWNARDS

🏨 BALLYNESTER HOUSE
$$
1A CARDY RD. (OFF MOUNT
STEWART RD.), BT22 2LS
TEL 028 4278 8386
FAX 028 4278 8986
E-MAIL geraldine.bailie@virgin.net
A welcoming guesthouse in a
beautiful location in the hills
above Strangford Lough, with
fine views. Choose from airy,
comfortable bedrooms in the
house, or the pitch pine beams
and wooden ambience of the
self-catering lodge next door.
🛏 3 🅿 9 🕭 MC, V

🏨 EDENVALE HOUSE
$$
130 PORTAFERRY RD. BT22 2AH
TEL 028 9181 4881
FAX 028 9182 6192
E-MAIL edenvalehouse@
hotmail.com
Peace and quiet are the key-
notes at this Georgian hide-
away with its large gardens and
views over Strangford Lough.
Bedrooms are decorated and
furnished in period style.
🛏 3 🅿 10 🕭 MC, V

PORTAFERRY

🏨 PORTAFERRY HOTEL
🍴 $$$
10 THE STRAND
BT22 1PE
TEL 028 4272 8231
FAX 028 4272 8999
E-MAIL info@portaferry
hotel.com
A very well-run hotel right on
the waterfront of charming
little Portaferry, overlooking the
Narrows of Strangford Lough
with superb views across the
bird-haunted sea lough. The
staff here are exceptionally
pleasant and friendly, and the
rooms with lough views are
wonderful. As at the Narrows,
it's the fish—especially the
scallops—that bring people to
the restaurant here from all
over the neighborhood.
🛏 14 🅿 6 🕐 Closed
Christmas 🕭 All major cards

🍴 THE NARROWS
$$$
8 SHORE RD.
BT22 1JY
TEL 028 4272 8148
FAX 028 4272 8405
E-MAIL info@narrows.co.uk
Good cooking with a light
touch (fresh fish don't have to
travel far). A friendly
atmosphere, and a great
loughside position.
🕭 AE, MC, V

SHOPPING IN IRELAND

Think of shopping in Ireland and the first things that spring to mind are usually the superb crafts that you find all over the island. Waterford Crystal, Aran knitwear, Donegal tweed, Belleek pottery, Claddagh rings, Connemara marble, and Ulster linen are lined up along with a host of less famous names who produce ceramics, lace, jewelry, sculptures, and paintings in countless artisans' workshops around the country. Kilkenny is an acknowledged center for all that is best in Irish craftsmanship, and the major tourist information centers around the country usually have a good selection on sale—the one at the Giant's Causeway Centre is particularly good. An excellent reminder of a trip to Ireland is to take home some recorded traditional music, evoking happy evenings spent in music pubs or at a ceilidh. Or, perhaps, something literary—poems by Yeats, a copy of *The Islandman* by Tomás O'Crohan, or an anthology of humorous articles by Flann O'Brien. Eason's is the bookstore chain with the biggest presence in Ireland.

Irish food and drink specialties include Bailey's liqueur, Cork Gin, and the famous Irish whiskeys (Bushmills, Powers, Jamesons, Paddy)—sure, you can buy them just about anywhere, but touring the distillery first makes it a very special shopping experience. There are also tasty farmhouse cheeses (try the Cashel Blue), smoked salmon, and delicious soda bread. More of an acquired taste, but certainly worth trying, is dulse, a kind of dried seaweed snack.

For those with a taste for the kitsch, there are still plenty of outlets full of bright green, shamrock-encrusted souvenirs, shilelaghs, and dancing leprechauns, along with various items of clothing that will declare in no uncertain terms to friends and neighbors back home that you have been to the Emerald Isle.

You will also find plenty of religious memorabilia, from gaudy plastic Virgin Marys to tasteful and artistic replicas of Celtic crosses; these reach peak proportions in places where storekeepers can trade on various stories of visions and miracles, such as at Knock in County Mayo.

Visitors in search of their Irish roots will also find plenty of genealogy centers, many with computerized research facilities, offering documents to take home that give information about your family name.

DUBLIN

Dublin has long been a good place to shop, particularly fashionable south of the river, and there is apparently no limit to the choices available: clothing includes classics, trendy designer innovations and the latest streetwise and club-wear; some of the finest arts and crafts in the world can be found here; and all manner of high-tech gadgetry. Traditional-style department stores, reflecting a bygone age, stand alongside glittering malls and one-of-a-kind stores run by people who really know their stuff and don't mind how long it takes to tell you about it. **Grafton Street** is undoubtedly the best place to start, full of character and bustling with shoppers and buskers. It leads to **St Stephen's Green shopping center**, a bright and spacious mall. Side streets in the area have plenty of places to eat and interesting stores. **Powerscourt Townhouse** is a unique mall, converted from a large town house, and containing upscale stores and eating places. The maze of narrow, cobbled lanes that comprise **Temple Bar** is a treasure trove of unique stores and galleries, interspersed with pubs and restaurants. North of the river is not quite so glitzy, but it's been getting a facelift, and wide **O'Connell Street** is full of character. The new **Liffey**

Boardwalks are worth a browse, and the street markets here give a flavor of old Dublin. There are a number of big shopping malls on the outskirts of the city—**Tallaght**, to the south, is the biggest.

ANTIQUES
One of the best areas for antiques shops is on and around Francis St., and there are regular antiques fairs in the city, notably at Newman House, 85–86 St. Stephen's Green (alternate Sundays all year).
Gerald Kenyon, 6 Great Strand St., tel 01 873 0488, specialises in the sale and restoration of fine furniture.
Ha'penny Bridge Galleries, at 15 Bachelor's Walk, tel 01 872 3950, has a huge selection of silver, china, and curios.

BOOKS
Books Upstairs, at 36 College Green, tel 01 679 6687, across from Trinity College, has a terrific selection of Irish literature and drama, minority interest, and popular fiction.
Eason's, 40 O'Connell St., tel 01 873 3811, has some Irish books, but mostly offers run-of-the-mill fiction, along with stationery and art supplies.
Hodges Figgis, 56–58 Dawson St., tel 01 677 4754, is the largest bookstore in Dublin, a historic emporium that was mentioned in *Ulysses*. It has a huge range of books and a coffee shop upstairs.

CRAFTS
Design Yard, 12 East Essex St., Temple Bar, tel 01 677 8453. A converted warehouse with a variety of modern, quality crafts, including an exceptional range of jewelry.
Irish Celtic Craftshop, 10–12 Lord Edward St., tel 01 679 9912, has a variety of crafts, including jewelry, knitwear, ceramics, and Celtic design T-shirts.
Kilkenny Shop, 6 Nassau St., tel 01 677 7066 has a very upscale selection of quality knitwear, woven goods, designer clothing, and pottery.

DEPARTMENT STORES

Arnotts, 12 Henry St., tel 01 872 1111. Long-established, with three floors of clothing, home wares, sporting goods, etc.

Brown Thomas, 88–95 Grafton St., tel 01 605 6666. By far the best and most exclusive in the city, with an aura of quality and class. Designer fashion, perfumes, crystal, home wares.

Clery and Co, 18–27 Lower O'Connell St., tel 01 878 6000, was once *the* place to shop in Dublin and is still interesting to wander round. Conservative fashions, household goods, etc.

FASHION

BT2, at 28–29 Grafton St., tel 01 605 6666, is the new generation Brown Thomas, located opposite it's parent store; likewise it deals in designer labels for the sons and daughters of the original store's customers.

Design Centre, in Powerscourt Townhouse Centre, 59 S. William St., tel 01 679 5718, is where you'll find the best Irish designers, including Louise Kennedy and Sharon Hoey.

Louis Copeland, at 39–41 Capel St., tel 01 872 1600, is the outlet for one of Europe's most renowned tailors, who provides slick suits for the rich and famous, including US presidents.

Louise Kennedy, 56 Merrion Sq., tel 01 662 3993: exclusive designs for women such as Enya, Meryl Streep, and Cherie Blair.

JEWELRY

Appleby's, at 5–6 Johnson's Court, Grafton St., tel 01 679 9572, is an exclusive jeweler with an excellent selection.

Weir's, at 96 Grafton St., tel 01 677 9678, has quality jewelry and watches, silver and leather goods.

MARKETS

Wandering around the markets of Dublin offers a great insight into the day-to-day life of the city. Try the artisan food market on **Meeting House Square** in Temple Bar (Saturdays) which has a great selection of cheeses, organic vegetables, fish, meat, and cakes; **Moore Street** market (Monday to Saturday) is famous for fruit, vegetables, and footwear; **Georges Arcade** (Monday to Saturday) has the same, plus clothing (new and secondhand), and fresh bread. There's a **book market** in Temple Bar Square on weekends; **Mother Redcap's Market** (Friday to Sunday) in Christ Church Place and Winetavern St. is famous for antiques and bric-a-brac.

MUSIC

Celtic Note, 12 Nassau St., tel 01 670 4157, has a huge range of Celtic music—traditional, pop and rock, ballads, classical—as well as videos and instruments.

Claddagh Records, 2 Cecilia St., Temple Bar, tel 01 677 0262, is an Aladdin's cave, full of CDs, tapes, and vinyl. Traditional Irish music, including some rare recordings., bluegrass, blues, and world music.

EAST IRELAND

ANTIQUES

Granny's Attic, 33 North Main St., Naas, Co. Kildare, tel 045 876988, is a treasure trove of antiques and curios.

Selskar Abbey Antiques, at Selskar Court, Wexford, tel 053 23630, specializes in old jewelry, but also has silver, paintings, china, and collectibles.

BOOKS

Kilkenny Bookshop, at 82 High St., Kilkenny, tel 056 772 3400, has a good range, from Irish interest to international bestsellers, as well as toys and games, and there's a café upstairs.

Willowsand Bookshop, at Ballyteigue, Kilmore Quay, Co. Wexford, tel 053 29655, has lots of secondhand books.

CLOTHING

Padmore and Barnes of Kilkenny, at Wolf Tone St., Kilkenny, tel 056 772 1037, specializes in handmade Irish shoes, exporting worldwide to U.S., Canada, Japan, and Europe.

CRAFTS

Avoca Handweavers, Millmount Mills, Avoca, Co. Wicklow, tel 0402 35105, sends their quality woven goods from this 18th-century watermill to craft outlets all over Ireland, but this is the original showroom. The tearoom is excellent too.

Irish Pewter Mill, at Timolin, near Moone, Co. Kildare, tel 059 8624164, has pewter jewelry, tableware, and gift items that are made here, in the mill of a 1,000-year-old nunnery.

Kilkenny is Ireland's principal center for top-quality original crafts, with many artists and artisans working in the area. The Kilkenny Design Centre, in the Castle Yard, tel 056 7722118, is their showcase. All kinds of wares, including ceramics, carving, jewelry, fabrics.

M2 Studios in Bray's Seaview Industrial Complex, tel 01 286 1368, is where Michael and Rebecca Murphy make decorative home furnishings using hardwoods and stained glass.

Pembroke Art Studio and Gallery at 1 Pembroke St., Carlow, Co. Carlow, tel 059 914 1562, has ceramics, paintings, bronze, and art workshops.

Waterford Crystal, on the N25 (Cork road), tel 051 332500, is world-famous for its glittering goblets, glasses, and chandeliers, and you can buy them from the showroom here.

JEWELRY

Murphy Jewellers of Kilkenny, on High St., tel 056 772 1127, has Irish-made Celtic gold and silver designs, diamond-set jewelry, and watches.

MARKETS

Kilkenny Market, in Market Yard, on Friday and Saturday mornings, has home produce, home baking, crafts, and plants.

SOUTHWEST IRELAND

This is home to some of the finest craftspeople and some of the longest-established craft businesses, including Blarney Woollen Mills (see below). Cork city has plenty of outlets, as does Killarney, further north, and there are little craft communities in various out-of-the-way places, like Ballydehob and Kinsale.

ANTIQUES
Georgian Antiques Ltd, at 21 Lavitt's Quay, Cork, tel 021 427 8153, does as its name implies, and specializes in the Georgian era furniture, clocks, porcelain, silver, writing boxes, and more.

BOOKS
Killarney Bookshop, on Main St., Killarney, tel 064 34108, specializes in books of Irish interest, but has thousands of others to choose from too.
Kinsale Bookshop, at 8 Main St., Kinsale, Co. Cork, tel 021 477 4244, is a charming little store with a wide range of titles, including plenty of Irish interest.

CRAFTS
Blarney Woollen Mills, Blarney, Co. Cork, tel 021 438 5280, has one of the largest craft shops in Ireland, stocking not only the said woollens, but also Waterford Crystal, Royal Tara china, Belleek Pottery, Irish Dresden, and other crafts.
Kinsale Crystal, tel 021 477 4493, is run by Gerry Dale, ex-Waterford Crystal craftsman, who has established a world-wide reputation.
Ladies View Industries, at Ladies View, near Killarney, Co. Kerry, tel 064 33430, has a superb selection of lace and other crafts, and a wonderful view.
Shandon Craft Centre, Buttermarket, Shandon, Cork, tel 021 4503936, has various crafts on sale, plus the chance to see jewelry, pottery, sculpture, and musical instruments being made.
The Weavers Shop, in Green St., Dingle, Co. Kerry, tel 066 915 1688, has a range of Lisbeth Mulcahy's designs in woven scarves, wall hangings, designer clothing … and you can watch handloom-weaving in action.

FOOD
West Cork **cheese** is well-known, and makers of quality include Carrigaline Farmhouse Cheese, Durrus Cheese from just west of Bantry, and Milleens, from the Beara Peninsula. And if you are in Clonakilty, Co. Cork, drop in at Edward Twomey's celebrated butcher store on Pearse St. and pick up a link or two of his tasty **black pudding** (blood pudding), made from a family recipe that dates back to the 1800s. **Mussels** are cultivated in Bantry Bay.

JEWELRY
Brian de Staic A craftsman who produces beautiful pieces of Celtic jewelry. He has outlets on Green St., Dingle, Co. Kerry, tel 066 915 1298, and 18 High St., Killarney, Co. Kerry, tel 064 33822.

MARKETS
The best shopping fun you are likely to have in Cork city is in the enclosed **English Market,** with entrances off Grand Parade, Patrick St., and Princes St.. An atmospheric place, brimming with goodies that include crafts, a delicatessen, and more mundane household items—with some good chat. Most towns of any size in this area will have a general market once or twice a week, . A particular highlight is the weekly farmer's market at Skibbereen.

MUSIC
The Living Tradition, at 40 MacCurtain St., Cork, tel 021 450 2040, has a huge collection of Irish and world music and instruments.

WEST IRELAND

Galway is the main city, with the **Eyre Square Shopping Centre** at its heart. and a cluster of shopping streets with lots of character. Country towns in this area, with their easy pace of life, no-pressure sales staff, and ready conversation, are a delight to stroll around: the narrow streets of **Ennis** in Co. Clare; the Georgian thoroughfares of

Westport in Co. Mayo. A different shopping experience is to be found at **Bunratty Village Mills** (tel 061 354321) in Co. Clare village—a big, modern complex, catering to the tourists who flock here for the castle and folk park. Stores range from tasteful and expensive to kitsch. If you're flying out of Shannon Airport, don't forget their **duty-free store** for souvenirs and gifts.

ANTIQUES
Arcadia Antiques, at Castle St., Galway, tel 091 561861, is a characterful place, full of ornaments, pictures, and a large range of antique jewelry.
Bygones of Ireland, at Lodge Rd., Westport, Co. Mayo, tel 098 26132 or 25701, has a huge showroom full of beautiful and genuine old pine furniture, plus china, copper, and brass.

BOOKS
Kenny's Bookshop and Art Gallery, High St., Galway, tel 091 534760, is a Galway institution, where the service from the Kenny family is personal and very helpful.

CLOTHING
The Coop, Inishmaan, tel 099 73010, produces Aran garments made by local knitters that are exported worldwide.
Mairéad Sharry, in Lurgan Village, Inis Oirr, Aran Islands, Co. Galway, tel 099 75101, is a designer who incorporates traditional Aran stitches into gorgeous modern garments. The shop also has Aran yarn, vintage tweed clothes, and books, and learning vacations and work-shops are available.

CRAFTS
Connemara Marble Industries, at their quarry at Moycullen, Co. Galway, tel 091 555102 or 555746, produces beautiful craft and household items, including jewelry and gifts.
Crannmór Pottery, in Bowgate St., Ballinrobe, Co. Mayo, tel 094 954 1663, is the workshop and showroom for beautiful

functional items and exhibition pieces by Hilary Jenkinson.

Galway Irish Crystal Heritage Centre, in Merlin Park on the edge of Galway city, tel 091 757311, offers guided tours of the workshop and a good gift shop.

FOOD

McCambridge's, at 38–39 Shop St., Galway, tel 091 562259, is a grocery and liquor store with a superb delicatessen counter; their cheese selection is outstanding.

JEWELRY

The big item in Galway, of course, is the famous **Claddagh Ring**, with its charming and distinctive motif of two hands encircling a heart, topped by a crown. Its long history is explained at the little museum behind **Dillon's Claddagh Ring Shop**, 1 Quay St., Galway, tel 091 566365, where you can buy rings in gold, silver, or platinum.

MARKETS

Galway hosts a market every Saturday morning near St Nicholas's Church, which is particularly strong on organic produce and homemade breads.

MUSIC

Custy's Ennis on Francis St., tel 065 682 1727, has traditional instruments, including whistles, fiddles, and squeeze-boxes.

Powells, at The Four Corners, Williams St., Galway, tel 091 562295, sells Irish music tapes and CDs, plus instruments and sheet music.

Roundstone Musical Instruments, at the IDA Craft Centre, Roundstone, Co. Galway, tel 095 35808, is most famous for the bodhráns (traditional Irish drums) that are made here. Also traditional music tapes and CDs.

NORTHWEST IRELAND

Sligo and **Donegal** towns have an enjoyable mix of upscale stores aimed at visitors and more down-to-earth shopping for locals: old-fashioned drapers and clothing stores (this is the home of Donegal tweed), plus traditional grocers and hardware stores with carved, wooden storefronts.

ANTIQUES

The Gallery, at Dunfahaghy, Co. Donegal, tel 074 913 6224, in a former fever hospital, and has two stories of antiques, paintings, and crafts.

Mourne Antiques, at 8 Port Rd., Letterkenny, Co. Donegal, tel 074 9126457, is crammed full of china, jewelry, silver, furniture, and other collectables.

CRAFTS

Donegal Craft Village, just outside Donegal on the Sligo road, tel 074 972 2225, comprises a cluster of workshops where you can see artisans at work and buy unique items: metalwork, jewelry, sculpture, batik, and a uilleann pipe maker.

Donegal Parian China, Ballyshannon, Co. Donegal, tel 071985 1826, produces fine, glossy china made with ground glass and coated with liquid glass. Tours of the factory end in the showroom.

Leitrim Design House, in the Market House Centre, Carrick-on-Shannon, Co. Leitrim, tel 071 965 0550, is a retail showroom and gallery for Leitrim craftspeople and artists.

DEPARTMENT STORES

McElhinney's, on Main St., Ballybofey, tel 074 913 1217, is the largest department store in the northwest, with a wide selection of quality goods.

Magee's, in The Diamond, Donegal town, tel 074 9722660, is the place for tweed—you can watch a weaver at work before buying top-quality jackets items.

FOOD

The Organic Centre, Rossinver, tel 071 985 4388, sells organic cheese, meat, herbs, vegetables, fruit, and candy.

JEWELRY

The Cat and the Moon, 4 Castle St., Sligo, tel 071 914 3686, is an all-encompassing craft and gift shop, including Celtic jewelry.

CENTRAL IRELAND

BOOKS

Bookwise Booksellers, in Metges Lane, Kennedy Rd., Navan, tel 046 902 7722, has a good selection, including Irish interest, local history, maps, and guides.

CRAFTS

Carna Craft, Baltrasna, Ashbourne, Co. Meath, tel 01 835 0273, sells Michael Mulkerrin's sculpral figurines made of horseshoe nails.

Carrickmacross Lace Gallery, in the Market Square, Carrickmacross, Co. Monaghan, tel 042 966 2506, has lace made in the traditional way; lace-making demonstration by appointment.

Cavan Crystal Visitor Centre, on Dublin Rd. in Cavan, tel 049 433 1800, is one of the oldest glassworks in Ireland, and you can see the master glassblowers and cutters in action before you buy.

Celtic Clays Workshop, at Riverside, Carlingford, Co. Louth, tel 042 938 3996, is one of Ireland's leading studio potteries, producing stoneware with rich, earthy glazes.

JEWELRY

Coldrick Jewellers, at 8 Trimgate St., Navan, Co. Meath, tel 046 902 3836, has top quality items, including Celtic designs.

NORTHERN IRELAND

Once, stores in Northern Ireland were reckoned bigger and better than any south of the border, but The Troubles saw the province's shopping facilities stagnate. Now, there is a welcome revival, though there's still some way to go to match the kind of upscale visitor stores of the Republic. Typical souvenirs and collectables here include Belleek pottery, Tyrone and Fermanagh crystal, Irish linen, and Bushmills whiskey.

BELFAST

The city has a number of vast Victorian stores, dating back to its real boom-time. At the other end of the timescale is the bright, ultramodern **Castle Court Shopping Centre** (02890 234591) encompassing 8.5 acres (3.5 ha) in the heart of the city

ANTIQUES
Donegall Pass is the center of the antiques area of Belfast. **Oakland Antiques**, at 135–137 Donegall Pass, tel 02890 230176, is the city's largest antiques store, with Georgian, Victorian, and Edwardian furniture, silver, glass, porcelain, and paintings.

BOOKS
Bookshop at Queens, 91 University Road, tel 02890 662552, is a general and academic bookstore, including a varied selection of poetry. **Waterstone's** is at Queen's Buildings, 8 Royal Ave., tel 02890 247355, and at 44–46 Fountain St., tel 02890 240159.

CRAFTS
Conway Mill Craft Shop and Exhibition Centre, within a restored historic flax mill, displays the work of the 22 craft workshops on site. It's at 5–7 Conway St., tel 02890 247276. **Ulster Weavers Gift Shop,** at 44 Montgomery Rd., Castlereagh, tel 02890 404236, is a good place to go for Irish linens, including bed linen and table and kitchen linens. **Workshops Collective for Arts and Crafts,** at 1a Lawrence St., tel 02890 234993, has 12 workshops, a showroom, and a coffee shop in an old stable block off Botanic Avenue.

FASHION
BT9, at 45 Bradbury Pl., tel 02890 239496, stocks classic designs by Irish designer, Paul Costello, and others including Irish linen garments.

The Bureau, at 4 Wellington St., tel 02890 439800, once a male preserve, now also has women's clothes. Clavin Klein, Dries Van Notel, Katherine Hamnet, and others.

FOOD
Aunt Sandra's Candy Factory, at 60 Castlereagh Rd., tel 02890 732868, sells hand-crafted candy, from old recipes … and you can watch it being made. **Sawyers,** at Unit 7 beneath the Fountain Centre, tel 02890 322021, is the best deli in town: huge range of cheeses, salamis, exotic meats (such as wild boar and ostrich), and patés. You can get fresh dulse (seaweed) here.

JEWELRY
Lauren May Jewellery, at 10 Queens Arcade, tel 02890 232681, has quality pieces by young designers.

MUSIC
Golden Discs, at 29 Donegall Pl., tel 02890 322653, specializes in Irish artistes: folk, rock and country. Also has chart toppers, blues, dance, classical. **Knight's,** at 33 Botanic Ave., tel 02890 322925 is a great antidote to the chain stores. Very little new stuff here, but a lot of secondhand vinyl and CDs, specializing in traditional jazz.

NORTHERN IRELAND COUNTIES

You'll find historic towns with traditional high streets, but there are also modern shopping facilities, such as the **Foyleside Shopping Centre** in Derry, anchored by Dunnes and Marks & Spencer.

ANTIQUES
Crannog Antiques, at 5 The Brook, Enniskillen, Co. Fermanagh, tel 02866 323509, has a lovely selection, including glass, china, furniture, jewelry, brass, and silver.

BOOKS
As in the rest of Ireland, you'll find branches of **Eason's** in all the major towns and cities. Those

listed below are alternatives that have good selections, including Irish and local interest.

Bell's Corner, 2 High St., Carrickfergus, Co. Antrim, tel 02893 351486. **Bookworm Community Bookshop,** at 18–20 Bishop St., Derry, Co. Londonderry, tel 02871 282727. **Cameron's,** 23–29 Broughshane St., Ballymena, Co. Antrim, tel 02825 648821. **L. Hall,** 34–36 Darling St., Enniskillen, Co. Fermanagh, tel 02866 322275.

CRAFTS
Belleek Pottery, at Belleek, Co. Fermanagh, tel 02868 658501, is one of Ireland's top visitor attractions, and is known worldwide for its delicate porcelain. **Buttermarket Craft and Design Centre,** at Down St., Enniskillen, Co. Fermanagh, tel 02866 324499, has 16 workshops, producing pottery, fishing flies, carvings, sculptures, fine art, etc.; there's a showroom and café. **Irish Linen Centre,** at Market Square, Lisburn, Co. Down, tel 02892 663377, has an exhibition about the production of Irish linen as well as a shop and café. **Island Turf Crafts,** at 25 Coalisland Enterprise Centre, 51 Dungannon Rd., Coalisland, Co. Tyrone, tel 02887 749041, make statues, Celtic crosses, jewelry, and more out of Irish turf (peat). **Tyrone Crystal,** at Killybrackey, Dungannon, Co. Tyrone, tel 02887 725335, has a glittering array of crystal, and you can see it being made. Showroom also stocks cutlery, tableware, and gifts.

JEWELRY
Faller the Jeweller, at 12 Strand Rd., Derry, Co. Londonderry, tel 02871 362710, is a family-run store with designer jewelry, watches, and gifts, including items made in their own workshop. **Inisor Jewellery,** at 62a Burn Road, Cookstown, Co. Tyrone, tel 02886 761606, produces hand-crafted jewelry. You can watch the jeweler at work.

TRAVELWISE **387**

SHOPPING IN IRELAND

ENTERTAINMENT & ACTIVITIES

Anyone who spends time in Ireland needs no persuading that the Irish are among the world's greatest natural entertainers. Not in the 'cap-and-bells' sense, but as a people absolutely in love with conversation, music, song, curiosity, argument, joking, and nonsense—the famous Irish *craic* (pronounced "crack"), in fact. And every town and village has a stage where anyone can be the star and everyone is part of the enthusiastically participating audience—the pub. There is so much recreation value, so much excellent *craic* in the Irish pub that many visitors don't bother looking anywhere else for their entertainment. An even more traditional venue for this kind of informal, come-all-ye gathering is the ceilidh (meeting) house, a cornerstone of Irish community life before television when neighbors and strangers would gather to chat, play music, and dance in some house known to be a venue for such goings-on. *Ceilidh* houses are enjoying something of a revival, and it's worth asking whether there is one in your locality.

The theater is extremely strong in Ireland, opera is gaining ground in the wake of the success of the annual Wexford Opera Festival, and Irish cinema has had extraordinary popularity in the past couple of decades. Traditional culture is perpetuated in many forms, and apart from the informal music sessions in pubs, you'll find it in civilized stage shows and tourist-oriented banquets. Almost anywhere you look there's some kind of festival going on: guzzling seaweed in Antrim or oysters in Galway; hooker (a kind of boat) racing in Connemara; poetry in Sligo; and storytelling in Cork.

Nightlife in the big cities—Dublin, Belfast, Cork, Limerick, Galway—has kept pace with its European counterparts in the shape of extreme-noise dance clubs, comedy venues, and late-license bars. But in the smaller communities that make up Ireland's country towns and villages, where the majority of visitors spend most of their time, it is still the pub that offers the best of music, dancing, talk, and laughter.

When it comes to sports, a day at the racetrack (horses or greyhounds) is a long-established and dearly cherished form of entertainment in Ireland, and Gaelic football, hurling and soccer draw big crowds. Golf, fishing, boating, and horseback riding are popular activities, and walking is gaining ground, so to speak.

DUBLIN

As the capital of Ireland, and a seedbed of a great literary tradition, Dublin is a cultured city with a long history of entertaining foreign visitors, vacationers, country folk come to town, and the Dubliners themselves. In common with most European cities, in recent years nightlife has become a lot noisier and bolder —Temple Bar leads the field in the rowdy party stakes, and there are plenty of clubs where you can rave till dawn. But Dublin has a lot more to offer than that.

BARS

Cool bars south of the river include **Fireworks** on Pearse St., in a former fire station just east of Trinity, the **Modern Green Bar** on Wexford St., a relaxed lounge with a DJ, on cool-as-ice South William Street the very hip, dark, and moody **Dakota,** and in Temple Bar the chic **Morgan Bar** at the Morgan Hotel. North of the river you could check out the African-themed **Zanzibar** on Lower Ormond Quay, and nearby the amusing Russian Communist-chic decor of **Pravda.**

NIGHTLIFE

Pure modern club dance is great at **POD** (tel 01 478 0166) on Harcourt Street; gentler Latin sounds are not too far away at the **Gaiety** (tel 01 677 1717) in South King Street. Across in Temple Bar an excellent dance club is **Club M** (tel 01 671 5485) on Anglesea St. As far as other nightlife is concerned, if you're under 50 and looking for a lively time you can scarcely escape the lure of **Temple Bar.** This is where stag and hen parties contest the cobbles with students, Celtic Tiger cubs, and cohorts of youngsters in from the suburbs—all good fun, mostly, but things can get a bit silly in the early hours. Clubs, pubs, sidewalk cafés, and other fun destinations seem to occupy all the buildings that don't house avant-garde or retro stores. Drinking and dancing places can change place overnight in the trendiness pecking order, but currently the cool **Front Lounge, Thomas Read's,** and the **Turk's Head,** all on Parliament St., are up in the popularity mix—as is **The Porterhouse,** a microbrewery that makes extremely palatable beer on the premises and providing live music every night. There's more live music at the **Viperoom Theatre Bar and Club** on Aston Quay.

PUBS

Older drinkers looking for a bit of conversation and some classic Dublin pub atmosphere will appreciate the **Horseshoe Bar** in the Shelbourne Hotel on St. Stephen's Green, and the conspiratorial chat of politicians and other city heavyweights in the Victorian comfort of **Doheny & Nesbitt's** on Lower Baggot St., **Mulligan's** of Poolbeg St., has long claimed to serve the best Guinness in Ireland. The theatrical but fun **Literary Pub Crawl** (tel 01 670 5602; nightly in summer; Thurs.–Sun. in winter), starts at the Duke pub on Duke St. and tours famous literary pubs, with actor-guides who offer information about the authors and act out scenes from their work.

THEATER

Three of Dublin's many theaters well worth making an effort to get to include the sometimes experimental, always interesting **Project Arts Centre** (tel 01 881 9613) on Henry Lane, and the well-regarded **Gate Theatre** (tel 01 874 4085) on Parnell Sq. And, of course, there's the one founded by W. B. Yeats, J. M. Synge, Lady Gregory, and others—the famous **Abbey Theatre** (tel 01 878 7222) on Lower Abbey Street, still putting on Irish works by the great classic playwrights as well as outstanding upcomers.

TRADITIONAL MUSIC
When it comes to finding the best session of traditional music, every enthusiast will give you a different answer. The city's *In Dublin* listings magazine will tell you what's where, and it's a question of trying your luck until you find what suits you. One really excellent, reliable venue is the unpretentious but friendly **Cobblestone Bar** (tel 01 872 1799) on North King Street north of the river, where the nightly sessions (all day Sundays) are memorable. The **Oliver St. John Gogarty** (tel 01 671 1822), at 58–59 Fleet St., Temple Bar, is also well known, with a popular session with brunch on Sundays. Also up there in the ratings is the **Brazen Head** (tel 01 677 9549) on Bridge St., an ancient pub (probably the city's oldest) with great beer and an exceptional atmosphere.

EAST IRELAND

GOLF
The east of Ireland with its large areas of level ground and low-lying coasts is great for golf and, as in the rest of the country, there are many championship courses. Down on the coast of County Waterford there's the **Tramore Golf Club** (tel 051 386170), 10 miles (16 km) south of Waterford town and open seven days a week.

HORSE RACING
Kildare is horse racing country,

home to the National Stud (see pp. 93–94) and the foremost race track—**The Curragh** (tel 045 441205). Northeast of Kildare town, off the N7, it's where most of Ireland's classic races are run. There are two tracks at Naas, Co. Kildare—the **Punchestown** track and the **Naas** town track—and **Leopardstown** in County Dublin. Not quite so prominent but just as much fun are the **Waterford and Tramore** and **Wexford** tracks.

IRISH CULTURE
The **Bru Boru Heritage Centre** (tel 062 61122) in Cashel is a cultural enclave in the shadow of the Rock of Cashel, set up to study and portray Irish music, song, dance, storytelling, and theater. Its resident group of musicians and artists are world famous.

OPERA
Don't miss **Wexford Opera Festival** (see p. 117) if you like your opera a little obscure and a lot of fun.

THEATER
The **Backstage Theatre and Centre for the Arts** (tel 043 47888) in Longford town, Co. Longford, is a small, custom-built theater that offers an excellent, varied program, including touring international theater companies, Irish drama, comedy, and music. The **Theatre Royal** (tel 051 874402) in Waterford is housed in the Georgian City Hall, and offers high quality drama, music and dance from Irish and international companies. There's another **Theatre Royal** (tel 053 22240) in Wexford, home of the Opera Festival (see above). Wexford also has an **Arts Centre** (tel 053 23764) in the Cornmarket, which has a rich program of music, theater, and film, and is central to the Fringe Festival. The **Watergate Theatre** (tel 056 61674) on Kilkenny's Parliament Street has a lovely, intimate auditorium and a very interesting program of

quality drama, music, and children's theater.

TRADITIONAL MUSIC
There are countless pubs for good traditional music. In County Kildare at Celbridge an enjoyable session takes place on Tuesday nights in the Kitchen Bar of the **Celbridge House** (tel 01 627 2729) on the Maynooth road (also live music on Friday nights and Saturday lunch in the lounge bar). In the beautiful Vale of Avoca in County Wicklow, **The Meetings** (tel 0402 35226) has music every weekend—every night April–Sep.—and has a traditional Irish *ceilidh* outdoors on summer Sunday afternoons. In the north of County Tipperary, on the shores of Lough Derg, you'll find traditional music every night from June to October in **Larkin's** (tel 067 23232) at Garrykennedy near Portroe. If you're down in Wexford town, try **The Sky and the Ground** (tel 053 21273), an excellent pub with a great atmosphere—sessions (Sun.–Thurs.) are often heavy on the songs. One of the most famous places (so it's often crowded) is **Johnny Fox's** (tel 01 295 5647) in Glencullen, high up in the Wicklow Mountains, where there is live music seven nights a week and on weekend afternoons too (and also a dinner show with traditional dancers).

SOUTHWEST IRELAND

CONCERTS
The **National Events Centre** (tel 064 36000) at Gleneagle Hotel on Muckross Rd., Killarney, Co. Kerry is the largest venue in Ireland and hosts concerts, shows and theater.

GAELIC FOOTBALL
Purely Irish entertainment! You may well be the only foreigner in attendance if you turn up on Sunday to Austin Stack Park on John Joe Sheehy Rd., in **Tralee,** Co. Kerry, to watch a blisteringly exciting game of Gaelic

football—like soccer, but with more thrills per minute (tel 066 712 1288 for fixture details).

GOLF
Golf fiends can cosset their addiction in Kerry on several notable courses, all agreeably scenic, some spectacularly so—try **Ballybunion** (tel 068 27146), **Tralee** (tel 066 713 6379), **Beaufort** (tel 064 44440), or **Ross** (tel 064 31125)—both of these near Killarney—or **Waterville** on the Iveragh Peninsula's Ring of Kerry (tel 066 947 4972). You could try two sports in one place at the **Killarney Golf and Fishing Club** (tel 064 31034).

GREYHOUND RACING
Be prepared to stand up and shout your head off at the dogs on an evening out with a wallet of flutter money at **Cork Greyhound Stadium** (tel 021 454 3095) in Curaheen Park on Curaheen Rd.

HORSE RACING
There are tracks at **Mallow**, Co. Cork, and at **Killarney** and **Tralee** in Co. Kerry, where you can enjoy the thrill of the sport among like-minded country folk.

IRISH CULTURE
Tralee in northern Co. Kerry is where you'll find **Siamsa Tíre** May–Oct.) at the National Folk Theatre on Ivy Terrace (tel 066 712 3055); this is a theatrical entertainment based round Ireland's rich culture of music, dance, and folklore.

PUBS
For that longed-for relaxing pint and conversation (firelit on chilly days), you can't do better than the cozy little first-floor **Hi-B Bar** opposite Cork city post office on Oliver Plunkett Street. Near Killarney, Co. Kerry, **Kate Kearney's Cottage** at the entrance to the Gap of Dunloe beauty spot is a nice old pub.

THEATER
Belltable Arts Centre (tel

061 319866) at 69, O'Connell St., Limerick city, offers a program that ranges from plays and concerts to dance, mime, poetry readings, and art exhibitions year-round. **Cork Opera House** (tel 021 427 0022) on Emmet Place is a handsome city-center theater that can seat 1,000 for opera, dance, and drama. The well-known **Everyman Palace** (tel 021 450 1673), MacCurtain St., is a gorgeous restored 630-seat Victorian theater with a varied program, majoring on Irish drama during the summer.

TRADITIONAL MUSIC
An Spailpín Fanach on South Main St., Cork, opposite the Beamish brewery, is great for music—often traditional, but just about anything might emerge. Music-lovers are spoiled for choice in West Cork: **De Barras** in Clonakilty, **McCarthy's** in Baltimore, **The Shanakee** in Kinsale, and **Barry Murphy's** pub in Bantry are good options.

In Co. Kerry traditional music in pubs is plentiful in Tralee—try **Paddy Mac's** on The Mall, **Baily's** on Ashe St., **Kirby's Brogue Inn** on Rock Street, or **Turner's** on Castle Street. In Dingle town head for **The Small Bridge**, **Dick Mack's** or the apparently tongue-tangling **Ua Flaithbheartaigh's** (don't panic—it's O'Flaherty's). In Killarney, on the High St., **O'Connor's Traditional Pub** puts on traditional music, as does the **Laurels** on Main St.

In Limerick city, there's **Dolan's Pub & Restaurant** on Dock Rd., **Nancy Blakes** of Denmark St., or **An Sibin** at the Royal George on O'Connell St.

WEST IRELAND

CLUBBING
If you're an over-21 clubber, the short trip west out of Galway to the **Warwick** in Salthill, Co. Galway (tel 091 521244; open from 10 p.m.) could be worth your while.

GREYHOUND RACING
Enjoy a bet on the dogs at **Galway Greyhound Track** (tel 091 562273) on College Rd.

HORSE RACING AND HORSEBACK RIDING
Galway has **Racing Festivals** in July and September each year when the racing world mingle with enthusiasts and visitors for a memorable Irish experience. If you want to explore Connemara on a Connemara pony, there are plenty of places. Try **Errislannan Manor** (tel 095 21134) on the west coast, just south of Clifden, which offers riding and trekking (for adults and children).

MEDIEVAL BANQUETS
In the west, especially in Co. Clare, there are lots of banquets, with groups of musicians and actors dressed in historical costume, often in castles and country houses. You really have to be in the mood, but when the *craic* and the company are right they can be very good fun. Try **Bunratty Castle** (tel 061 360788), where you feast (eating with your fingers) with the "Earl of Thomond," or take in a *Riverdance*-style show in the Corn Barn, and **Knappogue Castle** (tel 061 360788) near Quin (eating irons provided here). Reservations advised.

THEATER
In Galway city theater lovers will make for the **Town Hall Theatre** (tel 091 569777) in Court House Square, or for the more adventurous, **Druid Theatre** (tel 091 568660) nearby on Courthouse Lane.

TRADITIONAL MUSIC
The **Glór Irish Music Centre** (tel 065 684 3103) in Ennis, Co. Clare puts on performances of traditional Irish music with some of the country's top musicians. If you prefer to take your chances in a Clare pub—and Clare is renowned for it—get down to Doolin and **McGann's** (mostly tunes) and **O'Connor's** (more songs), or the pubs in Kilfenora,

Ennistymon, Lisdoonvarna, and many another town and village.

In Galway city, settle down with a pint at **Taaffes** of Shop St., **O'Malley's** on Prospect Hill, the **Roisin Dubh** on Upper Dominick St., or the wonderfully atmospheric **Crane** on Sea Road on the west bank of the river, where you might find an Irish dancing session upstairs.

Co. Mayo is great for music, too—**Westport** is probably the cream of the crop, with really lively sessions in **Matt Molloy's** (the flautist with The Chieftains), **Hoban's**, or **McHale's**.

NORTHWEST IRELAND

BOATING
Little Co. Leitrim depends on its lakes and waterways to attract visitors, and there are a couple of enjoyable **cruises** to take— **Moon River Cruise** (tel 078 21777 or 078 2610010) on Main St., Carrick-on-Shannon (floating bar and live music), and **Sliabh an Iarainn Sunset Riverbus and Davy's BBQ** (tel 078 44079) on Railway Rd., Ballinamore (live music on board, then a barbecue and more entertainment on land).

GOLF
For sheer scenic beauty, not to mention a respectable challenge, the **County Sligo Golf Club** (tel 071 77134), known here as Rosses Point, is hard to beat—it was even immortalized by W. B. Yeats, who dedicated a poem to the view from the 3rd tee.

IRISH CULTURE
Teac Jack (tel 075 31173) is a cultural centre at Derrybeg out by Gweedore in northwest Co. Donegal, where there are music sessions and *ceilidh* dancing. Sligo town gains tone from its associations with the famous Yeats brothers. Hence its **Yeats Summer School** and its **Arts Festival** (tel 071 42693).

SEAWEED BATHS
If you want a unique experience,

gol to Enniscrone on the Sligo coast for a sloppy and refreshing slither in **Kilcullen's Seaweed Baths** (tel 096 36238).

THEATER
High quality musicals, classical concerts, and dramas are staged at the **Hawk's Well Theatre** (tel 071 61526) on Temple St., Sligo. Letterkenny, Co. Donegal, offers the **Grianán Theatre** (tel 074 20777) on Port Rd., with regular music and drama.

TRADITIONAL MUSIC
Furey's on the bridge is the best music pub in Sligo town (it's owned by the Sligo band Dervish). In Co. Donegal the friendliest, most spontaneous spot is the **Scotsman** on Bridge Street. **Peter Oliver's** in Ardara, **An Teach Ceoil** at Fintown, and the **Central Bar** on Upper Main Street, Letterkenny, are great for music, too.

CENTRAL IRELAND

Entertainment tends to be less tourist-oriented than in the rest of Ireland—for the simple reason that this dairying and bog area sees fewer visitors.

FISHING
In Co. Meath, you can fish in any of a hundred lakes and rivers— **Clarke's Sports Den**, Trimgate St., Navan (tel 046 21130), offers permits and advice.

GOLF
Meath is a great golfing county. Try the **Royal Tara Golf Club,** Bellinter near Navan (tel 046 25508); **Headfort Golf Club,** Navan Rd., Kells (tel 046 40146), or **County Meath Golf Club** at Newtownmoyragh, Trim (tel 046 31463).

GREYHOUND RACING
In Co. Westmeath, small-town Ireland's passion for dog racing finds a noisy and enjoyable outlet in **Mullingar Greyhound Stadium** (tel 044 48348) at Ballinderry near Mullingar.

HORSERACING AND HORSE BACK RIDING
In Co. Meath, **Fairyhouse Racecourse,** Ratoath (tel 01 825 6167), is one of Ireland's major race tracks. For something less formal, there's a unique meeting at **Laytown** in June in which horses race along the beach while spectators watch from the dunes. If you want to ride, **Kells Equestrian Centre** at Normanstown, Carlanstown, near Kells (tel 046 46638), is one of the places to go.

IRISH CULTURE
At Ballyconnell in Co. Cavan there's the **Ballyhugh Arts and Cultural Centre** (tel 049 952 6044 or 049 952 6754) out on the Belturbet road, where exhibitions, live shows, and ceilidhs explore the native culture of west Cavan.

THEATER
Co. Monaghan has the **Garage Theatre** (tel 047 81597) in St Davnet's Complex, Monaghan town, where you can catch a wide program of drama, dance, music, and comedy. In Drogheda, Co. Louth, there's the **Droichead Arts Centre** (tel 041 33946 or 041 42054) on Stockwell Lane. In Dundalk, the **Spirit Store** (tel 042 935 2697) on Georges Quay offers a very varied mix of cultural activities.

TRADITIONAL MUSIC
There are tremendous music sessions (Sunday lunchtimes and Tuesday/Wednesday nights) in **C. ní Cairbre's** dark and characterful pub on North Strand, Dundalk, Co. Louth.

NORTHERN IRELAND

BELFAST

After years of apathy, neglect, and lack of investment brought about by the Troubles, Belfast has seized avidly on these more peaceful times to reinvent itself as just as much of a party city as Dublin. Every kind of entertainment is on offer here.

CONCERTS
The **Waterfront Hall** (tel 02890 334455) shows off its superb acoustics with mega-concerts and shows. while the **Ulster Hall** (tel 02890 329685) and **King's Hall** (tel 02890 665225) host big pop music shows.

NIGHTLIFE
The famed **Golden Mile** between the city center and the University is crammed with bars offering live entertainment.

PUBS
A great way to acquaint yourself with some of Belfast's oldest and most characterful pubs is to turn up outside the Northern Ireland Tourist Board's offices at 59 North Street at 2 p.m. on a Saturday and take part in a **Pub Walking Tour,** tel 028 9268 3665.

THEATER
Opera, musicals, pantomime, concerts, comedy shows, theater, and ballet can all be enjoyed in truly sumptuous surroundings at the **Grand Opera House** (tel 02890 241919) on Great Victoria St., There's excellent repertory theatre at the **Lyric Theatre** at Stranmillis (tel 02890 381081). The **Crescent Arts Centre** in the Golden Mile (tel 02890 242338) offers music, comedy, dance, and drama in a more intimate space.

TRADITIONAL MUSIC
The **Rotterdam** (tel 02890 746021) on Pilot Street, is, by general concensus, the home of live music in Belfast, and this includes traditional sessions on Sundays and Tuesdays. On a Friday night try the **Kitchen Bar** (tel 02890 324901), Victoria Square.

NORTHERN IRELAND COUNTIES

CLUBBING
Kelly's Complex (tel 02870 823539) on Bushmills Road at Portrush, Co. Antrim, has seven bars, three dance floors, and a popular club known as **Lush.**

FISHING AND BOATING
Fermanagh offers fishing or boating on Lough Erne (tel 02866 323110). Fishermen in Co. Down could try for a trout in the Mourne Mountains' Shimna River (permits from **Four Seasons** on Main St., Newcastle —tel 02843 725078).

GOLF
Downpatrick offers **golf** at the 18-hole **Downpatrick Golf Course** on Saul Road (tel 02844 615947), and at **Ardglass Golf Club** (tel 02844 841219). One of the best (and one of the oldest) courses is the **Royal County Down** (tel 02843 723314) at Newcastle, a championship links course beneath the Mountains of Mourne.

HORSE RACING
Co. Down is Northern Ireland's horse racing base, with **Down Royal** and **Downpatrick,** which bills itself as "the friendliest racecourse in Ireland."

IRISH CULTURE
Two excellent Co. Tyrone venues are **Dún Uladh Heritage** Centre (tel 02882 242777) on the outskirts of Omagh (Sat. evenings from 10 p.m.) and **An Creagán Visitor Centre** (tel 02880 761112), east of Omagh, on the Cookstown road. In south Armagh, tradition comes into its own in the admirable **Tí Chulainn Centre** (tel 02830 888828), in the village of Mullaghbane, where the rich culture of the area is explored in music, song, and storytelling.

NIGHTLIFE
In Derry city the **Gweedore Bar**, 59–63 Waterloo St., puts on live local bands and gets packed and sweaty. **Mullan's Bar** at 13, Little James Street (locally known as **Jackie Mullan's**) is a popular place with three bars on different levels where the music can be anything from jazz to disco. In Co. Tyrone, **Omagh** has plenty of music pubs, and McElroys Bar in Castle Street for the 18–25 crowd. If you're out on the town by night in Co. Down, try Bangor's **Café Ceol & Boom Boom Rooms** (tel 02891 468830)— hot, hard, and housey.

THEATER
Co. Antrim theaters include **Riverside Theatre** (tel 02870 351388) on the University of Ulster campus at Coleraine and the **McNeil Theatre** (tel 02828 260478) on Tower Rd., Larne. In Co. Armagh there's the **Market Place Theatre** (tel 028 3752 1821) in Armagh city. In Co. Fermanagh, there's Enniskillen's **Ardhowen Theatre** (tel 02866 323233) beside Lough Erne.

TRADITIONAL MUSIC
In Co. Antrim many of the small towns and villages have music pubs, in particular **McCollum's** (locally known as **Johnny Joe's**) at Cushendall. In Derry city **Peadar O'Donnells** is a characterful place with the decor of an old grocery store, and **Henry Joy McCracken's** at 10a, Magazine Street has sessions and good local bands.

Traditional music and the delights of the ceilidh house have revived recently in Co. Tyrone. **Fernagh Ceili House** (tel 02882 771551) out east of Omagh is wonderfully friendly— telephone first. **Teach Ceoil** (tel 02881 648882) in Rouskey is another music house in the foothills of the Sperrin Mountains, with a session usually held the last Saturday of every month.

In **Enniskillen,** Co. Fermanagh, you'll find live music at the **Crowe's Nest** in the High Street. **"Blakes of The Hollow,"** on Church St., is a gem, and regular sessions here are among the best. In the village of Derrygonnelly on the west side of Lower Lough Erne, try **McGovern's** or the **Cosy Bar.**

Co. Down boasts traditional music pubs in every town—a nice variant to the breakneck tunes is a singalong session, which you will find in the **Fiddlers Green** bar in Portaferry.

ILLUSTRATIONS CREDITS

Abbreviations for terms appearing below: (t) top; (b) bottom; (l) left; (c) center; (r) right

Front Cover, (l) AA Photo Library/S. McBridge. (c) World Pictures, Ltd. (r) The Travel Library. Spine, World Pictures Ltd. Back cover, AA Photo Library/S. McBride.

1, S. L. Day/AA Photo Lib. 2/3, L. Blake/AA Photo Lib. 4, M. Short/AA Photo Lib. 9, C. Coe/AA Photo Lib. 11, IFA-Bilderteam. 12/13 The Irish Image Coll. 14, Christopher Hill. 15, The Irish Image Coll. 16/17, The Irish Image Coll. 18/19, Martin McCullough/Rex Features. 20/21, Post Anna Susan/National Geographic Society. 22, The Irish Image Coll. 23, Michael Diggin. 25, National Museum of Ireland. 26, Private Collection/Bridgeman Art Lib. 27, The Irish Image Coll. 28/29, Hulton Archive. 29, Private Collection/Bridgeman Art Lib. 30, Hulton Archive. 31, Hulton Archive. 32/33, Hulton Archive/Getty Images. 33, Hulton Archive. 34, Hulton Archive/Getty Images. 35, C. Coe/AA Photo Lib. 37, Christopher Hill. 38(l), The Irish Image Coll. 38(r), Hulton Archive. 39(l), Rex Features. 39(r), Marius Alexander/Rex Features. 40, Rex Features. 41, The Irish Image Coll. 42/43, S. L. Day/AA Photo Lib. 44, Alex Maguire/Rex Features. 44/45, Joan Marcus, 2000/Abhann Productions. 46, S. McBride/AA Photo Lib. 47, The Irish Image Coll. 48, S. L. Day/AA Photo Lib. 49, Catherine Karnow. 50, S. Whitehorne/AA Photo Lib. 52, S. McBride/AA Photo Lib. 54/55, The Irish Image Coll. 55, S. McBride/AA Photo Lib. 56, The Board of Trinity College, Dublin, Ireland/ Bridgeman Art Lib. 57(bl), Board of Trinity College, Dublin, Ireland/Bridgeman Art Lib. 57(br), Board of Trinity College, Dublin, Ireland/Bridgeman Art Lib. 57(t), Hulton Archive. 58, National Museum of Ireland. 58/59, S. L. Day/AA Photo Lib. 59, National Museum of Ireland. 60(t), Michael Diggin. 60(b), National Museum of Ireland. 61, National Museum of Ireland. 62, S. L. Day/AA Photo Lib. 63, S. L. Day/AA Photo Lib. 64, S. Whitehorne/AA Photo Lib. 65(t), S. L. Day/AA Photo Lib. 65(b), Catherine Karnow. 66/67, S. L. Day/AA Photo Lib. 67, Chester Beatty Lib, Dublin/Bridgeman Art Lib. 68, Chester Beatty Lib, Dublin/Bridgeman Art Lib. 68/69, Chester Beatty Lib, Dublin/Bridgeman Art Lib. 70, The Irish Image Coll. 71, S. L. Day/AA Photo Lib. 72, S. L. Day/AA Photo Lib. 73, The Irish Image Coll. 74, Guinness Brewery and Storehouse. 75, The Irish Image Coll. 76, The Irish Image Coll. 76/77, Michael Corrigan/The Irish Image Coll. 78/79, S. McBride/AA Photo Lib. 79, S. McBride/AA Photo Lib. 81, S. McBride/AA Photo Lib. 82, M. Short/AA Photo Lib. 84, The Irish Image Coll. 84/85, L. Blake/AA Photo Lib. 86, The Irish Image Coll. 86/87, S. L. Day/AA Photo Lib. 88, S. L. Day/ AA Photo Lib. 89, C. Coe/AA Photo Lib. 92(t), The Irish Image Coll. 92(b), Slide File/AA Photo Lib. 93, S. McBride/AA Photo Lib. 94, Irish National Stud and Japanese Gardens. 94/95, S. L. Day/AA Photo Lib. 96/97, The Irish Image Coll. 97(l), Jill Jennings/Christopher Hill. 97(r), S. McBride/AA Photo Lib. 98/99, C. Coe/AA Photo Lib. 100, The Irish Image Coll. 102/103, M. Short/AA Photo Lib. 103, Jill Jennings/Christopher Hill. 104/105, The Irish Image Coll. 106/107, The Irish Image Coll. 108, The Irish Image Coll. 109, Michael Diggin. 110, The Irish Image Coll. 111, The Irish Image Coll. 112, The Irish Image Coll. 113, The Irish Image Coll. 114, Michael Diggin. 115(t), S. L. Day/AA Photo Lib. 115(b), Michael Diggin. 116, P. Zoeller/AA Photo Lib. 117, The Irish Image Coll. 118, P. Zoeller/AA Photo Lib. 119(t), C. Coe/AA Photo Lib. 119(b), AA Photo Lib. 120/121, The Irish Image Coll. 121, Michael Diggin. 122, Waterford Crystal Visitor Centre. 123(bl), Waterford Crystal Visitor Centre. 123(br), Waterford Crystal Visitor Centre. 123(t), The Irish Image Coll. 124/125, S. McBride/AA Photo Lib. 125, The Irish Image Coll. 126/127, The Irish Image Coll. 127, S. McBride/AA Photo Lib. 128, The Irish Image Coll. 129, The Irish Image Coll. 130, Michael Diggin. 132/133, S. McBride/AA Photo Lib. 133, The Irish Image Coll. 134/135, The Irish Image Coll. 136/137, The Irish Image Coll. 137, Irish Tourist Board/Cork/Kerry Tourism. 138, J. Blandford/AA Photo Lib. 140, S. McBride/AA Photo Lib. 140/141, S. McBride/AA Photo Lib. 141, S. Hill/AA Photo Lib. 142/143, The Irish Image Coll. 144/145, S. McBride/AA Photo Lib. 147, J. Blandford/AA Photo Lib. 148/149, The Irish Image Coll. 150/151, J. Blandford/AA Photo Lib. 151, S. McBride/AA Photo Lib. 152, Michael Diggin. 152/153, Michael Diggin. 153, Michael Diggin. 154/155, Michael Diggin. 155, Michael Diggin. 156/157, Powerstock/Superstock. 157, The Irish Image Coll. 158, The Irish Image Coll. 159, Thad Samuels II/National Geographic Society. 160/161, Michael Diggin. 161, Michael Diggin. 162/163, The Irish Image Coll. 165, The Irish Image Coll. 167, The Irish Image Coll. 168, The Irish Image Coll. 169, P. Zoeller/AA Photo Lib. 170/171, S. McBride/AA Photo Lib. 172, Michael Diggin. 173, Christopher Hill. 175, P. Zoeller/AA Photo Lib. 176/177, C. Coe/AA Photo Lib. 178(t), S. McBride/AA Photo Lib. 178(b), The Irish Image Coll. 179, S. McBride/AA Photo Lib. 180, Post Anna Susan/National Geographic Society. 180/181, S. Hill/AA Photo Lib. 182/183, The Irish Image Coll. 184, L. Blake/AA Photo Lib. 184/185, The Irish Image Coll. 186(t), L. Blake/AA Photo Lib. 186(b), Thad Samuels II/National Geographic Society. 187, Jill Jennings/Christopher Hill. 188, M. Diggin/AA Photo Lib. 189, S. L. Day/AA Photo Lib. 190, S. L. Day/AA Photo Lib. 191, Michael Diggin. 192/193, The Irish Image Coll. 194, The Irish Image Coll. 195, L. Blake/AA Photo Lib. 196, The Irish Image Coll. 198/199, The Irish Image Coll. 200/201, The Irish Image Coll. 201, The Irish Image Coll. 202/203, S. L. Day/AA Photo Lib. 203, Powerstock/Superstock. 205, Liam Blake/The Irish Image Coll. 207, The Irish Image Coll. 208, C. Hill/AA Photo Lib. 209, The Irish Image Coll. 210, Private Collection © Courtesy of the artist's estate/Bridgeman Art Library. 211(t), © Estate of Jack B. Yeats 2003. All rights reserved, DACS/Leeds Museums and Galleries (City Art Gallery), U.K./Bridgeman Art Lib. 211(b), © Estate of Jack B. Yeats 2003. All rights reserved, DACS/Crawford Municipal Art Gallery, Cork/Bridgeman Art Lib. 212/213, The Irish Image Coll. 214, C. Hill/AA Photo Lib. 214/215, The Irish Image Coll. 217, L. Blake/AA Photo Lib. 218/219, C. Coe/AA Photo Lib. 219, Christopher Hill. 220/221, C. Coe/AA Photo Lib. 222, The Irish Image Coll. 222/223, The Irish Image Coll. 224/225, Michael Diggin. 227, Jill Jennings/Christopher Hill. 229, The Irish Image Coll. 230/231, The Irish Image Coll. 232, The Irish Image Coll. 232/233, Adam Woolfitt/Corbis UK Ltd. 235, Christopher Hill. 236, S. L. Day/AA Photo Lib. 238, Strokestown Park House and Famine Museum. 238/239, M. Diggin/AA Photo Lib. 240/241, The Irish Image Coll. 242, Christopher Hill. 242/243, The Irish Image Coll. 244/245, BSK Photo Lib. 245, J. Jennings/AA Photo Lib. 246(t), S. McBride/AA Photo Lib. 246(b), L. Blake/AA Photo Lib. 247, The Irish Image Coll. 248/249, Michael Diggin. 250, The Irish Image Coll. 252, M. Diggin/AA Photo Lib. 253, Michael Diggin. 254/255, The Irish Image Coll. 255, C. Coe/AA Photo Lib. 256, The Irish Image Coll. 257, The Irish Image Coll. 258/259, The Irish Image Coll. 260, Michael Diggin. 260/261, M. Short/AA Photo Lib. 263, The Irish Image Coll. 264/265, The Irish Image Coll. 267, The Irish Image Coll. 268/269, The Irish Image Coll. 270, The Irish Image Coll. 272/273, Chris Hill/Christopher Hill. 273, Chris Hill/Christopher Hill. 274/275, The Irish Image Coll. 275, Michael Diggin. 277, Michael Diggin. 279, AA Photo Lib. 280, Christopher Hill. 282, Christopher Hill. 283, Jill Jennings/Christopher Hill. 284, The Irish Image Coll. 285, Christopher Hill/The Irish Image Coll. 286, Khara Pringle/Christopher Hill. 287, Jill Jennings/Christopher Hill. 288/289, Christopher Hill. 290, The Irish Image Coll. 291, The Irish Image Coll. 292, The Irish Image Coll. 293(bl), Richard Gardner/Rex Features. 293(br), The Irish Image Coll. 293(t), The Irish Image Coll. 294, Richard Gardner/Rex Features. 294/295, C. Coe/AA Photo Lib. 295, Christopher Hill/The Irish Image Coll. 296/297, Jill

Published by the National Geographic Society

John M. Fahey, Jr., *President and Chief Executive Officer*
Gilbert M. Grosvenor, *Chairman of the Board*
Nina D. Hoffman, *Executive Vice President,*
President, Books and School Publishing
Kevin Mulroy, *Vice President and Editor-in-Chief*
Elizabeth L. Newhouse, *Director of Travel Publishing*
Barbara A. Noe, *Senior Editor and Project Manager*
Cinda Rose, *Art Director*
Caroline Hickey, *Senior Researcher*
Carl Mehler, *Director of Maps*
Joseph F. Ochlak, *Map Coordinator*
Gary Colbert, *Production Director*
Richard S. Wain, *Production Project Manager*
Lawrence Porges, *Editorial Coordinator*
Judith Klein, Sallie Greenwood, Michele T. Callaghan, *Contributors*

Edited and designed by AA Publishing (a trading name of Automobile Association Developments Limited, whose registered office is Millstream, Maidenhead Road, Windsor, Berkshire, England SL4 5GD. Registered number: 1878835).
Virginia Langer, *Project Manager*
David Austin, *Senior Art Editor*
Allen Stidwill, *Editor*
Keith Russell, Bob Johnson, *Designers*
Keith Brook, *Senior Cartographic Editor*
Cartography by AA Cartographic Department
Richard Firth, *Production Director*
Sarah Reynolds, *Production Controller*
Carol Walker, *Picture Research Manager*
Picture Research by Zooid Pictures Ltd.
Drive maps drawn by Chris Orr Associates, Southampton, England
Cutaway illustrations drawn by Maltings Partnership, Derby, England
The Burren illustration drawn by Ann Winterbotham
Northern Ireland mapping reproduced by permission of the Director and Chief Executive, Ordnance Survey of Northern Ireland, acting on behalf of the Controller of Her Majesty's Stationery Office © Crown copyright 2003 (Permit No. 20252)
Republic of Ireland mapping reproduced by permission of the Director of Ordnance Survey Ireland © Ordnance Survey Ireland and Government of Ireland 2003 (Permit No. 7610)